FROM CALIGARI TO HITLER

A PSYCHOLOGICAL HISTORY OF THE GERMAN FILM

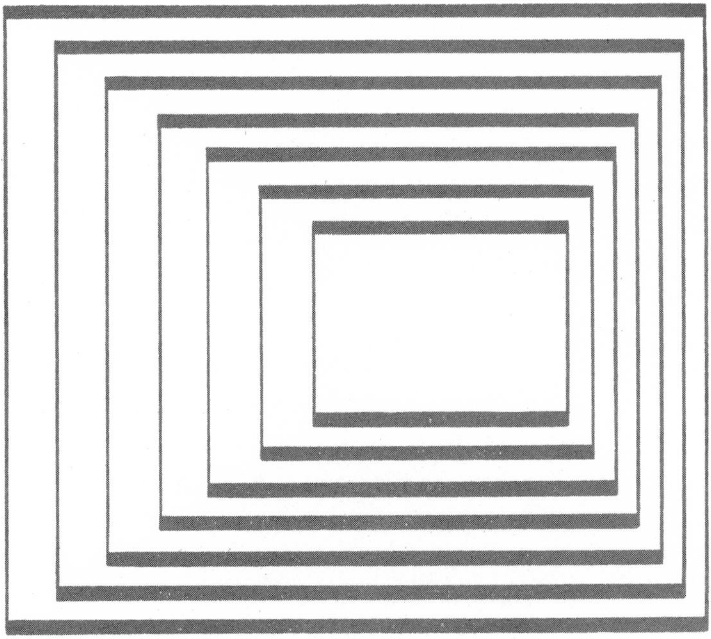

FROM CALIGARI TO HITLER

A PSYCHOLOGICAL HISTORY OF THE GERMAN FILM

By SIEGFRIED KRACAUER

PRINCETON UNIVERSITY PRESS

Library of Congress Catalog Card Number: 47-4412

ISBN 0-691-02505-3 (paperback edn.)

ISBN 0-691-08708-3 (hardcover edn.)

Printed in the United States of America
by Princeton University Press at Princeton, New Jersey

Fifth Princeton Paperback Printing, 1974

PREFACE

This book is not concerned with German films merely for their own sake; rather, it aims at increasing our knowledge of pre-Hitler Germany in a specific way.

It is my contention that through an analysis of the German films deep psychological dispositions predominant in Germany from 1918 to 1933 can be exposed—dispositions which influenced the course of events during that time and which will have to be reckoned with in the post-Hitler era.

I have reason to believe that the use made here of films as a medium of research can profitably be extended to studies of current mass behavior in the United States and elsewhere. I also believe that studies of this kind may help in the planning of films—not to mention other media of communication—which will effectively implement the cultural aims of the United Nations.

I am most indebted to Miss Iris Barry, Curator of the Museum of Modern Art Film Library, New York, to whom my book literally owes its existence; she not only suggested this study, but assisted generously and in many ways towards its realization. I am grateful to the Rockefeller Foundation, which enabled me to embark upon my enterprise, and to Mr. John Marshall of that office for his continued interest in its progress. I wish to express my deep gratitude to the John Simon Guggenheim Memorial Foundation, which honored me twice with a fellowship, and to Mr. Henry Allen Moe, Secretary General of this Foundation, who never tired of furthering my endeavors. Among those to whom I am very indebted for continual advice and help in the organization of the material and in matters of style, I expressly name Miss Barbara Deming, former analyst of the Library of Congress Film Project; and Miss Margaret Miller, Miss Ruth Olson and Mr. Arthur Rosenheimer, Jr., staff members of the Museum of Modern Art. Sincere thanks are also due to the Librarian of the Museum of Modern Art, Mr. Bernard Karpel, and the members of the Library staff; they patiently and expertly lent me a helping hand whenever I needed it and made me feel at home in this Library, with its invaluable facilities for studies of the film. Finally, I wish to thank my wife, though whatever I may say to thank her is insufficient. As always, she has helped me in the preparation of this book, and as always I have benefited greatly from her faculty of perceiving the essential and penetrating to its core.

SIEGFRIED KRACAUER

May, 1946
New York City

CONTENTS

ILLUSTRATIONS

FROM CALIGARI TO HITLER

A PSYCHOLOGICAL HISTORY OF THE GERMAN FILM

INTRODUCTION

I

WHEN, from 1920 on, German films began to break the boycott established by the Allies against the former enemy, they struck New York, London and Paris audiences as achievements that were as puzzling as they were fascinating.[1] Archetype of all forthcoming postwar films, THE CABINET OF DR. CALIGARI aroused passionate discussions. While one critic called it "the first significant attempt at the expression of a creative mind in the medium of cinematography," [2] another stated: "It has the odor of tainted food. It leaves a taste of cinders in the mouth." [3] In exposing the German soul, the postwar films seemed to make even more of a riddle of it. Macabre, sinister, morbid: these were the favorite adjectives used in describing them.

With the passage of time the German movies changed themes and modes of representation. But despite all changes they preserved certain traits typical of their sensational start—even after 1924, a year considered the beginning of a long period of decline. In the appraisal of these traits complete unanimity has been reached among American and European observers. What they most admire is the talent with which, from the time of CALIGARI, German film directors marshaled the whole visual sphere: their outspoken feeling for impressive settings, their virtuosity in developing action through appropriate lighting. Connoisseurs also appreciate the conspicuous part played in German films by a camera which the Germans were the first to render completely mobile. In addition, there is no expert who would not acknowledge the organizational power operative in these films—a collective discipline which accounts for the unity of

[1] Lubitsch's historical costume film PASSION—the first German production to be brought to this country—was shown at New York late in 1920. In April 1921, there followed the New York release of THE CABINET OF DR. CALIGARI.

[2] Rotha, *Film Till Now*, p. 178.

[3] Amiguet, *Cinéma! Cinéma!*, p. 37.

narrative as well as for the perfect integration of lights, settings and actors.[4] Owing to such unique values, the German screen exerted world-wide influence, especially after the total evolution of its studio and camera devices in THE LAST LAUGH (1924) and VARIETY (1925). "It was the German camera-work (in the fullest sense of that term) which most deeply impressed Hollywood." [5] In a characteristic expression of respect, Hollywood hired all the German film directors, actors and technicians it could get its hands on. France, too, proved susceptible to screen manners on the other side of the Rhine. And the classic Russian films benefited by the German science of lighting.[6]

Admiration and imitation, however, need not be based on intrinsic understanding. Much has been written about the German cinema, in a continual attempt to analyze its exceptional qualities and, if possible, to solve the disquieting problems bound up with its existence. But this literature, essentially aesthetic, deals with films as if they were autonomous structures. For example, the question as to why it was in Germany that the camera first reached complete mobility has not even been raised. Nor has the evolution of the German cinema been grasped. Paul Rotha, who along with the collaborators of the English film magazine *Close Up* early recognized the artistic merits of German films, confines himself to a merely chronological scheme. "In surveying the German cinema from the end of the war until the coming of the American dialogue film," he says, "the output may roughly be divided into three groups. Firstly, the theatrical costume picture; secondly, the big middle period of the studio art films; and thirdly, the decline of the German film in order to fall into line with the American 'picture-sense' output." [7] Why these three groups of films were bound to follow each other, Rotha does not try to explain. Such external accounts are the rule. They lead straight into dangerous misconceptions. Attributing the decline after 1924 to the exodus of important German film people and American interference in German film business, most authors dispose of the German pictures of the time by qualifying them as "Americanized" or "international-

[4] Rotha, *Film Till Now*, pp. 177–78; Barry, *Program Notes*, Series I, program 4, and Series III, program 2; Potamkin, "Kino and Lichtspiel," *Close Up*, Nov. 1929, p. 388; Vincent, *Histoire de l'Art Cinématographique*, pp. 139–40.

[5] Barry, *Program Notes*, Series I, program 4.

[6] Jahier "42 Ans de Cinéma," *Le Rôle intellectuel du Cinéma*, p. 86.

[7] Rotha, *Film Till Now*, p. 177.—It should be noted that Rotha expresses the views then held of the German movies by French and English film aesthetes, although his book is more vigorous and perceptive than those which had preceded it.

ized" products.[8] It will be seen that these allegedly "Americanized" films were in fact true expressions of contemporaneous German life. And, in general, it will be seen that the technique, the story content, and the evolution of the films of a nation are fully understandable only in relation to the actual psychological pattern of this nation.

II

The films of a nation reflect its mentality in a more direct way than other artistic media for two reasons:

First, films are never the product of an individual. The Russian film director Pudovkin emphasizes the collective character of film production by identifying it with industrial production: "The technical manager can achieve nothing without foremen and workmen and their collective effort will lead to no good result if every collaborator limits himself only to a mechanical performance of his narrow function. Team work is that which makes every, even the most insignificant, task a part of the living work and organically connects it to the general task."[9] Prominent German film directors shared these views and acted accordingly. Watching the shooting of a film directed by G. W. Pabst in the French Joinville studios, I noticed that he readily followed the suggestions of his technicians as to details of the settings and the distribution of lights. Pabst told me that he considered contributions of that kind invaluable. Since any film production unit embodies a mixture of heterogeneous interests and inclinations, teamwork in this field tends to exclude arbitrary handling of screen material, suppressing individual peculiarities in favor of traits common to many people.[10]

Second, films address themselves, and appeal, to the anonymous multitude. Popular films—or, to be more precise, popular screen motifs—can therefore be supposed to satisfy existing mass desires. It has occasionally been remarked that Hollywood manages to sell films which do not give the masses what they really want. In this opinion Hollywood films more often than not stultify and misdirect a public persuaded by its own passivity and by overwhelming publicity into accepting them. However, the distorting influence of

[8] Bardèche and Brasillach, *History of Motion Pictures,* p. 258 ff.; Vincent, *Histoire de l'Art Cinématographique,* pp. 161–62; Rotha, *Film Till Now,* pp. 176–77; Jeanne, "Le Cinéma Allemand," *L'Art Cinématographique,* VIII, 42 ff.; etc.

[9] Pudovkin, *Film Technique,* p. 136.

[10] Balázs, *Der Geist des Films,* pp. 187–88.

Hollywood mass entertainment should not be overrated. The manipulator depends upon the inherent qualities of his material; even the official Nazi war films, pure propaganda products as they were, mirrored certain national characteristics which could not be fabricated.[11] What holds true of them applies all the more to the films of a competitive society. Hollywood cannot afford to ignore spontaneity on the part of the public. General discontent becomes apparent in waning box-office receipts, and the film industry, vitally interested in profit, is bound to adjust itself, so far as possible, to the changes of mental climate.[12] To be sure, American audiences receive what Hollywood wants them to want; but in the long run public desires determine the nature of Hollywood films.[13]

III

What films reflect are not so much explicit credos as psychological dispositions—those deep layers of collective mentality which extend more or less below the dimension of consciousness. Of course, popular magazines and broadcasts, bestsellers, ads, fashions in language and other sedimentary products of a people's cultural life also yield valuable information about predominant attitudes, widespread inner tendencies. But the medium of the screen exceeds these sources in inclusiveness.

Owing to diverse camera activities, cutting and many special devices, films are able, and therefore obliged, to scan the whole visible world. This effort results in what Erwin Panofsky in a memorable lecture defined as the "dynamization of space": "In a movie theater . . . the spectator has a fixed seat, but only physically. . . . Aesthetically, he is in permanent motion, as his eye identifies itself with the lens of the camera which permanently shifts in distance and direction. And the space presented to the spectator is as movable as the spectator is himself. Not only do solid bodies move in space, but space itself moves, changing, turning, dissolving and recrystallizing. . . ."[14]

[11] See the analyses of these films in the Supplement.

[12] Cf. Farrell, "Will the Commercialization of Publishing Destroy Good Writing?" *New Directions*, 9, 1946, p. 26.

[13] In pre-Hitler Germany, the film industry was less concentrated than in this country. Ufa was preponderant without being omnipotent, and smaller companies carried on beside the bigger ones. This led to a diversity of products, which intensified the reflective function of the German screen.

[14] Panofsky, "Style and Medium in the Moving Pictures," *transition*, 1937, pp. 124–25.

In the course of their spatial conquests, films of fiction and films of fact alike capture innumerable components of the world they mirror; huge mass displays, casual configurations of human bodies and inanimate objects, and an endless succession of unobtrusive phenomena. As a matter of fact, the screen shows itself particularly concerned with the unobtrusive, the normally neglected. Preceding all other cinematic devices, close-ups appeared at the very beginning of the cinema and continued to assert themselves throughout its history. "When I got to directing films," Erich von Stroheim told an interviewer, "I would work day and night, without food, without sleeping sometimes, to have every detail perfect, even to descriptions of how facial expressions should change." [15] Films seem to fulfill an innate mission in ferreting out minutiae.

Inner life manifests itself in various elements and conglomerations of external life, especially in those almost imperceptible surface data which form an essential part of screen treatment. In recording the visible world—whether current reality or an imaginary universe —films therefore provide clues to hidden mental processes. Surveying the era of silent films, Horace M. Kallen points to the revealing function of close-ups: "Slight actions, such as the incidental play of the fingers, the opening or clenching of a hand, dropping a handkerchief, playing with some apparently irrelevant object, stumbling, falling, seeking and not finding and the like, became the visible hieroglyphs of the unseen dynamics of human relations. . . ." [16] Films are particularly inclusive because their "visible hieroglyphs" supplement the testimony of their stories proper. And permeating both the stories and the visuals, the "unseen dynamics of human relations" are more or less characteristic of the inner life of the nation from which the films emerge.

That films particularly suggestive of mass desires coincide with outstanding box-office successes would seem a matter of course. But a hit may cater only to one of many coexisting demands, and not even to a very specific one. In her paper on the methods of selection of films to be preserved by the Library of Congress, Barbara Deming elaborates upon this point: "Even if one could figure out . . . which were the most popular films, it might turn out that in saving those at the top, one would be saving the same dream over and over again . . . and losing other dreams which did not happen to appear in the

[15] Lewis, "Erich von Stroheim . . ," *New York Times*, June 22, 1941.
[16] Kallen, *Art and Freedom*, II, 809.

most popular individual pictures but did appear over and over again in a great number of cheaper, less popular pictures."[17] What counts is not so much the statistically measurable popularity of films as the popularity of their pictorial and narrative motifs. Persistent reiteration of these motifs marks them as outward projections of inner urges. And they obviously carry most symptomatic weight when they occur in both popular and unpopular films, in grade B pictures as well as in superproductions. This history of the German screen is a history of motifs pervading films of all levels.

IV

To speak of the peculiar mentality of a nation by no means implies the concept of a fixed national character. The interest here lies exclusively in such collective dispositions or tendencies as prevail within a nation at a certain stage of its development. What fears and hopes swept Germany immediately after World War I? Questions of this kind are legitimate because of their limited range; incidentally, they are the only ones which can be answered by an appropriate analysis of the films of the time. In other words, this book is not concerned with establishing some national character pattern allegedly elevated above history, but it is concerned with the psychological pattern of a people at a particular time. There is no lack of studies covering the political, social, economic and cultural history of the great nations. I propose to add to these well-known types that of a psychological history.

It is always possible that certain screen motifs are relevant only to part of the nation, but caution in this respect should not prejudice one against the existence of tendencies affecting the nation as a whole. They are the less questionable as common traditions and permanent interrelationship between the different strata of the population exert a unifying influence in the depths of collective life. In pre-Nazi Germany, middle-class penchants penetrated all strata; they competed with the political aspirations of the Left and also filled the voids of the upper-class mind. This accounts for the nation-wide appeal of the German cinema—a cinema firmly rooted in middle-class mentality. From 1930 to 1933, the actor Hans Albers played

[17] Deming, "The Library of Congress Film Project: Exposition of a Method," *Library of Congress Quarterly*, 1944, p. 20.

the heroes of films in which typically bourgeois daydreams found outright fulfillment; his exploits gladdened the hearts of worker audiences, and in MÄDCHEN IN UNIFORM we see his photograph worshiped by the daughters of aristocratic families.

Scientific convention has it that in the chain of motivations national characteristics are effects rather than causes—effects of natural surroundings, historic experiences, economic and social conditions. And since we are all human beings, similar external factors can be expected to provoke analogous psychological reactions everywhere. The paralysis of minds spreading throughout Germany between 1924 and 1929 was not at all specifically German. It would be easy to show that under the influence of analogous circumstances a similar collective paralysis occurs—and has occurred—in other countries as well.[18] However, the dependence of a people's mental attitudes upon external factors does not justify the frequent disregard of these attitudes. Effects may at any time turn into spontaneous causes. Notwithstanding their derivative character, psychological tendencies often assume independent life, and, instead of automatically changing with ever-changing circumstances, become themselves essential springs of historical evolution. In the course of its history every nation develops dispositions which survive their primary causes and undergo a metamorphosis of their own. They cannot simply be inferred from current external factors, but, conversely, help determine reactions to such factors. We are all human beings, if sometimes in different ways. These collective dispositions gain momentum in cases of extreme political change. The dissolution of political systems results in the decomposition of psychological systems, and in the ensuing turmoil traditional inner attitudes, now released, are bound to become conspicuous, whether they are challenged or endorsed.

V

That most historians neglect the psychological factor is demonstrated by striking gaps in our knowledge of German history from World War I to Hitler's ultimate triumph—the period covered in this book. And yet the dimensions of event, milieu and ideology have

[18] Of course, such similarities never amount to more than surface resemblances. External circumstances are nowhere strictly identical, and whatever psychological tendency they entail comes true within a texture of other tendencies which color its meaning.

been thoroughly investigated. It is well known that the German "Revolution" of November 1918 failed to revolutionize Germany; that the then omnipotent Social Democratic Party proved omnipotent only in breaking the backbone of the revolutionary forces, but was incapable of liquidating the army, the bureaucracy, the big-estate owners and the moneyed classes; that these traditional powers actually continued to govern the Weimar Republic which came into shadowy being after 1919. It is also known how hard the young Republic was pressed by the political consequences of the defeat and the stratagems of the leading German industrialists and financiers who unrestrainedly upheld inflation, impoverishing the old middle class. Finally, one knows that after the five years of the Dawes Plan —that blessed era of foreign loans so advantageous to big business— the economic world crisis dissolved the mirage of stabilization, destroyed what was still left of middle-class background and democracy, and completed the general despair by adding mass unemployment. It was in the ruins of "the system" which had never been a true structure that the Nazi spirit flourished.[19]

But these economic, social and political factors do not suffice to explain the tremendous impact of Hitlerism and the chronic inertia in the opposite camp. Significantly, many observant Germans refused until the last moment to take Hitler seriously, and even after his rise to power considered the new regime a transitory adventure. Such opinions at least indicate that there was something unaccountable in the domestic situation, something not to be inferred from circumstances within the normal field of vision.

Only a few analyses of the Weimar Republic hint at the psychological mechanisms behind the inherent weakness of the Social Democrats, the inadequate conduct of the communists and the strange reactions of the German masses.[20] Franz Neumann is forced to explain the failure of the communists partly in terms of "their inability to evaluate correctly the psychological factors and sociological trends operating among German workers. . . ." Then he adds to a statement on the Reichstag's limited political power the revealing remark: "Democracy might have survived none the less—but only if the democratic value system had been firmly rooted in the soci-

[19] Cf. Rosenberg, *Geschichte der Deutschen Republik;* Schwarzschild, *World in Trance;* etc.

[20] Outstanding among these analyses is Horkheimer, ed., *Studien über Autorität und Familie;* see especially Horkheimer, "Theoretische Entwürfe über Autorität und Familie," pp. 3–76.

ety. . . ."[21] Erich Fromm amplifies this by contending that the German workers' psychological tendencies neutralized their political tenets, thus precipitating the collapse of the socialist parties and the trade-unions.[22]

The behavior of broad middle-class strata also seemed to be determined by overwhelming compulsions. In a study published in 1930 I pointed out the pronounced "white-collar" pretensions of the bulk of German employees, whose economic and social status in reality bordered on that of the workers, or was even inferior to it.[23] Although these lower middle-class people could no longer hope for bourgeois security, they scorned all doctrines and ideals more in harmony with their plight, maintaining attitudes that had lost any basis in reality. The consequence was mental forlornness: they persisted in a kind of vacuum which added further to their psychological obduracy. The conduct of the petty bourgeoisie proper was particularly striking. Small shopkeepers, tradesmen and artisans were so full of resentments that they shrank from adjusting themselves. Instead of realizing that it might be in their practical interest to side with democracy, they preferred, like the employees, to listen to Nazi promises. Their surrender to the Nazis was based on emotional fixations rather than on any facing of facts.

Thus, behind the overt history of economic shifts, social exigencies and political machinations runs a secret history involving the inner dispositions of the German people. The disclosure of these dispositions through the medium of the German screen may help in the understanding of Hitler's ascent and ascendancy.

21 Neumann, *Behemoth*, pp. 18–19, 25.
22 Fromm, *Escape from Freedom*, p. 281.
23 Cf. Kracauer, *Die Angestellten*.

THE ARCHAIC PERIOD
(1895–1918)

1. PEACE AND WAR

It was only after the first World War that the German cinema really came into being. Its history up to that time was prehistory, an archaic period insignificant in itself. However, it should not be overlooked. During that period—especially during the course of the war—certain conditions materialized which account for the extraordinary power of the German film after 1918.

Theoretically speaking, the German cinema commenced in 1895, when, almost two months before Lumière's first public performance, the Brothers Skladanovsky showed their "Bioscop" in the Berlin Wintergarten—bits of scenes shot and projected with apparatus they had built.[1] But this beginning was of little consequence; for until 1910 Germany had virtually no film industry of its own. Films of French, Italian and American origin—among them those of Méliès—ingratiated themselves with the audiences of the early tent-shows (*Wanderkinos*), poured into the nickelodeons (*Ladenkinos*) after 1900, and then passed across the screen of the primitive movie theaters proper which slowly began to evolve.[2] One French celluloid strip of 1902, The Beggar's Pride, features a noble Paris beggar who, after rescuing a lady, contemptuously refuses the money she offers him, because she has previously indicted him for being a thief.[3] These films of high moral standards competed with pornographic ones which, of course, never lived up to their exciting promises. Between 1906 and 1908, the films increased in length, and spoken comments gave way to printed titles. Owing to such improvements, these years were marked by the opening of many new theaters and the advent of German film distributors.[4]

[1] Olimsky, *Filmwirtschaft*, p. 20; Kalbus, *Deutsche Filmkunst*, I, 11.

[2] Olimsky, *Filmwirtschaft*, p. 14; Kalbus, *Deutsche Filmkunst*, I, 12.

[3] Shown by Hans Richter in a New York lecture, May 25, 1943.

[4] Messter, *Mein Weg*, p. 98; Boehmer and Reitz, *Film in Wirtschaft und Recht*, pp. 4–5

The outstanding figure among the few native producers of the period was Oskar Messter, who makes no effort in his autobiography to belittle any of his merits.[5] Messter began working in a modest apartment studio in the Berlin Friedrichstrasse, later the headquarters for numerous film-makers of low caliber and questionable business ethics. He possessed the eagerness of a pioneer to experiment, to try every innovation. At a time in which close-ups were still unusual, one of his early comedies intermingled with long shots of several female cyclists a close shot of their fidgeting legs—a procedure anticipating a favorite German camera usage.[6] Messter also promoted the fashion of "sound films." Originating in France and America, this species flourished in Germany about 1908–1909. A costumed tenor standing before a painted canvas pretended to sing, endeavoring to synchronize the movements of his mouth with a hidden gramophone. In addition to grand-opera scenes, folk-songs and musical parodies, one could listen to Otto Reutter, the incomparable cabaret artist, whose songs cloaked bitter criticism of life with good-natured humor. Sound films of this kind had already been exhibited during the Paris World's Fair of 1900, but proved too expensive and intricate to be continued.[7] The particular interest they met with in Germany doubtless resulted from the traditional German concern with all forms of musical expression.

During that whole era the film had the traits of a young street arab; it was an uneducated creature running wild among the lower strata of society. Many people enticed by the movies had never attended artistic spectacles before; others were lured from the stage to the screen. About 1910 the theater of the provincial town of Hildesheim reported having lost 50 per cent of those customers who previously frequented the three cheapest categories of seats. Variety and circus shows complained of similar setbacks.[8] An attraction for young workers, salesgirls, the unemployed, loafers and social nondescripts, the movie theaters were in rather bad repute. They afforded a shelter to the poor, a refuge to sweethearts. Sometimes a crazy intellectual would stray into one.

In France, the freedom of the film from cultural ties and intellectual prejudices enabled artists like Georges Méliès or Émile Cohl

[5] Cf. Messter, *Mein Weg.*

[6] This scene is included in S. Licot's cross-section film, *Quarante Ans de Cinéma.* See also Messter, *Mein Weg*, p. 98.

[7] Ackerknecht, *Lichtspielfragen*, p. 151; Zaddach, *Der literarische Film*, pp. 14–16; Messter, *Mein Weg*, pp. 64–66, 78–79.

[8] Zimmereimer, *Filmzensur*, pp. 27–28; see also Altenloh, *Soziologie des Kinos.*

to prosper, but in Germany it seems not to have stirred the cinematic sense. Then, after 1910, in response to a movement which started in France, that freedom vanished. On November 17, 1908, the newly founded French film company Film d'Art released THE ASSASSINATION OF THE DUC DE GUISE, an ambitious creation acted by members of the Comédie Française and accompanied by a musical score of Saint-Saëns.[9] This was the first of innumerable films which were to be mistaken for works of art because, spurning cinematic potentialities, they imitated the stage and adapted celebrated literary productions. Italy followed the French example, and the American screen temporarily favored famous players in famous plays.

The same thing happened in Germany. The upper world of stage directors, actors and writers began to show interest in the cinema after having despised it as an inferior medium. Their change of mind must be traced, in part, to the missionary zeal of Paul Davidson, the great promoter of the early German film, who, under the spell of the new Danish film actress Asta Nielsen, firmly proclaimed the cinema's artistic future. He headed the Projektion-A. G. Union, which steadily extended its ownership of movie theaters and turned to producing films of its own even before the war. To boost the movies, Davidson made contact with Max Reinhardt, the leading Berlin stage producer, and, about 1911/1912, participated in the founding of a kind of guild which was to regulate the relations between film-makers and playwrights.[10] Of course, the prospect of tangible advantages did much to soften the resistance of many formerly hostile to films. Young actors from the Berlin stages were not unwilling to make a little extra money in the studios. Stage directors for their part profited by reducing the wages of these actors; moreover, they realized, not without satisfaction, that the theaters could now appeal to moviegoers anxious to adore their screen favorites in the flesh.[11]

Admission of films into the realm of the officially sanctioned arts went hand in hand with the evolution of a native film industry. During the last four prewar years, big film studios were constructed at Tempelhof and Neubabelsberg in the immediate neighborhood of Berlin, on grounds reserved to this day for the production of films —studios whose removable glass walls made possible the combination

[9] Bardèche and Brasillach, *History of Motion Pictures,* p. 42.

[10] Boehmer and Reitz, *Film in Wirtschaft und Recht,* p. 5; Davidsohn, "Wie das deutsche Lichtspieltheater entstand," *Licht Bild Bühne,* pp. 7–8; Diaz, *Asta Nielsen,* pp. 34–35; Zaddach, *Der literarische Film,* p. 23.

[11] Kalbus, *Deutsche Filmkunst,* I, 13.

of indoor and outdoor work favored at the time.[12] All looked bright and promising. Max Reinhardt himself was engaged in directing motion pictures. Hugo von Hofmannsthal was writing a "dream-play," DAS FREMDE MÄDCHEN (THE STRANGE GIRL, 1913),[13] among the first of the fantastic films soon to become a German institution. From Arthur Schnitzler's comedy *Liebelei* to Richard Voss's obsolete middle-class novel *Eva,* few reputable works were being overlooked by the screen.

But this elevation of the film to literary high life proved, as might be expected, a blunder. Traditionally attached to the ways of the theater, the stage people were incapable of grasping the different laws of the new cinematic medium. Their behavior towards the movies was condescending. They welcomed them as a means of emphasizing the art of the actor, and moreover, as a wonderful opportunity to popularize theatrical productions. What the screen meant to them was simply the stage again. In the summer of 1910, Reinhardt's pantomime *Sumurun* was made into a film which bored its audience by wasting 2,000 meters on an exact duplication of the original stage performance.

The so-called film reformers (*Kinoreformbewegung*), including teacher associations, Catholic societies and all kinds of *Vereine* in pursuit of cultural aims, exerted an analogous influence. From 1912 on, these pressure groups set out to justify their existence by opposing the immorality of the films and denouncing them as a source of corruption of the youth. The resemblance to the American Puritan leagues is obvious. However, the German movement differed from all similar movements abroad in that it drew much delicious indignation from the carelessness with which most films treated literary masterpieces.[14] It happened, in 1910, that a DON CARLOS film suppressed two main characters of Schiller's drama. In the eyes of the film reformers this was a crime. For any "literary" film had but one duty: to preserve the full integrity of its model. Was it for the sake of art that these spokesmen of the educated middle class shielded Schiller so ardently? Rather, classic literature enjoyed an awe-inspiring authority, and in defending it they yielded to the truly

[12] "25 Jahre Filmatelier," *25 Jahre Kinematograph,* p. 66.

[13] In all cases where a German film has been shown in the United States under an English title accepted by the trade, this title will be used in the text. If no American trade title exists, the translation appearing in parentheses is the author's own. The date given with a title always refers to the year of release.

[14] For a discussion of the arty and literary-minded film and the film reformers, see Zaddach, *Der literarische Film,* pp. 17, 22–29, 30–33.

German desire to serve the established powers. Harassing the motion picture industry with their cultured demands, the film reformers survived the war and continued to stigmatize what they considered trash on the screen through numerous pamphlets, invariably couched in metaphysical terms.

Fortunately, all efforts to ennoble the film by dragging it into the sphere of stage and literature aroused the scepticism of film experts and encountered the salutary indifference of the masses. The film version of *Sumurun* was reproached by its audiences for a complete lack of details and close-ups offered by even the average film. Discouraged by such reactions, Ernst von Wolzogen, a German poet, desisted from contributing further film scenarios on the grounds that the crowd always favors the banal. People preferred to these elevated screen adaptations the current output of historical films and melodramas which dealt in a primitive way with popular themes. Of most films of the time only the titles and perhaps a few stills remain to us; but it can be presumed that they somewhat resembled the exercises of a student who has not yet learned to express himself with facility.

In 1913 the detective film emerged, a genre obviously inspired by the French *ciné-romans*, which were adopted in America during the war.[15] The first German master-detective to be serialized was Ernst Reicher as eagle-eyed Stuart Webbs, who, with the peaked cap and the inevitable shag pipe, had all the trademarks of Sherlock Holmes. Since he enjoyed an immense popularity, he was soon followed by competitors vainly trying to outdo him. They called themselves "Joe Deebs" or "Harry Higgs," were on excellent terms with Scotland Yard, and lived up to their English names by looking exactly like tailor-made gentlemen.[16]

It is noteworthy that, while the French and Americans succeeded in creating a national counterpart of Conan Doyle's archetype, the Germans always conceived of the great detective as an English character. This may be explained by the dependence of the classic detective upon liberal democracy. He, the single-handed sleuth who makes reason destroy the spider webs of irrational powers and decency triumph over dark instincts, is the predestined hero of a civilized world which believes in the blessings of enlightenment and individual freedom. It is not accidental that the sovereign detective is disap-

[15] Jahier, "42 Ans de Cinéma," *Le Rôle intellectuel du Cinéma*, p. 26.
[16] Kalbus, *Deutsche Filmkunst*, I, 39.

pearing today in films and novels alike, giving way to the tough "private investigator": the potentialities of liberalism seem, temporarily, exhausted. Since the Germans had never developed a democratic regime, they were not in a position to engender a native version of Sherlock Holmes. Their deep-founded susceptibilities to life abroad enabled them, nevertheless, to enjoy the lovely myth of the English detective.

Despite the evolution of domestic production, foreign films continued to flood German movie theaters, which had considerably increased in number since 1912.[17] A new Leipzig *Lichtspiel* palace was inaugurated with QUO VADIS, an Italian pageant that actually received press reviews as if it were a real stage play.[18] Towards the end of the prewar period, the Danish films gained more and more influence. Greatly indebted to Asta Nielsen, they appealed to German audiences by focusing upon psychological conflicts unfolded in natural settings. The success of the American Westerns was particularly sweeping. Broncho Bill and Tom Mix conquered the hearts of the young German generation, which had devoured, volume after volume, the novels of Karl May—novels set in an imaginary Far West and full of fabulous events involving Indian tribes, covered wagons, traders, hunters, tramps and adventurers. To staid and settled adults the spell this shoddy stuff exerted on boys in the early teens was inexplicable; but youngsters would shed tears of delight when the noble Indian chief Winnetou, having become a Christian, died in the arms of his friend Old Shatterhand, a righter of wrongs, and a German, of course. By their simple manner and untroubled outlook, their ceaseless activity and heroic exploits, the American screen cowboys also attracted many German intellectuals suffering from lack of purpose. Because they were mentally tossed about, the intelligentsia welcomed the simplifications of the Westerns, the life in which the hero has but one course to follow. In the same fashion, at the outbreak of the war, numerous students enthusiastically rushed to volunteer in the army. They were drawn not so much by patriotism as by a passionate desire to escape from vain freedom into a life under compelling pressure. They wished to serve.

Besides the Westerns, short comedies featuring Max Linder, Fatty and Tontolini were the vogue of those years. All strata of Ger-

[17] Jason, "Zahlen sehen uns an," *25 Jahre Kinematograph*, p. 67.
[18] Olimsky, *Filmwirtschaft*, p. 21.

man moviegoers participated in the gay laughter they aroused. The Germans liked that sort of visual fun. It is all the more surprising, therefore, that they themselves were incapable of producing a popular film comedian. As early as 1921, a German writer stated plainly that the Germans were short of comical film ideas—a domain which, he admitted, the French and after them the Americans had learned to explore with mastery.[19]

This strange deficiency may be connected with the character of the old screen buffooneries. Whether or not they indulged in slapstick, they invariably exposed their hero to all kinds of pitfalls and dangers, so that he depended upon one lucky accident after another to escape. When he crossed a railroad, a train would approach, threatening to crush him, and only in the very last moment would his life be spared as the train switched over to a track hitherto invisible. The hero—a sweet, rather helpless individual who would never harm anyone—pulled through in a world governed by chance. The comedy adjusted itself in this way to the specific conditions of the screen; for more than any other medium the film is able to point up the contingencies of life. It was a truly cinematic type of comedy. Had it a moral to impart? It sided with the little pigs against the big bad wolf by making luck the natural ally of its heroes. This, incidentally, was comforting to the poor. That such comedy founded on chance and a naïve desire for happiness should prove inaccessible to the Germans arises from their traditional ideology, which tends to discredit the notion of luck in favor of that of fate. The Germans have developed a native humor that holds wit and irony in contempt and has no place for happy-go-lucky figures. Theirs is an emotional humor which tries to reconcile mankind to its tragic plight and to make one not only laugh at the oddities of life but also realize through that laughter how fateful it is. Such dispositions were of course incompatible with the attitudes underlying the performances of a Buster Keaton or Harold Lloyd. There exists, moreover, a close interrelationship between intellectual habits and bodily movements. The German actors may have felt that, owing to their credos, they were hardly the type for gags and gestures similar to those of the American film comedians.

The war began. Not only part of the German youth, but also the clan of the film reformers firmly believed that it would imbue their

[19] Möllhausen, "Aufstieg des Films," *Ufa-Blätter*.

drab life with a new and marvelous meaning. Hermann Häfker's preface to his book on the cinema and the cultured classes is illuminating in this respect. Dated September 1914, it extols the war as a sure means of realizing the noble designs of the film reformers, and finally turns into one of those bellicose dithyrambs not at all unusual then. "May it [i.e., the war] purify our public life as a thunderstorm does the atmosphere. May it allow us to live again, and make us eager to risk our lives in deeds such as this hour commands. Peace had become insupportable." [20] Häfker and his like were in a frenzy.

Peace, to be sure, had seen the German film industry caught in a crisis. The domestic output was far too insignificant to compete with the foreign films crowding the movie theaters, which had seemed to increase for the sole purpose of absorbing the influx from abroad. Products of Pathé Frères and Gaumont inundated the German market. The Danish Nordisk went to the limit to ruin Davidson's Projektion-A.G. Union.[21]

This embarrassing situation was reversed by the war, which abruptly freed the native industry from the burden of foreign competition. After the frontiers had been shut, Germany belonged to the German film producers, faced now with the task of satisfying on their own all internal demands. These were immense. In addition to the regular movie theaters numerous military ones spreading behind the front lines demanded a permanent supply of fresh films. It was lucky for the film-makers that just before the war large and modern studio plants had been completed. A boom set in, and new film companies cropped up with incredible speed. According to a seemingly reliable survey, the number of these companies rose from 28 in 1913 to 245 in 1919. Movie theaters also flourished and grew more and more luxurious. It was a period of abundant dividends. The middle class began to pay some attention to the cinema.[22]

Thus the German film was offered a unique chance: it became autonomous; it no longer needed to emulate foreign products to sustain its market value. One would think that under such auspicious circumstances Germany might have succeeded in creating a cinema of her own, of truly national character. Other countries did. During

[20] Häfker, *Der Kino und die Gebildeten,* p. 4.

[21] Boehmer and Reitz, *Film in Wirtschaft und Recht,* p. 5; Kalbus. *Deutsche Filmkunst,* I, 23.

[22] Boehmer and Reitz, *Film in Wirtschaft und Recht,* pp. 5–6; Olimsky, *Filmwirtschaft,* pp. 23–24; Jason, "Zahlen sehen uns an," *25 Jahre Kinematograph,* p. 67; Bardèche and Brasillach, *History of Motion Pictures,* pp. 135–36.

those war years, D. W. Griffith, Chaplin and Cecil B. De Mille developed the American film, and the Swedish industry took shape.

But the German evolution was not similar. From October 1914 on, Messter substituted for the prewar newsreels of Pathé Frères, Gaumont and Éclair weekly film reports which pictured diverse war events with the help of documentary shots. Disseminated among the neutrals as well as in the fatherland, these illustrated bulletins were supplemented by staged propaganda films in which extras put into British uniforms surrendered to valiant German troops. The government encouraged efforts of that kind as a means to make people "stick to it." Later in the course of the war the High Command ordered selected cameramen to participate in military actions. The design was to obtain impressive pictorial material which would also serve as an historic record. One reel which was taken from a submarine, and closely detailed the sinking of Allied ships, gained a wide reputation.[23] But these cinematic activities were by no means peculiar to the Germans. The French had nearly the same ideas about the utility of war documentaries, and realized them with no less determination.[24]

In the domain of the fictional film, scores of patriotic dramas, melodramas, comedies and farces spread over the screen—rubbish filled to the brim with war brides, waving flags, officers, privates, elevated sentiments and barracks humor. When, about the middle of 1915, it became obvious that the gay war of movement had changed into a stationary war of uncertain issues, the moviegoers apparently refused to swallow the patriotic sweets any longer. A marked shift in entertainment themes occurred. The many pictures exploiting patriotism were superseded by films which concentrated upon peacetime subjects. By resuming part of their normal interests, people adjusted themselves to the stabilized war.

A multitude of comedies emerged, transferring to the screen popular Berlin stage comedians in proved theatrical plays. They laid hold of such stereotyped figures as the Prussian lieutenant or the adolescent girl, and, in the main, indulged in wanton sex fun. Ernst Lubitsch started his amazing career in the field of these slight comedies. Not content with minor stage roles in classic dramas, he, the Reinhardt actor, found an outlet for his nimble wit and ingenuity by

[23] Rohde, "German Propaganda Movies," *American Cinematographer*, Jan. 1943, p. 10; Ackerknecht, *Lichtspielfragen*, pp. 21–22; Messter, *Mein Weg*, pp. 128–30.

[24] Bardèche and Brasillach, *History of Motion Pictures*, p. 93.

playing the comic in screen farces. One of them features him as a Jewish apprentice in a Berlin shop who, always on the verge of being fired, ends as the son-in-law of his boss. He soon took pleasure in directing, himself, such one-reel comedies. Although, under the Nazis, Kalbus denounced Lubitsch for displaying "a pertness entirely alien from our true being," the contemporary German audience did not feel at all scandalized, but enjoyed the actor and his films wholeheartedly.[25]

The war failed to provoke vital innovations, nor did it engender additional film types, with the exception, perhaps, of a group of cheap serials promoting favorite actors such as Fern Andra and Erna Morena.[26] The German film-makers continued to explore mines opened by prewar activities, and, at best, played new variations on old tunes. Occasionally, a sure instinct seized upon a story that later would be picked up again and again. Sudermann's outmoded novels and theatrically effective plays were first translated to the screen during that period.[27] They were full of dramatic suspense, good roles and a bourgeois outlook, abounded in realistic details, and rendered the melancholy East Prussian landscape painstakingly—qualities which made them attractive to film producers for many years to come.

Only towards the end of the war did the events take place that caused the birth of the German film proper, but that they proved so effective was due to the whole development prior to their intervention. Although this development lacked strong impulses and striking results, it nevertheless established traditions that facilitated the final breakthrough.

The decisive contribution of the war and prewar years was the preparation of a generation of actors, cameramen, directors and technicians for the tasks of the future. Some of these old-timers continued under Hitler; among them was Carl Froelich, a pre-eminent German director who did not mind occupying a key post in the Nazi film industry. He entered one of the first Messter studios as an electrician, then cranked a camera, and, as early as 1911 or 1912, began directing films.[28] Many others gained practice by making primitive

[25] Kalbus, *Deutsche Filmkunst,* I, 34. Kalbus deals extensively with the German war output; cf. pp. 18–19, 32–37.

[26] *Ibid.*, pp. 25–26.

[27] Zaddach, *Der literarische Film,* p. 34.

[28] Messter, *Mein Weg,* pp. 57, 99 ff.

films long since passed into oblivion. They learned by their own mistakes. Emil Jannings—he, too, subsequently prominent in Nazi Germany—writes about his debut as a film actor during the war: "When I watched myself for the first time on the screen, the impression was crushing. Did I really look as stupid as that?" [29]

Jannings was only one of numerous actors who underwent their basic training in the course of the archaic period. They all were later to build up a sort of repertory company. Indeed, the cast of every film to be released in Germany would include members of this "guild," which, in spite of continually acquiring new recruits, kept its old guard intact. While Hollywood cultivates stars rather than ensemble effects, and the Russian cinema often uses laymen as film figures, the German film is founded upon a permanent body of players—highly disciplined professionals who adjust themselves to all changes in style and fashion.[30]

To meet actors familiar to contemporary moviegoers in a past that has become history is an uncanny experience: what was once our life is now stored away, and we have somehow unknowingly moved on. Not the predecessors of Werner Krauss or Albert Bassermann, but they themselves passed across the screen during the first World War—figures irrevocably separated from the present day. One of their companions was Henny Porten who—she was a rare exception—began her film career without any previous stage experience. From about 1910 on, this ingenious blonde, much praised as the ideal type of German woman, maintained herself in the favor of the public, playing with equal ease comic and tragic parts, vulgar farmer's wives and sensitive ladies.[31] Another figure of those early days was Harry Piel, called the German Douglas Fairbanks. He appeared in the middle of the war as the hero of UNTER HEISSER SONNE (UNDER A HOT SUN), a film in which he forced several lions (from Hamburg's Hagenbeck Zoo) to yield to his spell.[32] From the very beginning Piel seems to have been true to the type he was to impersonate in the future: that of a chivalrous daredevil who excels in defeating re-

[29] Jannings, "Mein Werdegang," *Ufa-Magazin,* Oct. 1–7, 1926.

[30] C. A. Lejeune, the English film writer, comments on this point in an interesting way. The German repertory company, she says, "is right for the mood of Germany, and will always be the type for any segment of cinema that works from the psychological-fantastic basis, any production that builds up a whole from the materials of the studio rather than cleaving out a meaning from the raw materials of life."—Lejeune, *Cinema,* p. 142.

[31] Kalbus, *Deutsche Filmkunst,* I, 19–21.

[32] *Ibid.,* pp. 89–90.

sourceful criminals and rescuing innocent maidens. When he showed up in evening attire, he epitomized an immature girl's daydream of a perfect gentleman, and the boyish charm he radiated was as sweet as the colored sugar-sticks which, in European fairs, are the delight of children and blasé aesthetes. His films were in the black-and-white style of the dime novels rather than the shadings of psychological conflicts; they superseded tragic issues with happy endings, and, on the whole, presented a German variation of the Anglo-American thriller. This bright and pleasing trash stands isolated against a mass of somber "artistic" products.

The most fascinating personality of the primitive era was the Danish actress Asta Nielsen. In 1910, after years of stage triumphs, she made her screen debut in AFGRUNDEN (ABYSS), a Copenhagen Nordisk film directed by her husband, Urban Gad. This film, distinguished by a length which was then unusual, has left no trace other than an enthusiastic comment on some footage devoted to her pantomime—a sign that she must have been predestined for the cinema. Convinced of her future, Paul Davidson offered Asta Nielsen fabulous salaries and working conditions if she would agree to put her gifts at the disposal of his film company, Union. She agreed, settled in Berlin, and there, about 1911, began to appear in films which during the war stirred French as well as German soldiers to adorn their dugouts with her photograph. What they obscurely felt, Guillaume Apollinaire expressed in a torrent of words: "She is all! She is the vision of the drinker and the dream of the lonely man. She laughs like a girl completely happy, and her eye knows of things so tender and shy that one could not speak of them," and so forth.

This exceptional artist enriched the German film in more than one way. At a time when most actors still clung to stage devices, Asta Nielsen developed an innate film sense which could not but inspire her partners. Her knowledge of how to produce a definite psychological effect by means of an adequately chosen dress was as profound as her insight into the cinematic impact of details. Diaz, her early biographer, wondered at the confusion of futile objects piled up in her home—a collection including semielegant articles of men's clothing, optical instruments, little walking sticks, distorted hats and impossible wrappers. "What I am playing," she told him, "I am throughout. And I like to form so detailed an idea of my characters that I know them down to the last externals, which consist precisely of all these many bagatelles. Such bagatelles are more revealing than obtrusive exaggerations. I really build up my characters—and here you find the most decorative, most effective elements of which to compose the façade." The German screen world would be incomplete without the characters Asta Nielsen created during the silent era.[33]

[33] Diaz, *Asta Nielsen*, p. 61. For the Apollinaire quotation, see Diaz, p. 7. See also Möllhausen, "Aufstieg des Films," *Ufa-Blätter;* Kalbus, *Deutsche Filmkunst*, I, 15.

2. FOREBODINGS

From the junk heap of archaic films four call for special attention because they anticipated important postwar subjects. Three of them mirrored fantastic worlds full of chimerical creatures; this was in harmony with the progressive German film theories of the time. Many a contemporary writer encouraged the film-makers to substantiate the specific possibilities of their medium by rendering not so much existing objects as products of pure imagination. Hermann Häfker—he who praised war as the salvation from the evils of peace —advised film poets to interweave real and unreal elements. The war enthusiast fond of fairy tales: it was a truly German phenomenon. Similarly, Georg Lukacs, who was later to change from a bourgeois aesthete into a Marxist thinker (going to the extreme in both cases), wrote in 1913 that he considered the film tantamount to the fairy tale and the dream.[1]

The first to put in practice the doctrines of his contemporaries was Paul Wegener, a Reinhardt actor whose Mongolian face told of the strange visions that haunted him.[2] His desire to represent them on the screen resulted in films that were true innovations. They swept into regions ruled by other laws than ours; they rendered events which only the film could make seem real. Wegener was animated by the same cinematic passion which had inspired Georges Méliès to make such films as A Trip to the Moon and The Merry Frolics of Satan. But while the amiable French artist enchanted all childlike souls with his bright conjuring tricks, the German actor proved a sinister magician calling up the demoniac forces of human nature.

Wegener started, as early as 1913, with Der Student von Prag (The Student of Prague), a pioneer work also in that it inaugurated the exploitation of old legends. Hanns Heinz Ewers who wrote

[1] Cf. Pordes, *Das Lichtspiel,* p. 10.

[2] Mack, *Wie komme ich zum Film?,* p. 114.

the script, in collaboration with Wegener himself, possessed a real film sense. He had the good fortune to be a bad author with an imagination reveling in gross sensation and sex—a natural ally for the Nazis, for whom he was to write, in 1933, the official screen play on Horst Wessel. But precisely this kind of imagination forced him into spheres rich in tangible events and sensual experiences—always good screen material.

Borrowing from E. T. A. Hoffmann, the Faust legend and Poe's story "William Wilson," Ewers presents us with the poor student Baldwin signing a compact with the queer sorcerer Scapinelli. This incarnation of Satan promises Baldwin an advantageous marriage and inexhaustible wealth on condition that he, Scapinelli, be given the student's mirror reflection. It was a brilliant film idea to have the reflection, lured out of the looking-glass by the wizard, transform itself into an independent person. According to the terms of the compact, Baldwin meets a beautiful countess and falls in love with her; whereupon her official suitor challenges him. A duel is inevitable. At the demand of the countess' father, the student, who is reputed to be an excellent fencer, agrees to spare the life of his adversary. But as Baldwin hurries to the rendezvous—having been prevented by Scapinelli's machinations from reaching it at the appointed time—he learns that his ghostly counterpart has supplanted him and slain the unhappy suitor. Baldwin is disgraced. He tries to convince the countess of his innocence; but all attempts at rehabilitating himself are ruthlessly frustrated by his double. Obviously the double is nothing more than a projection of one of the two souls inhabiting Baldwin. The greedy self that makes him succumb to devilish temptations assumes a life of its own and sets out to destroy the other and better self he has betrayed. At the end the desperate student shoots his reflection in the same attic from which he once emerged. The shot fired at the apparition kills only himself. Then Scapinelli enters and tears the compact; its pieces drop down and cover Baldwin's corpse.[3]

The cinematic novelty of THE STUDENT OF PRAGUE seems to have stirred contemporaries. One critic compared it with paintings of Ribera—a praise that was to be crudely reversed by a reviewer who, on the occasion of a revival in 1926, called the film "incredibly naïve

[3] Cf. Ewers, *Der Student von Prag*; Kalbus, *Deutsche Filmkunst*, I, 17; Wesse, *Grossmacht Film*, p. 125 ff. For Stellan Rye, the director of the film, see Coböken, "Als ich noch rund um die Friedrichstrasse ging . . ," *25 Jahre Kinematograph*, p. 18.

and often ridiculous." [4] The film belongs among the many lost ones. Much as this may be regretted, its significance undoubtedly rests less on the camera-work than on the story proper, which despite all its Anglo-American affiliations attracted the Germans as irresistibly as if it had been exclusively drawn from native sources.

THE STUDENT OF PRAGUE introduced to the screen a theme that was to become an obsession of the German cinema: a deep and fearful concern with the foundations of the self. By separating Baldwin from his reflection and making both face each other, Wegener's film symbolizes a specific kind of split personality. Instead of being unaware of his own duality, the panic-stricken Baldwin realizes that he is in the grip of an antagonist who is nobody but himself. This was an old motif surrounded by a halo of meanings, but was it not also a dreamlike transcription of what the German middle class actually experienced in its relation to the feudal caste running Germany? The opposition of the bourgeoisie to the Imperial regime grew, at times, sufficiently acute to overshadow its hostility towards the workers, who shared the general indignation over the semi-absolutist institutions in Prussia, the encroachments of the military set and the foolish doings of the Kaiser. The current phrase, "the two Germanys," applied in particular to the differences between the ruling set and the middle class—differences deeply resented by the latter. Yet notwithstanding this dualism the Imperial government stood for economic and political principles which even the liberals were not unwilling to accept. Face to face with their conscience they had to admit that they identified themselves with the very ruling class they opposed. They represented both Germanys.

The determination with which THE STUDENT OF PRAGUE treats its horror story as a case of individual psychology is also revealing. The whole external action is merely a mirage reflecting the events in Baldwin's soul. Baldwin is not part of the world; the world is contained in Baldwin. To depict him thus, nothing was more appropriate than to locate the play in a fantastic sphere where the demands of social reality did not have to be considered. This explains, in part, the predilection of the German postwar cinema for imaginary subjects. The cosmic significance attributed to Baldwin's interior life reflects the profound aversion of all German middle-class

[4] Seeber, "Szenen aus dem Film meines Lebens," *Licht Bild Bühne*, p. 16. The quotation comes from the Hanover newspaper, *Volkswille*, Winter 1926–1927 (clipping in the possession of Mr. Henrik Galeen, New York).

strata to relating their mental dilemma to their ambiguous social plight. They shrank from tracing ideas or psychological experiences to economic and social causes after the fashion of the socialists. Founded upon the idealist concept of the autonomous individual, their attitude was in perfect harmony with their practical interests. Since any concession to the materialist thinking of the socialists might have undermined these interests, they instinctively avoided one by exaggerating the autonomy of the individual. This led them to conceive outer duplicities as inner dualities, but they preferred such psychological complications to issues involving a loss of their privileges. Nevertheless they seem to have sometimes doubted whether their retreat into the depth of the soul would save them from a catastrophic breakthrough of social reality. Baldwin's ultimate suicide mirrors their premonitions.

Wegener produced his second film, Der Golem (The Golem; like his first film, remade after the war), with the assistance of Henrik Galeen, an imaginative artist who wrote the script, directed the film and also played a role in it. Released at the beginning of 1915, the film exemplified anew Wegener's genuine passion for drawing screen effects from fantastic themes. This time the legend behind the film was the medieval Jewish one in which Rabbi Loew of Prague infuses life into a Golem—a statue he had made of clay—by putting a magic sign on its heart. In the film, workmen digging a well in an old synagogue excavate the statue and take it to an antique dealer. The dealer subsequently comes upon a report on Rabbi Loew's procedures in some cabalistic volume, and, following its directions, he achieves the miraculous metamorphosis. Now the story turns to modern psychology. While the Golem functions as the dealer's servant, a second transformation occurs: he, the dull robot, falls in love with the daughter of his master and thus changes into a human being with a soul of his own. The frightened girl tries to escape her eerie suitor, whereupon he realizes his terrible isolation. This rouses him to fury. A raging monster, he pursues the daughter, blindly destroying all obstacles in his way. At the end he perishes by falling from a tower; his corpse is the shattered statue of clay.[5]

The motifs of The Golem reappear in Homunculus (1916), a thriller in six parts which enjoyed an enormous success during

[5] Based on information offered by Mr. Henrik Galeen. For Wegener's other films, see Kalbus, *Deutsche Filmkunst*, I, 63, and Zaddach, *Der literarische Film*, p. 36.

the war. Its title role was taken by the popular Danish actor Olaf Fønss, whose romantic attire in the film reportedly influenced the fashions of elegant Berlin. Since this serial, an early forerunner of the Frankenstein films, sprang from quite other sources than Wegener's screen legend THE GOLEM, the analogies between the two movies are particularly striking.

Like the Golem, Homunculus is an artificial product. Generated in a retort by the famous scientist Professor Hansen and his assistant, Rodin, he develops into a man of sparkling intellect and indomitable will. However, no sooner does he learn the secret of his birth than he behaves as the Golem had. Homunculus is a Golem figure in the sphere of consciousness. He feels like an outcast and yearns for love to rid himself of his fatal loneliness. This overpowering desire drives him to far countries where he expects his secret to be safe, but the truth leaks out, and whatever he does to conquer their hearts, people recoil in horror, saying: "It is Homunculus, the man without a soul, the devil's servant—a monster!" When they happen to kill his dog, even Rodin, his sole friend, cannot keep the deluded Homunculus from despising all mankind. In elaborating his further career, the film foreshadows Hitler surprisingly. Obsessed by hatred, Homunculus makes himself the dictator of a large country, and then sets out to take unheard-of revenge for his sufferings. Disguised as a worker, he incites riots which give him, the dictator, an opportunity to crush the masses ruthlessly. Finally he precipitates a world war. His monstrous existence is cut short by nothing less than a thunderbolt.[6]

Both HOMUNCULUS and THE GOLEM portray characters whose abnormal traits are presented as the result of abnormal origins. But the postulate of such origins is actually a poetic subterfuge rationalizing the seemingly inexplicable fact that these heroes are, or feel themselves to be, different from their fellow creatures. What makes them so different? Homunculus formulates the reason of which the Golem is only obscurely aware: "I am cheated out of the greatest thing life has to offer!" He hints at his inability to offer and receive love—a defect which cannot but give him a strong feeling of inferiority. At about the time HOMUNCULUS appeared, the German philosopher Max Scheler lectured in public meetings on the causes of the hatred which Germany aroused everywhere in the

[6] Cf. Fønss, *Krig, Sult Og Film.* See also note on the film in Museum of Modern Art Library, clipping files.

world. The Germans resembled Homunculus: they themselves had an inferiority complex, due to an historic development which proved detrimental to the self-confidence of the middle class. Unlike the English and the French, the Germans had failed to achieve their revolution and, in consequence, never succeeded in establishing a truly democratic society. Significantly, German literature offers not a single work penetrating an articulated social whole after the manner of Balzac or Dickens. No social whole existed in Germany. The middle-class strata were in a state of political immaturity against which they dreaded to struggle lest they further endanger their already insecure social condition. This retrogressive conduct provoked a psychological stagnation. Their habit of nurturing the intimately associated sensations of inferiority and isolation was as juvenile as their inclination to revel in dreams of the future.

The two artificial screen figures react to frustration in a similar way. In the case of Homunculus the impulses prompting him to action are quite obvious. He combines lust for destruction with sado-masochistic tendencies manifesting themselves in his wavering between humble submission and revengeful violence. Rodin's much-stressed friendship with him adds a touch of homosexuality that rounds out the picture. Modern psychoanalysis is undoubtedly justified in interpreting these perversions as means of escape from the specific suffering Homunculus undergoes. That both films dwell upon such outlets reveals a strong predisposition on the part of the Germans to utilize them.

Having gone berserk, the Golem and Homunculus die deaths as remote from the normal as their origins. That of Homunculus is strictly supernatural, although he might well have been killed by an act of revenge or justice. Isolating him definitely from the rest of humanity, his end testifies not only, as did THE STUDENT OF PRAGUE, to the desire of the middle-class German to exalt his independence of social exigencies, but also to his pride in this self-chosen isolation. Like Baldwin's suicide, the deaths of both monsters betray gloomy forebodings.

The fourth archaic film denoting psychological unrest was DER ANDERE (THE OTHER), a realistic counterpart of the three fantasies. Released in 1913, it was based on Paul Lindau's stage play of the same title, which dramatized a Dr. Jekyll-and-Mr. Hyde case, drawing it into a stuffy bourgeois atmosphere. The Dr. Jekyll is here an enlightened Berlin lawyer, Dr. Hallers, who, during a house party, smiles sceptically at an account of a split personality. Nothing of that kind, he contends, can ever happen to him. But, overworked, Hallers falls from a horse, and, as a consequence, becomes increasingly often the victim of a compulsory sleep from which he emerges as "the other." This other self of his, a rogue, joins a burglar to break into the lawyer's own flat. The police interfere, arresting the burglar. While they examine him, his accomplice falls asleep and awakes as Dr. Hallers—a Hallers completely unconscious of his participation in the crime. He collapses after being forced to identify himself as the burglar's partner. The story has a happy ending. Hallers regains his health and gets married: the prototype of a citizen immune to all psychological disturbances.[7]

Hallers' adventure intimates that anyone can fall prey to mental disintegration like Baldwin, and thereby become an outcast like Homunculus. Now, Hallers is defined as a middle-class German. Owing to his spiritual kinship with the fantastic figures of the other films, it seems all the more justifiable to consider them middle-class representatives as well. Instead of elaborating on this kinship, THE OTHER treats it as a temporary one. Hallers' disintegration appears as a curable disease, and far from ending tragically, he returns to the calm haven of normal life. This difference must be laid to a change of perspective. While the fantastic films spontaneously reflect certain attitudes symptomatic of collective uneasiness, THE OTHER approaches the same attitudes from the standpoint of banal middle-class optimism. Guided by this optimism, the story minimizes the existing uneasiness, and, in consequence, symbolizes it through an ephemeral accident which cannot invalidate confidence in everlasting security.

[7] Publicity program for the film; Kalbus, *Deutsche Filmkunst,* I, 14. The part of Dr. Hallers was Albert Bassermann's first film role.

3. GENESIS OF UFA

The birth of the German film proper resulted in part from organizational measures taken by the German authorities. These measures must be traced to two observations all informed Germans were in a position to make during World War I. First, they became increasingly aware of the influence anti-German films exerted everywhere abroad—a fact which startled them all the more as they themselves had not yet realized the immense suggestive power inherent in this medium. Second, they recognized the insufficiency of the domestic output. To satisfy the enormous demands, incompetent producers had flooded the market with films which proved inferior in quality to the bulk of foreign pictures [1]; moreover, the German film had not been animated by the propagandistic zeal that those of the Allies evinced.

Aware of this dangerous situation, the German authorities tried to change it by intervening directly in the production of motion pictures. In 1916 the government, with the support of associations promoting economic, political and cultural objectives, founded Deulig (*Deutsche Lichtspiel-Gesellschaft*), a film company which, through appropriate documentary films, was to publicize the fatherland at home and abroad.[2] At the beginning of 1917, there followed the establishment of Bufa (*Bild- und Filmamt*); set up purely as a government agency, it supplied the troops at the front with movie theaters and also assumed the task of providing those documentaries which recorded military activities.[3]

This was something, but not enough. When after the entrance of the United States into the war American movies swept over the world, impressing hatred of Germany with an unrivaled force upon

[1] Boehmer and Reitz, *Film in Wirtschaft und Recht*, p. 6.
[2] *Ibid.*, p. 6; Kalbus, *Deutsche Filmkunst*, I, 42.
[3] Kalbus, *ibid.*, p. 44; Bardèche and Brasillach, *History of Motion Pictures*, p. 135.

enemies and neutrals alike, leading German circles agreed that only an organization of tremendous proportions would be able to counteract that campaign. The omnipotent General Ludendorff himself took the initiative by recommending a merger of the main film companies, so that their scattered energies might be channeled in the national interest. His suggestions were orders. On the strength of a resolution adopted in November 1917 by the German High Command in close touch with prominent financiers, industrialists and shipowners, Messter Film, Davidson's Union and the companies controlled by Nordisk—with backing from a group of banks—merged into a new enterprise: Ufa (*Universum Film A. G.*). Its stock of shares amounted to about 25 million marks, of which the Reich took over one-third, i.e., 8 million. The official mission of Ufa was to advertise Germany according to government directives. These asked not only for direct screen propaganda, but also for films characteristic of German culture and films serving the purpose of national education.[4]

To attain its aims, Ufa had to raise the level of domestic production, because only films of high standards could be expected to compete with, let alone outstrip, foreign achievements in effective propaganda. Animated by this interest, Ufa assembled a team of talented producers, artists and technicians, and organized the studio work with that thoroughness upon which the success of any propagandistic campaign depends. In addition, Ufa had to sell its goods. Conscious of this task, it began to infiltrate the occupied Ukraine as early as March 1918.[5]

In its effort to make the German film a propaganda weapon, the government had not reckoned with defeat and revolution. However, the events of November left this weapon intact, except, of course, for Bufa which, as a residue of the Imperial administration, was dissolved at the end of 1918. In the case of Ufa, a transfer of property took place: the Reich renounced its partnership, and the Deutsche Bank began to acquire most of the shares, including those of Nordisk.[6] Yet this economic shift did not imply a change of conduct. Since the new masters of Ufa scarcely differed from the

[4] *Jahrbuch der Filmindustrie,* 1922/3, p. 26, and 1923/25, p. 12; Neumann, *Film-"Kunst"*, pp. 36–37; Olimsky, *Filmwirtschaft,* p. 24; Vincent, *Histoire de l'Art Cinématographique,* p. 139.

[5] *Jahrbuch der Filmindustrie,* 1922/3, p. 27; Jacobs, *American Film,* p. 303.

[6] Neumann, *Film-"Kunst"*, pp. 36–37; *Jahrbuch der Filmindustrie,* 1922/3, p. 28, and 1923/25, p. 12.

old ones, they were inclined to perpetuate on the screen the conservative and nationalist pattern set by the former regime. Only a slight retouching was desirable: in view of the actual domestic situation the films to be promoted would have to make it absolutely clear that the Germany of which Ufa dreamed was by no means identical with the Germany of the socialists.

Owing to Ufa's transformation into a private company, its concern with propaganda was somewhat overshadowed by purely commercial considerations, especially those of export. But export was of propagandistic use, too, and precisely in the interest of economic expansion there now remained, as before, the task of perfecting the German film, so that it might be forced upon a world utterly disinclined to accept any such contribution. German postwar films encountered a stiff international boycott calculated to last several years. To run this blockade, Ufa began immediately after the war to secure rights to movie theaters in Switzerland, Scandinavia, Holland, Spain and other neutral countries. Deulig, which like Ufa continued working under the Republic, adopted the same policy by building up contacts in the Balkans.[7]

The genesis of Ufa testifies to the authoritarian character of Imperial Germany. Although, in wartime, the authorities of all belligerent countries assume virtually unlimited powers, the use they can make of these powers is not everywhere the same. When the German war lords ordered the foundation of Ufa, they initiated activities which in democracies result from the pressure of public opinion. Manipulated as this opinion may be, it preserves a certain spontaneity which no democratic government can afford to disregard. After America's entrance into the war, anti-German films were officially encouraged, but the administration relied on existing emotional trends.[8] These films expressed what the people actually felt. No such consideration for popular sentiments influenced decisions in favor of a similar screen campaign in Germany. Dictated by the necessities of the war, they were based exclusively upon the arguments of experts. The German authorities took it for granted that public opinion could be molded into any pattern they desired. Symptomatically, the Germans were so accustomed to an authoritive handling of their affairs that they believed the enemy screen propaganda also to be the outcome of mere government planning.

[7] Kalbus, *Deutsche Filmkunst,* I, 42.
[8] Jacobs, *American Film,* p. 253 ff.

Any framework of organizational measures has to be filled out with life. The birth of the German film originated not only in the foundation of Ufa, but also in the intellectual excitement surging through Germany after the war. All Germans were then in a mood which can best be defined by the word *Aufbruch*. In the pregnant sense in which it was used at the time, the term meant departure from the shattered world of yesterday towards a tomorrow built on the grounds of revolutionary conceptions. This explains why, as in Russia, expressionist art became popular in Germany during that period.[9] People suddenly grasped the significance of *avant-garde* paintings and mirrored themselves in visionary dramas announcing to a suicidal mankind the gospel of a new age of brotherhood.

Intoxicated by such prospects, which now seemed within reach, intellectuals, students, artists and whoever felt the call set out to solve all political, social and economic problems with equal ease. They read *Capital* or quoted Marx without having read him; they believed in international socialism, pacifism, collectivism, aristocratic leadership, religious community life or national resurrection, and frequently presented a confused mixture of these variegated ideals as a brand-new creed. But whatever they advocated seemed to them a universal remedy for all evils, particularly in cases in which they owed their discovery to inspiration rather than knowledge. When in a meeting after the Armistice Max Weber, the great scholar and German democrat, criticized the humiliating peace conditions which the Allies had in store, a sculptor of local reputation shouted: "Germany should let the other nations crucify her for the sake of the world!" The eagerness with which the sculptor jumped into this Dostoievsky-like declaration was quite symptomatic. Innumerable manifestoes and programs spread all over Germany, and the smallest meeting room resounded with the roar of heated discussion. It was one of those rare moments in which the soul of a whole people overflows its traditional bounds.

In the wake of this uproarious *Aufbruch* the last prejudices against the cinema melted away. Even more important, the cinema attracted creative energies which longed for an opportunity to express adequately the new hopes and fears of which the era was full. Young writers and painters just back from the war approached the film studios, animated, like the rest of their generation, by the desire to commune with the people. To them the screen was more than a

[9] Kurtz, *Expressionismus*, p. 61.

medium rich in unexplored possibilities; it was a unique means of imparting messages to the masses. Of course, the film producers and big executives interfered with such upward flights, engineering all kinds of compromises. But even so this postwar effervescence enriched the German screen with singular content and a language of its own.

THE POSTWAR PERIOD
(1918–1924)

4. THE SHOCK OF FREEDOM

To call the events of November 1918 a revolution would be abusing the term. There was no revolution in Germany. What really took place was the breakdown of those in command, resulting from a hopeless military situation and a sailors' revolt which gained momentum only because people were sick of the war. The Social Democrats who took over were so unprepared for a revolution that they originally did not even think of establishing a German Republic. Its proclamation was improvised.[1] These leaders, in whom Lenin had placed such hope, proved incapable of removing the big landowners, the industrialists, the generals, the judiciary. Instead of creating a people's army, they relied on the antidemocratic Freikorps formations to crush Spartacus. On January 15, 1919, Freikorps officers murdered Rosa Luxemburg and Karl Liebknecht—a crime soon to be followed by the series of notorious *Feme*-murders, not one of which was ever punished. After the first weeks of the new Republic the old ruling classes began to re-establish themselves. Except for a few social reforms not much had been changed.[2]

However, the sweep of intellectual excitement accompanying even this abortive revolution reveals the cataclysm Germany endured after the collapse of the old hierarchy of values and conventions. For a brief while the German mind had a unique opportunity to overcome hereditary habits and reorganize itself completely. It enjoyed freedom of choice, and the air was full of doctrines trying to captivate it, to lure it into a regrouping of inner attitudes.

In the domain of public life nothing was settled as yet. People suffered from hunger, disorder, unemployment and the first signs of inflation. Street fighting became an everyday event. Revolutionary solutions seemed now remote, now just around the corner. The ever-smoldering class struggle kept fears and hopes aflame.

[1] Schwarzschild, *World in Trance,* pp. 51–53.

[2] Rosenberg, *Geschichte der Deutschen Republik,* pp. 48, 71–73.

Of the two types of films in vogue immediately after the war the first elaborated upon matters of sex life with an undeniable penchant for pornographic excursions. Films of this kind took advantage of the sexual enlightenment officially promoted in prewar Germany. In those days eighteen-year-old boys did not leave high school for a university without being initiated by some medical man into the dangers of venereal diseases and the use of prophylactics. During the war, Richard Oswald, a versatile film director with a flair for the needs of the market, divined that the hour had come to transfer this indoctrination to the screen. He wisely managed to have the Society for Combatting Venereal Diseases (*Gesellschaft zur Bekämpfung der Geschlechtskrankheiten*) sponsor his film Es WERDE LICHT (LET THERE BE LIGHT) which dealt with the destructive nature of syphilis. This was in 1917. As box-office receipts justified his hygienic zeal, Oswald continued to keep the light burning by adding, in 1918, a second and third part.[3] The film was drawn out like an accordion. In the same year Davidson's Union, obviously stimulated by Oswald's success, released KEIMENDES LEBEN (GERMINATING LIFE); featuring Jannings, it advertised hygiene under the auspices of a high-ranking medical officer.[4] This dignified patronage of course bewitched the censors.

When, immediately after the war, the Council of People's Representatives abolished censorship—a measure revealing that government's confused ideas about revolutionary exigencies—the effect was not a transformation of the screen into a political platform, but a sudden increase of films which pretended to be concerned with sexual enlightenment. Now that they had nothing to fear from official supervision, they all indulged in a copious depiction of sexual debaucheries. Refreshed by the atmosphere of freedom, Richard Oswald felt in so creative a mood that he annexed a fourth part to LET THERE BE LIGHT, and also made a film called PROSTITUTION. Scores of similar products swarmed out under such alluring titles as VOM RANDE DES SUMPFES (FROM THE VERGE OF THE SWAMP), FRAUEN, DIE DER ABGRUND VERSCHLINGT (WOMEN ENGULFED BY THE ABYSS), VERLORENE TÖCHTER (LOST DAUGHTERS), HYÄNEN DER LUST (HYENAS OF LUST), and so forth. One of them, GELÜBDE DER KEUCHHEIT (VOW OF CHASTITY), intermingled pictures detailing the love affairs of a Catholic priest with shots of devotees reciting

[3] Kalbus, *Deutsche Filmkunst*. I, 40–41.
[4] *Ibid.*, p. 41; *Jahrbuch der Filmindustrie*, 1922/3, p. 28.

the rosary for the sake of the priest's soul. Two other films, significantly entitled Aus eines Mannes Mädchenjahren (A Man's Girlhood) and Anders als die Andern (Different from the Others), dwelt upon homosexual propensities; they capitalized on the noisy resonance of Dr. Magnus Hirschfeld's campaign against Paragraph 175 of the penal code which exacted punishment for certain abnormal sex practices.[5]

The appeal to sensual curiosity proved a sound commercial speculation. According to the balance sheets, many a movie theater doubled its monthly revenues whenever it exhibited outspoken sex films.[6] These were naturally advertised in suitable terms. For instance, the film Das Mädchen und die Männer (The Girl and the Men) was played up as "a very spicy picture drawn from the life of a girl who storms through her youth in the arms of men, and fades away with a nostalgic longing for the greatness of unattainable purity." [7] Films of that ilk attracted the multitude of demobilized soldiers not yet adjusted to a civilian life which seemed to reject them, the numerous youngsters who had grown up like weeds while their fathers were in the war, and all those who in times out of joint always come to the fore, seeking jobs, gambling, waiting for opportunities or simply prowling the streets. The more privileged also enjoyed these stimulants, as can be inferred from the success of Opium, which ran in an expensive Berlin movie theater with the house sold out for three weeks.[8] Of course, one avoided being seen on such occasions.

The sex films testified to primitive needs arising in all belligerent countries after the war. Nature itself urged that people who had, for an eternity, faced death and destruction, reconfirm their violated life instincts by means of excesses. It was an all but automatic process; equilibrium could not be reached at once. However, since the Germans survived the slaughter only to undergo the hardships of a sort of civil war, this fashion of sex films cannot be explained fully as a symptom of sudden release from pressure. Nor did it convey a revolutionary meaning. Even though some affected to be scandalized by the penal code's intolerance, these films had nothing in common with the prewar revolt against outmoded sexual conven-

[5] Kalbus, *Deutsche Filmkunst,* I, 41; Eger, *Kinoreform,* pp. 17–18; Zimmereimer, *Filmzensur,* p. 76.

[6] Eger, *Kinoreform,* p. 23.

[7] *Ibid.,* p. 17.

[8] *Ibid.,* p. 18.

tions. Nor did they reflect the revolutionary erotic feelings that quivered in contemporary literature. They were just vulgar films selling sex to the public. That the public demanded them rather indicated a general unwillingness to be involved in revolutionary activities; otherwise interest in sex would have been absorbed by interest in the political aims to be attained. Debaucheries are often an unconscious attempt to drown the consciousness of deep, inner frustration. This psychological mechanism seems to have forced itself upon many Germans. It was as if they felt paralyzed in view of the freedom offered them, and instinctively withdrew into the unproblematic pleasures of the flesh. An aura of sadness surrounded the sex films.

With the favorable response to these films mingled, as might be expected, stiff opposition. In Düsseldorf the audience of VOW OF CHASTITY went so far as to tear the screen; in Baden the public prosecutor seized the copies of Oswald's PROSTITUTION and recommended his indictment.[9] Elsewhere youth took the lead. Dresden demonstrated against the film FRÄULEIN MUTTER (MAIDEN MOTHER), while the Leipzig boy scouts (*Wandervögel*) issued a manifesto disapproving of all screen trash and its promoters among the actors and owners of movie theaters.[10]

Were these crusades the outcome of revolutionary austerity? That the demonstrating Dresden youth distributed anti-Semitic leaflets reveals this local campaign to have been a reactionary maneuver calculated to turn the resentments of the suffering petty bourgeoisie away from the old ruling class. By making the Jews responsible for the sex films, the wire-pullers in Dresden could be fairly sure to influence lower middle-class people in the desired direction. For these orgies and extravagances were condemned with a moral indignation which was all the more poisonous as it cloaked envy of those who embraced life unhesitatingly. The socialists too launched attacks against the sex films. In the National Assembly as well as in most diets they declared that their move to socialize and communalize the film industry would best serve to exterminate the plague on the screen.[11] But to suggest socialization for reasons of conventional morality was an argument that discredited the cause it supported. The cause was a revolutionary shift; the argument suited the

[9] Kalbus, *Deutsche Filmkunst*, I, 41–42.
[10] Eger, *Kinoreform*, pp. 27–28.
[11] *Ibid.*, p. 31; Moreck, *Sittengeschichte*, pp. 37–39.

mind of philistines. This exemplifies the cleavage between the convictions of many socialists and their middle-class dispositions.

The plague raged through 1919 and then subsided. In May 1920, the National Assembly rejected several motions in favor of socialization, and simultaneously passed a law governing all film matters of the Reich. National censorship was resumed.[12]

The other type of film in vogue after the war was the historical pageant. While the sex films crowded the lower depths of the screen world, the histories self-assuredly settled themselves in the higher realms reserved for art. Whether they really represented summits of artistic perfection or not, they were planned as such by the founding fathers of Ufa who, as has been seen, promoted the idea of putting art to the service of propaganda.

An interesting article published in January 1920 by Rudolf Pabst testifies to the thoroughness with which the Germans prepared for the reconquest of a prominent economic and cultural position.[13] Pabst severely criticized the current advertising shorts for subordinating entertainment to propaganda. Since any audience, he argued, desires to be entertained, these shorts were resented as boring interludes. He explained the tremendous success of most foreign propaganda films precisely by the fact that they were feature films full of suspense and action—films, he emphasized, which implied propaganda subtly instead of shouting it from the rooftops. His conclusion was that the Germans should not outrightly advertise to people abroad their unbroken economic efficiency, but should rather lure them into recognizing it through full-length pictures offering outstanding entertainment. To serve as a means to an end this screen entertainment would have to seem an end in itself. It was not by mere chance that, about 1920, Deulig, which until now had specialized in propagandistic documentaries, began to include in its production program films of fiction.[14]

No sooner had Ufa been founded than its masters went ahead in the direction Pabst's article praised as good policy. There existed a pattern of entertainment strongly appealing to their taste for all that was *kolossal*: the Italian superspectacle. Such films as Quo Vadis and Cabiria had been the rage of two continents. Of

[12] *Jahrbuch der Filmindustrie*, 1922/3, p. 31.

[13] Pabst, "Bedeutung des Films," *Moderne Kinematographie*, 1920, p. 26 ff. See also Vincent, *Histoire de l'Art Cinématographique*, p. 140.

[14] Boehmer and Reitz, *Film in Wirtschaft und Recht*, p. 6.

course, their cost was exorbitant; but Ufa could afford to spend millions. It began investing them in the film VERITAS VINCIT made by Joe May in 1918—a gigantic nonentity which resorted to the theory of the transmigration of souls to drag a love story through three pompously staged historic ages.[15]

More important achievements followed this first attempt at grandiloquence; they were inspired by Davidson who, after the great merger of November 1917, had become one of Ufa's chief executives. Davidson dreamed of gorgeous dramas featuring his new favorite, Pola Negri, and since he considered Lubitsch the only one to handle such a superior woman, he tried hard to make the project alluring to him. "No, dear director," Lubitsch answered, "this is not for me. I am going on with my comedies." But he finally yielded to Davidson's wishes. While the war was slowly approaching its end, Lubitsch directed Pola Negri in two films, DIE MUMIE MA (THE EYES OF THE MUMMY) and CARMEN (GYPSY BLOOD). These films, which co-starred his actor-friends Emil Jannings and Harry Liedtke, established his reputation as a dramatic director and revealed him to be a true disciple of Max Reinhardt, whose stage devices he adapted to the screen.[16]

The response to GYPSY BLOOD was sufficiently promising to encourage further production of spectacular dramas. In the first two postwar years Lubitsch made four of them which thoroughly justified the hopes Davidson had for their international success. This famous series began with MADAME DU BARRY (PASSION), released in Berlin's largest movie theater, the Ufa-Palast am Zoo, on September 18, 1919, the very day of its opening to the public.[17] Huge demonstrations swept continuously through the Berlin streets at that time; similar throngs of aroused Parisians were unleashed in PASSION to illustrate the French Revolution. Was it a revolutionary film? Here are the salient points of the plot: After becoming the omnipotent mistress of King Louis XV, Countess du Barry, a former milliner's apprentice, frees her lover, Armand de Foix, who has been imprisoned for slaying his adversary in a duel, and ap-

[15] Tannenbaum, "Der Grossfilm," *Der Film von Morgen,* p. 65; Kalbus, *Deutsche Filmkunst,* I, 44.

[16] Davidson, "Wie das deutsche Lichtspieltheater entstand," and Lubitsch, "Wie mein erster Grossfilm entstand," *Licht Bild Bühne,* pp. 8, 13–14; Kalbus, *Deutsche Filmkunst,* I, 45 ff. For Davidson, see "Was is los?" *Ufa Magazin,* April 8–14, 1927. For Pola Negri, see Kalbus, *Deutsche Filmkunst,* I, 31–32, and Balázs, *Der sichtbare Mensch,* p. 67.

[17] *Jahrbuch der Filmindustrie,* 1922/3, p. 29.

points him a royal guard at the palace. But, as the Ufa synopsis puts it, "Armand cannot bear these new conditions, and plots, making the cobbler Paillet head of the revolutionary plans." Paillet leads a deputation to the palace at the very moment when the King falls prey to deadly smallpox. Meeting the cobbler on a stairway, Madame du Barry sends him to the Bastille. A little later—the story's contempt for historic facts is matched only by its disregard for their meaning—Armand incites the masses to storm that symbol of absolutist power. Louis XV dies, and his mistress, now banished from the court, is dragged to the revolutionary tribunal over which Armand presides. He tries to rescue her. However, Paillet forestalls this tender project by killing Armand and having Madame du Barry sentenced to death. At the end, she is seen on the scaffold surrounded by innumerable vengeful fists that emerge from a crowd fanatically enjoying the fall of her beautiful head.

This narrative of Hans Kräly's, who also fashioned the rest of the Lubitsch pageants in collaboration with Norbert Falk and others, drains the Revolution of its significance. Instead of tracing all revolutionary events to their economic and ideal causes, it persistently presents them as the outcome of psychological conflicts. It is a deceived lover who, animated by the desire for retaliation, talks the masses into capturing the Bastille. Similarly, Madame du Barry's execution is related not so much to political reasons as to motives of personal revenge. PASSION does not exploit the passions inherent in the Revolution, but reduces the Revolution to a derivative of private passions. If it were otherwise, the tragic death of both lovers would hardly overshadow the victorious rising of the people.[18]

Lubitsch's three subsequent superproductions were in the same vein. In ANNA BOLEYN (DECEPTION, 1920) he spent 8½ million marks on an elaborate depiction of Henry VIII's sex life, setting it off against a colorful background which included court intrigues, the Tower, two thousand extras and some historic episodes. In this particular case he did not have to distort the given facts very much to make history seem the product of a tyrant's private life. Here, too, despotic lusts destroy tender affections: a hired cavalier kills Anne Boleyn's lover, and finally she herself mounts the executioner's block. To intensify the sinister atmosphere torture episodes were

[18] "Passion," *Exceptional Photoplays*, Nov. 1920; *Ufa Verleih-Programme*, 1923, I, 2.

inserted which an early reviewer called a "terse suggestion of medieval horror and callous infliction of death." [19]

All these ingredients reappeared in DAS WEIB DES PHARAO (THE LOVES OF PHARAOH, 1921), which nevertheless impressed the audience as new, because it substituted the Sphinx for the Tower, and considerably increased the number of extras and intrigues. Its tyrant figure, the Pharaoh Amenes, is so infatuated with the Greek slave Theonis that he refuses to hand the girl back to her legitimate owner, an Ethiopian king; whereupon the two nations become involved in a bloody war. That Theonis prefers a young man named Ramphis to the Pharaoh adds the desired final touch to the emotional and political confusion. In a state of absent-mindedness the story unexpectedly heads for a happy ending, but at the last moment the tragic sense prevails, and instead of surviving their troubles, the lovers are stoned by the people, while Amenes dies from a stroke or inner exhaustion.[20]

SUMURUN (ONE ARABIAN NIGHT, 1920), a screen version of Reinhardt's stage pantomime *Sumurun* with Pola Negri in the title role, withdrew from the realms of history into Oriental fairy-tale surroundings, making an old sheik in search of sex adventures the comical counterpart of Amenes and Henry VIII. The sheik surprises his son and his mistress, a young dancer, in each other arms—an incident prearranged by a hunchbacked juggler who wants to take revenge for the indifference the dancer has shown him. In a fit of jealousy the sheik kills the sinful couple, whereupon the sensitive hunchback, in turn, feels urged to stab the sheik. Loaded with kisses and corpses, this showy fantasy pretended superiority to its theme by satirizing it pleasantly.[21]

The whole series gave rise to numerous historical pageants which invariably adopted the standardized plot Lubitsch and his collaborators had fashioned. Buchowetski's much-praised DANTON (ALL FOR A WOMAN, released in 1921)outdid even PASSION in its contempt for the French Revolution. Envying Danton his popularity, the Robespierre of this film accuses him of debauchery and connivance with the aristocrats, but Danton's masterful speech during

[19] Quotation from "Deception," *Exceptional Photoplays*, April 1921, p. 4. See also Tannenbaum, "Der Grossfilm," *Der Film von Morgen*, pp. 66, 68, 71; *Ufa Verleih-Programme*, 1923, I, 10. For Henny Porten in this film, see Amiguet, *Cinéma! Cinéma!*, pp. 61–62.

[20] Program to this film; Kalbus, *Deutsche Filmkunst*, I, 47.

[21] Program to this film; Jacobs, *American Film*, p. 306; *Film Index*, p. 300b.

the trial transforms the suspicious audience into a crowd of ecstatic followers. To avert this threat Robespierre spreads the rumor that food has arrived and will be gratuitously distributed. The trick works: the people run away, leaving Danton to the mercy of his pitiless enemy. According to this film, the masses are as despicable as their leaders.[22]

The international reception of any achievement depends upon its capacity for arousing fertile misunderstandings everywhere. Lubitsch's films—the first German postwar productions to be shown abroad—possessed this capacity. Towards the end of 1920, they began to appear in America, enthusiastically received by a public which at that time rather repudiated costume drama. All contemporary reviewers were unanimous in praising as the main virtue of these films their sense of authenticity, their outstanding "historical realism." "History," a critic wrote of DECEPTION, "is presented to us naked and real and unromanticized in all its grandeur and its barbarism." Uneasy about the failure of Wilson's policy, the American people had obviously such a craving for history debunked that they were attracted by films which pictured great historic events as the work of unscrupulous wire-pullers. Consequently, Lubitsch was called the "great humanizer of history" and the "Griffith of Europe." [23]

The French had suffered too much from Germany to react as naïvely as the Americans. Obsessed by distrust, they imagined that anything coming from beyond the Rhine was intended to poison them. They therefore considered Lubitsch a clever propagandist rather than a great humanizer, and suspected his films of deliberately smearing the past of the Allies. In these films, the Paris film writer Canudo declared, "French history . . . was depicted by the perverted and sexual pen of the Germans." The same opinion prevailed in other countries neighboring Germany. Although Fréd.-Ph. Amiguet of Geneva was amiable enough to admire the verve of the Lubitsch spectacles, he bluntly stigmatized them as "instruments of vengeance." [24] These emotional judgments were hardly justified.

[22] "All for a Woman," *Exceptional Photoplays*, Nov. 1921, pp. 4–5; Zaddach, *Der literarische Film*, p. 41.

[23] Quotation about DECEPTION comes from "Deception," *Exceptional Photoplays*, April 1921, p. 4; quotation about Lubitsch cited by Jacobs, *American Film*, p. 305.

[24] Canudo quotation from Jahier, "42 Ans de Cinéma," *Le Rôle intellectuel du Cinéma*, pp. 59–60. Amiguet, *Cinéma! Cinéma!*, pp. 33–34; Bardèche and Brasillach, *History of Motion Pictures*, p. 189; Vincent, *Histoire de l'Art Cinématographique*, p. 142.

That the Lubitsch films did not aim at discrediting French or English history follows conclusively from the vital interest Ufa had in selling them to the Allies.

In his history of German film art, a Nazi-minded product with some remnants of pre-Nazi evaluations, Oskar Kalbus connects the vogue of historical pageants with the moment of their production; they were produced, he contends, "because in times of national emergency people are particularly susceptible to representations of great historic periods and personalities." [25] He completely overlooks the fact that this susceptibility was betrayed by films representing not so much historic periods as personal appetites and seeming to seize upon history for the sole purpose of removing it thoroughly from the field of vision.[26] It is not as if the historical films of Italian or American origin had ever achieved miracles of perspicacity; but the sustained lack of comprehension in the Lubitsch films is significant inasmuch as they emerged at a moment when it would have been in the interest of the new democratic regime to enlighten the people about social and political developments. All these German pageants which the Americans mistook for summits of "historical realism" instinctively sabotaged any understanding of historic processes, any attempt to explore patterns of conduct in the past.

A hint of the true meaning of the Lubitsch films can be found in the fact that Lubitsch played the hunchback in ONE ARABIAN NIGHT. It was at that time quite exceptional for him to take a role himself. After stabbing the sheik and freeing all the women in his harem, the hunchback returns from the scene of wholesale murder to his fair booth. "He must dance and gambol again," the Ufa prospectus states, "for the public wants a laugh." Through his identification with a juggler who drowns horrors in jokes, Lubitsch involuntarily deepens the impression that the vogue he helped to create originated in a blend of cynicism and melodramatic sentimentality. The touch of melodrama made the implications of this cynicism more palatable. Its source was a nihilistic outlook on world affairs, as can be inferred from the stern determination with which the Lubitsch films and their like not only put insatiable rulers to death, but also destroyed young lovers representative of all that counts in life. They characterized history as meaningless. History, they seemed to say, is an arena reserved for blind and ferocious

[25] Kalbus, *Deutsche Filmkunst,* I, 51.

[26] Cf. Chowl, "The French Revolution," *Close Up,* May 1929, p. 49.

instincts, a product of devilish machinations forever frustrating our hopes for freedom and happiness.

Designed for mass consumption, this nihilistic gospel must have satisfied widespread wants. It certainly poured balm on the wounds of innumerable Germans who, because of the humiliating defeat of the fatherland, refused any longer to acknowledge history as an instrument of justice or Providence. By degrading the French Revolution to a questionable adventure in both PASSION and ALL FOR A WOMAN, that nihilism moreover revealed itself as a symptom of strong antirevolutionary, if not antidemocratic, tendencies in postwar Germany. It was, for once, a nihilism that did not scare the nation. Why? The only tenable explanation is that, whether consciously or not, the majority of people lived in fear of social changes and therefore welcomed films which defamed not only bad rulers but also good revolutionary causes. These films outrightly encouraged the existing resistance to any emotional shift that might have enlivened the German Republic. Their basic nihilism made them indulge also in images of utter destruction, which, like those of THE STUDENT OF PRAGUE or HOMUNCULUS, reflected forebodings of a final doom.

American observers admired the free use made of the camera in these Lubitsch pageants. Lewis Jacobs remarks of them that it was revolutionary in those days "to tilt a camera toward the sky or turn it toward an arabesque mosaic in a floor, and to see the backs of a crowd was unorthodox; quick cutting, too, was shocking." [27] His statement mistakenly suggests that the Lubitsch films were the first to develop this camera initiative, but it was the war that had aroused the camera's curiosity by making it focus upon subjects of military importance. Photographs of a shell crater with a few pairs of legs at the upper margin or an agglomeration of rifles, truck wheels and torsos were then quite common.[28] While traditional aesthetics would have condemned such photographs as incoherent, the war generation which had become accustomed to them began enjoying their singular power of expression. This change of visual habits emboldened the camera to emphasize parts of bodies, to capture objects from unusual angles.

Lubitsch's method of furthering the dramatic action through

[27] Jacobs, *American Film,* p. 306. Surprisingly, Jacobs forgets to mention in this connection D. W. Griffith, whose film techniques surpassed those of Lubitsch.

[28] Gregor, *Zeitalter des Films,* pp. 81–82.

shots of this kind was an additional innovation. Shaken by catastrophe, the Germans had to adjust their conventional notions to the needs of the moment. In the wake of any such metamorphosis perspectives change: things consecrated by tradition lose their prestige, while others that have been as yet overlooked suddenly come to the fore. Since the Lubitsch pageants substituted for the old conception of history one that dissolved history into psychology, they were naturally obliged to resort to a new set of pictorial elements. Their psychological tendency made them single out such details as the arabesque mosaic or the backs of a crowd—seeming bagatelles which, however, effectively underlined major emotional events.

What fascinated the public most was "Mr. Lubitsch's indisputable talent for handling crowds." [29] Many years after the release of his films moviegoers still remembered as their main attraction the throngs of the Paris rabble in PASSION, the agitated battle scenes in THE LOVES OF PHARAOH and that episode of DECEPTION which showed all London before the Tower attending Anna Boleyn's solemn entrance.[30] Lubitsch had of course learned from Max Reinhardt, who early proved himself a master in the art of surrounding his stage crowds with appropriate space and orchestrating their movements dramatically. Perhaps Reinhardt sensed coming events, for crowds were to develop from an element of his stage into one of German everyday life—a process that reached its climax after the war, when no one could avoid encountering them on streets and squares. These masses were more than a weighty social factor; they were as tangible as any individual. A hope to some and a nightmare to others, they haunted the imagination. Ernst Toller's "speaking chorus" tried to endow them with a voice of their own, and Reinhardt himself paid tribute to them by founding his short-lived "Theater of the Five Thousand." [31]

The moment for rendering crowds on the screen was well chosen inasmuch as they now assumed the aspect of dynamic units sweeping through large spaces—an aspect which the screen rather than the stage was able to mirror. Lubitsch knew how to handle such crowds, and even showed true originality in elaborating a feature familiar

[29] Quotation from "The Loves of Pharaoh," *Exceptional Photoplays,* Jan.–Feb. 1922, p. 3. See also "Passion," *ibid.*, Nov. 1920, p. 3.

[30] Birnbaum, "Massenscenen im Film," *Ufa-Blätter*; Tannenbaum, "Der Grossfilm," *Der Film von Morgen,* p. 66.

[31] Birnbaum, "Massenscenen im Film," *Ufa-Blätter*; Samuel and Thomas, *Expressionism in German Life,* pp. 46–47; Freedley and Reeves, *History of the Theatre,* esp. p. 529.

to all postwar Germans: the contrast between the individual in the crowd and the crowd itself as a solid mass. To this end he used an exclusively cinematic device which cannot better be described than in the following words of Miss Lejeune: "Lubitsch had a way of manipulating his puppets that gave multitude, and in contrast, loneliness, a new force. No one before had so filled and drained his spaces with the wheeling mass, rushing in the figures from every corner to cover the screen, dispersing them again like a whirlwind, with one single figure staunch in the middle of the empty square." [32] The mass scene typical of the Lubitsch films decomposed the crowd to exhibit as its nucleus "one single figure" who, after the crowd's dissolution, was left alone in the void. Thus the individual appeared as a forlorn creature in a world threatened by mass domination [Illus. 1]. Paralleling the stereotyped plot of all those pageants, this pictorial device treated the pathetic solitude of the individual with a sympathy which implied aversion to the plebeian mass and fear of its dangerous power. It was a device that testified to the anti-democratic inclinations of the moment.

In the Lubitsch films and their derivatives—these portrayed, in addition to Danton, such characters as Lucrezia Borgia and Lady Hamilton—two disparate tendencies constantly intermingled.[33] One manifested itself in architectural structures, costumes and genre scenes which resurrected bygone surface life. With this extrovert tendency an introvert one competed: the depiction of certain psychological configurations with an utter disregard for given facts. But this medley did not disturb anyone. The film-makers were expert at molding the ingredients of a film into a prepossessing mixture that would conceal divergences rather than expose them. What this mixture did reveal, of course, was the inherent nihilism of which I have spoken.

The deceptive blend of conventional realism and overweening psychology Lubitsch and his followers devised was never generally adopted. In most important German postwar films introspection outweighed the extrovert tendency. Influenced not so much by Lubitsch's pseudo-realistic PASSION as by Wegener's fantastic STU-

[32] Lejeune, *Cinema*, p. 64; Tannenbaum, "Der Grossfilm," *Der Film von Morgen*, p. 66.

[33] For LUCREZIA BORGIA (1922), see Tannenbaum, *ibid.*, p. 67, and Zaddach, *Der literarische Film*, pp. 45–49. For LADY HAMILTON (1921), see Tannenbaum, *ibid.*, p. 67, and Birnbaum, "Massenscenen im Film," *Ufa-Blätter*. See also Kalbus, *Deutsche Filmkunst*, I, 52–53, 60.

DENT OF PRAGUE, these films reflected major events in emotional depths with an intensity that transformed customary surroundings into strange jungles. They predominated between 1920 and 1924, a period which will be considered as a consecutive whole.

But before examining the essential achievements of the postwar period, some attention must be given to films of secondary importance. To characterize them in this way is a verdict on their symptomatic rather than aesthetic value. They satisfied wants of the moment or obsolete tastes, seized upon provincial peculiarities as well as upon themes of world-wide interest. Significantly, they did not follow the introvert tendency of the time, but dealt with subjects that allowed them more or less to preserve the usual aspects of life. Among them, flourishing from 1919 to 1920, was a group of popular films concerned with sensational adventures encountered at every known or unknown spot on earth. The unknown spots were preferred because of their exotic spell. In DIE HERRIN DER WELT (MISTRESS OF THE WORLD), a serial in eight parts, a valiant German girl traveled from the unexplored interior of China to the legendary country of Ophir to find there the fabulous treasure of the Queen of Sheba.[34]

Other films of this kind—such as the gay DER MANN OHNE NAMEN (MAN WITHOUT A NAME) and Fritz Lang's first picture, DIE SPINNEN (THE SPIDERS)—also assumed the form of lengthy serials, perhaps tempted by the immensity of geographical space they covered.[35] Even though Joe May's 20-million-mark film DAS INDISCHE GRABMAL (THE INDIAN TOMB) modestly confined itself to India and normal footage, it outdid the serials in thrilling episodes. This superproduction, which imparted the same sinister moral as the Lubitsch pageants, not only adapted the miraculous practices of yoga to the screen, but showed rats gnawing the fetters of its captive hero, elephants forming a gigantic lane and an all-out fight against tigers.[36] Circuses at that time made nice profits out of animal rentals.

The whole group of films, with its craving for exotic sceneries, resembled a prisoner's daydream. The prison was of course the muti-

[34] Program to this film; Kalbus, *ibid.*, pp. 47–48.

[35] Kalbus, *ibid.*, p. 48. For other exotic adventurer films of this kind, see Birnbaum, "Massenscenen im Film," *Ufa-Blätter*, and Kalbus, *ibid.*, pp. 90–91.

[36] Kalbus, *ibid.*, pp. 49, 94; Mühsam, "Tiere im Film," *Ufa-Blätter;* Tannenbaum, "Der Grossfilm," *Der Film von Morgen*, p. 71; Balázs, *Der sichtbare Mensch,* p. 112.

lated and blockaded fatherland; at least, this was the way most Germans felt about it. What they called their world mission had been thwarted, and now all exits seemed barred. These space-devouring films reveal how bitterly the average German resented his involuntary seclusion. They functioned as substitutes; they naïvely satisfied his suppressed desire for expansion through pictures that enabled his imagination to reannex the world, including Ophir. As for Ophir, the prospectus of MISTRESS OF THE WORLD did not forget to note that the idea of locating this mythical kingdom in Africa had been advocated by Karl Peters. Since Karl Peters was the promoter of the German Colonization Society (*Deutscher Kolonialverein*) and one of the founders of German East Africa, the mention of his name overtly indicated the film's timely connotations. Inflation prevented the film producers at that moment from sending costly expeditions to the edge of the world.[37] The consequence was that a Chinese pagoda topped a German hill, and Brandenburg's sandy plain served as a genuine desert. This extensive faking proved a vehicle of progress inasmuch as it forced the German studio teams to develop many a new craft.

In the interest of completeness—a mania too boring to be cultivated, yet too rewarding to be altogether suppressed—one should not overlook the comedies produced during that period of introvert films. It was again Lubitsch who took the lead in this field, which he had left only to oblige Davidson. Had he left it? While he was inciting a mass of extras to curse Madame du Barry and cheer Anne Boleyn, he was also directing a sort of film operetta, DIE PUPPE (THE DOLL, 1919), and the satire DIE AUSTERNPRINZESSIN (THE OYSTER PRINCESS, 1919) which is said to have clumsily ridiculed American habits within spectacular settings.[38] Thus he put into practice the philosophy of his hunchback in SUMURUN who "must dance and gambol again, for the public wants a laugh." Considering the speed with which Lubitsch exchanged murders and tortures for dancing and joking, it is highly probable that his comedies sprang from the same nihilism as his historical dramas. This tendency made it easy for him to drain great events of their seriousness and realize comical potentialities in trifles. Seasoned by him, such trifles became truffles. From 1921 on, having done away

[37] Kalbus, *Deutsche Filmkunst,* I, 102–4.

[38] Vincent, *Histoire de l'Art Cinématographique,* p. 142; Bardèche and Brasillach, *History of Motion Pictures,* pp. 189–90; Kalbus, *Deutsche Filmkunst,* I, 85–86.

with history, Lubitsch devoted himself almost exclusively to the savory entertainment of which he was master. In his coolly received DIE BERGKATZE (MOUNTAIN CAT, 1921), Pola Negri moved, a catlike brigand's daughter, between swollen architectural forms which assisted in a parody of boastful Balkan manners, pompous militarism and, perhaps, the expressionist vogue.[39]

If it were not for Lubitsch, the German film comedies of the time would hardly be worth mentioning. Adaptations of operettas and stage plays—among these the indestructible ALT HEIDELBERG (STUDENT PRINCE, 1923)—prevailed over products of genuine screen humor, and American comedies ingratiated themselves more effectively than the native ones with a public eager for a moment's laughter.[40] This proves again that in Germany the natural desire for happiness was not so much catered to as tolerated.

Escapist needs were somewhat balanced by the urge to take sides in the conflict of opinions. A true expression of philistine indignation, several films deplored the general postwar depravity, the craze for dancing and the *nouveaux riches*.[41] Outright propaganda messages intermingled with these moral verdicts. Two films discredited the French army, causing the French government to send sharp notes to Berlin; others incurred the censor's veto by spreading anti-Semitic and antirepublican views.[42] Owing to the tense atmosphere of those years, even remote themes occasionally aroused political passions. In 1923, the Munich performance of a film version of Lessing's *Nathan the Wise* had to be discontinued because of anti-Semitic riots—an incident foreshadowing the notorious Berlin Nazi demonstrations which, nine years later, were to result in the prohibition of Remarque's ALL QUIET ON THE WESTERN FRONT.[43] However, all these screen events are of a merely ideological interest; they characterize group intentions rather than group dispositions.

As early as 1919 Dr. Victor E. Pordes, a German writer on aesthetics, complained of the awkwardness with which the German screen shaped stories involving scenes of society life and questions of *savoir-faire*. Whenever civilized manners are to be mirrored, he

[39] Kalbus, *ibid.*, p. 86; Kurtz, *Expressionismus*, p. 82.

[40] Kalbus, *Deutsche Filmkunst*, I, esp. 77. For early German film comedies, see also *Ufa Verleih-Programme*, 1923/1924, p. 63 ff.

[41] Kalbus, *Deutsche Filmkunst*, I, 58.

[42] *Jahrbuch der Filmindustrie*, 1922/3, pp. 33, 41.

[43] *Jahrbuch der Filmindustrie*, 1922/3, p. 46; Kalbus, *Deutsche Filmkunst*, I, 68; Zaddach, *Der literarische Film*, pp. 49–50.

said, Danish, French and American films by far surpass the German ones "in the social education and quality of the bulk of players, in the tone, shading and artistic discretion of acting, and finally in the precise knowledge and observance of manners." [44] But it was certainly not sheer inability that interfered with the rendering of manners on the German screen. Rather, Pordes' criticism corroborates what has already been stated about the introvert tendency of all representative films up to 1924. They were not intended to record given phenomena; their failure to do so was an inevitable consequence of their intrinsic design. The progressive literary products and paintings of the time manifested exactly the same aversion to realism. Yet this similarity of style did not exclude differences of content and meaning; on the contrary, in all such essentials the screen went its own, independent way. The introvert tendency it followed up must be traced to powerful collective desires. Millions of Germans, in particular middle-class Germans, seem to have shut themselves off from a world determined by Allied pressure, violent internal struggles and inflation. They acted as if under the influence of a terrific shock which upset normal relations between their outer and inner existence. On the surface, they lived on as before; psychologically, they withdrew within themselves.

This retreat into a shell was favored by several circumstances. First, it admirably suited the interests of the German ruling set, whose chances of survival depended upon the readiness of the masses to pass over the reasons for their sufferings. Secondly, the middle-class strata had always been content with being governed, and now that political freedom had come overnight, they were theoretically as well as practically unprepared to assume responsibilities. The shock they experienced was caused by the inroads of freedom. Thirdly, they entered the arena at a moment when any attempt to make up for the aborted bourgeois emancipation was bound to precipitate a socialist solution. And would the Social Democrats themselves venture on revolutionary experiments? The whole situation seemed so thorny that no one felt bold enough to cope with it.

Nevertheless, it would be an undue simplification to label the psychological exodus from the outer world a merely retrogressive move. During the period of its retreat, the German mind was shaken by convulsions which upset the whole emotional system. While this mind neglected, or obstructed, all external revolutionary possibilities,

[44] Pordes, *Das Lichtspiel,* p. 106.

it made an extreme effort to reconsider the foundations of the self, to adjust the self to the actual conditions of life. Qualms about those deep-rooted dispositions which had supported the collapsed authoritative regime constantly interfered with the desire to keep them alive. It is true that during the postwar years introspection dealt solely with the isolated individual. But this does not necessarily mean that the Germans insisted upon perpetuating the individual's autonomy at the expense of his social liabilities. Rather, the German conception of the individual was so rich in traditional values that it could not unhesitatingly be thrown overboard.

The films of the postwar period from 1920 to 1924 are a unique *monologue intérieur*. They reveal developments in almost inaccessible layers of the German mind.

5. CALIGARI

THE Czech Hans Janowitz, one of the two authors of the film DAS CABINET DES DR. CALIGARI (THE CABINET OF DR. CALIGARI), was brought up in Prague—that city where reality fuses with dreams, and dreams turn into visions of horror.[1] One evening in October 1913 this young poet was strolling through a fair at Hamburg, trying to find a girl whose beauty and manner had attracted him. The tents of the fair covered the Reeperbahn, known to any sailor as one of the world's chief pleasure spots. Nearby, on the Holstenwall, Lederer's gigantic Bismarck monument stood sentinel over the ships in the harbor. In search of the girl, Janowitz followed the fragile trail of a laugh which he thought hers into a dim park bordering the Holstenwall. The laugh, which apparently served to lure a young man, vanished somewhere in the shrubbery. When, a short time later, the young man departed, another shadow, hidden until then in the bushes, suddenly emerged and moved along—as if on the scent of that laugh. Passing this uncanny shadow, Janowitz caught a glimpse of him: he looked like an average bourgeois. Darkness reabsorbed the man, and made further pursuit impossible. The following day big headlines in the local press announced: "Horrible sex crime on the Holstenwall! Young Gertrude . . . murdered." An obscure feeling that Gertrude might have been the girl of the fair impelled Janowitz to attend the victim's funeral. During the ceremony he suddenly had the sensation of discovering the murderer, who had not yet been captured. The man he suspected seemed to recognize him, too. It was the bourgeois—the shadow in the bushes.

Carl Mayer, co-author with Janowitz of CALIGARI, was born in the Austrian provincial capital of Graz, where his father, a wealthy

[1] The following episode, along with other data appearing in my pages on CALIGARI, is drawn from an interesting manuscript Mr. Hans Janowitz has written about the genesis of this film. I feel greatly indebted to him for having put his material at my disposal. I am thus in a position to base my interpretation of CALIGARI on the true inside story, up to now unknown.

businessman, would have prospered had he not been obsessed by the idea of becoming a "scientific" gambler. In the prime of life he sold his property, went, armed with an infallible "system," to Monte Carlo, and reappeared a few months later in Graz, broke. Under the stress of this catastrophe, the monomaniac father turned the sixteen-year-old Carl and his three younger brothers out into the street and finally committed suicide. A mere boy, Carl Mayer was responsible for the three children. While he toured through Austria, peddling barometers, singing in choirs and playing extras in peasant theaters, he became increasingly interested in the stage. There was no branch of theatrical production which he did not explore during those years of nomadic life—years full of experiences that were to be of immense use in his future career as a film poet. At the beginning of the war, the adolescent made his living by sketching Hindenburg portraits on postcards in Munich cafés. Later in the war, Janowitz reports, he had to undergo repeated examinations of his mental condition. Mayer seems to have been very embittered against the high-ranking military psychiatrist in charge of his case.

The war was over. Janowitz, who from its outbreak had been an officer in an infantry regiment, returned as a convinced pacifist, animated by hatred of an authority which had sent millions of men to death. He felt that absolute authority was bad in itself. He settled in Berlin, met Carl Mayer there, and soon found out that this eccentric young man, who had never before written a line, shared his revolutionary moods and views. Why not express them on the screen? Intoxicated with Wegener's films, Janowitz believed that this new medium might lend itself to powerful poetic revelations. As youth will, the two friends embarked on endless discussions that hovered around Janowitz' Holstenwall adventure as well as Mayer's mental duel with the psychiatrist. These stories seemed to evoke and supplement each other. After such discussions the pair would stroll through the night, irresistibly attracted by a dazzling and clamorous fair on Kantstrasse. It was a bright jungle, more hell than paradise, but a paradise to those who had exchanged the horror of war for the terror of want. One evening, Mayer dragged his companion to a side-show by which he had been impressed. Under the title "Man or Machine" it presented a strong man who achieved miracles of strength in an apparent stupor. He acted as if he were hypnotized. The strangest thing was that he accompanied his feats with utterances which affected the spellbound spectators as pregnant forebodings.

Any creative process approaches a moment when only one additional experience is needed to integrate all elements into a whole. The mysterious figure of the strong man supplied such an experience. On the night of this show the friends first visualized the original story of CALIGARI. They wrote the manuscript in the following six weeks. Defining the part each took in the work, Janowitz calls himself "the father who planted the seed, and Mayer the mother who conceived and ripened it." At the end, one small problem arose: the authors were at a loss as to what to christen their main character, a psychiatrist shaped after Mayer's archenemy during the war. A rare volume, *Unknown Letters of Stendhal,* offered the solution. While Janowitz was skimming through this find of his, he happened to notice that Stendhal, just come from the battlefield, met at La Scala in Milan an officer named Caligari. The name clicked with both authors.

Their story is located in a fictitious North German town near the Dutch border, significantly called Holstenwall. One day a fair moves into the town, with merry-go-rounds and side-shows—among the latter that of Dr. Caligari, a weird, bespectacled man advertising the somnambulist Cesare. To procure a license, Caligari goes to the town hall, where he is treated haughtily by an arrogant official. The following morning this official is found murdered in his room, which does not prevent the townspeople from enjoying the fair's pleasures. Along with numerous onlookers, Francis and Alan—two students in love with Jane, a medical man's daughter—enter the tent of Dr. Caligari, and watch Cesare slowly stepping out of an upright, coffinlike box. Caligari tells the thrilled audience that the somnambulist will answer questions about the future. Alan, in an excited state, asks how long he has to live. Cesare opens his mouth; he seems to be dominated by a terrific, hypnotic power emanating from his master. "Until dawn," he answers. At dawn Francis learns that his friend has been stabbed in exactly the same manner as the official. The student, suspicious of Caligari, persuades Jane's father to assist him in an investigation. With a search warrant the two force their way into the showman's wagon, and demand that he end the trance of his medium. However, at this very moment they are called away to the police station to attend the examination of a criminal who has been caught in the act of killing a woman, and who now frantically denies that he is the pursued serial murderer.

Francis continues spying on Caligari, and, after nightfall, secretly peers through a window of the wagon. But while he imagines he sees Cesare lying in his box, Cesare in reality breaks into Jane's bedroom, lifts a dagger to pierce the sleeping girl, gazes at her, puts the dagger away and flees, with the screaming Jane in his arms, over roofs and roads. Chased by her father, he drops the girl, who is then escorted home, whereas the lonely kidnaper dies of exhaustion. As Jane, in flagrant contradiction of what Francis believes to be the truth, insists on having recognized Cesare, Francis approaches Caligari a second time to solve the torturing riddle. The two policemen in his company seize the coffinlike box, and Francis draws out of it— a dummy representing the somnambulist. Profiting by the investigators' carelessness, Caligari himself manages to escape. He seeks shelter in a lunatic asylum. The student follows him, calls on the director of the asylum to inquire about the fugitive, and recoils horror-struck: the director and Caligari are one and the same person.

The following night—the director has fallen asleep—Francis and three members of the medical staff whom he has initiated into the case search the director's office and discover material fully establishing the guilt of this authority in psychiatric matters. Among a pile of books they find an old volume about a showman named Caligari who, in the eighteenth century, traveled through North Italy, hypnotized his medium Cesare into murdering sundry people, and, during Cesare's absence, substituted a wax figure to deceive the police. The main exhibit is the director's clinical records; they evidence that he desired to verify the account of Caligari's hypnotic faculties, that his desire grew into an obsession, and that, when a somnambulist was entrusted to his care, he could not resist the temptation of repeating with him those terrible games. He had adopted the identity of Caligari. To make him admit his crimes, Francis confronts the director with the corpse of his tool, the somnambulist. No sooner does the monster realize Cesare is dead than he begins to rave. Trained attendants put him into a strait jacket.

This horror tale in the spirit of E. T. A. Hoffmann was an outspoken revolutionary story. In it, as Janowitz indicates, he and Carl Mayer half-intentionally stigmatized the omnipotence of a state authority manifesting itself in universal conscription and declarations of war. The German war government seemed to the authors the prototype of such voracious authority. Subjects of the Austro-Hungarian monarchy, they were in a better position than most citizens of the Reich to penetrate the fatal tendencies inherent in the German system. The character of Caligari embodies these tendencies; he stands for an unlimited authority that idolizes power as such, and, to satisfy its lust for domination, ruthlessly violates all human rights and values [Illus. 2]. Functioning as a mere instrument, Cesare is not so much a guilty murderer as Caligari's innocent victim. This is how the authors themselves understood him. According to the pacifist-minded Janowitz, they had created Cesare with the dim design of portraying the common man who, under the pressure of compulsory military service, is drilled to kill and to be killed. The revolutionary meaning of the story reveals itself unmistakably at the end, with the disclosure of the psychiatrist as Caligari: reason overpowers unreasonable power, insane authority is symbolically abolished. Similar ideas were also being expressed on the contemporary stage, but the authors of CALIGARI transferred them to the screen without including any of those eulogies of the authority-freed "New Man" in which many expressionist plays indulged.

A miracle occurred: Erich Pommer, chief executive of Decla-Bioscop, accepted this unusual, if not subversive, script. Was it a miracle? Since in those early postwar days the conviction prevailed that foreign markets could only be conquered by artistic achievements, the German film industry was of course anxious to experiment in the field of aesthetically qualified entertainment.[2] Art assured export, and export meant salvation. An ardent partisan of this doctrine, Pommer had moreover an incomparable flair for cinematic values and popular demands. Regardless of whether he grasped the significance of the strange story Mayer and Janowitz submitted to him, he certainly sensed its timely atmosphere and interesting scenic potentialities. He was a born promoter who handled screen and business affairs with equal facility, and, above all, excelled in stimulating the creative energies of directors and players. In 1923, Ufa was to make him chief of its entire production.[3] His behind-the-scenes activities were to leave their imprint on the pre-Hitler screen.

Pommer assigned Fritz Lang to direct CALIGARI, but in the middle of the preliminary discussions Lang was ordered to finish his serial THE SPIDERS; the distributors of this film urged its completion.[4] Lang's successor was Dr. Robert Wiene. Since his father, a

[2] Vincent, *Histoire de l'Art Cinématographique,* p. 140.

[3] *Jahrbuch der Filmindustrie,* 1922/3, pp. 35, 46. For an appraisal of Pommer, see Lejeune, *Cinema,* pp. 125–31.

[4] Information offered by Mr. Lang. Cf. p. 56.

once-famous Dresden actor, had become slightly insane towards the end of his life, Wiene was not entirely unprepared to tackle the case of Dr. Caligari. He suggested, in complete harmony with what Lang had planned, an essential change of the original story—a change against which the two authors violently protested. But no one heeded them.[5]

The original story was an account of real horrors; Wiene's version transforms that account into a chimera concocted and narrated by the mentally deranged Francis. To effect this transformation the body of the original story is put into a framing story which introduces Francis as a madman. The film CALIGARI opens with the first of the two episodes composing the frame. Francis is shown sitting on a bench in the park of the lunatic asylum, listening to the confused babble of a fellow sufferer. Moving slowly, like an apparition, a female inmate of the asylum passes by: it is Jane. Francis says to his companion: "What I have experienced with her is still stranger than what you have encountered. I will tell it to you." [6] Fade-out. Then a view of Holstenwall fades in, and the original story unfolds, ending, as has been seen, with the identification of Caligari. After a new fade-out the second and final episode of the framing story begins. Francis, having finished the narration, follows his companion back to the asylum, where he mingles with a crowd of sad figures—among them Cesare, who absent-mindedly caresses a little flower. The director of the asylum, a mild and understanding-looking person, joins the crowd. Lost in the maze of his hallucinations, Francis takes the director for the nightmarish character he himself has created, and accuses this imaginary fiend of being a dangerous madman. He screams, he fights the attendants in a frenzy. The scene is switched over to a sickroom, with the director putting on horn-rimmed spectacles which immediately change his appearance: it seems to be Caligari who examines the exhausted Francis. After this he removes his spectacles and, all mildness, tells his assistants that Francis believes him to be Caligari. Now that he understands the case of his patient, the director concludes, he will be able to heal him. With this cheerful message the audience is dismissed.

Janowitz and Mayer knew why they raged against the framing story: it perverted, if not reversed, their intrinsic intentions. While

[5] Extracted from Mr. Janowitz's manuscript. See also Vincent, *Histoire de l'Art Cinématographique*, pp. 140, 143–44.

[6] Film license, issued by Board of Censors, Berlin, 1921 and 1925 (Museum of Modern Art Library, clipping files); *Film Society Programme*, March 14, 1926.

the original story exposed the madness inherent in authority, Wiene's CALIGARI glorified authority and convicted its antagonist of madness. A revolutionary film was thus turned into a conformist one—following the much-used pattern of declaring some normal but troublesome individual insane and sending him to a lunatic asylum. This change undoubtedly resulted not so much from Wiene's personal predilections as from his instinctive submission to the necessities of the screen; films, at least commercial films, are forced to answer to mass desires. In its changed form CALIGARI was no longer a product expressing, at best, sentiments characteristic of the intelligentsia, but a film supposed equally to be in harmony with what the less educated felt and liked.

If it holds true that during the postwar years most Germans eagerly tended to withdraw from a harsh outer world into the intangible realm of the soul, Wiene's version was certainly more consistent with their attitude than the original story; for, by putting the original into a box, this version faithfully mirrored the general retreat into a shell. In CALIGARI (and several other films of the time) the device of a framing story was not only an aesthetic form, but also had symbolic content. Significantly, Wiene avoided mutilating the original story itself. Even though CALIGARI had become a conformist film, it preserved and emphasized this revolutionary story—as a madman's fantasy. Caligari's defeat now belonged among psychological experiences. In this way Wiene's film does suggest that during their retreat into themselves the Germans were stirred to reconsider their traditional belief in authority. Down to the bulk of social democratic workers they refrained from revolutionary action; yet at the same time a psychological revolution seems to have prepared itself in the depths of the collective soul. The film reflects this double aspect of German life by coupling a reality in which Caligari's authority triumphs with a hallucination in which the same authority is overthrown. There could be no better configuration of symbols for that uprising against the authoritarian dispositions which apparently occurred under the cover of a behavior rejecting uprising.

Janowitz suggested that the settings for CALIGARI be designed by the painter and illustrator Alfred Kubin, who, a forerunner of the surrealists, made eerie phantoms invade harmless scenery and visions of torture emerge from the subconscious. Wiene took to the idea of painted canvases, but preferred to Kubin three expressionist artists: Hermann Warm, Walter Röhrig and Walter Reimann. They were affiliated with the Berlin Sturm group, which, through Herwarth Walden's magazine *Sturm*, promoted expressionism in every field of art.[7]

Although expressionist painting and literature had evolved years before the war, they acquired a public only after 1918. In this respect the case of Germany somewhat resembled that of Soviet Russia where, during the short period of war communism, diverse currents of abstract art enjoyed a veritable heyday.[8] To a revolutionized people expressionism seemed to combine the denial of bourgeois traditions with faith in man's power freely to shape society and nature. On account of such virtues it may have cast a spell over many Germans upset by the breakdown of their universe.[9]

"Films must be drawings brought to life": this was Hermann Warm's formula at the time that he and his two fellow designers were constructing the CALIGARI world.[10] In accordance with his beliefs, the canvases and draperies of CALIGARI abounded in complexes of

[7] Mr. Janowitz's manuscript; Vincent, *Histoire de l'Art Cinématographique*, p. 144; Rotha, *Film Till Now*, p. 43.

[8] Kurtz, *Expressionismus*, p. 61.

[9] In Berlin, immediately after the war, Karl Heinz Martin staged two little dramas by Ernst Toller and Walter Hasenclever within expressionist settings. Cf. Kurtz, *ibid.*, p. 43; Vincent, *Histoire de l'Art Cinématographique*, pp. 142–43; Schapiro, "Nature of Abstract Art," *Marxist Quarterly*, Jan.–March 1937, p. 97.

[10] Quotation from Kurtz, *Expressionismus*, p. 66. Warm's views, which implied a verdict on films as photographed reality, harmonized with those of Viking Eggeling, an abstract Swedish painter living in Germany. Having eliminated all objects from his canvases, Eggeling deemed it logical to involve the surviving geometrical compositions in rhythmic movements. He and his painter friend Hans Richter submitted this idea to Ufa, and Ufa, guided as ever by the maxim that art is good business or, at least, good propaganda, enabled the two artists to go ahead with their experiments. The first abstract films appeared in 1921. While Eggeling—he died in 1925—orchestrated spiral lines and comblike figures in a short he called DIAGONAL SYMPHONY, Richter composed his RHYTHM 21 of squares in black, gray and white. One year later, Walter Ruttmann, also a painter, joined in the trend with OPUS I, which was a dynamic display of spots vaguely recalling X-ray photographs. As the titles reveal, the authors themselves considered their products a sort of optical music. It was a music that, whatever else it tried to impart, marked an utter withdrawal from the outer world. This esoteric *avant-garde* movement soon spread over other countries. From about 1924, such advanced French artists as Fernand Léger and René Clair made films which, less abstract than the German ones, showed an affinity for the formal beauty of machine parts, and molded all kinds of objects and motions into surrealistic dreams.—I feel indebted to Mr. Hans Richter for having permitted me to use his unpublished manuscript, "Avantgarde, History and Dates of the Only Independent Artistic Film Movement, 1921–1931." See also *Film Society Programme*, Oct. 16, 1927; Kurtz, *Expressionismus*, pp. 86, 94; Vincent, *Histoire de l'Art Cinématographique*, pp. 159–61; Man Ray, "Answer to a Questionnaire," *Film Art*, no. 7, 1936, p. 9; Kraszna-Krausz, "Exhibition in Stuttgart, June 1929, and Its Effects," *Close Up*, Dec. 1929, pp. 461–62.

jagged, sharp-pointed forms strongly reminiscent of gothic patterns. Products of a style which by then had become almost a mannerism, these complexes suggested houses, walls, landscapes. Except for a few slips or concessions—some backgrounds opposed the pictorial convention in too direct a manner, while others all but preserved them—the settings amounted to a perfect transformation of material objects into emotional ornaments. With its oblique chimneys on pell-mell roofs, its windows in the form of arrows or kites and its treelike arabesques that were threats rather than trees, Holstenwall resembled those visions of unheard-of cities which the painter Lyonel Feininger evoked through his edgy, crystalline compositions.[11] In addition, the ornamental system in CALIGARI expanded through space, annuling its conventional aspect by means of painted shadows in disharmony with the lighting effects, and zigzag delineations designed to efface all rules of perspective. Space now dwindled to a flat plane, now augmented its dimensions to become what one writer called a "stereoscopic universe." [12]

Lettering was introduced as an essential element of the settings—appropriately enough, considering the close relationship between lettering and drawing. In one scene the mad psychiatrist's desire to imitate Caligari materializes in jittery characters composing the words "I must become Caligari"—words that loom before his eyes on the road, in the clouds, in the treetops. The incorporation of human beings and their movements into the texture of these surroundings was tremendously difficult. Of all the players only the two protagonists seemed actually to be created by a draftman's imagination. Werner Krauss as Caligari had the appearance of a phantom magician himself weaving the lines and shades through which he

[11] Mr. Feininger wrote to me about his relation to CALIGARI on Sept. 13, 1944: "Thank you for your . . . letter of Sept. 8. But if there has been anything I never had a part in nor the slightest knowledge of at the time, it is the film CALIGARI. I have never even seen the film. . . . I never met nor knew the artists you name [Warm, Röhrig and Reimann] who devised the settings. Some time about 1911 I made, for my own edification, a series of drawings which I entitled: 'Die Stadt am Ende der Welt.' Some of these drawings were printed, some were exhibited. Later, after the birth of CALIGARI, I was frequently asked whether I had had a hand in its devising. This is all I can tell you. . . ."

[12] Cited by Carter, *The New Spirit*, p. 250, from H. G. Scheffauer, *The New Spirit in the German Arts.*—For the CALIGARI décor, see also Kurtz, *Expressionismus*, p. 66; Rotha, *Film Till Now*, p. 46; Jahier, "42 Ans de Cinéma," *Le Rôle intellectuel du Cinéma*, pp. 60–61; "The Cabinet of Dr. Caligari," *Exceptional Photoplays*, March 1921, p. 4; Amiguet, *Cinéma! Cinéma!*, p. 50. For the beginnings of Werner Krauss and Conrad Veidt, see Kalbus, *Deutsche Filmkunst*, I, 28, 30, and Veidt, "Mein Leben," *Ufa-Magazin*, Jan. 14–20, 1927.

paced, and when Conrad Veidt's Cesare prowled along a wall, it was as if the wall had exuded him [Illus. 3]. The figure of an old dwarf and the crowd's antiquated costumes helped to remove the throng on the fair's tent-street from reality and make it share the bizarre life of abstract forms.

If Decla had chosen to leave the original story of Mayer and Janowitz as it was, these "drawings brought to life" would have told it perfectly. As expressionist abstractions they were animated by the same revolutionary spirit that impelled the two scriptwriters to accuse authority—the kind of authority revered in Germany—of inhuman excesses. However, Wiene's version disavowed this revolutionary meaning of expressionist staging, or, at least, put it, like the original story itself, in brackets. In the film CALIGARI expressionism seems to be nothing more than the adequate translation of a madman's fantasy into pictorial terms. This was how many contemporary German reviewers understood, and relished, the settings and gestures. One of the critics stated with self-assured ignorance: "The idea of rendering the notions of sick brains . . . through expressionist pictures is not only well conceived but also well realized. Here this style has a right to exist, proves an outcome of solid logic." [13]

In their triumph the philistines overlooked one significant fact: even though CALIGARI stigmatized the oblique chimneys as crazy, it never restored the perpendicular ones as the normal. Expressionist ornaments also overrun the film's concluding episode, in which, from the philistines' viewpoint, perpendiculars should have been expected to characterize the revival of conventional reality. In consequence, the CALIGARI style was as far from depicting madness as it was from transmitting revolutionary messages. What function did it really assume?

During the postwar years expressionism was frequently considered a shaping of primitive sensations and experiences. Gerhart Hauptmann's brother Carl—a distinguished writer and poet with expressionist inclinations—adopted this definition, and then asked how the spontaneous manifestations of a profoundly agitated soul might best be formulated. While modern language, he contended, is too perverted to serve this purpose, the film—or the bioscop, as he termed it—offers a unique opportunity to externalize the fermentation of inner life. Of course, he said, the bioscop must feature only those

[13] Review in *8 Uhr Abendblatt,* cited in *Caligari-Heft,* p. 8.

gestures of things and of human beings which are truly soulful.[14]

Carl Hauptmann's views elucidate the expressionist style of CALIGARI. It had the function of characterizing the phenomena on the screen as phenomena of the soul—a function which overshadowed its revolutionary meaning. By making the film an outward projection of psychological events, expressionist staging symbolized—much more strikingly than did the device of a framing story—that general retreat into a shell which occurred in postwar Germany. It is not accidental that, as long as this collective process was effective, odd gestures and settings in an expressionist or similar style marked many a conspicuous film. VARIETY, of 1925, showed the final traces of them.[15] Owing to their stereotyped character, these settings and gestures were like some familiar street sign—"Men at Work," for instance. Only here the lettering was different. The sign read: "Soul at Work."

After a thorough propaganda campaign culminating in the puzzling poster "You must become Caligari," Decla released the film in February 1920 in the Berlin Marmorhaus.[16] Among the press reviews—they were unanimous in praising CALIGARI as the first work of art on the screen—that of *Vorwärts*, the leading Social Democratic Party organ, distinguished itself by utter absurdity. It commented upon the film's final scene, in which the director of the asylum promises to heal Francis, with the words: "This film is also morally invulnerable inasmuch as it evokes sympathy for the mentally diseased, and comprehension for the self-sacrificing activity of the psychiatrists and attendants." [17] Instead of recognizing that Francis' attack against an odious authority harmonized with the Party's own antiauthoritarian doctrine, *Vorwärts* preferred to pass off authority itself as a paragon of progressive virtues. It was always the same psychological mechanism: the rationalized middle-class propensities of the Social Democrats interfering with their rational socialist designs. While the Germans were too close to CALIGARI to appraise its symptomatic value, the French realized that this film was more than just an exceptional film. They coined the term "*Caligarisme*" and

[14] Carl Hauptmann, "Film und Theater," *Der Film von Morgen*, p. 20. See also Alten, "Die Kunst in Deutschland," *Ganymed*, 1920, p. 146; Kurtz, *Expressionismus*, p. 14.

[15] Cf. p. 127.

[16] *Jahrbuch der Filmindustrie*, 1922/3, p. 31.

[17] Quoted from *Caligari-Heft*, p. 23.

applied it to a postwar world seemingly all upside down; which, at any rate, proves that they sensed the film's bearing on the structure of society. The New York première of CALIGARI, in April 1921, firmly established its world fame. But apart from giving rise to stray imitations and serving as a yardstick for artistic endeavors, this "most widely discussed film of the time" never seriously influenced the course of the American or French cinema.[18] It stood out lonely, like a monolith.

CALIGARI shows the "Soul at Work." On what adventures does the revolutionized soul embark? The narrative and pictorial elements of the film gravitate towards two opposite poles. One can be labeled "Authority," or, more explicitly, "Tyranny." The theme of tyranny, with which the authors were obsessed, pervades the screen from beginning to end. Swivel-chairs of enormous height symbolize the superiority of the city officials turning on them, and, similarly, the gigantic back of the chair in Alan's attic testifies to the invisible presence of powers that have their grip on him. Staircases reinforce the effect of the furniture: numerous steps ascend to police headquarters, and in the lunatic asylum itself no less than three parallel flights of stairs are called upon to mark Dr. Caligari's position at the top of the hierarchy [Illus. 4]. That the film succeeds in picturing him as a tyrant figure of the stamp of Homunculus and Lubitsch's Henry VIII is substantiated by a most illuminating statement in Joseph Freeman's novel, *Never Call Retreat*. Its hero, a Viennese professor of history, tells of his life in a German concentration camp where, after being tortured, he is thrown into a cell: "Lying alone in that cell, I thought of Dr. Caligari; then, without transition, of the Emperor Valentinian, master of the Roman world, who took great delight in imposing the death sentence for slight or imaginary offenses. This Caesar's favorite expressions were: 'Strike off his head!'—'Burn him alive!'—'Let him be beaten with clubs till he expires!' I thought what a genuine twentieth century ruler the emperor was, and promptly fell asleep." [19] This dreamlike reasoning penetrates Dr. Caligari to the core by conceiving him as a counterpart of Valentinian and a premonition of Hitler. Caligari is a very specific premonition in the sense that he uses hypnotic power to force his will upon his tool—a technique foreshadowing, in content and purpose, that

[18] Quotation from Jacobs, *American Film,* p. 303; see also pp. 304–5.
[19] Freeman, *Never Call Retreat,* p. 528.

manipulation of the soul which Hitler was the first to practice on a gigantic scale. Even though, at the time of CALIGARI, the motif of the masterful hypnotizer was not unknown on the screen—it played a prominent role in the American film TRILBY, shown in Berlin during the war—nothing in their environment invited the two authors to feature it.[20] They must have been driven by one of those dark impulses which, stemming from the slowly moving foundations of a people's life, sometimes engender true visions.

One should expect the pole opposing that of tyranny to be the pole of freedom; for it was doubtless their love of freedom which made Janowitz and Mayer disclose the nature of tyranny. Now this counterpole is the rallying-point of elements pertaining to the fair —the fair with its rows of tents, its confused crowds besieging them, and its diversity of thrilling amusements. Here Francis and Alan happily join the swarm of onlookers; here, on the scene of his triumphs, Dr. Caligari is finally trapped. In their attempts to define the character of a fair, literary sources repeatedly evoke the memory of Babel and Babylon alike. A seventeenth century pamphlet describes the noise typical of a fair as "such a distracted noise that you would think Babel not comparable to it," and, almost two hundred years later, a young English poet feels enthusiastic about "that Babylon of booths—the Fair." [21] The manner in which such Biblical images insert themselves unmistakably characterizes the fair as an enclave of anarchy in the sphere of entertainment. This accounts for its eternal attractiveness. People of all classes and ages enjoy losing themselves in a wilderness of glaring colors and shrill sounds, which is populated with monsters and abounding in bodily sensations—from violent shocks to tastes of incredible sweetness. For adults it is a regression into childhood days, in which games and serious affairs are identical, real and imagined things mingle, and anarchical desires aimlessly test infinite possibilities. By means of this regression the adult escapes a civilization which tends to overgrow and starve out the chaos of instincts—escapes it to restore that chaos upon which civilization nevertheless rests. The fair is not freedom, but anarchy entailing chaos.

Significantly, most fair scenes in CALIGARI open with a small iris-in exhibiting an organ-grinder whose arm constantly rotates, and, behind him, the top of a merry-go-round which never ceases its cir-

[20] Kalbus, *Deutsche Filmkunst*, I, 95.
[21] McKechnie, *Popular Entertainments*, pp. 33, 47.

cular movement.[22] The circle here becomes a symbol of chaos. While freedom resembles a river, chaos resembles a whirlpool. Forgetful of self, one may plunge into chaos; one cannot move on in it. That the two authors selected a fair with its liberties as contrast to the oppressions of Caligari betrays the flaw in their revolutionary aspirations. Much as they longed for freedom, they were apparently incapable of imagining its contours. There is something Bohemian in their conception; it seems the product of naïve idealism rather than true insight. But it might be said that the fair faithfully reflected the chaotic condition of postwar Germany.

Whether intentionally or not, CALIGARI exposes the soul wavering between tyranny and chaos, and facing a desperate situation: any escape from tyranny seems to throw it into a state of utter confusion. Quite logically, the film spreads an all-pervading atmosphere of horror. Like the Nazi world, that of CALIGARI overflows with sinister portents, acts of terror and outbursts of panic. The equation of horror and hopelessness comes to a climax in the final episode which pretends to re-establish normal life. Except for the ambiguous figure of the director and the shadowy members of his staff, normality realizes itself through the crowd of insane moving in their bizarre surroundings. The normal as a madhouse: frustration could not be pictured more finally. And in this film, as well as in HOMUNCULUS, is unleashed a strong sadism and an appetite for destruction.[23] The reappearance of these traits on the screen once more testifies to their prominence in the German collective soul.

Technical peculiarities betray peculiarities of meaning. In CALIGARI methods begin to assert themselves which belong among the special properties of German film technique. CALIGARI initiates a long procession of 100 per cent studio-made films. Whereas, for instance, the Swedes at that time went to great pains to capture the actual appearance of a snowstorm or a wood, the German directors, at least until 1924, were so infatuated with indoor effects that they built up whole landscapes within the studio walls. They preferred the command of an artificial universe to dependence upon a haphazard outer world. Their withdrawal into the studio was part of

[22] Rotha, *Film Till Now*, p. 285. For the role of fairs in films, see E. W. and M. M. Robson, *The Film Answers Back*, pp. 196–97.—An iris-in is a technical term for opening up the scene from a small circle of light in a dark screen until the whole frame is revealed.

[23] Cf. p. 33.

the general retreat into a shell. Once the Germans had determined to seek shelter within the soul, they could not well allow the screen to explore that very reality which they abandoned. This explains the conspicuous role of architecture after CALIGARI—a role that has struck many an observer. "It is of the utmost importance," Paul Rotha remarks in a survey of the postwar period, "to grasp the significant part played by the architect in the development of the German cinema." [24] How could it be otherwise? The architect's façades and rooms were not merely backgrounds, but hieroglyphs. They expressed the structure of the soul in terms of space.

CALIGARI also mobilizes light. It is a lighting device which enables the spectators to watch the murder of Alan without seeing it; what they see, on the wall of the student's attic, is the shadow of Cesare stabbing that of Alan. Such devices developed into a specialty of the German studios. Jean Cassou credits the Germans with having invented a "laboratory-made fairy illumination," [25] and Harry Alan Potamkin considers the handling of the light in the German film its "major contribution to the cinema." [26] This emphasis upon light can be traced to an experiment Max Reinhardt made on the stage shortly before CALIGARI. In his *mise-en-scène* of Sorge's prewar drama *The Beggar* (*Der Bettler*)—one of the earliest and most vigorous manifestations of expressionism—he substituted for normal settings imaginary ones created by means of lighting effects.[27] Reinhardt doubtless introduced these effects to be true to the drama's style. The analogy to the films of the postwar period is obvious: it was their expressionist nature which impelled many a German director of photography to breed shadows as rampant as weeds and associate ethereal phantoms with strangely lit arabesques or faces. These efforts were designed to bathe all scenery in an unearthly illumination marking it as scenery of the soul. "Light has breathed soul into the expressionist films," Rudolph Kurtz states in his book on the expressionist cinema.[28] Exactly the reverse holds true: in those films the soul was the virtual source of the light. The task of switching on this inner illumination was somewhat facilitated by powerful romantic traditions.

[24] Rotha, *Film Till Now*, p. 180. Cf. Potamkin, "Kino and Lichtspiel," *Close Up*, Nov. 1929, p. 387.

[25] Cited in Leprohon, "Le Cinéma Allemand," *Le Rouge et le Noir*, July 1928, p. 135.

[26] Potamkin, "The Rise and Fall of the German Film," *Cinema*, April 1930, p. 24.

[27] Kurtz, *Expressionismus*, p. 59.

[28] *Ibid.*, p. 60.

The attempt made in CALIGARI to co-ordinate settings, players, lighting and action is symptomatic of the sense of structural organization which, from this film on, manifests itself on the German screen. Rotha coins the term "studio constructivism" to characterize "that curious air of completeness, of finality, that surrounds each product of the German studios." [29] But organizational completeness can be achieved only if the material to be organized does not object to it. (The ability of the Germans to organize themselves owes much to their longing for submission.) Since reality is essentially incalculable and therefore demands to be observed rather than commanded, realism on the screen and total organization exclude each other. Through their "studio constructivism" no less than their lighting the German films revealed that they dealt with unreal events displayed in a sphere basically controllable.[30]

In the course of a visit to Paris about six years after the première of CALIGARI, Janowitz called on Count Etienne de Beaumont in his old city residence, where he lived among Louis Seize furniture and Picassos. The Count voiced his admiration of CALIGARI, terming it "as fascinating and abstruse as the German soul." He continued: "Now the time has come for the German soul to speak, Monsieur. The French soul spoke more than a century ago, in the Revolution, and you have been mute. . . . Now we are waiting for what you have to impart to us, to the world." [31]

The Count did not have long to wait.

[29] Rotha, *Film Till Now*, pp. 107–8. Cf. Potamkin, "Kino and Lichtspiel," *Close Up*, Nov. 1929, p. 388, and "The Rise and Fall of the German Film," *Cinema*, April 1930, p. 24.

[30] Film connoisseurs have repeatedly criticized CALIGARI for being a stage imitation. This aspect of the film partly results from its genuinely theatrical action. It is action of a well-constructed dramatic conflict in stationary surroundings—action which does not depend upon screen representation for significance. Like CALIGARI, all "indoor" films of the postwar period showed affinity for the stage in that they favored inner-life dramas at the expense of conflicts involving outer reality. However, this did not necessarily prevent them from growing into true films. When, in the wake of CALIGARI, film technique steadily progressed, the psychological screen dramas increasingly exhibited an imagery that elaborated the significance of their action. CALIGARI's theatrical affinity was also due to technical backwardness. An immovable camera focused upon the painted décor; no cutting device added a meaning of its own to that of the pictures. One should, of course, not forget the reciprocal influence CALIGARI and kindred films exerted, for their part, on the German stage. Stimulated by the use they made of the iris-in, stage lighting took to singling out a lone player, or some important sector of the scene. Cf. Barry, *Program Notes*, Series III, program 1; Gregor, *Zeitalter des Films*, pp. 134, 144–45; Rotha, *Film Till Now*, p. 275; Vincent, *Histoire de l'Art Cinématographique*, p. 139.

[31] From Janowitz's manuscript.

6. PROCESSION OF TYRANTS

Caligari was too high-brow to become popular in Germany. However, its basic theme—the soul being faced with the seemingly unavoidable alternative of tyranny or chaos—exerted extraordinary fascination. Between 1920 and 1924, numerous German films insistently resumed this theme, elaborating it in various fashions.

One group specialized in the depiction of tyrants. In this film type, the Germans of the time—a people still unbalanced, still free to choose its regime—nursed no illusions about the possible consequences of tyranny; on the contrary, they indulged in detailing its crimes and the sufferings it inflicted. Was their imagination kindled by the fear of bolshevism? Or did they call upon these frightful visions to exorcise lusts which, they sensed, were their own and now threatened to possess them? (It is, at any rate, a strange coincidence that, hardly more than a decade later, Nazi Germany was to put into practice that very mixture of physical and mental tortures which the German screen then pictured.)

Among the films of this first group, Nosferatu, released in 1922, enjoyed particular fame for initiating the fashion of screen vampires. The film was an adaptation of Bram Stoker's novel *Dracula*, but Henrik Galeen, the script writer, managed to impregnate it with ideas of his own.

A real estate agent in Bremen sends his recently married clerk to Nosferatu, who, living far away in the Carpathian woods, wants to settle some business matter. The clerk's travel across these woods—macabre with mists, shying horses, wolves and eerie birds—proves but an innocent prelude to the adventures awaiting him in Nosferatu's castle. The day after his arrival he wanders, in search of his host, through abandoned rooms and cellars, and eventually discovers Nosferatu lying in a sarcophagus—like a corpse with eyes wide open in a ghastly face. Nosferatu is a vampire, and vampires sleep by day. By night the monster approaches the slumbering clerk to suck his blood.

At this very moment Nina, the clerk's wife, awakens in Bremen with the name of her husband on her lips, whereupon Nosferatu withdraws from his victim. It was Galeen's idea to demonstrate through this telepathic phenomenon the supernatural power of love. After the clerk's escape, the vampire, who comes to appear more and more as an incarnation of pestilence, leaves his castle to haunt the world. Wherever he emerges, rats swarm out and people fall dead. He goes aboard a sailing ship: the crew dies, and the ship continues cutting the waves on its own. Finally Nosferatu makes his entrance in Bremen and there meets Nina—in an episode which symbolizes Galeen's credo that the deadly evils for which Nosferatu stands cannot defeat those who encounter them fearlessly. Instead of fleeing the vampire's presence, Nina, her arms extended, welcomes him into her room. As she does so, a supreme miracle occurs: the sun breaks through, and the vampire dissolves into thin air [1] [Illus. 5].

F. W. Murnau, who directed NOSFERATU, had already a few films to his credit—among them JANUSKOPF (JANUS-FACED, 1920), a version of *Dr. Jekyll and Mr. Hyde;* SCHLOSS VOGELÖD (VOGELÖD CASTLE, 1921), a crime picture visibly influenced by the Swedes; and the realistic farm drama BRENNENDER ACKER (BURNING SOIL, 1922), in which he is said to have furthered the action through sustained close shots of facial expressions. In VOGELÖD CASTLE, too, he knowingly used faces to reveal emotional undercurrents and orchestrate suspense. This early film moreover testified to Murnau's unique faculty of obliterating the boundaries between the real and the unreal. Reality in his films was surrounded by a halo of dreams and presentiments, and a tangible person might suddenly impress the audience as a mere apparition.[2]

Béla Balázs, a German film writer of Hungarian descent, wrote in 1924 that it was as if "a chilly draft from doomsday" passed through the scenes of NOSFERATU.[3] To obtain this effect Murnau and his cameraman, Fritz Arno Wagner, used all kinds of tricks. Strips of negative film presented the Carpathian woods as a maze of ghostlike white trees set against a black sky; shots taken in the

[1] Based on information offered by Mr. Galeen, who also permitted me to use the manuscript of his lecture on the fantastic film. Cf. *Film Society Programme,* Dec. 16, 1928; Dreyfus, "Films d'épouvante," *Revue du Cinéma,* May 1, 1930, p. 29; Vincent, *Histoire de l'Art Cinématographique,* p. 151.

[2] Vincent, *ibid.,* p. 151; "Auch Murnau . . ," *Filmwelt,* March 22, 1931; "Der Regisseur F. W. Murnau," *Ufa-Magazin,* Oct. 15–21, 1926; Kalbus, *Deutsche Filmkunst,* I, 58.

[3] Balázs, *Der sichtbare Mensch,* p. 108.

"one-turn-one-picture" manner transformed the clerk's coach into a phantom vehicle uncannily moving along by jerks. The most impressive episode was that in which the spectral ship glided with its terrible freight over phosphorescent waters. It is noteworthy that such an amount of picture sense and technical ingenuity served the sole purpose of rendering horrors. Of course, film sensations of this kind are short-lived; at the end of 1928, the Film Society in London revived the film with the remark that it "combined the ridiculous and the horrid." [4]

When speaking of NOSFERATU, the critics, even more than in the case of CALIGARI, insisted upon bringing in E. T. A. Hoffmann.[5] However, this reference to the film's romantic antecedents does not account for its specific meaning. The horrors NOSFERATU spreads are caused by a vampire identified with pestilence. Does he embody the pestilence, or is its image evoked to characterize him? If he were simply the embodiment of destructive nature, Nina's interference with his activities would be nothing more than magic, meaningless in this context. Like Attila, Nosferatu is a "scourge of God," and only as such identifiable with the pestilence. He is a blood-thirsty, blood-sucking tyrant figure looming in those regions where myths and fairy tales meet. It is highly significant that during this period German imagination, regardless of its starting-point, always gravitated towards such figures—as if under the compulsion of hate-love. The conception that great love might force tyranny into retreat, symbolized by Nina's triumph over Nosferatu, will be discussed later.[6]

VANINA, also released in 1922, dwelt upon the psychological causes and effects of tyranny. Carl Mayer, who fashioned the script after Stendhal's story *Vanina Vanini,* termed the film a "ballad." The Germans had then a penchant for ballads and legends, which, because of their unreal character, were as timely as the expressionist films proper. This predilection for an imagined world was early recognized and praised as a German feature. "The strength of the German film lies in the fantastic drama," the program-magazine of the Ufa theaters contended in 1921, lest its readers worry about the

[4] *Film Society Programme,* Dec. 16, 1928. See also Rotha, *Film Till Now,* pp. 197, 276; Oswell Blakeston, "Comment and Review," *Close Up,* Jan. 1929, pp. 71–72.

[5] Vincent, *Histoire de l'Art Cinématographique,* p. 151; Canudo, *L'Usine aux Images,* p. 138.

[6] Cf. pp. 90, 109.

superiority of the Americans, Italians and Swedes in other departments of screen entertainment.[7]

Vanina is the daughter of a royalist governor who wields his power so tyrannically that the people, exasperated, rebel against him and storm his feudal palace. The governor is a cripple, walking with crutches: this bodily defect makes him a counterpart of Homunculus. Like Homunculus, he is a tyrant whose sadism appears to stem from a basic inferiority complex. If this explanation of tyranny had not touched something in the Germans, it would hardly have been resumed. The rebellion is crushed, and the governor imprisons Octavio, its leader, with whom Vanina has fallen in love. Surprisingly, she succeeds in persuading her father to free Octavio and arrange for their marriage. However, his apparent generosity turns out to be sadistic finesse. While the wedding is still going on, the governor orders Octavio to be thrown again into the dungeon and then hanged. Enraged by this perfidy, Vanina strikes her crippled father and extorts from him Octavio's pardon. She runs to the dungeon, fetches her lover and heads with him for the portal of the palace. But in the meantime the governor, too, moves along with his crutches. On the strength of his counterorder the young lovers are seized just as they reach the last gate that separates them from freedom. Octavio, accompanied by Vanina, is dragged to the gallows, and the governor, convulsed with laughter, pronounces his death-sentence. Vanina drops dead; she cannot survive her lover.[8]

Supported by such actors as Asta Nielsen and Paul Wegener, Arthur von Gerlach made this study in sadism into a film which emphasized certain emotional complexes rampant under a tyrannical regime. Conspicuous in that respect is the sequence of the lovers' flight from the dungeon. Instead of giving the impression of speed, this sequence shows the couple walking endlessly through endless corridors. It is an escape in slow motion. Whereas an American reviewer complained of these boring "miles of passages,"[9] Béla Balázs, who was more familiar with the climate of the film, considered each new passage a "mysterious and uncanny aspect of doom."[10] There is, at any rate, no doubt that the corridors are intended to be

[7] Quotation from Möllhausen, "Der Aufstieg des Films," *Ufa-Blätter*.—For film ballads and legends of the time, see Jahier, "42 Ans de Cinéma," *Le Rôle intellectuel du Cinéma*, p. 61; Kalbus; *Deutsche Filmkunst*, I, 64, 66.

[8] *Ufa Verleih-Programme*, 1923, p. 18; Weinberg, *Scrapbooks*, 1928.

[9] Weinberg, *Scrapbooks*, 1928.

[10] Balázs, *Der sichtbare Mensch*, p. 134; see also p. 53.

symbolic rather than realistic. Their uninterrupted succession, which is certainly not in the interest of suspense, delineates the dread of ever-impending punishment at the hand of a merciless tyrant. This dread decomposes the traditional hierarchy of feelings. The terrorized fugitives experience one moment as an eternity, and limited space as space beyond any limits. Hope drives them towards the portal, but panic, which under the reign of terror is inseparable from hope, transforms their route into a monotonous repetition of blind alleys.[11]

The third important tyrant film appearing in 1922 was Fritz Lang's DR. MABUSE, DER SPIELER (DR. MABUSE, THE GAMBLER), a screen version of a much-read novel by Norbert Jacques. Lang and his wife, Thea von Harbou, collaborated on the script, as was their custom. Their design was to portray contemporary life. Two years after the release of DR. MABUSE, Lang himself called the film a document about the current world, and attributed its international success to its documentary virtues rather than to the many thrills it offered.[12] Whether or not the film lived up to this claim, Dr. Mabuse, its main character, was a contemporary tyrant. His appearance proves that those remote tyrants of NOSFERATU and VANINA also had topical significance.

Dr. Mabuse's family likeness to Dr. Caligari cannot be overlooked. He, too, is an unscrupulous master-mind animated by the lust for unlimited power. This superman heads a gang of killers, blind counterfeiters and other criminals, and with their help terrorizes society—in particular the postwar multitude in search of easy pleasures. Proceeding scientifically, Dr. Mabuse hypnotizes his presumptive victims—another resemblance to Dr. Caligari—and evades identification by impersonating diverse characters, such as a psychiatrist, a drunken sailor, a financial magnate. No one would even suspect his existence, if it were not for Dr. Wenk, the public prose-

[11] Potamkin praised VANINA for its fluidity. Cf. Potamkin, "Kino and Lichtspiel," *Close Up*, Nov. 1929, p. 391, and "The Rise and Fall of the German Film," *Cinema*, April 1930, p. 25.—Similar tyrant films were LUISE MILLERIN (1922) and PETER DER GROSSE (PETER THE GREAT, 1923). For the former, see *Decla-Bioscop Verleih-Programme*, 1923, p. 34. For the latter: Zaddach, *Der literarische Film*, p. 50; Kalbus, *Deutsche Filmkunst*, I, 70; "Peter the Great," *Exceptional Photoplays*, Feb.–March 1924, pp. 1–2.

[12] Lang, "Kitsch—Sensation—Kultur und Film," *Kulturfilmbuch*, p. 30. According to *Jahrbuch der Filmindustrie*, 1922/3, p. 46, the film's London première was a big success.

cutor, who is determined to track down the mystery man. Wenk has found an able helper in the degenerate Countess Told, while Mabuse relies on his mistress, Cara Carozza, a dancer slavishly devoted to him. A gigantic duel takes place: it is set against a background of swanky gambling haunts, and involves a considerable amount of violence and cunning. In its course Mabuse abducts the countess, with whom he has fallen in love, ruins her husband systematically, and orders the jailed Cara to poison herself, which she gladly does. It looks as if Mabuse is to triumph, for, after two unsuccessful attempts on Wenk's life, he finally hypnotizes him into a suicidal state: Wenk drives his car at high speed towards a perilous quarry. However, the police intervene in time, and, led by Wenk, storm Mabuse's house, kill the members of the gang and free the countess. Where is Mabuse himself? Days afterwards, they find him, a raving maniac, in the secret cellar which served the blind counterfeiters as a workshop. Like Caligari, Mabuse has gone mad.[13]

Owing to its two parts, the film is of an extraordinary length—a dollar-dreadful rather than a penny-dreadful. Trash need not be untrue to life; on the contrary, life may culminate in heaps of trash, such as no writer could ever amass. However, instead of making DR. MABUSE reflect familiar surroundings, Lang frequently stages the action in settings of pronounced artificiality. Now the scene is an expressionist club-room with painted shadows on the wall, now a dark back street through which Cesare might have slipped with Jane in his arms. Other decorative forms help these expressionist ones to mark the whole as an emotional vision. DR. MABUSE belongs in the CALIGARI sphere [Illus. 6]. It is by no means a documentary film, but it is a document of its time.

The world it pictures has fallen prey to lawlessness and depravity. A night-club dancer performs in a décor composed of outright sex symbols. Orgies are an institution, homosexuals and prostitute children are everyday characters. The anarchy smoldering in this world manifests itself clearly in the admirably handled episode of the police attack against Mabuse's house—an episode which through its imagery intentionally recalls the tumultuous postwar months with their street fights between Spartacus and the Noske troops. Circular ornaments emerge prominently time and again. Both the tricky floor in a new gambling club and the chain of hands formed during a

[13] Program brochure to the film; *Decla-Bioscop Verleih-Programme*, 1923, pp. 10–14.

spiritualist séance are shown from above to impress their circular appearance upon the spectator. Here, as in the case of CALIGARI, the circle denotes a state of chaos.[14]

The relation between Dr. Mabuse and this chaotic world is revealed by a shot to which Rudolf Arnheim has drawn attention. A small bright spot, Mabuse's face gleams out of the jet-black screen, then, with frightening speed, rushes to the foreground and fills the whole frame, his cruel, strong-willed eyes fastened upon the audience.[15] This shot characterizes Mabuse as a creature of darkness, devouring the world he overpowers. Much as Mabuse resembles Caligari, he surpasses him in that he continually changes his identity. Commenting upon this film, Lang once remarked that he was guided by the idea of rendering the whole of society, with Mabuse everywhere present but nowhere recognizable. The film succeeds in making of Mabuse an omnipresent threat which cannot be localized, and thus reflects society under a tyrannical regime—that kind of society in which one fears everybody because anybody may be the tyrant's ear or arm.

Throughout the film Mabuse is stigmatized as a man of genius who has become Public Enemy No. 1. The final scene depicts the outbreak of his madness in grandiose terms. Trapped in the cellar, Mabuse finds himself surrounded by all the persons he murdered—pale apparitions who urge him to join their company and cheat at cards. In the middle of the game the ghosts vanish; whereupon the lonely Mabuse amuses himself by throwing scores of banknotes into the air. They flutter about, flow around him. In vain, he tries to fend them off. Then Wenk arrives. . . . Wenk himself is scarcely more than a smart representative of the law, a kind of legal gangster, with the police functioning as his gang. Unlike Francis, who pursues Caligari for strong and just reasons, Wenk is morally so indifferent that his triumph lacks significance. To be sure, Mabuse is wrecked; but social depravity continues, and other Mabuses may follow. Here as well as in CALIGARI not the slightest allusion to true freedom interferes with the persistent alternative of tyranny or chaos.

DR. MABUSE adds to CALIGARI only in one respect: it attempts to show how closely tyranny and chaos are interrelated. The program brochure Decla-Bioscop published on the occasion of the film's première describes the Mabuse world as follows: "Mankind, swept

[14] Cf. p. 74.
[15] Arnheim, *Film als Kunst*, p. 124.

about and trampled down in the wake of war and revolution, takes revenge for years of anguish by indulging in lusts . . . and by passively or actively surrendering to crime." [16] That is, chaos breeds tyrants like Mabuse who, for their part, capitalize on chaos. One should not overlook the seemingly harmless word "and" through which the prospectus chooses to connect the weighty terms "war" and "revolution": this "and" throws a dazzling light on Dr. Mabuse's origin in the middle-class mind.

To stress the film's documentary value the prospectus also states: "This Dr. Mabuse . . . was not possible in 1910 and, perhaps, will not be possible any more in 1930—let us hope so, one should like to say. But with regard to the year 1920 he is a bigger-than-life portrait. . . ." The hope for the future proved illusory. In 1932, Lang, in THE LAST WILL OF DR. MABUSE,[17] resuscitated his supercriminal to mirror the obvious Mabuse traits of Hitler. Through this second Mabuse film the first one is revealed to be not so much a document as one of those deep-rooted premonitions which spread over the German postwar screen.

The cycle of imaginary tyrant films came to a close with DAS WACHSFIGURENKABINETT (WAXWORKS). Released as late as November 1924—at a time when life was just beginning to look normal again—WAXWORKS marked the end of that period in which the harassed German mind retreated into a shell. The script was written by Henrik Galeen, who, in NOSFERATU, had identified the tyrant with pestilence. He peopled the new film with no less than three tyrants, but reduced all of them to wax figures.[18]

As in CALIGARI, the scene is a fair, with a booth in which these figures are exhibited. A starved young poet (William Dieterle) approaches the showman, who has advertised that he wants someone to write stories about the waxworks. The showman takes this promising aspirant into the dark booth and slowly lights up one figure after another. Entranced by the sight of them, the poet sits down and writes and writes, with the showman's daughter sympathetically peeping over his shoulder. What he concocts emerges in the form of three successive episodes. The first, devoted to the figure of Harun-

[16] "Vorwort," program brochure to the film.

[17] Cf. p. 248 ff.

[18] Vincent, *Histoire de l'Art Cinématographique*, p. 153; *Film Society Programme*, Oct. 25, 1925. Besides the three tyrant figures of the film, Galeen's original script also included the figure of Rinaldo Rinaldini.

al-Rashid (Emil Jannings), is an Oriental burlesque ridiculing the manner of tyrants. They make passes at every pretty woman; in a fit of temper they order innocent people beheaded, and a moment later magnanimously pardon unpardonable crimes. This burlesque—it displays Harun's dealings with a jealous pastry-cook and his coquettish wife—turns out to be a rather insignificant prelude to the following more serious variations on the same theme.

The second episode animates the wax figure of Ivan the Terrible (Conrad Veidt), presenting him as an incarnation of insatiable lusts and unheard-of cruelties [Illus. 8]. Compared with him, the governor in VANINA is somewhat unimaginative. Ivan not only derives pleasure from interrupting a wedding party to make the bride his mistress for a night, but also shows true ingenuity in combining mental and physical tortures. He places an hourglass before each of his poisoned victims, so that these unfortunates may anticipate the precise moment of their death, calculated to coincide with the running-down of the last grain of sand. The Marquis de Sade would have liked that one. Owing to the machinations of a revengeful conspirator, Ivan finally believes himself poisoned and moreover comes upon a sandglass labeled "Ivan." Horror-stricken, the tyrant turns it incessantly to postpone the end. His mind out of joint, he shares the fate of Mabuse and Caligari.

In the third episode, the figure of Jack-the-Ripper (Werner Krauss) and the characters of the framing story are interlinked by means of a dream. Falling asleep from exhaustion, the poet dreams that, while he is taking a walk with the showman's daughter, Jack-the-Ripper appears and pursues them relentlessly. This is about all; but chase and flight perfectly render the nightmarish character life assumes under any Ivan. To round out the framing story, the film concludes with the heartening intimation that the poet and the girl please each other.

WAXWORKS was staged by Paul Leni, a former Reinhardt collaborator and one of the outstanding film directors of the postwar era. He had a special gift for designing sets.[19] In the case of WAXWORKS, he developed a décor which, in its attempt to create a fantastic atmosphere, borrowed much from expressionism. The halo of unreality with which Leni surrounded the film's three episodes was the more appropriate as these episodes center around wax figures. Such figures usually counterfeit kings, murderers or heroes who

[19] For Leni, see Vincent, *Histoire de l'Art Cinématographique*, p. 153.

belong in the past—counterfeit them to permit contemporaries to enjoy the shudders of awe or fright they once aroused. Their waxen appearance in a fair booth characterizes Harun and Ivan as phantoms that are remote in time as well as remote from reality.

The three episodes seize upon types of tyrants haunting a bygone period. (Haunting also former films: Jack-the-Ripper originates in CALIGARI, the Harun episode recalls Lubitsch's SUMURUN, and Ivan is an offspring of both the CALIGARI and the Lubitsch sphere.[20]) However, since dreams as a rule bear on the dreamer's current plight, the dream character of the Jack-the-Ripper episode arouses the suspicion that Jack and his confreres are not merely figures of the past, but tyrants still among us.

Like the imagery of MABUSE, VANINA and similar films, that of WAXWORKS culminates in scenes which, exceeding their task of illustrating the plot, penetrate the nature of tyrannical power. The insistence with which, during those years, pictorial imagination reverted to this subject indicates that the problem of absolute authority was an intrinsic concern of the collective mind. One shot in the Ivan episode reveals the magic spell power radiates: Ivan appears in a folding-door, the portrait of a saint in life-size on each leaf, and as he stands there, vested with all the insignia of his dignity, he seems a living icon between the two painted ones. Another picture unit of the same episode shows the bride whom Ivan wants to make his mistress looking through the iron bars of a window into the torture-chamber where her husband is undergoing terrible sufferings; and the shot of her face, distorted with horror, is followed by a close-up of Ivan's well-groomed, ring-adorned hand clasping those iron bars. This unit foreshadows a device common to all Russian screen epics of the Revolution: they never tire of contrasting the degraded oppressed with the smug Czarist oppressor in such a way that the latter's appearance exemplifies the dreadful alliance between culture and atrocity. Here the Germans intuitively visualize an aspect of tyranny which the Russians, doubtless on the strength of experience, were to emphasize as a basic one.

The most significant episode is that of Jack-the-Ripper—a very short sequence which must be counted among the greatest achieve-

[20] In their book, *The Film Answers Back,* p. 196, though questionable in both premises and conclusions, the English authors E. W. and M. M. Robson noted this point: "If it is permissible to describe the Caligari and the Lubitsch trends as thesis and antithesis in the early German film, we may say that *Waxworks* represents the synthesis of these two influences. . . ."

ments of film art.[21] It evolves outside the waxworks, in the fair with which the audience has already been familiarized by the framing story. But what in the framing story was nothing more than a crowded pleasure spot is now a deserted hunting ground for specters. Expressionist canvases, ingenious lighting effects and many other devices at hand in 1924 have been used to create this eerie phantasmagoria, which substantiates more forcibly than the analogous décor in CALIGARI the notion of chaos. Disparate architectural fragments form pell-mell complexes, doors open of their own accord and all proportions and relations depart from the normal. Much as the episode recalls CALIGARI, it goes beyond its model in stressing the role of the fair: the fair that in CALIGARI merely served as a background is here the very scene of action. In the course of their flight, the poet and the girl hurry past the constantly circling merry-go-round, while Jack-the-Ripper himself, Caligari and Cesare in one, pursues them on miraculous dream paths, hovering through a gigantic Ferris wheel that also turns without pause. [Illus. 7]. Completing the kindred pictorial efforts of DR. MABUSE, these images symbolize the interpenetration of chaos and tyranny in a definite manner. WAXWORKS adds the final touch to the tyrant films proper.

[21] Barry, *Program Notes,* Series II, program 4; Kurtz, *Expressionismus,* p. 80; Vincent, *Histoire de l'Art Cinématographique,* p. 153 ff.

7. DESTINY

In its attempt to reconsider the foundations of the self, German imagination did not confine itself to elaborating upon tyranny, but also inquired into what might happen if tyranny were rejected as a pattern of life. There seemed a sole alternative: for the world to turn into a chaos with all passions and instincts breaking loose. From 1920 through 1924—years in which the German screen never championed or even visualized the cause of liberty—films depicting the sway of unchecked instincts were as current as those devoted to tyrants. The Germans obviously held that they had no choice other than the cataclysm of anarchy or a tyrannical regime. Either possibility appeared pregnant with doom. In this plight contemporaneous imagination resorted to the ancient concept of Fate. Doom decreed by an inexorable Fate was not mere accident but a majestic event that stirred metaphysical shudders in sufferers and witnesses alike. As an outcome of superior necessity doom at least had grandeur. General susceptibility to this aspect is proved by the sweeping success of Spengler's *The Decline of the West* during that period. Even though many prominent German philosophers and scientists launched vigorous anathemas against the book, they were not able to weaken the overwhelming appeal of a vision that seemed to derive its timely prophecy of decline from laws inherent in history itself. This vision conformed to the emotional situation so perfectly that all counter-arguments sounded thin.

The second group of films in the wake of Caligari is composed of two films by Fritz Lang, both playing up the role of Fate. Der müde Tod (Destiny), the first of them, appeared in 1921, one year before Dr. Mabuse. Lang again wrote the script in collaboration with Thea von Harbou. After the release of the film, which in Germany is called The Tired Death, a sarcastic Berlin critic thought it fit to entitle his review "The Tiresome Death." However, when a little later the French praised the work for being truly German, the Germans also discovered its value, and what had at first looked like a failure developed into a complete victory on the home front.[1]

Part legend, part fairy tale, the romantically involved story starts with a girl and her young lover putting up at the inn of a small old town. An uncanny stranger joins them. According to a flashback, this man has long ago bought land bordering the nearby cemetery, and has surrounded it with a huge wall entirely bare of doors. In the inn, the girl pays a short visit to the kitchen; when she returns, her lover has disappeared with the stranger. Terrified, she hurries to the huge wall, swoons there, and after a while is found by the town's old pharmacist, who takes her to his home. While he is preparing a tonic, the girl in her despair lifts a poison cup to her mouth. But before the liquid wets her lips, she dreams a long dream, in which the huge wall re-emerges. This time there is a door in it, and behind the door an endless flight of stairs appears. At the top of the steps the stranger is waiting for the girl. As she wants her lover back from him, the stranger—he is the Angel of Death and as such the agent of Fate, if not Fate itself—leads her to a dark hall filled with burning candles, each representing a human soul. Her wish will be satisfied, he says, if she can prevent three flaring candle-lights from being extinguished. Now the authors utilize a compositional device later adopted in WAXWORKS: three longish episodes narrating the stories of these lights interrupt the course of the main action.[2] The first episode is located in a Moslem city, the second in the Venice of the Renaissance, the third in a fantastic China. In all three episodes, as if passing through successive stages of the transmigration of souls, the girl and her lover are pursued by a jealous, greedy and cruel tyrant; which, incidentally, makes these episodes resemble the Lubitsch pageants. Three times the girl tries to outwit the tyrant intent on killing her lover; three times the tyrant realizes his murderous design with the aid of Death, alias Fate, who in each case is incarnated in the executioner. . . . The three candle-lights die away, and again the girl implores the mercy of Death; whereupon Death offers her a last chance: if she can bring him another life, he is willing to return that of her lover. Here the dream of a split second ends, with the pharmacist snatching the poison cup away from the

[1] Based on information offered by Mr. Lang himself. Cf. Zaddach, *Der literarische Film*, pp. 41–42.

[2] Cf. p. 84 ff.

girl's mouth. He intimates that he himself feels tired of life; but when the girl asks him to sacrifice his life, he throws her out of his house. A weary beggar and several infirm old women in a hospital likewise refuse to make such a sacrifice. Fire breaks out in the hospital and after their flight the inmates learn that a baby has been left behind. Touched by the grief of the mother, the girl fights her way through the flames. At the very moment she seizes the baby, Death, keeping his promise, extends his arms to take this life. But the girl reneges; instead of ransoming her lover, she hands the baby out of a window to the happy mother. Amidst the blaze in the crashing house Death finally guides the dying girl to her dead lover, and, forever united, their souls wander heavenward over a blossoming hill.[3]

This plot forces one point strongly upon the audience: that, however arbitrary they seem, the actions of tyrants are realizations of Fate. The agent of Fate supports tyranny not only in all three episodes but also in the story proper. The death he inflicts upon the young lover appears so senseless that it is as if some unscrupulous tyrant had pulled the strings. There is an old fairy tale about a traveler startled by the misdeeds of his companion; this enigmatic fellow sets an inhabited house afire, obstructs justice and persistently returns evil for good. At the end he reveals himself as an angel and initiates the traveler into the true meaning of those apparent misdeeds; they were measures of Providence to protect the very people they wronged from future catastrophes. No such paradoxical meaning can be read into the shocking actions of Fate in DESTINY. The film ends with the girl's self-renunciation accompanied by a caption that emphasizes its religious significance: "He who loses his life gains it." This sacrifice conveys about the same message as Nina's final surrender in NOSFERATU.[4]

The long-lived power of DESTINY's imagery is the more amazing as all had to be done with the immovable, hand-cranked camera, and night shots were still impossible. These pictorial visions are so precise that they sometimes evoke the illusion of being intrinsically real. A "drawing brought to life," the Venetian episode resuscitates genuine Renaissance spirit through such scenes as the carnival procession—silhouettes staggering over a bridge—and the splendid cockfight radiating bright and cruel Southern passion in the mode of Stendhal

[3] Vincent, *Histoire de l'Art Cinématographique*, p. 147; Weinberg, *Scrapbooks*, 1925–27; Rotha, *Film Till Now*, p. 192.

[4] Cf. p. 79.

or Nietzsche. The Chinese episode abounds in miraculous feats. It is well known that its magic steed, its Liliputian army and its (jerkily) flying carpet inspired Douglas Fairbanks to make his THIEF OF BAGDAD, a spectacular revue of similar conjuring tricks.

The imagery rather than the plot brings the humane character of Death to the fore. With infinite care Death lifts the light of a candle, softly separating a child's soul from his body. This gesture as well as the tenderness he shows for the girl betrays his inner opposition to the duty enjoined on him. He is sick of his duty. Precisely by humanizing the agent of Fate, the film emphasizes the irrevocability of Fate's decisions. Different pictorial devices serve an analogous purpose; it is as if the visuals were calculated to impress the adamant, awe-inspiring nature of Fate upon the mind. Besides hiding the sky, the huge wall Death has erected runs parallel with the screen, so that no vanishing lines allow an estimate of the wall's extent [Illus. 9]. When the girl is standing before it, the contrast between its immensity and her tiny figure symbolizes Fate as inaccessible to human entreaties. This inaccessibility is also denoted by the innumerable steps the girl ascends to meet Death.

A very ingenious device makes it clear that no one can hope to evade Fate. In the Chinese episode the girl and her lover try to escape the revenge of the emperor who is deeply hurt by the girl's insensibility to his feelings. But instead of speeding their flight, the girl uses her magic wand to call upon the slowest means of transportation—an elephant. While they move along on the elephant, troops sent out by the emperor are following them with the speed of a snail, and there is obviously not the slightest danger of the couple's being recaptured. This operatic pursuit—it vaguely recalls the escape in slow motion in VANINA [5]—characterizes the inscrutable ways of Fate. No matter what people do or fail to do, Fate strikes when the time has come and not a moment before. The mock chase ends in a scene corroborating this meaning. On the emperor's command, his archer, who is none other than the agent of Fate, mounts a magic steed, rides through the skies, and in a trice overtakes the couple. Now that Fate wants to strike, all magic artifices prove ineffective: the archer's arrow pierces the lover.

Released at the beginning of 1924, Fritz Lang's world-famous DIE NIBELUNGEN (NIBELUNGEN) was produced by Decla-Bioscop,

[5] Cf. p. 80 f.

which by then had merged with Ufa. The preparation of this film classic took two years. Thea von Harbou, who had a propensity for titanic themes, fashioned the script freely after ancient sources, attempting to imbue them with current meaning. The Nordic myth became a gloomy romance featuring legendary characters in the grip of primitive passions. Notwithstanding its monumental style, NIBELUNGEN was by no means intended to compete with what Lang, in a statement published on the occasion of the film's première, called "the external enormousness of the American costume film." According to him NIBELUNGEN had quite another mission: to offer something strictly national, something that, like the Lay of the Nibelungs itself, might be considered a true manifestation of the German mind.[6] In short, Lang defined this film as a national document fit to publicize German culture all over the world. His whole statement somewhat anticipated the Goebbels propaganda.

Even though the NIBELUNGEN film differs entirely from *The Ring of the Nibelung*, it is rich in events which no one can witness without being haunted by Wagnerian leitmotivs. In SIEGFRIED, the film's first part, the hero goes through his adventures with the dragon and Alberic, and then visits the court of Burgundy to propose to Kriemhild, sister of King Gunther. But Hagen, the king's black-minded confidant, demands that, before marrying Kriemhild, Siegfried help conquer the fierce Brunhild for Gunther. Siegfried agrees, and by means of his magic hood cheats Brunhild into becoming Gunther's wife. The denouement is well known: Brunhild, learning of this base transaction from Kriemhild, insists upon Siegfried's death, and Hagen contrives to kill the hero. At the bier of her husband Kriemhild swears revenge. KRIEMHILD'S REVENGE, the film's second part, shows her marrying Attila, king of the barbarian Huns, and persuading him to invite Gunther to visit them. No sooner has Gunther arrived, than Kriemhild incites the Huns to attack him and his clan. A terrible mass slaughter ensues, with the Burgundians trapped in a hall which on Attila's order is shot afire. The end is an orgy of destruction: Kriemhild slays Gunther and Hagen, then she is killed, and Attila with her corpse in his arms buries himself in the burning hall.[7]

[6] Lang, "Worauf es beim Nibelungen-Film ankam," *Die Nibelungen*, p. 15. See also Vincent, *Histoire de l'Art Cinématographique*, pp. 146–47; Willy Haas, "Das letzte Filmjahr," *Das grosse Bilderbuch*, p. 8.

[7] Program to the film; "Inhaltsangabe für die Nibelungen . . ," *Die Nibelungen*, p. 17 ff.

In an article on NIBELUNGEN, Thea von Harbou remarked of her screen version that it was designed to stress "the inexorability with which the first guilt entails the last atonement." [8] In DESTINY Fate manifests itself through the actions of tyrants; in NIBELUNGEN, through the anarchical outbursts of ungovernable instincts and passions. To mark as fateful the doom these impulses bring about, the story closely interlinks causes and effects. From the moment when the dying dragon with a movement of his tail makes the ominous leaf drop on Siegfried's back down to the moment of Attila's self-chosen death, nothing seems left to mere chance. An inherent necessity predetermines the disastrous sequence of love, hatred, jealousy and thirst for revenge. Fate's pace-maker is Hagen, whose sinister presence suffices to prevent any good luck from slipping in and altering the inevitable. On the surface, he is nothing but Gunther's loyal vassal; but his whole behavior reveals that his loyalty is motivated by a nihilistic lust for power. Foreshadowing a well-known type of Nazi leader, this screen figure augments the mythic compactness of the Nibelungen world—a compactness impenetrable to enlightenment or Christian truth. The cathedral of Worms, which in SIEGFRIED appears rather frequently, forms a mute background without significance.

This Fate-conditioned story materializes through scenes which seem to be staged after decorative paintings of a bygone period. The scene of Siegfried riding on horseback in studio-built, heroic woods vividly recalls Böcklin's "Great Pan." It is amazing that despite their too pronounced beauty and their somewhat outmoded taste—a taste already outmoded in 1924—these pictures are still effective. The constructional austerity they breathe may account for it. Lang knew why, instead of resorting to Wagner's picturesque opera style or to some kind of psychological pantomime, he relied upon the spell of such decorative compositions: they symbolize Fate. The compulsion Fate exerts is aesthetically mirrored by the rigorous incorporation of all structural elements into a framework of lucid forms.

There are many elaborate scenic details, such as the marvelous ground-mists in the Alberic episode, the flaming waves protecting Brunhild's castle, and the young birch trees surrounding the spring at which Siegfried is murdered.[9] But far from pretending to self-

[8] Harbou, "Vom Nibelungen-Film und seinem Entstehen," *Die Nibelungen*, p. 8. Cf. *Decla-Bioscop Verleih-Programme*, 1923, pp. 44–57.

[9] Kalbus, *Deutsche Filmkunst*, I, 67, 114. Cf. Balthasar, "Die Dekoration," *Der Film von Morgen*, p. 80.

sufficiency, each of these details assumes its specific function only within the composition as a whole. To heighten the impression of pictorial unity, extensive use is made of simple, large and solemn architectural structures dominating the scene. Before Siegfried and his vassals enter Gunther's palace, they are seen, little figures, on a bridge which appears at the upper margin of the screen, and it is the relation of this bridge to the deep ravine beneath it that determines the picture. Other compositions, too, reduce human beings to accessories of primeval landscapes or vast buildings.

As if the inherent ornamental character of these compositions were not sufficient, primitive ornaments cover the walls, curtains, ceilings and costumes. Similar patterns appear everywhere. SIEGFRIED includes Kriemhild's "Dream of the Hawks," a short insert made by Ruttmann: it is nothing but an animated heraldic design involving two black hawks and a white dove in rhythmic movements.[10] Frequently the players themselves form ornamental figures. One scene shows Gunther's hall, with the king and his retinue sitting like statues in symmetrically arranged recesses. The camera eagerly exploits every opportunity of capturing figures of this kind. When Siegfried pays his first visit to Gunther, his entrance into the hall is shot from an elevation, so as to reveal the ornamental aspect of the ceremony.[11]

These patterns collaborate in deepening the impression of Fate's irresistible power. Certain specific human ornaments in the film denote as well the omnipotence of dictatorship. These ornaments are composed of vassals or slaves. Gunther's men support the landing-stage on which Brunhild goes ashore; standing up to their waists in the water, they are living pillars of mathematical precision. Particularly striking is the picture of the chained dwarfs serving as a decorative pedestal of the giant urn which contains Alberic's treasures: cursed by their master, the enslaved creatures are metamorphosed into stone figures. It is the complete triumph of the ornamental over the human [Illus. 10]. Absolute authority asserts itself by arranging people under its domination in pleasing designs. This can also be seen in the Nazi regime, which manifested strong ornamental inclinations in organizing masses. Whenever Hitler ha-

[10] Rotha, *Film Till Now*, p. 62.

[11] A similar ornamental style had already asserted itself in HAMLET (1920), a German film directed by Sven Gade and featuring Asta Nielsen in the title role. Cf. Barry, *Program Notes*, Series III, program 2. "The interior scenes," Miss Barry says of HAMLET, ". . . often predict the settings for Fritz Lang's *Siegfried*."

rangued the people, he surveyed not so much hundreds of thousands of listeners as an enormous ornament consisting of hundreds of thousands of particles.[12] TRIUMPH OF THE WILL, the official Nazi film of the Nuremberg Party Convention in 1934, proves that in shaping their mass-ornaments the Nazi decorators drew inspiration from NIBELUNGEN. SIEGFRIED's theatrical trumpeters, showy steps and authoritarian human patterns reappear, extremely magnified, in the modern Nuremberg pageant [Illus. 11 and 12].

NIBELUNGEN unfolds in lingering scenes that have all the qualities of stills.[13] Their slow procession, which characterizes the mythic realm as a static one, is calculated to draw attention to the action proper. This intrinsic action does not coincide with the succession of treacheries and murders, but is to be found in the development of smoldering instincts and imperceptibly growing passions. It is an all but vegetative process through which Fate realizes itself.

[12] Cf. p. 302 f.

[13] Jahier, "42 Ans de Cinéma," *Le Rôle intellectuel du Cinéma,* p. 61.

8. MUTE CHAOS

THE third group of films emanating from CALIGARI emphasizes the surge of disorderly lusts and impulses in a chaotic world. They may be called instinct films, in contrast to the tyrant films. The most significant achievements among them are based upon the scripts of Carl Mayer—scripts written with a view to specifically cinematic means. Except for THE LAST LAUGH, the concluding film of the series, Mayer's screen poems have met with little response outside the circle of the intellectuals. However, the insistence with which they all center round one and the same theme is sufficient proof of their symptomatic value.

Immediately after CALIGARI, Robert Wiene, meaning to strike while the iron was hot, engaged Carl Mayer and the painter Césare Klein for the production of another expressionist film: GENUINE (1920). This fantasy, in which an exuberant décor competes with a far-fetched, bizarre story, is of importance only in that it marks a turning-point thematically. Genuine, a sanguinary priestess for sale in an Oriental slave-market, is bought by a queer old man, who jealously confines her in a sort of glass cage inaccessible to visitors. But Genuine manages to lure a young barber into cutting the old tyrant's throat, and then carries on as a supervamp, ruining all the men available.[1] The narrative shows Mayer's interest shifting from the tyrant to the instinct theme.

All instinct films Mayer made after GENUINE have one feature in common: they are laid in a lower middle-class world which is the meaningless remnant of a disintegrated society. The lower middle class appears in Mayer's films as a breeding ground for stunned, oppressed creatures who, reminiscent of Büchner's Wozzek figure, are unable to sublimate their instincts. This was undoubtedly the plight of the German petty bourgeoisie during those years. It is true

[1] Kurtz, *Expressionismus*, pp. 70–73; Vincent, *Histoire de l'Art Cinématographique*, p. 145.

that in an era of anarchy the preponderance of instinctive life does not confine itself to one single stratum of the population. But this kind of life is nowhere as conspicuous and aggressive as in the lower middle class where greed and jealousy are supplemented by deep social resentments and inherited moral impulses that have lost any vital function. Mayer conceives his lower middle-class characters as instinct-possessed denizens of a shattered universe, and he seizes upon them to reveal the destruction and self-destruction they necessarily bring about. Their doom is laid to the workings of Fate. In NIBELUNGEN, Fate is symbolized by a strictly decorative style; in Mayer's films, by extreme simplicity in psychological construction. A few persons, each incarnating some particular instinct, are involved in a rigidly composed action. While foreign observers criticized this simplicity as artificial and poor, German connoisseurs, tired of the screen pageants they had to endure, praised these films as "chamber plays," exhibiting the very depths of the soul.[2] As late as 1924, when expressionism was definitely fading away, Professor Paul Hildebrandt agreed with Carl Hauptmann in contending: "In the sphere of the fantastic, the film . . . must represent what can be represented only within this medium . . . : the primitive passions."[3]

In 1921, Carl Mayer began his series with two films, one of which was HINTERTREPPE (BACKSTAIRS). Staged by Leopold Jessner, this film is a veritable excess of simplicity. It sets three characters in motion: a hired girl absorbed in housekeeping activities; her lover, promising to send the girl letters from afar; a partly paralyzed, subnormal postman who out of morbid love for the girl intercepts these letters. Believing herself abandoned, she is stirred by a sort of maternal pity to call on the postman in his nearby basement. Her visit there is interrupted by the returning lover. In the ensuing quarrel between the two men the frantic postman slays his rival with an ax; whereupon the girl, in a state of complete bewilderment, walks up to the roof and throws herself down to the cobblestones. The public was rather annoyed by such an accumulation of violence and misery.[4]

[2] Tannenbaum, "Der Grossfilm," *Der Film von Morgen*, pp. 71–72; Möllhausen, "Der Aufstieg des Films," *Ufa-Blätter*.

[3] Hildebrandt, "Literatur und Film," *Das Kulturfilmbuch*, p. 85.

[4] Weinberg, *Scrapbooks*, 1925–27; Vincent, *Histoire de l'Art Cinématographique*, p. 153; Kalbus, *Deutsche Filmkunst*, I, 73.

The other film released in 1921 was SCHERBEN (SHATTERED). Lupu Pick directed it with an innate affinity for Mayer's intentions. At the beginning, a railroad trackwalker (Werner Krauss), his wife and his daughter are living in the solitude of snow-covered, wooded hills—a solitude accented by the man's ever-repeated walks along the track, and the occasional passing of a train. The arrival of a railway inspector controlling this section changes stagnant monotony to ferment. It all starts with a love affair between the inspector and the quickly yielding daughter. After surprising the two in tender intimacy, the pious mother goes out into the cold night to pray before a votive tablet, and there freezes to death. The daughter implores the inspector to take her with him to town, meets with a plain rebuff, and, humiliated, avenges herself on him by informing her father of what has happened. Deep-rooted awe of the authorities causes the trackwalker to knock at the inspector's door; moral convention, having become instinct, makes him strangle the seducer of his daughter. Then he patrols the track, swinging his signal lantern to stop the express. (Here an ingenious color effect is used: the lantern radiates a bright red, rendering the man's emotional turmoil to perfection.) Although the travelers in the dining-car wonder at the unexpected stop, they are not at all interested in a humble trackwalker's affairs. By emphasizing their indifference, the film marks the dissolution of society into incompatible social spheres. "I am a murderer," the trackwalker says to the engine driver; it is the sole caption in the entire film. From a rock above the track the daughter, gone mad, watches the express with her father in it rush by.[5]

After VANINA, his last tyrant film, Carl Mayer resumed his felicitous collaboration with Lupu Pick in the domain of the instinct films; the result was SYLVESTER (NEW YEAR'S EVE, 1923). A quotation from the Tower-of-Babel story heads the script, which has since been published as a book: "Go to, let us go down, and there confound their language, that they may not understand one another's speech." This motto clearly indicates Mayer's design to continue in NEW YEAR'S EVE what he had begun in SHATTERED: the representation of social chaos by two social spheres separated by an abysmal gulf. One sphere materializes in a cheap café, the meeting-place of lower

[5] Kalbus, *ibid.*, p. 73; Weinberg, *Scrapbooks*, 1925–27; "Shattered," *Exceptional Photoplays*, Jan.–Feb. 1922, pp. 4–5; Vincent, *Histoire de l'Art Cinématographique*, p. 149.

middle-class people; the other in the street, in a nearby elegant restaurant and on the adjacent town square—places populated with merry crowds celebrating New Year's Eve. To these two spheres a third one is added: nature. Pictures of a cemetery, the heath and the sea emerge every now and then in the manner of a leitmotiv—great and silent landscapes which make human agitation seem still more extreme. The story proper shows the café-owner suffering from the discord between his wife and his mother. In her despotic love of the son, the mother hates the wife with whom she has to share what she considers her exclusive property; in the interest of peace at home, the wife in turn wants the son to send his mother away.

As the conflict reaches its climax, something almost inconceivable occurs: unable to make a decision, the man breaks down, and while his mother caresses him as if he were a child, he rests his head helplessly on her bosom. This gesture, followed (and corroborated) by the suicide of the man [Illus. 13], betrays his intense desire to return to the maternal womb. He has never attained maturity. It is noteworthy that, far from being repudiated, his singular gesture of capitulation reappeared, almost unchanged, in various German films,[6] indicating that his instinctive reluctance to attempt emancipation might be considered a typical German attitude. It is an attitude which results from the prolonged dependence of the Germans upon a feudal or half-feudal military regime—not to mention the current social and economic motives enforcing the perpetuation of this attitude within the middle class. When the café-owner capitulates, he overflows with a self-pity entirely to the point. Self-pity is the given emotional outlet for undeveloped or repressed characters.

The film ends with a few scenes confronting part of the merry crowd with the corpse of the ill-fated café-owner; but the two social spheres are made to overlap for the sole purpose of stressing their utter estrangement. Indifferent to human affairs, the moon shines over the sea.[7]

The series culminates in DER LETZTE MANN (THE LAST LAUGH; released at the end of 1924). This powerful film—the outcome of teamwork by Carl Mayer, F. W. Murnau and the cameraman Karl

[6] Cf. pp. 112, 114, 122, 157 f., 171.

[7] Cf. Pick, "Vorwort des Regisseurs," *Sylvester*, pp. 9–11; Mayer, "Sylvester," *ibid.*, pp. 17–96; Faure, "Cinéma," *Le Rôle intellectuel du Cinéma*, p. 209; Balázs, *Der Geist des Films*, p. 53; Rotha, *Film Till Now*, p. 204; Vincent, *Histoire de l'Art Cinématographique*, p. 149.

Freund—resumes the basic motif of its forerunners by contrasting two buildings: a gloomy tenement house crowded with lower middle-class people, and a palace hotel for the rich, who keep the revolving door and the elevators in permanent motion. Yet THE LAST LAUGH differs from the previous films in that it shows the two social spheres united by strong ties. Wearing his sparkling uniform with an inimitable dignity, Emil Jannings as the old hotel porter not only ushers the guests through the revolving door, but also offers candies to the children in the yard of the tenement house where he lives with some relatives. All the tenants, in particular the female ones, are awed by his uniform which, through its mere presence, seems to confer a mystic glamour upon their modest existence. They revere it as a symbol of supreme authority and are happy to be allowed to revere it. Thus the film advances, however ironically, the authoritarian credo that the magic spell of authority protects society from decomposition.

In the case of the porter, however, this spell is suddenly destroyed. The hotel manager, watching him stagger under the burden of a heavy trunk, orders the old man to exchange his uniform for the white blouse of a—lavatory attendant. This rather humane administrative measure entails a catastrophe. Since the film implies that authority, and authority alone, fuses the disparate social spheres into a whole, the fall of the uniform representing authority is bound to provoke anarchy. No sooner do the tenants learn about the ignominious white blouse than they feel alienated from that upper world with which they communed through the uniform. They resent being socially abandoned and thrown back into the gloominess of their flats and of their souls. All evil lower middle-class instincts are unleashed against the porter. The gossiping housewives maliciously ridicule him; his own relatives turn him out onto the street. The porter's reactions resemble those of the café-owner in NEW YEAR'S EVE. He believes himself humiliated by the loss of his uniform, and instead of maturely putting up with his plight, he falls into a self-pity tantamount to complete self-renunciation [Illus. 14]. At the end he is seen in the hotel's dark lavatory, with the night-watchman tenderly wrapping him in a cover. It is a moving gesture of solidarity between two human wrecks—a gesture, though, that does not alter anything.

Here everyone would expect the film to come to a close. But Mayer grafts upon this natural conclusion an ingenious second one, prefaced by a few sentences which form the film's sole caption. They tell the audience that the author, out of pity for the poor porter's fate in real life, wants to guide him towards a better, if unreal, future. What follows is a nice farce jeering at the happy ending typical of the American film. One should not forget that in 1924 Hollywood had begun to exert its influence on the German screen. The farce opens with the richly dressed porter dining in the grill room of the hotel. While he tries to cope with intricate dishes, the amused guests show each other a newspaper notice to the effect that an American millionaire bequeathed his fortune to the last person present at his death, and that this person happened to be the lavatory attendant. The rest of the fairy tale exhibits the naïve kindness with which the old porter showers money on the worthy and unworthy alike. After having enjoyed their triumph in the hotel, he and his crony, the night-watchman, leave in a carriage drawn by four horses: two bragging profiteers, in reality sweet angels.[8]

The farcical character of this concluding sequence corroborates its introductory caption in that it expresses the author's disbelief in a happy ending involving such categories as chance and good luck. If there should exist a way out for hotel porters degraded to lavatory attendants, it is certainly not identical with any solution rooted in the superficial concepts of Western civilization. Through its second ending the film underscores the significance of its first one, and moreover rejects the idea that the "decline of the West" could be remedied by the blessings of the West.

Mayer's films reveal their remoteness from realism by the insistent use made in them of a specifically expressionist device. No character bears a name: the mother is "the Mother," the trackwalker just "the Trackwalker." Instead of portraying individuals, all these characters incarnate impulses and passions—allegoric figures required for the externalization of inner visions. This requirement determines the whole staging. The décor of BACKSTAIRS would have been impossible without CALIGARI; the snow-covered sceneries in SHATTERED—their insertion may have been due to the influence of the Swedish film—look exactly as if they were studio-built struc-

[8] Rotha, "It's in the Script," *World Film News,* Sept. 1938, p. 205; Potamkin, "The Rise and Fall of the German Film," *Cinéma,* April 1930, p. 25, and "Kino and Lichtspiel," *Close Up,* Nov. 1929, p. 387–88. For the rupture between Mayer and Pick on the occasion of THE LAST LAUGH, see Vincent, *Histoire de l'Art Cinématographique,* p. 149.

tures; the bizarre lower middle-class scenes in The Last Laugh counterbalance the film's concessions to the realistic current gaining momentum in 1924.[9]

Because of its world success The Last Laugh has usually been considered the source of cinematic innovations which, in fact, are peculiar to the whole series of instinct films. Among these innovations —they can all be traced to Carl Mayer's suggestions—one struck the public immediately: the lack of any captions. Except for the two mentioned above, the stories are told exclusively through pictures.[10] Here again the interrelationship between the method of representation and the content to be represented is striking. It is not so much the technical ingenuity as the subject-matter of the instinct films that causes the film-makers to introduce titleless narration. Instincts and passions flourish beneath the dimension of discursive reasoning, and therefore lend themselves to being pictured without verbal explanations. This holds particularly true for Mayer's films, with their purposefully simplified plot. They are displays of essentially mute events. Captions in them would not only be superfluous, but would interfere with pictorial continuity. That contemporaries were aware of this structural necessity is shown by a review of New Year's Eve published in the German film magazine *Licht Bild Bühne* after the film's première: "What counts is not so much the actual omission of titles . . . as the fact that, owing to its whole structure, New Year's Eve can and even must do without them."[11]

Mayer's films are also the first to seize upon the world of objects —until then explored only by slapstick comedy—in the interest of dramatic action. When Backstairs was released in New York, one of the reviewers pointed to the important role of the hired girl's alarm clock. She "is shown being awakened by her alarm clock at six in the morning. She sets it back five minutes, and then the idea that it is ringing again is depicted by the key in the back of the timepiece slowly turning. . . ."[12] The alarm clock reappears in Shattered

[9] Kurtz, *Expressionismus,* pp. 83–84. For the influence of the Swedish film, see Möllhausen, "Der Aufstieg des Films," *Ufa-Blätter*; Balthasar, "Die Dekoration," *Der Film von Morgen,* pp. 78–79.—That Murnau himself inclined towards realism is proved by his film comedy Die Finanzen des Grossherzogs (The Grand Duke's Finances, winter 1923–4). The magazine *Licht Bild Bühne* (Jan. 8, 1924) acknowledged this comedy with a sigh of relief: "At last a film without deeper significance!" Quoted from Zaddach, *Der literarische Film,* p. 56.

[10] Rotha, *Film Till Now,* p. 298.

[11] Quoted from Zaddach, *Der literarische Film,* p. 54.

[12] See Weinberg, *Scrapbooks,* 1925–27.

along with such significant objects as the miserable scarcecrow trembling in the wind before the trackwalker's house, and the shining boots of the inspector. While the daughter goes on her knees to clean the staircase, these boots leisurely descend the steps, and almost touch her—the first view she has of her future lover. In addition, SHATTERED offers details of locomotives, wheels, telegraph wires, signal bells and other pertinent items destined to degenerate into the standardized adornments of innumerable railway scenes to come.

In NEW YEAR'S EVE, the motif of the clock acquires its full meaning. Even more important than the clock on the town square is a pendulum clock in the café-owner's room. As with twelve strokes it marks the beginning of the new year, the camera turns from it to the corpse of the café-owner, thus forcing upon us our simultaneous existence in the outer and the inner world, the *temps espace* and the *temps durée*. It is as if the objects watched attentively the spectacle of raging human passions or even participated in it. The perambulator in the room where the café-owner's mother and wife fight each other assumes a restless life of its own, and the revolving door of the elegant restaurant is both entrance-way and background for the merry crowds on the street.

In THE LAST LAUGH this revolving door becomes an obsession.[13] The film opens with a magnificent traveling shot showing the hotel guests streaming through the ever-turning door, a device employed time and again until the very end—something between a merry-go-round and a roulette wheel [Illus. 15]. A *pièce de résistance* like the door, the porter's ubiquitous uniform seems endowed with the power of luring scores of other objects out of their seclusion. The trunks intervene energetically; the walls in the nocturnal hotel seem to breathe. Even fragments of human bodies are dragged into the realm of objects: owing to big close-ups, no one can tell the open mouths of gossips from fuming craters. This irresistible tendency to involve inanimate objects in the action springs from the intrinsic nature of Mayer's instinct-possessed characters. Incapable of sublimating their impulses, they inhabit a region determined by physical sensations and material stimulants—a region in which objects loom high, taking on the function of stumbling-blocks or signal-posts, enemies or partners. These films are bound to call upon alarm clocks and revolving doors: the clock obsesses

[13] Cf. Lejeune, *Cinema*, pp. 122–23.

the mind of the hired girl, and in swinging the door, the porter, one with his uniform, sways his scepter.

It is true that many an object seems to be exhibited merely for the sake of cheap symbolism. The repeated close-ups of broken glass in SHATTERED have no purpose other than to denote the fragility of human design in the face of Fate; they mean nothing by themselves. But these obvious failures arise from the same source as the solid attainments—from Mayer's passion for objects. By conquering the domain of objects for the screen, he enriched its pictorial vocabulary lastingly; it was a conquest which, in harmony with his effort to cancel all captions, paved the way for truly cinematic narration.

In his preface to the publication of NEW YEAR'S EVE, Lupu Pick makes an elucidating remark about its subtitle, "*Ein Lichtspiel*" ("A Play of Light"). Carl Mayer, he states, "may well have intended to disclose brightness and darkness . . . within the soul itself, that eternal alternation of light and shadow characterizing the psychological relations between human beings." [14] Pick's statement reveals that in Mayer's series, no less than in the expressionist film proper, the light is an unreal light, one that illuminates interior landscapes. "The illumination seemed to emanate from the objects themselves," the Belgian film writer Carl Vincent comments on BACKSTAIRS.[15] Creating not so much sharply contoured forms as fluctuating complexes, this light helps emphasize the irrational events of instinctive life. Such events draw near or dissolve like any elemental phenomenon, and the light illustrates that agitation. In THE LAST LAUGH impenetrable shadows transform the lavatory entrance into a dark abyss, and the appearance of the night-watchman is forecast by the circle of light his lantern projects on the walls.

All these achievements are topped by the mobilization of the camera in Mayer's films. Owing to complete camera mobility, THE LAST LAUGH strongly influenced Hollywood's motion-picture technique.[16] Yet this film only brought to perfection what had already announced itself in SHATTERED—at a time when no one else thought of moving a camera firmly fastened to its fixed tripod. In SHATTERED, so-called pan shots—shots ranging from one point of the scene to another, so as to make the spectator survey a whole panorama—deliberately advance the narrative. For instance, the camera pans

[14] Pick, "Vorwort des Regisseurs," *Sylvester*, p. 9.

[15] Vincent, *Histoire de l'Art Cinématographique*, p. 153.

[16] Rotha, *Film Till Now*, p. 177; Jacobs, *American Film*, p. 307; Potamkin, "Kino and Lichtspiel," *Close Up*, Nov. 1929, pp. 390–91.

from the trembling scarecrow to a corner window, with the silhouettes of the inspector and the daughter behind it, in a slow and steady movement designed not only to divulge the starting love affair, but also to relate its meaning to that of the desolate effigy in the wind. By connecting successive visual elements in such a way that they are forced to illuminate each other, the freed camera develops an activity entirely consistent with the omission of titles and the promotion of objects: it intensifies that pictorial continuity through which instinctive life manifests itself. In the case of Mayer's films, camera movements are the more needed as the instincts unfold in a chaotic world. These movements serve to familiarize the spectator with spheres and events irretrievably separated from each other. Guided by the camera, he is in a position to survey the frantic whole without going astray in the labyrinth.

Carl Mayer himself was quite conscious of what he achieved in unchaining the camera. In his preface to NEW YEAR'S EVE, he first defines the spheres of the merry crowds and the natural scenery as the "surroundings" of the café-owner's rooms, and then states that certain movements of the camera are calculated to express the idea of a world including the "surroundings" as well as the scene of action proper. "As the events progress, these movements are . . . to encompass depths and heights, so as to picture the frenzy shaking the whole human world amidst nature." [17] To realize Mayer's directives for NEW YEAR'S EVE, Lupu Pick's cameraman, Guido Seeber, introduced a tripod moving on rails.[18]

When, a little later, Murnau staged THE LAST LAUGH, he had a fully automatic camera at his disposal, an instrument capable of all sorts of movements. Throughout this film it pans, travels and tilts up and down with a perseverance which not only results in a pictorial narrative of complete fluidity, but also enables the spectator to follow the course of events from various viewpoints.[19] The roving camera makes him experience the glory of the uniform as well as the misery of the tenement house, metamorphoses him into the hotel porter, and imbues him with the author's own feelings. He is psychologically ubiquitous. However, despite its eagerness for ever-changing aspects, the camera, at home in the dimension of instincts, refrains from penetrating that of consciousness. Conscious acting is not allowed to

[17] Mayer, "Technische Vorbemerkungen des Autors," *Sylvester*, pp. 15–16.

[18] Kalbus, *Deutsche Filmkunst*, I, 111–12.

[19] Potamkin, "The Rise and Fall of the German Film," *Cinema*, April 1930, p. 25: "Die Entfesselte Kamera," *Ufa-Magazin*, March 25–31, 1927.

prevail. The player is the passive subject of the camera. In a retrospective article on F. W. Murnau, Kenneth White elaborates this point by referring to a scene in which the porter gets drunk: "The pantomime everyone had thought to be the derived art of the movies was not discoverable in THE LAST LAUGH. The doorman got drunk, but not in the way a pantomimic actor with subordinate properties got drunk; the camera did it for him." [20]

During the whole postwar period the theme of Mayer's instinct films proved so attractive that any literary work showing some affinity for it was immediately transferred to the screen—from Strindberg's *Lady Julia* (FRÄULEIN JULIE, 1922) to Tolstoy's *Power of Darkness* (DIE MACHT DER FINSTERNIS, 1924), from Gerhart Hauptmann's peasant drama *Rose Bernd* (ROSE BERND, 1919) to that of his brother Carl, *Driven from Home* (AUSTREIBUNG, 1923).[21] When ROSE BERND appeared in New York, the *National Board of Review Magazine* commented on it in terms which somehow cover the whole trend of kindred films, regardless of their different aesthetic qualities. "It is a picture . . . with no moral other than that which . . . is implied by the fate of its characters, and by the forces leading to that fate. It is also a picture . . . in which one may feel blind impulses welling from their springs of animal need and instinct." [22] The bulk of these adaptations was followed by a brilliant straggler, CHRONIK VON GRIESHUUS (CHRONICLES OF THE GRAY HOUSE, 1925); made after Theodor Storm's story of the same title, it breathed the atmosphere of a sinister medieval saga.[23]

[20] White, "Film Chronicle: F. W. Murnau," *Hound & Horn*, July–Sept. 1931, p. 581.

[21] For these films, see Zaddach, *Der literarische Film*, pp. 42–43, 53; Kalbus, *Deutsche Filmkunst*, I, 72–73; *Decla-Bioscop Verleih-Programme*, 1923, pp. 64–67.

[22] "Rose Bernd," *National Board of Review Magazine*, Feb. 1927, p. 16.

[23] Barrett, "Grey Magic," *National Board of Review Magazine*, Dec. 1926, pp. 4–6. Films in a similar vein were SAPPHO (MAD LOVE, 1921)—see *Ufa Verleih-Programme*, 1923, p. 17—and Lupu Pick's WILDENTE (THE WILD DUCK, 1925). For the latter film, see *Film Society Programme*, Nov. 18, 1928.

9. CRUCIAL DILEMMA

The German soul, haunted by the alternative images of tyrannic rule and instinct-governed chaos, threatened by doom on either side, tossed about in gloomy space like the phantom ship in NOSFERATU.

While tyrant and instinct films were still flourishing, the German screen began to offer films manifesting an intense inner desire to find a way out of the dilemma. It was a desire pervading the whole sphere of consciousness. Whoever lived through those crucial years in Germany will remember the craving for a spiritual shelter which possessed the young, the intellectuals. The Church won over many, and the enthusiasm these converts manifested over their newly acquired security contrasted strangely with the attempt by a group of young men born in the Catholic faith to influence ecclesiastic policy in favor of leftist tendencies. There is also no doubt that the increase of communist sympathizers was in part the result of the spell the orthodox character of the Marxist doctrine cast over many mentally unprotected who were in search of a solid refuge. In their dread of being left in the open, scores of people rushed to mushroom prophets, who were to sink into oblivion a few years later. The theosophist Rudolf Steiner was a particular rage of the time; he resembled Hitler in that he zealously advertised inflated visions in execrable, petty-bourgeois German.

On the screen diverse efforts were being made to discover a *modus vivendi*, a tenable pattern of inner existence. Two films by Ludwig Berger, both released in 1923, are typical of one of these attempts: EIN GLAS WASSER (A GLASS OF WATER), fashioned after Scribe's comedy of that title, and DER VERLORENE SCHUH (CINDERELLA), which transferred the ancient fairy tale to the screen with many arabesques and detours.[1] To justify the choice of such bright subjects in so dark a world, Berger cited the Romantics as a precedent.

[1] Programs to these films. For CINDERELLA, see also *Film Society Programme*, Nov. 22, 1925.

In the prospectus of A Glass of Water he wrote: "In times of misery and oppression even more than in times of security and wealth, we long for serenity and light play. There has been much talk about the 'flight of the Romantics.' But what outwardly appeared to be a flight, was in reality the deepest self-examination . . . , was food and strength during decades of external poverty, and at the same time a bridge to a better future." [2] Berger's reference to the Romantics only emphasizes the escapist character of his own products.

While inflation grew all-devouring and political passion was at its height, these films provided the illusion of a never-never land in which the poor salesgirl triumphs over the conniving queen, and the kind fairy godmother helps Cinderella win Prince Charming. It was, of course, enjoyable to forget harsh reality in tender daydreams, and Cinderella in particular satisfied the longing for "serenity and light play" by concocting, with the aid of special cinematic devices, a sweet mixture of human affairs and supernatural miracles. However, this never-never land was not beyond the range of politics.

Both films developed within settings staged by Rudolf Bamberger in the warm and gay style of South German baroque—settings of a pronounced symmetry, to which Paul Rotha early drew attention. "Doorways, windows, gateways, alley-ways, etc., were always set in the centre of the screen, the remainder of the composition moving about them." [3] This baroque décor, with its stress on symmetry, conveyed the spirit of patriarchal absolutism reigning in the old Catholic principalities: the two films conceived the "better future" as a return to the good old days. Berger was not wrong in leaning on the Romantics; they, too, inclined to glorify the past, and in consequence had strong affiliations with the traditional powers [Illus. 16]. These films were pleasant digressions. But their inherent romanticism was unable to meet the wants of a collective mind definitely expelled from that baroque paradise.

A second effort to establish an adequate psychological pattern consisted in the suggestion that all suffering springing from tyranny or chaos should be endured and overcome in the spirit of Christlike love. This suggestion recommended itself by its implication that inner metamorphosis counts more than any transformation of the outer world—an implication justifying the aversion of the middle

[2] Program brochure to A Glass of Water.
[3] Rotha, *Film Till Now*, p. 199.

class to social and political changes. Here it becomes clear why, in NOSFERATU, Nina's love alone succeeds in defeating the vampire, and why, in DESTINY, the girl's union with her lover in the hereafter is made dependent upon her supreme self-sacrifice.[4] It was the solution of Dostoievsky. His works—edited by Moeller van den Bruck, who supplied the Nazis with the basic concept of the "Third Reich" —were then so popular with the middle class that their red covers adorned every drawing room. What James T. Farrell writes about *The Brothers Karamazov* also applies to this emotional trend in postwar Germany: "The revolution will only produce catastrophe. Man must suffer. The noblest man is he who suffers not only for himself but for all his fellow-men. Since the world cannot be changed, man must be changed by love."[5] As early as 1920, a fragment of the Karamazov novel was transferred to the screen.[6] Robert Wiene seized upon *Crime and Punishment*; his RASKOLNIKOW (CRIME AND PUNISHMENT), released in 1923, was performed by a group of the Moscow Art Players adapting themselves to stylized settings reminiscent of CALIGARI. Conspicuous are the scenes in which Raskolnikow indulges in self-accusing fantasies before the judge; a spider's web ornamenting the corner of a wall actively participates in the "physiognomic duel" between the oily judge and the delirious murderer.[7]

Other films, too, plunged into the depths of religious experience. With the aid of Asta Nielsen, Henny Porten, Werner Krauss and Gregori Chmara, Robert Wiene staged I.N.R.I. (1923), a passion play that was framed by scenes showing a murderer sentenced to death. Meditating on the story of Christ's Passion, the murderer—he has shot a minister to free his people from oppression—comes to abjure his revolutionary methods.[8] The political significance of many a religious conversion could not have been exhibited more directly. In a similar vein were several balladlike films with a certain Dos-

[4] Cf. pp. 79, 90.

[5] Farrell, "Dostoievsky and 'The Brothers Karamazov' Revalued," *New York Times Book Review*, Jan. 9, 1944, p. 28.

[6] DIE BRÜDER KARAMASOFF (THE BROTHERS KARAMAZOV), directed by Carl Froelich. Cf. Zaddach, *Der literarische Film*, pp. 38–39; Amiguet, *Cinéma! Cinéma!*, p. 50.

[7] "Crime and Punishment," *National Board of Review Magazine*, June 1927, pp. 10–11; *Film Society Programme*, Dec. 20, 1925; Vincent, *Histoire de l'Art Cinématographique*, p. 145; Kurtz, *Expressionismus*, pp. 75, 76, 78. A similar "physiognomic duel"—this phrase was coined by Balázs—occurred in Joe May's DIE TRAGÖDIE DER LIEBE (LOVE TRAGEDY, 1923); cf. Balázs, *Der sichtbare Mensch*, p. 70, and Kurtz, *ibid.*, pp. 78–79.

[8] *Film Society Programme*, Jan. 8, 1928; Kalbus, *Deutsche Filmkunst*, I, 54.

toievsky touch; DER HENKER VON ST.-MARIEN (THE HANGMAN OF ST.-MARIEN, 1920), DER GRAF VON CHAROLAIS (THE COUNT OF CHAROLAIS, 1922, a screen version of Richard Beer-Hofmann's play) and DER STEINERNE REITER (THE STONE RIDER, 1923).[9] They demonstrated that true love is capable of working miracles, or that heavenly miracles may intervene in favor of true love. But notwithstanding the relatively broad appeal of these films, the form of inner existence they endorsed proved attainable only to a small, predisposed minority. The way of Christlike love was for the Germans a mirage rather than a solution.

A third attempt to cope with the existing plight manifested itself through a film genre which was exclusively German: the mountain films. Dr. Arnold Fanck, a native of Freiburg i. Br., discovered this genre and all but monopolized it throughout the republican era. He was originally a geologist infatuated with mountain climbing. In his zeal for spreading the gospel of proud peaks and perilous ascents, Fanck relied increasingly on actors and technicians who were, or became, outstanding alpinists and skiers. Among his foremost collaborators were Leni Riefenstahl, Luis Trenker and Sepp Allgeier.

Mountains had already been featured in HOMUNCULUS and CALIGARI. Homunculus is seen standing on a mountain top when lightning strikes him for blasphemy; and when Dr. Caligari makes his first appearance, it is as if he emerged from the conical mountain towering over Holstenwall and the fair. However, these mountains were primarily symbolic, and Fanck was interested in real ones. He began with three films devoted to the joys and beauties of mountain sport: WUNDER DES SCHNEESCHUHS (MARVELS OF SKI, 1920), IM KAMPF MIT DEN BERGEN (STRUGGLE WITH THE MOUNTAINS, 1921) and FUCHSJAGD IM ENGADIN (FOX HUNT IN THE ENGADINE, 1923), a film depicting a paper chase on skis.[10] These films were extraordinary in that they captured the most grandiose aspects of nature at a time when the German screen in general offered nothing but studio-made scenery. In subsequent films, Fanck grew more and more keen on combining precipices and passions, inaccessible steeps and insoluble human conflicts; every year brought a new drama in the mountains. But the fictional ele-

[9] For THE HANGMAN OF ST.-MARIEN, see *Illustrierter Film-Kurier;* for THE COUNT OF CHAROLAIS, program to this film; for THE STONE RIDER, *Decla-Bioscop Verleih-Programme,* 1923, p. 26. See also Kalbus, *Deutsche Filmkunst,* I, 64, 66.

[10] Kalbus, *ibid.,* p. 91. Cf. Fanck, *Kampf mit dem Berge.*

ment, rampant as it was, did not interfere with an abundance of documentary shots of the silent world of high altitudes. As documents these films were incomparable achievements. Whoever saw them will remember the glittering white of glaciers against a sky dark in contrast, the magnificent play of clouds forming mountains above the mountains, the ice stalactites hanging down from roofs and windowsills of some small chalet, and, inside crevasses, weird ice structures awakened to iridescent life by the torchlights of a nocturnal rescue party.

The message of the mountains Fanck endeavored to popularize through such splendid shots was the credo of many Germans with academic titles, and some without, including part of the university youth. Long before the first World War, groups of Munich students left the dull capital every weekend for the nearby Bavarian Alps, and there indulged their passion. Nothing seemed sweeter to them than the bare cold rock in the dim light of dawn. Full of Promethean promptings, they would climb up some dangerous "chimney," then quietly smoke their pipes on the summit, and with infinite pride look down on what they called "valley-pigs"—those plebeian crowds who never made an effort to elevate themselves to lofty heights. Far from being plain sportsmen or impetuous lovers of majestic panoramas, these mountain climbers were devotees performing the rites of a cult[11] [Illus. 17]. Their attitude amounted to a kind of heroic idealism which, through blindness to more substantial ideals, expended itself in tourist exploits.

Fanck's dramas carried this attitude to such an extreme that the uninitiated could not help feeling irritated at the mixture of sparkling ice-axes and inflated sentiments. In BERG DES SCHICKSALS (PEAK OF DESTINY, 1924), a fanatical mountain climber considers it the mission of his life to conquer the impregnable Guglia del Diavolo. He is killed in action. His son promises the mourning mother never to approach that "peak of destiny." Unfortunately, his sweetheart approaches it, and of course goes astray. As her signals of distress are seen in the village, the mother releases the son from his promise with the words: "If you succeed in rescuing this human life, the death of your father had a meaning." The son

[11] This strange cult never fails to puzzle outsiders. In James R. Ullman's pompous mountain novel, *The White Tower* (p. 72), a Swiss guide says to an American pilot: "We Swiss—yes, and the English and French and Americans, too—we climb mountains for sport. But the Germans, no. What it is they climb for I do not know. Only it is not for sport."

succeeds and even heightens the meaning of his father's death by setting his foot on the top of the devilish Guglia amidst a terrific blizzard.[12]

The conduct of another model mountaineer, featured in Der Heilige Berg (The Holy Mountain, 1927), shows that Fanck's fanciful heroes were sometimes able to master their fiery instincts. During a stunt ascent made in the company of his young friend Vigo, this alpinist learns that Vigo is wooing the very girl with whom he himself is in love. In a fit of jealousy, he turns on Vigo, who involuntarily moves backwards and loses his foothold. With his companion hanging in mid-air on the rope that connects them, the alpinist reconsiders and, obedient to the code of mountain climbers, tries to rescue him at the expense of his own life.[13] Although this kind of heroism was too eccentric to serve as a pattern for the people in the valleys, it was rooted in a mentality kindred to Nazi spirit. Immaturity and mountain enthusiasm were one. When, in The Holy Mountain, the girl tells Vigo that she is willing to gratify any wish he might express, Vigo goes down on his knees and puts his head in her lap. It is the gesture of the café-owner in New Year's Eve. In addition, the idolatry of glaciers and rocks was symptomatic of an antirationalism on which the Nazis could capitalize.

Particularly memorable is a fourth attempt at inner adjustment —the only progressive one made during the immediate postwar years. It aimed at endowing rational thinking with executive powers, so that it would be able to dispel the dark inhibitions and unchecked impulses of which the collective soul was possessed. If this attempt to enthrone reason had been successful, reason would have denounced the phantom character of the torturing alternative of tyranny or chaos, and eventually have done away with those traditional authoritarian dispositions that obstructed true emancipation. But interest in mobilizing reason was apparently so limited that it reached the screen only in two isolated instances, one of which was nothing more than an episode of Wegener's second Golem (1920).

Professor Pölzig had devised the settings for this enlarged version of the old prewar film. In it the Hapsburg emperor issues an order that the Jews are to be expelled from their ghetto, a dream-

[12] Program to this film; Kalbus, *Deutsche Filmkunst*, I, 91.
[13] Program to this film.

like maze of crooked streets and stooped houses. To soothe the emperor's mind, Rabbi Loew, by means of magic, conjures up a procession of Biblical figures—among them Ahasuerus, who proceeds to trespass on the domain of reality, starting to destroy the imperial palace. The emperor, panic-stricken, agrees to withdraw his order of expulsion if the rabbi will avert the danger; thereupon the latter directs the Golem, his servant, to prevent walls and ceilings from falling down. The Golem obeys with the automatic promptness of a robot [Illus. 18]. Here reason avails itself of brute force as a tool to liberate the oppressed. But instead of following up this motif, the film concentrates upon the Golem's emancipation from his master, and becomes increasingly entangled in half-truths.[14]

The other instance of concern with reason was SCHATTEN (WARNING SHADOWS, 1922), which in its German version bore the subtitle "A Nocturnal Hallucination" ("*Eine nächtliche Halluzination*"). This film, directed by Arthur Robison, resembled Carl Mayer's screen poems in that it involved nameless characters in an all but titleless narration. Similarities of style originate in a similarity of theme. To a large extent, WARNING SHADOWS is nothing but an instinct film, which accounts for the marked role assigned in it to the display of lights and shadows. Their marvelous fluctuations seem to engender this extraordinary drama.

Fashioned after an idea by Albin Grau, the film opens with a few scenes showing a jealous count exasperated at the favors his wife bestows on her four courtiers. One of them, called "the Lover," is on the point of passing beyond the stage of mere hope. While the count and his wife entertain this amorous quartet, a strolling juggler asks permission to present shadow-plays. The juggler soon senses disaster in the air, and discontinues his performance to forestall a tragedy arising out of the steady growth of conflicting passions. A sagacious wizard, he removes the shadows cast by the party alongside the table, and simultaneously hypnotizes all six persons, so that they follow their shadows into the realm of the subconscious [Illus. 19]. In a state of trance, they anticipate the future by doing exactly what they would do if their passions continued to determine their actions. The drama develops into a "nocturnal hallucination"; it reaches its climax when the count, mad with

[14] "The Golem," *Exceptional Photoplays*, June 1921, pp. 3–4; *Ufa Verleih-Programme*, 1923, p. 14; Vincent, *Histoire de l'Art Cinématographique*, p. 143; Rotha, *Film Till Now*, p. 284; Barry, *Program Notes*, Series III, program 1.

jealousy, compels the courtiers to stab his fettered wife. Here again the immaturity of instinct-possessed beings manifests itself in the customary way: the count rests his head on the Lover's chest and weeps bitterly over what has happened. The hallucination ends with the furious courtiers throwing the count out of the window. Then the scene shifts back to the hypnotized party alongside the table, and the shadows are seen returning to their owners, who slowly awaken from their collective nightmare. They are cured. White magic has enabled them to grasp the hidden springs and terrible issue of their present existence. Owing to this magical therapy—it recalls model cases of psychoanalytical treatment—the count changes from a puerile berserk into a composed adult, his coquettish wife becomes his loving wife, and the Lover takes silent leave. Their metamorphosis at the very end of the film coincides with the beginning of a new day whose sober natural lighting splendidly symbolizes the light of reason.[15]

Even though it belongs among the masterpieces of the German screen, WARNING SHADOWS passed almost unnoticed. Contemporaries may have felt that any acknowledgment of the healthy shock effect of reason was bound to result in an adjustment to the ways of democracy. In a retrospective comment on WARNING SHADOWS, Fritz Arno Wagner, its cameraman, states: "It only found response from the film aesthetes, making no impression on the general public." [16]

[15] Rotha, *Film Till Now*, p. 200; Potamkin, "The Rise and Fall of the German Film," *Cinema*, April 1930, p. 25.

[16] Wagner, "I Believe in the Sound Film," *Film Art*, 1936, no. 8, p. 11.

10. FROM REBELLION TO SUBMISSION

STILL another attempt to overcome the unbearable inner dilemma was made during the postwar years. It advocated the resumption of authoritarian behavior, presupposing a mentality that would prefer even a tyrannical regime to chaos. Typical of the authoritarian tendency were two films springing from almost opposite camps and reflecting very different surroundings. Despite their discrepancies, both promote the same psychological pattern.

One of the two films was FRIDERICUS REX, an opulent, if cinematically trivial, Ufa product, released in 1922. No one could overlook its purpose: it was pure propaganda for a restoration of the monarchy. Directed by Arzèn von Cserèpy, the film depicted the life of Frederick the Great in a succession of loosely connected episodes, with little regard for historic truth. At the beginning, the young crown prince is seen revolting against the rigorous discipline his father enjoins on him; but instead of exhibiting the rebel's unpatriotic passion for French philosophy and literature, Ufa cunningly emphasizes a neutral love affair to demonstrate his sense of independence. Subsequent episodes record his attempt to run away, his arrest and those terrible minutes during which, by order of his father, Frederick witnesses the execution of his friend Katte. Much footage is devoted to displaying the fortunate results of this barbarian punishment: Frederick submits so completely to his father's will that he even marries the unloved princess of Brunswick-Bevern, whereupon the father closes his eyes with the certitude of leaving behind a worthy successor. That certitude is not belied. No sooner does he ascend the throne, than the former rebel continues the work of his father [Illus. 20].

This screen Frederick is given two major virtues. He appears as the father of his people—a patriarchal ruler using his absolute power to mitigate legal hardships, further general welfare and protect the poor from exploitation by the rich. Simultaneously, he appears as the national hero who, through several successful wars, elevates little Prussia to the rank of a great power. The whole construction overtly aims at convincing the audience that another Frederick might not only prove an effective antidote against the virus of socialism, but also realize Germany's national aspirations. To strengthen the emotional ties between the audience and this timely figure, Ufa elaborates upon his inner suffering. The episodes of the Seven Years' War characterize Frederick as a tragic genius involved in a seemingly hopeless fight and abandoned by his most reliable followers. In addition, there is a continuous display of military parades and victorious battles—just the kind of spectacle that would elate patriots in distress over the lost war, the disarmament and that odious confusion called democracy.[1]

FRIDERICUS REX was met by heavy opposition in the press. *Vorwärts* and the communist *Freiheit* invited the masses to boycott the film, while the democratic *Berliner Tageblatt* called for police intervention.[2] It is also hardly believable that South Germany took a liking to this piece of Prussian self-glorification. However, South Germany was not the Reich, and political protests do not prove much about psychological reactions. During the production of the film, two thousand extras were assigned to cheer the newly crowned king in the courtyard of the Berlin Old Palace (*Altes Schloss*). When he stepped out onto the balcony in his regalia, they manifested an enthusiam that could not have been ordered by any director. "Here the people act themselves," an eyewitness stated.[3] Even in workers' quarters, the performances of the film are reported to have drawn full houses.[4] A sure sign of its success was the eagerness with which Ufa as well as other film companies repeated the formula. In the years to come, numerous similar films were launched, the last ones under Hitler. Whether they featured Frederick as the rebellious youth, the charming host of Sans Souci or the "Old Fritz," they all more or less adopted the pattern of the first Fridericus film. And in all but one of them Otto Gebühr portrayed the king. Perhaps it is more correct to say that he resurrected him. Whenever he played the flute, fastened his great sparkling eyes on some ambassador, rode on a white horse at the head of his troops, or, a stooped figure in a

[1] Program to the film's first two parts; *Ufa Verleih-Programme*, 1923, pp. 26–29 (also including synopsis of Parts 3 and 4); Tannenbaum, "Der Grossfilm," *Der Film von Morgen*, p. 67.

[2] Kalbus, *Deutsche Filmkunst*, I, 55; Vincent, *Histoire de l'Art Cinématographique*, p. 142; Bardèche and Brasillach, *History of Motion Pictures*, p. 189.

[3] Birnbaum, "Massenscenen im Film," *Ufa-Blätter*.

[4] Kalbus, *Deutsche Filmkunst*, I, 55.

dirty uniform, moved about with his crutch among his generals, it was as if Frederick himself passed across the screen—at least, it was so until 1930, when the actor's sonorous stage voice began to conflict with his appearance.

Towards the end of the twenties, Werner Hegemann published a book on Frederick the Great violently attacked by all nationalists for debunking the current Frederick legend.[5] But even though many intellectuals on the left took sides with Hegemann, the "true" Frederick he painstakingly excavated never succeeded in upsetting the legendary one. Any legend immune to rational arguments can be supposed to rest upon powerful collective desires. The spurious Frederick obviously conformed to psychological dispositions widespread among the people. This accounts for the symptomatic value of the Fridericus films—to be more precise, of the elaborate pattern of inner existence implied by them.

Throughout the Fridericus series the psychological course leading from the rebellion of the crown prince to his final submission is strongly emphasized. It was a theme, or rather a complex of themes, long familiar to the Germans. Kleist's *Prinz Friedrich von Homburg* had dealt with the conflict between the individual's moral right to unauthorized initiative and his moral duty to submit to the authority of the state. Then, following the example of Wedekind's *Frühlings Erwachen* (*The Awakening of Spring*, 1891), several early expressionist dramas had advocated the rebellion of the son against the father, and at about the same time a whole generation of young Germans had set out to practice this rebellion in the form of the idealistic Youth Movement.[6] In stressing the development from rebellion to submission, the Fridericus films adapted themselves to current circumstances. Owing to the postwar revolutionary situation, the masses were not ready to believe unhesitatingly in the necessity for authoritarian behavior. All Fridericus films therefore resorted to a detour. They began by sanctioning rebellious, if not revolutionary, conduct so as to captivate the minds in turmoil; but they did so only to pass off this conduct as the first stage of an evolution in the course of which it would have to be suppressed. The son's rebellion, which in the expressionist dramas prepared the

[5] Cf. English translation: Hegemann, *Frederick the Great*, London, 1929.

[6] For the father-son conflict in early expressionism, see Hain, *Studien*, pp. 83–86. For the German Youth Movement, see Weniger, "Die Jugendbewegung," *Geist der Gegenwart*, pp. 1–54.—See also Erikson, "Hitler's Imagery . . ," *Psychiatry*, Nov. 1942, p. 478 ff.

ground for the "new man," was here to increase the father's sovereignty. These films presented the rebel as the pupa of the dictator, and approved of anarchy inasmuch as it made authority desirable. They offered a way out of the dilemma between chaos and tyranny by transforming the dilemma itself into an evolutionary process—a process including rebellion as a legitimate phase. This legalization undoubtedly served to repress the old trauma of the unsuccessful bourgeois revolution, which now more than ever before was bound to haunt the collective mind. The reality of a rebellion incorporated into the system of social life could not but overshadow that trauma. What the screen postulated came true in life. In the postwar period, the Youth Movement developed from a spontaneous uprising into an officially confirmed institution, which rapidly disintegrated, parts of it being absorbed by the existent political and religious groups. As if to demonstrate their instinctive desire to do away with the traumatic image of the revolution, many genuine followers of the Movement were to join the marching Nazi columns.

The moral of the Fridericus films was to submit unconditionally to absolute authority. Here a contradiction arises. On the one hand, a majority of Germans—in particular middle-class Germans—tried to fend off socialist notions by insisting upon the idealistic concept of the autonomous individual. On the other hand, the same people were keen on giving up individual autonomy in favor of total dependence upon an autocratic ruler, provided, of course, that he prevent any encroachments on private property. Provoked by interest in safeguarding vital privileges, this paradox seemed unavoidable. There remained only one way to preserve a semblance of self-determination while actually relinquishing it: one could participate in the ruler's glory and thus drown the consciousness of one's submission to him. The halo of glamour surrounding the screen Frederick lured the audience into acts of identification with this supergenius.

Since all those who, consciously or not, adopted the pattern of the Fridericus films did so in a period in which they were offered a unique chance of freedom, their renunciation of individual autonomy was tantamount to a grave retrogression—no doubt the gravest since the unification of Germany. Even though it was by no means a foregone conclusion that the price of a mature acceptance of democracy would be the loss of their social status, they preferred to fall back on a state of immaturity. The Fridericus films not only played up the old king's solitude in a juvenile manner—recalling the mountain films' exaltation of some lonely mountaineer on a lofty peak—but also testified to the inferiority complex bound up with retrogressive behavior. Feelings of inferiority expressed themselves through the aggrandizement of Frederick's power politics as well as through the depreciation of Voltaire's significance. Episodes showing Voltaire in Frederick's company were inserted in FRIDERICUS REX and several other films of the series. Besides distorting the facts, these episodes stressed his depravity rather than his superiority; the Voltaire they set up seemed designed to intimate the decay of French civilization and to justify the resentment of an authoritarian-minded public against enlightening reason.

The other standard film suggesting authoritarian behavior was Ufa's DIE STRASSE (THE STREET, 1923). That it was a nonpolitical *avant-garde* product indicates that the moral implications of FRIDERICUS REX did not appeal merely to those who applauded its political propositions. THE STREET sprang from the same deep psychological layers as the films by Carl Mayer or the genuine expressionist films. Karl Grune, a former Reinhardt disciple, who was its script writer and director in one, has himself told how he happened to discover the cinema. The vicissitudes of the war had forced him to live for long years among foreign soldiers; but, instead of learning their language, he had simply watched their gestures and faces so as to become familiar with their intentions. His experiences aroused his desire to develop on the screen a pictorial language as communicative as the spoken one.[7] This may help explain why THE STREET, made completely without titles, was particularly rich in significant pictures. It ingratiated itself with a rather broad public composed mainly of intellectuals.

Exactly like the first half of FRIDERICUS REX, Grune's simple story illustrates development from rebellion to submission. It starts in a dim plush parlor sheltering a middle-class, middle-aged philistine, who desperately longs for the sensations and splendors of the nocturnal city. His wife enters with the soup tureen, and as if this ritual action has impressed upon him the infinite monotony of his existence, he suddenly runs away. The street engulfs the would-be rebel. A prostitute lures him into a night-club, done in inflation style, and there introduces him to two "friends": her *souteneur* and his chum. While they start gulling him, a provincial bourgeois naïvely

[7] Vincent, *Histoire de l'Art Cinématographique*, p. 150.

exhibiting his wallet swollen with banknotes joins the party. Both he and the rebellious philistine are predestined to be plucked. The subsequent episodes—among them a game of cards with beautifully lit close-ups of the assembled faces—result in a terrible showdown: the two criminals kill the provincial and, using the prostitute as bait, contrive to make the man from the plush parlor appear the murderer. At the police station, the man proves so helpless that he does not even think of asserting his innocence; he simply succumbs to his despair and, left alone in a cell, tries to end his life. Owing to the real murderer's confession, this second attempt to run away is frustrated. Released, the man staggers along the street, which at dawn is a vacuum, except for scraps of waste paper occasionally stirred by the wind. When he reappears in the parlor, his wife silently puts the warmed-up soup on the table. And the man now willingly submits to the domestic regime, including all soups to come. The street calls him no longer. It is as if he considered the ordeal he has undergone a well-deserved punishment for his vain rebellion.[8]

The staging is of interest in that it manifests two different intentions of style.[9] In the conception of the philistine, for instance, expressionist mentality still predominates. Eugen Klöpfer moves about in this part like a somnambulist, and whenever he expresses joy, bewilderment or horror, his gestures seem to be determined by hallucinations rather than by actual experiences. These gestures would undoubtedly appear less exaggerated if, as in the case of CALIGARI, the whole film were nothing but an outward projection of inner events. However, realistic designs interfere with the expressionist ones. Far from being a sheer fantasy or a forthright psychological construction, the plot is an episode of everyday life handled in an almost realistic spirit. This spirit also animates the settings—they awkwardly endeavor to give the impression of normal surroundings—and moreover transforms the characters, except for the philistine, into individuals who, notwithstanding their lack of names, might well exist outside the picture frame. Here a realism breaks through which has nothing in common with the cheap realism of conventional productions; it is a militant realism challenging the penchant for introspection. The rise of this realistic tendency in THE STREET clearly indicates that the general retreat into a shell, symptomatic

[8] Program brochure to the film; "The Street," *National Board of Review Magazine*, June 1927, p. 9.

[9] Kurtz, *Expressionismus*, p. 123; Jahier, "42 Ans de Cinéma," *Le Rôle intellectuel du Cinéma*, pp. 62–63.

of the postwar period, was about to be revoked. It was as if with the acceptance of the formula "From rebellion to submission" that retreat had attained its aim, and as if now that the process of inner adjustment had come to a close the collective soul desired to resume contact with outer reality.

Various pictorial devices help to characterize the street into which the rebellious philistine ventures as a jungle swept by unaccountable instincts. At the beginning, when the man still lingers in his plush parlor, the ceiling becomes luminous with lights reflecting those of the street outside the window; they herald the street, and he nostalgically watches their display above him. In this famous scene light assumes exactly the same function as in Carl Mayer's instinct films: its iridescent fluctuations symbolize the irrational alternations in the sphere of instinctive life. The excited man goes to the window and, looking out, sees—not the street itself, but a hallucinated street. Shots of rushing cars, fireworks and crowds form, along with shots taken from a speeding roller coaster, a confusing whole, made still more confusing by the use of multiple exposures and the insertion of transparent close-ups of a circus clown, a woman and an organ-grinder.[10] Through this ingeniously cut montage sequence the street is defined as a sort of fair, that is, as the region of chaos. The circle usually serving as a symbol of chaos has yielded to the straight line of a city street; since chaos here is not so much an end in itself as a passage ending in the realm of authority, this change of symbols is well-founded.

On the street itself, all kinds of objects take on life, awakened, as in Carl Mayer's films, by the presence of instinct-possessed beings. A wavy line on the pavement—it carries the same meaning as the oscillating light on the ceiling—tempts the man to follow its course, and the two intermittently glowing eyes of an optician's shop almost frighten him into retreat, as if they were the eyes of an invisible bogey [Illus. 21]. For the first time on the German screen window-dressings participate in the action. The man gazes through an art-shop window at nudities that make him dream of ideal beauty, and then, transported by his dreams, sails to faraway countries aboard the ship model in a nearby travel agency.

Instead of acknowledging the values of anarchical life, the film deprecates this life by marking the street as a region where the law of the jungle rules and happiness is sought in gambling and in futile

[10] Cf. Wesse, *Grossmacht Film*, pp. 229–32.

sex affairs. This verdict on anarchy goes hand in hand with the glorification of the police. One scene, destined to reappear in many a film to come, is very significant. While ever-new waves of vehicles hurl onwards, a little child, lost in the crowd, sets out to cross the street. With an imperious gesture a policeman stops the waves and, like Moses leading the Jews across the Red Sea, pilots the child safely through the petrified traffic. Then hell breaks loose anew, submerging the miraculous lane. Again it is the police who reveal the terrified philistine's innocence and send him back home. What a change of concepts since CALIGARI! Whereas CALIGARI scoffs at the police to stigmatize official authority, here just and wise authority realizes itself through police overpowering the sinister forces of anarchy.

In exposing the psychological mechanisms involved in the would-be rebel's submission, THE STREET corroborates the Fridericus films to the full. Particularly conclusive is the final scene showing the man back in his parlor. At this crucial moment, when the slightest reaction is telling, the man anticipates the gesture of the café-owner in NEW YEAR'S EVE: he rests his head upon his wife's shoulder, and she, in turn, caresses his arm as maternally as if he were her child [11] [Illus. 22]. The shot does not conceal that he experiences his frustration with voluptuous masochism and a feeling of inferiority increased by that of guilt. To these rather familiar traits a new one is added: retrogression assumes the character of resignation. When, before re-entering his room, the man hesitatingly walks upstairs, scattered lights from the street play all over him, seem to say farewell. The mood of resignation is so conspicuous that it induced an American reviewer to formulate the film's moral as follows: "Better stay where you are. Life in the haunts you are unused to, is dangerous. Romance may always be around the corner, but the effort to find it is hardly worth the candle you must burn to light the way." [12] This mood is about the opposite of the banal optimism pervading THE OTHER, of 1913. In that old film, the lawyer, Dr. Hallers, returns from his subconscious escapade involving him in criminal actions with the pleasant sensation of regaining his normal middle-class status; ten years later, in THE STREET, the return from a similar escapade amounts to a sad renunciation of life. The contrast between the two kindred films strikingly reveals the rapid decline of

[11] Cf. p. 99.

[12] "The Street," *National Board of Review Magazine*, June 1927, p. 9.

the middle class and its determination to deny this decline at any cost. Under the given circumstances, the philistine cannot help looking out for a shining new Fridericus to chase away the sadness from his plush parlor.

The philistine may easily turn into a sort of split personality. Just before the war, THE STUDENT OF PRAGUE had mirrored the duality of any liberal under the Kaiser; now THE STREET foreshadowed a duality provoked by the retrogressive move from rebellion to submission. Besides resulting in feelings of inferiority and the like, this particular shift of balance upset the whole inner system and, in consequence, favored mental dissociation. The surprising frequency of dual roles in German films—among them Murnau's JANUS-FACED (1920) mentioned above, Lubitsch's KOHLHIESL'S TÖCHTER (KOHLHIESL'S DAUGHTERS, 1920) featuring Henny Porten as both the fine lady and her blunt maid, Grune's DIE BRÜDER SCHELLENBERG (TWO BROTHERS, 1926) and the world-famous DER KONGRESS TANZT (CONGRESS DANCES, 1931)—would suggest that cases of duality occurred then in real life on a rather large scale.[13] And in fact, throughout the whole republican era no unbiased observer was able to overlook a phenomenon bearing out the screen's ample evidence: the widespread discrepancy between theory and practice, thinking and living. Instead of being aware of two Faustian souls in his breast, as in the past, the individual was dragged in contradictory directions and did not know it. This dissociation seemed to him only a new facet of the old inner abundance. It is probable—a hint of that kind has already been made—that the middle-class German's reluctance to emancipate himself originated in the fear of losing not only his social privileges, but also those multifaceted potentialities he thought he had discovered within himself.[14]

Derivative of the street theme are a number of aesthetically valuable films which, notwithstanding substantial differences, have one motif in common: in all of them the leading character breaks away from the social conventions to grasp life, but the conventions prove stronger than the rebel and force him into either submission or suicide. However inconspicuous a role this motif may play in the films under consideration, its frequency corroborates what can be

[13] For JANUS-FACED, see p. 78; for CONGRESS DANCES, p. 208. Cf. Kalbus, *Deutsche Filmkunst,* I, 115.

[14] Cf. p. 60.

inferred from the figures of Frederick and the philistine: that powerful collective dispositions urged the resumption of authoritarian behavior.[15]

As early as 1920, the motif began its screen career in VON MORGENS BIS MITTERNACHT (FROM MORN TO MIDNIGHT), an expressionist experiment fashioned after Georg Kaiser's play of that title and reportedly shown in no country other than Japan. In it, the philistine of THE STREET is anticipated in the character of a teller, who in his desire to exchange everyday life for something great and beautiful wastes the money of his bank on prostitutes and in night-clubs, and at the end, disappointed, kills himself to escape the police.[16] Murnau, too, was infatuated with the motif. In his PHANTOM (1922)—a screen version of a novel by Gerhart Hauptmann—a humble town clerk longs to become a famous poet and marry a charming girl he has seen driving past him in a pony-drawn phaeton. Possessed by his longing, he sleeps with a prostitute resembling the unattainable girl and sinks ever deeper, until in the solitude of his prison cell he learns to renounce all phantoms. Murnau's film reached its pictorial climax with a montage sequence that fused street impressions into a vision of chaos.[17]

[15] These dispositions asserted themselves in places and on occasions where no one would have suspected them. In 1919, Max Weber, who after the armistice had joined the staff of *Frankfurter Zeitung* to help prepare a German democracy, went to Versailles and then paid a visit to General Ludendorff, trying to persuade him that he must deliver himself up to the Allies. Ludendorff refused. Their subsequent dialogue, quoted from Meyer Schapiro's article "A Note on Max Weber's Politics" (*Politics*, Feb. 1945, p. 44), confirms the testimony of all these authoritarian-minded films.

Ludendorff: "There's your fine democracy! You and the *Frankfurter Zeitung* are responsible for it! What good has come of it?"

Weber: "Do you believe then that I consider the mess we are in now democracy?"

L.: "If that's how you talk, perhaps we can come to an understanding."

W.: "But the mess before was also no monarchy."

L.: "What do you understand then by democracy?"

W.: "In a democracy the people elects the leader (*Führer*) whom it trusts. Then the elected one says: 'Now shut up and obey. People and parties must no longer butt in.' "

L.: "Such 'democracy' is all right with me."

W.: "Afterwards the people can judge—if the leader has made mistakes, to the gallows with him!"

Max Weber was quite able to foresee that first the people would be sent to the gallows by their leader. But his intrinsic urges apparently interfered with his sociological judgment.—See also Kurtz, *Expressionismus*, p. 12.

[16] Kurtz, *ibid.*, pp. 15–17, 69–70; Zaddach, *Der literarische Film*, p. 39; Berstl, ed., *25 Jahre Berliner Theater*, p. 94.—The motif under consideration also asserted itself in Berthold Viertel's fantastic film DIE PERRÜCKE (THE WIG, 1923?).

[17] Program brochure to the film; *Jahrbuch der Filmindustrie*, 1922/3, p. 41; *Decla-Bioscop Verleih-Programme*, p. 18; Wesse, *Grossmacht Film*, pp. 132–35; Balázs, *Der sichtbare Mensch*, p. 85.

In 1923, Lubitsch took over. He promoted the motif in DIE FLAMME (MONTMARTRE), which, laid in last-century Paris, narrated the love affair between a naïve young composer and a cocotte with a pure soul. The composer leaves his austere mother for the cocotte, but since he fails to leave his bourgeois inhibitions behind, his new life turns into a troublesome adventure from which he penitently flees back to his loving mother. The original version ends with the cocotte throwing herself out of the window with the words: "The street calls me." One genuine "Lubitsch touch" was the scene in which the cocotte prepared her brothel room for the composer's first visit by shifting the furniture so that the room suddenly looked as respectable as he then believed her to be.[18]

The motif reappeared in NJU (HUSBANDS OR LOVERS? 1924), a psychological study based upon a play by Ossip Dimov. It was Paul Czinner's first film with Elisabeth Bergner, who played in it a married woman hungry for love. The action begins with a stranger (Conrad Veidt) gazing up from the street to her window. Enticed by him, she parts with husband and child, and moves into a furnished room, which seems to her a paradise compared to her home; but after a while the stranger tires of the paradise and his mistress, and bluntly advises her to return to her husband. In her desolation, she prefers to drown herself. Finally, the stranger is seen standing in her furnished room, while an old charwoman cleans it for the subsequent lodger. The whole film breathed a sadness surpassing that of THE STREET. It was as if hope had deserted the world of the middle-class home as well as the middle-class rebel's enchanted street world: at home, Emil Jannings as the vulgar husband walked about with his suspenders hanging down, and the street merely led from a furnished room to the river.[19]

The motif materialized yet again in VARIÉTÉ (VARIETY), released toward the end of 1925—that year which marked the rise of a realistic-minded era. Even though this world-renowned music-hall film indulged in the new realism, it still radiated the spirit of bygone days. VARIETY was a belated product of the postwar period, an end rather than a beginning.

The film, made after a popular prewar novel by Felix Holländer,

[18] *Ufa Verleih-Programme*, 1923/4, pp. 48–51; Kalbus, *Deutsche Filmkunst*, I, 60; Balázs, *Der sichtbare Mensch*, p. 104; "Montmartre," *Exceptional Photoplays*, Feb.–March 1924, p. 5; Berstl, ed., *25 Jahre Berliner Theater*, p. 93.

[19] Publicity sheet to the film; *Film Society Programme*, Feb. 14, 1926; Weinberg, *Scrapbooks*, 1927; Rotha, *Film Till Now*, p. 195; Leprohon, "Le Cinéma Allemand," *Le Rouge et le Noir*, July 1928, p. 142.

opens with a sequence inside a penitentiary. Emil Jannings as "Boss" Huller has been pardoned before the end of his prison term, and now agrees to tell the prison director the story of his crime. This prefacing sequence is significant in that it emphasizes Huller's ultimate submission. At the outset of the story proper, Huller is running a shabby show in an amusement park, but neither that nor his faded wife can compensate for the sensations he had once experienced as a trapeze artist. One day, a sailor brings Huller a girl from a remote southern country. Huller hires her, and soon her sensuous beauty stirs him to rebel against his humdrum existence. He runs away with her. While they are working on the trapeze in a Berlin fair, Artinelli, a music-hall artist of international reputation, approaches the couple to engage them for the Berlin Wintergarten. They act as his partners when he performs a triple somersault blindfolded. Fatally, Artinelli and the girl extend their partnership into leisure time between the performances. No sooner does Huller learn of the girl's betrayal, than he turns into one of those instinct-possessed characters who destroy each other so eagerly in the films of Carl Mayer. A reincarnation of the trackwalker in SHATTERED,[20] he kills Artinelli and surrenders to the police. Here the flashback ends. In the final scene, the prison gates open symbolically before Huller; but nothing indicates that, in stepping out of them, he will be freed from the prison of his self.[21] The plot confines itself to interweaving the motif of rebellion and submission with the familiar theme of the instinct dramas in a rather banal manner.

Nevertheless, VARIETY aroused a "white heat of enthusiasm" among American moviegoers.[22] The film, as Harry Alan Potamkin puts it, "burnt its way through these United States and came near demoralizing the matter-of-fact technique of Hollywood."[23] Accustomed to that matter-of-fact technique, the American public may have been struck by the intensity everyday life assumed in VARIETY. Such accustomed settings as a music hall, a café and a stuffy hotel corridor seemed to glow from within. It was as if one had never before seen these commonplace surroundings.

E. A. Dupont had staged VARIETY under Erich Pommer's in-

[20] Cf. p. 98.

[21] Weinberg, *Scrapbooks*, 1925–27; Moussinac, *Panoramique du Cinéma*, pp. 49–50.

[22] Quoted from Jacobs, *American Film*, p. 307.

[23] Potamkin, "The Rise and Fall of the German Film," *Cinema*, April 1930, p. 24. For the influence of the German school in this country, see Jacobs, *American Film*, pp. 331–32, and "Die entfesselte Kamera," *Ufa-Magazin*, March 25–31, 1927.

spiring supervision.[24] Dupont was not an innovator, but he was a brilliant adaptor. Assisted by Karl Freund, the cameraman of THE LAST LAUGH, he adapted the methods of the expressionist postwar period to the exigencies of the realistic Dawes Plan period. (Traces of expressionism can still be found in the framing prison scenes of VARIETY.) Dupont's achievement lay in that, in shaping his music-hall film, he penetrated outer reality by means of devices used originally in the outward projection of inner reality. This transplanting of techniques had, of course, amazing results. It has been rightly observed that in VARIETY the actors seem to be unaware of the presence of the camera; Jannings' bulky back, for instance, plays as conspicuous a part as any close-up of his face[25] [Illus. 23]. Such truth to reality could hardly be achieved without the incessant camera movements typical of this film; for they alone enable the spectator to break into the magic circle of the action. Led by the inquisitive camera, he rushes through space as if he were one of the trapeze artists, sneaks about rooms full of tension, identifies himself with Artinelli when he lies in wait for the girl, and spies on her hasty endeavor to renew her make-up before rejoining Jannings [Illus. 24]. Unusual camera angles, multiple exposures and sagacious transitions help transport the spectator to the heart of the events.[26] Thus Dupont superseded the conventional realism of the past by a realism that captured along with visible phenomena the psychological processes below their surface. However, nothing he offered was essentially new. Psychological ubiquity as well as fluidity of pictorial narration: all sprang from THE LAST LAUGH.[27] VARIETY was a derivative of this fundamental film; it resumed in the realistic sphere what THE LAST LAUGH had accomplished in the sphere of introspection.

Numerous less important films of the postwar period have al-

[24] For Dupont and his first film, DAS ALTE GESETZ (THE ANCIENT LAW, 1923), see Vincent, *Histoire de l'Art Cinématographique*, p. 157; Museum of Modern Art Library, clipping files.

[25] Moussinac, *Panoramique du Cinéma*, pp. 51–52; Arnheim, *Film als Kunst*, pp. 58–59; Vincent, *Histoire de l'Art Cinématographique*, pp. 157–58; Leprohon, "Le Cinéma Allemand," *Le Rouge et le Noir*, July 1928, pp. 138, 141.

[26] Karl Freund himself comments on the camera angles: "In *Variety*, the unaccustomed angle was stressed by necessity, owing to cramped quarters in the Berlin Winter Palace, where the picture was made, and this film, curiously enough, was an original source-book of the lying-on-the-stomach school of photography, which has today reached the proportions of a national craze." Quoted from B. C. Crisler, "The Friendly Mr. Freund," *New York Times*, Nov. 21, 1937.

[27] Cf. p. 105 f.

ready been mentioned. It remains to complete their survey. The need for adaptations was so urgent that even Hermann Bang's esoteric novel *Michael* was made into a film—perhaps because of its tinge of homosexuality (MICHAEL, 1924).[28] Rather frequent were such films as DIE LIEBESBRIEFE DER BARONIN S. (THE LOVE LETTERS OF BARONESS S., 1924) and KOMÖDIE DES HERZENS (COMEDY OF THE HEART, 1924), which offered a convenient mixture of love life and society life. Harry Piel thrillers, detective films with Ernst Reicher as Stuart Webbs, Ossi Oswalda comedies and Henny Porten dramas were institutions.[29] Outshining all these stars, Asta Nielsen played characters ennobled by love, with an intensity that made one ignore the affinity of her films with bad magazine stories. In the concluding scenes of ABSTURZ (DOWNFALL, 1923), she was a worn-out old woman trying desperately to look young again for her lover who was returning from a ten-year prison term; no one who watched her vain attempt will ever forget her acting.[30] At the end of the inflation period, there was a new vogue of historical pageants and a sudden mania for films centering round folk-songs—just the right thing for small-town people and salesgirls with warm hearts and nothing else.[31] In a tiny realm of her own, Lotte Reiniger swung her scissors diligently, preparing one sweet silhouette film after another.[32]

[28] Willy Haas, *Skizzen zu Michael's Welt*, a publicity booklet for the film.—In this context, Berthold Viertel's film, NORA (Winter, 1923/4), with Olga Tschechowa in her first film role, may be mentioned. Cf. Kalbus, *Deutsche Filmkunst*, I, 72; Arnheim, *Film als Kunst*, p. 109; Zaddach, *Der literarische Film*, p. 50.

[29] For Harry Piel and Ernst Reicher films, see "Die Produktion des Jahres," *Das grosse Bilderbuch des Films*, 1925, pp. 168–70. For Henny Porten films of the time, see Porten, "Mein Leben," *Ufa-Magazin*, April 22–28, 1927.—Jannings was featured in ALLES FÜR GELD (ALL FOR MONEY, 1923); cf. *Ufa Verleih-Programme*, 1923/4, pp. 52–55.

[30] Cf. Balázs, *Der sichtbare Mensch*, pp. 163, 165–67. For the Nielsen film DAS FEUER (THE FIRE, 1924), see Moreck, *Sittengeschichte*, pp. 165–68.

[31] Among the historical pageants of the time were HELENA (1924), CARLOS UND ELISABETH (CARLOS AND ELISABETH, 1924), and DIE SKLAVENKÖNIGIN (MOON OF ISRAEL, 1924). Synopsis of the latter film in *Illustrierter Film-Kurier*. For the foregoing films, cf. Zaddach, *Der literarische Film*, pp. 55–56, and Kalbus, *Deutsche Filmkunst*, I, 67. —Kalbus, *ibid.*, p. 59, lists a number of films featuring folk-song themes as a peculiarity of the year 1924.

[32] Reiniger, "Lebende Schatten," *Film-Photos*, pp. 45–46; *Film Society Programme*, Dec. 11, 1927; etc.

THE STABILIZED PERIOD

(1924–1929)

11. DECLINE

In 1924, after the mark had been stabilized, Germany accepted the Dawes Plan, which arranged for the payment of reparations and effected Germany's incorporation into the financial system of the Allies. Normal life began to reassert itself, and soon the inflation seemed a remote nightmare. This stabilized or Dawes Plan period lasted until 1929, when the crash put an end to false prosperity. While it lasted, Stresemann embarked upon a clever policy of rehabilitation, marked by such successes as the Treaty of Locarno and Germany's entrance into the League of Nations. At home, things did not look too bad either. Even though the Hitlerites and their like tried hard to undermine the "system," as they called the Weimar regime, no one would listen to them. The oblivion into which they sank resulted not so much from any inner strength of the Republic as from an abundance of foreign loans that helped reduce unemployment by engendering feverish activity.

With the aid of these loans, which were granted to public corporations, communities and businessmen alike, the German industrialists modernized and expanded their plants systematically. Towards the end of the stabilized period, Germany commanded an industrial apparatus with a capacity far beyond her immediate needs. Its creation was bound up with an enormous increase of administrative functions. From 1924 to 1928, the number of the employees was augmented fivefold, while that of the workers was scarcely doubled. The white-collar class developed into an important social stratum. Simultaneously, another change took place which contemporaries spoke of as the streamlining of big business (*Rationalisierung der Wirtschaft*): the methods of the assembly line were transferred to the workrooms of the administration buildings. This meant that with regard to their occupational and economic plight innumerable employees were no better off than the workers. Yet instead of acknowledging their proletarian existence, they endeavored to maintain their old middle-class status. Compared to the workers with their firm beliefs and hopes, these three and a half million employees were mentally shelterless; all the more so as the middle class itself had begun to falter. They filled the cities and belonged nowhere.[1] Considering their crucial position within the social structure, much depended upon their reactions. The films would have to take notice of them.

From 1924 on, economic exigencies influenced the development of the German film more directly than in the previous years. To understand this a few retrospective remarks are indispensable. During the inflation, the film industry managed to get along without serious disturbances. It is true that the domestic market yielded only 10 per cent of the production costs. However, two circumstances compensated for this ruinous situation. First, people eagerly spent their money, which was lost anyway, on every pleasure available; in consequence, movie theaters were crowded and even increased in number. Secondly, the export of films, much furthered by "dumping," proved exceedingly lucrative. A Swiss license, which in normal times would have amounted to nothing, represented a value almost equivalent to the cost of an average film. Tempted by such opportunities, numerous unpleasant profiteers squeezed into the film business, and minor banks readily supported brand-new joint-stock companies, whose supervisory boards usually included some Excellency highly paid for the attractiveness of his title. Fritz Olimsky states in his thesis on German film economics that at that time the cultural standards in the film industry were lower than in all other industries of similar size.[2] This testifies to the relative independence of art from its environment; for amidst the weeds there blossomed such films as THE STREET and NEW YEAR'S EVE.

No sooner was the mark stabilized than the film industry suffered a severe setback, caused by the sudden discontinuance of all exports. It was the so-called stabilization crisis. In 1924 and 1925, many new joint-stock companies went bankrupt, and the Excellencies retired, leaving behind ruined stockholders. The distributors felt the blow more than anyone. With box-office receipts dwindling

[1] Cf. Rosenberg, *Geschichte der Deutschen Republik*, p. 181 ff.; Schwarzschild, *World in Trance*, pp. 227, 243, 247, 261–62; Samuel and Thomas, *Expressionism in German Life*, p. 171; Kracauer, *Die Angestellten.*

[2] Olimsky, *Filmwirtschaft*, p. 28; see also pp. 26–27, 29. Jason, "Zahlen sehen uns an . . ," *25 Jahre Kinematograph*, p. 68.

and the banks demanding exorbitant rates of interest, the surviving film companies hardly knew where to turn.[3] But man's extremity is God's opportunity. God in this case was Hollywood.

The big Hollywood industrialists recognized that after the re-establishment of the gold standard in Germany the German market would offer them pleasant possibilities. They were determined to step in, and began flooding Germany with American pictures. In the course of this large-scale invasion, they not only founded their own distributing agencies there, but also purchased big German movie theaters and even built several new ones. To stem the flood, the German government decreed that for every foreign film released a German film should be produced. But this decree had quite an unexpected effect: it gave rise to the widespread species of "quota films" (*Kontingentfilme*). Many a quota film was never released, its sole reason for existence being the acquisition of a "quota certificate" (*Kontingentschein*) that would authorize its holder to import a foreign picture. In the cafés where the film agents met, these certificates were traded like stocks. Of course, the Americans had a vital interest in getting as many certificates as possible; they therefore produced their own quota films in Germany, and in addition financed or bought up a number of German film companies. No doubt, these methods of infiltration were unscrupulous, but they did enable the native film industry to surmount a perilous crisis.[4]

The case of Ufa illustrates the whole situation. In 1925, Ufa was in such a lamentable predicament that it would have failed without the intervention of Paramount and Loew's Inc. (Metro-Goldwyn). The two Hollywood companies urged Ufa to sign the so-called "Parufamet agreement," which provided that in return for a considerable loan Ufa should put its quota certificates as well as its numerous movie theaters at the disposal of the American creditors. These terms proved the more disastrous as, with the millions it acquired, Ufa had not only to fulfill its new obligations but also to liquidate its old debt to the Deutsche Bank. In 1927, as a result of both external pressure and internal mismanagement, Ufa was again on the verge of ruin. Then Hugenberg came to its rescue—Hugenberg, the Prussian conservative and reactionary, who through

[3] Olimsky, *Filmwirtschaft*, p. 30.

[4] Olimsky, *ibid.*, pp. 43–45, 54–55; Jason, "Zahlen sehen uns an . . ," *25 Jahre Kinematograph*, pp. 68–69; Neumann, *Film-'Kunst,'* p. 60; Fawcett, *Die Welt des Films*, p. 121; Berr, "Etat du Cinéma 1931: Etats-Unis et Allemagne," *Revue du Cinéma*, July 1931, p. 50.

the newspapers in his possession controlled a vast domain of public opinion. He wanted to extend his influence by swallowing the leading German film company. After the ensuing revision of the Parufamet agreement, Ufa was free to become a propaganda instrument in Hugenberg's hands. Yet as long as the Republic seemed firmly established, Hugenberg neither utilized this instrument to the full nor even expected all Ufa executives to share his views.[5] He was also a businessman, after all. This does not mean that the Hugenberg Ufa took a liking to the democratic ways of life. It merely chose to obstruct them under the mask of neutrality.

Occasionally, the mask covering reactionary behind-the-scenes activities was lifted. In 1927, when Phoebus went bankrupt, the public learned that this important film company had been financed, and ruled, by a certain Captain Lohmann. And the republican and leftist press revealed that his money had come from—the secret funds of the Reichswehr. The Phoebus affair turned into a Reichswehr scandal, and for a moment the smoldering conspiracy of the militarists seemed seriously compromised. It was not, of course. Hindenburg fired the democrat Gessler, until then in charge of the Reichswehr ministry, and appointed General Groener in his place. And there the matter ended.[6]

With the commencement of the Dawes Plan period the character of the German film changed markedly. Now that life had resumed normal aspects and social revolution was no longer impending, the fantastic figures and unreal settings of the postwar screen dissolved into thin air like the vampire in NOSFERATU. To be sure, studio-minded products persisted long after 1924.[7] But on the whole the films of the stabilized period turned towards the outer world, shifting the emphasis from apparitions to actual appearances, from imaginary landscapes to natural surroundings. They were essentially realistic.

A change in aesthetic standards took place also. Compared to the postwar films those of the stabilized period were aesthetically dubious. "The true German film died quietly," Paul Rotha comments on

[5] Olimsky, *Filmwirtschaft*, pp. 29–30; Fawcett, *Die Welt des Films*, pp. 122–26; Schwarzschild, *World in Trance*, p. 283; Schlesinger, "Das moderne deutsche Lichtspiel-theater," *Das grosse Bilderbuch*, 1925, p. 28.

[6] Rosenberg, *Geschichte der Deutschen Republik*, p. 212; see also *New York Times*, from Berlin, Aug. 9, 1927 (clipping in Weinberg, *Scrapbooks*, 1927).

[7] Cf. Potamkin, "The Rise and Fall of the German Film," *Cinema*, April 1930, p. 25.

the output after VARIETY.[8] Observers were unanimous in remarking this decline. The problem is how to explain it.

One explanation offered is the exodus of many prominent German film artists and technicians about the middle of the twenties. Hollywood bought them up, as it did other foreign talents. Among the first to answer the call were Lubitsch, Pola Negri, Hans Kräly and Buchowetski. In 1925 and 1926 they were joined by a whole crowd, including the star directors E. A. Dupont, Ludwig Berger, Lupu Pick, Paul Leni and Murnau, and such actors as Veidt and Jannings. Erich Pommer, too, could not resist the temptation. There is no doubt that Hollywood effected this wholesale importation not solely to heighten its own standards; the main idea was to eliminate a competitor extremely dangerous at the time.[9] But much as the mass desertions added to the difficulties of the German screen, they did not cause its decline. This can be evidenced by the fact that, after the mark was stabilized, several brilliant directors of the postwar period—among them Murnau and Lang—wasted their craftsmanship on insignificant products. Murnau then left Germany, but Lang stayed at home, and new talents also began to emerge. The decline was not due to the lack of talent; rather, many a talent declined for reasons still to be explored.

Another explanation has been found in the tendency, then widespread, to "Americanize" the German film. This tendency flowed from the need to export. Since Hollywood seemed to have discovered the secret of pleasing all the world, the German producers dreamed of imitating what they believed to be the genuine Hollywood manner. The result was pitiful. And yet when G. W. Pabst, outstanding figure among the film directors of the stabilized period, was obliged to film his DIE LIEBE DER JEANNE NEY (THE LOVE OF JEANNE NEY) in the American style, he succeeded in making it a fascinating picture.[10] The decline cannot be attributed to the penchant for films after the current Hollywood manner. Even though this penchant may well have accelerated the decline, it was nothing more than one of its symptoms.

The attempt at Americanization went hand in hand with an effort

[8] Rotha, *Film Till Now*, pp. 176, 181.

[9] Rotha, *ibid.*, pp. 30, 204; Jacobs, *American Film*, pp. 306–8; Vincent, *Histoire de l'Art Cinématographique*, p. 161; Olimsky, *Filmwirtschaft*, p. 43; Barry, *Program Notes*, Series III, program 2; Kalbus, *Deutsche Filmkunst*, II, 98.

[10] MacPherson, "Die Liebe der Jeanne Ney," *Close Up*, Dec. 1927, p. 18. See also Rotha, *Film Till Now*, p. 208.

to internationalize the German film business. Franco-German and Anglo-German alliances prospered during that period. They devoted themselves to joint productions, which as a rule indulged in a shallow cosmopolitanism. Most of them—including such exceptions as Renoir's NANA and Feyder's THÉRÈSE RAQUIN—were shot in the German studios because of the superior technical resources there. Neubabelsberg, Staaken and Geiselgasteig became the favorite meeting-places of international teams.[11] Since the German film industry also admitted numerous foreigners among its personnel, several observers have come to believe that the decline of the German screen was caused by a process of "denationalization." In his *Histoire du Cinéma,* Robert Brasillach—the French collaborationist executed in February 1945—denounces a "host of rascals of dubious nationality" as the ultimate source of all evils. A certain René Jeanne is even more precise; he blames "the Jews and the aliens" for the preponderance of German films that lost all "German character." [12] The "German character" must have been exhausted, then, if it would simply yield to a handful of parasites. But the whole argument is unfounded, for in their concern with racial discrimination Brasillach and his like have overlooked a few weighty facts. Without the Austrian Jew Carl Mayer the German film would never have come into its own. The Viennese Fritz Lang, no pure Aryan either, made films so truly German that even Hitler admired them, and he was a connoisseur. It has also been seen that during the inflation, when a "host of rascals" meddled in all film matters, the German screen was far from declining artistically.

Nor can the decline after 1924 be traced to those legal provisions which called forth the multitude of cheap "quota films." These films had characteristics in common with many an expensive superproduction. And on the other hand, Ruttmann's BERLIN, one of the most remarkable achievements of the period, was made as a quota film for Fox Europe.

As Harry A. Potamkin puts it, "the real cause of the decline is an interior one." [13] Modes of inner existence brought about the grandeur of the German screen throughout the postwar era; they also were responsible for its misery in subsequent years. As impor-

[11] Rotha, *ibid.,* p. 182; Fawcett, *Die Welt des Films,* pp. 128–29; Vincent, *Histoire de l'Art Cinématographique,* p. 162.

[12] Bardèche and Brasillach, *History of Motion Pictures,* pp. 258–59; Jeanne, "Le Cinéma Allemand," *L'Art Cinématographique,* VIII, 45.

[13] Potamkin, "The Rise and Fall of the German Film," *Cinema,* April 1930, p. 25.

tant postwar films testify, the outcome of the desperate struggle for psychological adjustment was a general strengthening of the old authoritarian tendencies. The masses, that is, were basically authoritarian-minded when they entered the stabilized period. But the republican regime of the period rested upon democratic principles that repudiated those mass tendencies. Prevented from finding an outlet and yet too persistent to yield, authoritarian dispositions fell into a state of paralysis. This naturally affected the whole of the collective mind. Instead of breathing life into the republican institutions, the masses drained themselves of life. They preferred the neutralization of their primary impulses to the transformation of these impulses. The decline of the German screen is nothing but the reflection of a widespread inner paralysis.

12. FROZEN GROUND

The films of the stabilized period can be divided into three groups. The first simply testifies to the existence of a state of paralysis. The second group sheds light on the tendencies and notions that are paralyzed. The third reveals the inner workings of the paralyzed collective soul.

The innumerable films of the first group form the main bulk of the whole output. Whether quota films or not, they never advanced anything that could disturb the fragile peace of the republican regime. Nor did they take sides with the regime emphatically. To them the "system" was a matter of indifference, and even if they went so far as to justify its capitalistic structure and the ways of the rich, they did so in a superficial, lukewarm manner. This kind of indifference is their chief characteristic. They avoid touching upon any essentials, except in a few instances where they infallibly blur the issues. Apart from such stray attempts at profundity, these films appear to be concerned merely with doling out entertainment in an atmosphere of neutrality. They seem cut off from all inner roots. The emotional grounds are frozen.

Undeniably, most American and French films of the time were in a similar vein. But in the wake of Locarno it was natural for conditions in all countries involved to approximate each other. And since the strange character of the German postwar screen and the suddenness of its decline are symptoms of a unique development, resemblances between German and foreign films should not be overrated. They were surface resemblances, produced in the case of Germany by the paralysis of primary impulses. Below the surface, these impulses persisted. Under such peculiar circumstances many German films preserved a character of their own even during these years of international complacency.

Before discussing the films of the first group, several series of little interest in this context but still part of the record may at least be mentioned. The resumption, about 1924, of the immediate postwar vogue of sex films and adventurous travel films indicates that after the stabilization of the mark most people experienced the same appetites as after the end of the war.[1] Simultaneously, a host of military films, rich in barracks humor, dull-witted privates and dashing lieutenants, swept across the screen. Drawn from outdated prewar novels and plays, they mirrored the average German's confidence in the return of the normal, which to him was unimaginable without a regular army and the sight of uniforms blossoming everywhere.[2] While these film types as mere fashions were too short-lived to characterize the period, others failed in the same respect because of their perennial nature. The species of mystery films proved indestructible, and now that times had changed attracted even a director like Lupu Pick, who once had known how to arouse less ephemeral shudders.[3] Berlin local comedies featuring the good heart and bright wit of the native population also flourished throughout the stabilized period and longer; a fixed folk genre, they evolved untouched by the course of events.[4]

Many films of the group which evidenced society's state of paralysis simply ignored social reality. The comedies among them pretended to be comedies because they consisted of ingredients usually found in comedies. Fred loves Lissy, but does not want to marry her. To stir his jealousy, Lissy engages the gigolo Charley to court her ostentatiously. Charley on his part hankers after the dancer Kitty, and Kitty herself is coveted by the fickle Fred. A double wedding uniting the right couples straightens out matters at the very last moment. This intrigue, which ran under the title BLITZZUG DER LIEBE (EXPRESS TRAIN OF LOVE, 1925), roughly illustrates what the comedies were like.[5] They were located nowhere and void of genuine life. When they reproduced a French boulevard comedy, the framework remained and the spirit evaporated.

A change of ingredients, and the outcome was dramas as stillborn as the comedies. To simulate liveliness, they often resorted to brisk

[1] Cf. "Ufa," *Das grosse Bilderbuch*, 1926, p. 186; Kalbus, *Deutsche Filmkunst*, I, 49; *Ufa Verleih-Programme*, 1923/4, pp. 56–59.

[2] For the vogue of military films, see Kalbus, *Deutsche Filmkunst*, I, 77–78.

[3] Besides Pick's DAS PANZERGEWOELBE (THE ARMORED VAULT, 1926), Kalbus, *ibid.*, pp. 87–88, lists a series of mystery films.

[4] Cf. Potamkin, "Kino and Lichtspiel," *Close Up*, Nov. 1929, p. 395.

[5] Synopsis of EXPRESS TRAIN OF LOVE in *Illustrierter Film-Kurier*. For other comedies of the time, see, for instance, "Les Présentations de l'Alliance Cinématographique Européenne," *Cinéa-Ciné*, April 1927, p. 14 ff.; Buchner, *Im Banne des Films*, p. 140; "Saucy Suzanne," *Close Up*, Nov. 1927, pp. 65–66.

and picturesque surroundings. A circus, for instance, offered *divertissement*. But no feat of horsemanship sufficed to make the circus films breathe. Except, perhaps, for Max Reichmann's MANEGE (1927) with its valid emotional content, they invariably handled the stereotyped figures of the clown, the girl and the lover in pure clichés.[6] The same clichés unfolded within music-hall settings, made popular by Dupont's VARIETY. Dupont himself exploited his success in MOULIN ROUGE (1928), which he tried to enliven by means of daredevil driving in a racing car and documentary shots of Paris. Russian milieus, too, were in vogue. In HEIMWEH (HOMESICKNESS, 1927), one saw Russian exiles gather in a Paris boardinghouse and listen nostalgically to national folk-songs played on the piano. It was an exhibition of sentiment fashioned after a commonplace recipe.[7] All these dramas and comedies were manufactured mechanically.

The escapist tendency to which they testified seems to have been very strong during those years. A multitude of films owed their very existence to outright escapism. The favorite method was to metamorphose certain real towns or landscapes into imaginary locales where all one's yearnings would be fulfilled. German popular songs praised Heidelberg and the Rhine as the eternal playgrounds of a youth immersed in love and the joys of life. These songs were made into films which differed only with regard to the beverages raising the spirits. DER FRÖHLICHE WEINBERG (THE GAY VINEYARD, 1927), based upon Zuckmayer's play of the same title, was a record accumulation of moistened throats and amorous hearts.[8] Paris, the city of light, appeared on the screen as a city of neon lights and frivolous adventures. When in the Paris films a woman feared to lose her inconstant husband, she just disguised herself, went to the Moulin Rouge and there captivated the fugitive anew.

[6] For MANEGE, see Kracauer, "Der heutige Film und sein Publikum," *Frankfurter Zeitung*, Nov. 30, 1928. Other circus films were LOOPING THE LOOP, 1928 (cf. program to the film, and Rotha, *Film Till Now*, p. 201); DIE DREI CODONAS (cf. synopsis in *Illustrierter Film-Kurier*); DIE ZIRKUSPRINZESSIN (mentioned in *Jahrbuch der Filmindustrie*, 1923/25, p. 37); etc.

[7] For MOULIN ROUGE, see Moussinac, *Panoramique du Cinéma*, pp. 75–76; for HOMESICKNESS, "Heimweh," *Close Up*, Dec. 1927, pp. 74–76. Other films featuring Russian motifs: WOLGA-WOLGA (1928), cf. program to the film; DER KURIER DES ZAREN (THE TSAR'S COURIER, 1926), cf. "'Mütterchen' Russland," *Ufa-Magazin*, Aug. 27–Sept. 2, 1926; HOCHVERRAT (HIGH TREASON, 1929), cf. "Hochverrat," *Film-Magazin*, Sept. 29 and Nov. 17, 1929.

[8] Program to THE GAY VINEYARD. Kalbus, *Deutsche Filmkunst*, *I*, 78–79, lists numerous films based upon popular songs.

These films had nothing in common with René Clair's graceful screen poems; rather, they resembled those de luxe "Paris-at-night" buses which in prewar times transported packets of sightseers from one pleasure spot to another.[9]

The paradise of paradises was Vienna. Any obsolete Viennese operetta was dragged to the screen as long as it offered the public an opportunity of escaping from the prosaic republican world to the days of the late Hapsburg monarchy. Trained in romanticizing the past, Ludwig Berger staged EIN WALZERTRAUM (WALTZ DREAM, 1925) after an operetta by Oscar Strauss—one of the few German films to become a hit in America. This model film operetta not only satirized court life with a charm kindred to Lubitsch's, but also established that enchanted Vienna which was to haunt the screen from then on.[10] Its components were gentle archdukes, tender flirtations, baroque décors, Biedermeier rooms, people singing and drinking in a suburban garden restaurant, Johann Strauss, Schubert and the venerable old Emperor.[11] The persistent image of this retrospective utopia overshadowed the misery of twentieth century Vienna. Incidentally, most Fridericus films included episodes with Austrian officers who might well have appeared in those Vienna concoctions. They were easygoing, music-loving fellows; the patronizing benevolence with which they were depicted implied that such effeminate enemies would be a pushover.

Escapist needs determined as well the shape of the documentary films—the *Kulturfilme* as they were called in Germany. From about 1924 on, when no other country yet cared much about films of this kind, Ufa produced them with a zeal due mainly to economic factors. The specific difficulties of the stabilization crisis entailed temporary reduction of feature-length entertainment films. The surviving film companies with Ufa in the lead therefore found it expedient to step

[9] Paris films of this kind: LIEBE MACHT BLIND (LOVE MAKES ONE BLIND, 1925), cf. synopsis in *Illustrierter Film-Kurier*; DIE RATTE VON PARIS (THE RAT OF PARIS, 1925), cf. "Emelka-Ronzern," *Das grosse Bilderbuch*, 1926, p. 53; DAS MODELL VON MONTPARNASSE (THE MODEL OF MONTPARNASSE, 1929), cf. "Das Modell von Montparnasse," *Film-Magazin*, April 21, 1929; DER DOMINOSPIELER VON MONTMARTRE (THE DOMINO PLAYER OF MONTMARTRE, 1928), cf. "Comment and Review," *Close Up*, May 1928, pp. 80–82; PANAME (1927), cf. Weyher, "Wir drehen in Paris," *Ufa-Magazin*, March 25–31, 1927.

[10] Synopsis in *Illustrierter Film-Kurier*; Rotha, *Film Till Now*, p. 199; Fawcett, *Die Welt des Films*, p. 126. Berger also made a Hans Sachs film, DER MEISTER VON NÜRNBERG (THE MASTER OF NUREMBERG, 1927); cf. program brochure to this film.

[11] For film operettas, see Kalbus, *Deutsche Filmkunst*, I, 82–83; Kracauer, "Der heutige Film und sein Publikum," *Frankfurter Zeitung*, Nov. 30, 1928; etc.

up the production of short subjects, and in the wake of this development documentaries naturally gained in importance.[12] Perhaps they also owed something to the curiosity about externals prevalent now after years of introspection.

According to an Ufa brochure of the time, the *Kulturfilme* included the following items: "The heart at work . . . bundles of palpitating nerves . . . ghostly hissing snakes, iridescent beetles . . . infusoria . . . rutting deer, sluggishly staring frogs . . . Oriental cult rites . . . fire-worshipers and Tibetan monasteries, living Buddhas . . . gigantic bridges . . . powerful ships, railways, sluices . . . machines . . . colossal mountains, glaciers luminous with a bewitching alpenglow . . . Mexico's wild buffalo herds . . . nimble-footed Chinese before palanquins, fanning and tea-drinking Japanese women lit by Chinese lanterns . . . the Neva Prospect . . . races in Auteuil . . . confusion of the time. . . ." The adjective-laden prospectus ends with the assertion: "The world is beautiful; its mirror is the *Kulturfilm*." [13]

The first *Kulturfilm* to impress itself upon audiences abroad was Ufa's WEGE ZU KRAFT UND SCHÖNHEIT (WAYS TO HEALTH AND BEAUTY)—a feature-length documentary, released in 1925 and reissued, one year later, in a somewhat altered version. Made with the financial support of the German government, this film circulated in the schools because of what was considered its educational value. In an Ufa publicity pamphlet devoted to its merits, a professional eulogist states that WAYS TO HEALTH AND BEAUTY promotes the concept of the "regeneration of the human race." [14] As a matter of fact, the film simply promoted calisthenics and sport. This was done in an omnivorous manner: not content with recording actual achievements in the fields of athletics, hygienic gymnastics, rhythmic gymnastics, dancing, and so forth, Ufa resurrected the Roman thermae and an antique Greek gymnasium crowded with adolescents posing as the contemporaries of Pericles [Illus. 25]. The masquerade was

[12] Jason, "Zahlen sehen uns an . . ," *25 Jahre Kinematograph*, p. 68.

[13] Quoted from "30 Kulturfilme," *Ufa-Leih.* For *Kulturfilme* of the time, see *Jahrbuch der Filmindustrie*, 1923/25, pp. 24, 28, 34–37; Thomalla, "Der Kulturfilm," *Das grosse Bilderbuch*, 1925 p. 24; Kaufmann, *Filmtechnik und Kultur*, pp. 26–27; *Film Society Programmes*, Dec. 1 and Dec. 14, 1930; "New Educational Films from Ufa," *Close Up*, Sept. 1929, pp. 252–54; "Silberkondor über Feuerland," *Close Up*, Dec. 1929, pp. 542–43; Weiss, "The Secret of the Egg-Shell," *Close Up*, May 1930, pp. 421–22; etc. The *Kulturfilme* are commented upon by Kracauer, "Der heutige Film und sein Publikum," *Frankfurter Zeitung*, Nov. 30, 1928.

[14] Quotation from Holländer, "The Road to Beauty and Strength," *Wege zu Kraft und Schönheit*, p. 50. See also *Film Society Programme*, Nov. 13, 1927.

easy inasmuch as many of the athletes performed stark naked. Of course, this sight offended the prudish, but Ufa held that perfect bodily beauty was bound to evoke joys of a purely aesthetic order, and found its idealism rewarded by good box-office takes. Aesthetically speaking, the reconstructions of antiquity were tasteless, the sport pictures excellent, and the bodily beauties so massed together that they affected one neither sensually nor aesthetically.

Owing to their scientific thoroughness and competent photography, the Ufa *Kulturfilme* developed into a German specialty in great demand on the international market.[15] Yet their workmanship could not compensate for their amazing indifference to human problems. By passing off calisthenics as a means to regenerate mankind, WAYS TO HEALTH AND BEAUTY diverted contemporaries from the evils of the time which no calisthenics would remedy. All these documentaries excelled in evasiveness. They mirrored the beautiful world; but their concern with the beauty of "nimble-footed Chinese before palanquins" made them overlook the misery these beautiful coolies endured. They mirrored "the confusion of the time"; but instead of penetrating the confusion, they gloated over it, thus leaving the audience more confused than ever. They spread information on wild buffalo herds and fire-worshipers; but their insistence upon exotic matters of no use to the spectator enabled them to withhold from him any essential information regarding his everyday life. Through their escapist neutrality the Ufa *Kulturfilme* revealed that their submission to the rules of the republican "system" was by no means tantamount to true acceptance.

Not all films refrained from facing social reality. The so-called Zille films—a species flourishing in 1925 and 1926—showed themselves much concerned with real-life incidents. Heinrich Zille was a Berlin draftsman who, driven by pity for the underdog, specialized in portraying the human fauna crowding Berlin's proletarian quarters. His drawings of undernourished children, workers, wretched girls, organ-grinders in ugly backyards, destitute women and nondescripts idling away their time enjoyed great popularity among the Germans. Gerhart Lamprecht brought these drawings to life in DIE VERRUFENEN (SLUMS OF BERLIN, 1925), which he built around personal observations retailed to him by Zille. An engineer who has committed perjury to shield his fiancée finds himself an outcast after leaving prison. Unable to get a job, he attempts sui-

[15] Jason, "Zahlen sehen uns an . . ," *25 Jahre Kinematograph*, p. 68.

cide, and is saved by a good-hearted girl who promptly falls in love with him. She belongs to a Zille milieu characterized by such figures as a kind photographer and a gang of minor criminals. The engineer becomes attached to these people and begins to make his living as a simple factory worker. Soon he rises again: the factory owner discovers his talents and promotes him to a socially respectable position. To complete the engineer's happiness the good-hearted girl conveniently dies, so that he need feel no compunction about marrying the socially respectable sister of the factory owner.[16]

The formula underlying this plot is compounded of two ingredients. On the one hand, the film-makers pretend to tackle the social problem by harping on the sufferings of the proletariat; on the other, they evade the social problem by giving one particular worker (who is not even really of that class) a lucky break. Their design is obviously to trick the spectator into the illusion that he, too, might be upwardbound, and thus make him stick to the "system." Perhaps class differences are fluid after all, the plot suggests, and its sham frankness in exposing the predicament of the lower classes serves to invigorate that daydream of social redemption.

Films based upon this formula not only explored the picturesque Zille world, but also penetrated the sphere of the white-collar workers to promote a manicurist or switchboard operator among them: one Lotte landing in the arms of a rich bridegroom would reward the wishful thinking of all Lottes.[17] To be sure, such daydreams were produced elsewhere as well; but the German specimens advertised the existing regime in a particularly detached, if not absent-minded, manner. They relied on the alluring effect of promotions to a higher social level at a time when, because of the streamlining of big business, promotions of that kind had become extremely scarce. They presented upper-class people in such a way that choice night-clubs and shining cars appeared as the ultimate goal of all human endeavor. When Hollywood dealt with similar themes, events and characters at least preserved a faint vestige of liveliness. These

[16] Program brochure to the film. Cf. Weinberg, *Scrapbooks*, 1925–27; "Wissen Sie schon?" *Das grosse Bilderbuch*, p. 145. Kalbus, *Deutsche Filmkunst*, I, 59, lists a number of such "Zille" films. Among them may be mentioned DIE GESUNKENEN (THE SUNKEN, 1926) with Asta Nielsen, and DAS ERWACHEN DES WEIBES (WOMAN'S AWAKENING, 1927). Cf. programs to these films.

[17] For critical comment on the whole trend, see Kracauer, "Der heutige Film und sein Publikum," *Frankfurter Zeitung*, Nov. 30, 1928.

German films were artificial and oblique products. And yet they found response. Spirits were barren.

Other films aimed at manipulating those who were too discontented with the general social and political conditions to let themselves be drugged by Zille films and the like. The recipe was primitive: one tried to neutralize pent-up indignation by directing it against evils of small importance. Several films of the time stigmatized rigors of the penal code. KREUZZUG DES WEIBES (UNWELCOME CHILDREN, 1926) attacked the provisions against unlawful abortion, while the Nero film GESCHLECHT IN FESSELN (SEX IN FETTERS, 1928) campaigned for prison reform.[18] Since both films, moreover, emphasized sex matters, they were bound to arouse a mixture of indignation and sensuality which could not but increase their value as safety valves.

If, as it happened, some film or other assumed a radical attitude, that radicalism invariably turned against powers long since overthrown. Two mediocre screen versions of Gerhart Hauptmann plays —DIE WEBER (THE WEAVERS, 1927) and DER BIBERPELZ (THE BEAVER COAT, 1928)—combated the early capitalists and the conceited authorities under the Kaiser.[19] Among these anachronistic affairs was one of the best films of the period: Hans Behrendt's DIE HOSE (ROYAL SCANDAL, 1927), fashioned after a prewar comedy by Carl Sternheim. It concerned a romantic intrigue between the sovereign of a small principality and the wife of a petty official who, instead of objecting to being cuckolded, felt highly elated over his fate because the wise sovereign did not forget to promote and decorate him. Even though film experts held that ROYAL SCANDAL was too high-brow to be good business, this "blend of grand burlesque and satire," as Potamkin called it, ingratiated itself with German moviegoers.[20] They relished the acting of Werner Krauss, who endowed the petty official with all the traits of the German philistine. When they laughed at him, they may have believed that they laughed at a former, pretty ridiculous stage of their own existence. But their laughter was mixed with emotional concern, for they could not help secretly craving that lost era with its protective sovereigns and sparkling medals.

[18] For UNWELCOME CHILDREN, see Buchner, *Im Banne des Films*, p. 142; for SEX IN FETTERS, B., "Geschlecht in Fesseln," *Close Up*, Dec. 1928, pp. 69–71.

[19] Cf. Zaddach, *Der literarische Film*, p. 71, and Kracauer, "Der heutige Film und sein Publikum," *Frankfurter Zeitung*, Nov. 30, 1928.

[20] Potamkin, "Kino and Lichtspiel." *Close Up*, Nov. 1929, p. 395. See also program to ROYAL SCANDAL, and Freedley and Reeves, *History of the Theatre*, p. 514.

The testimony of film content was borne out by that of methods of presentation: they, too, betrayed the paralysis of the collective mind. It was as if, along with sensibility to essential content, the whole film sense had weakened. Instead of narrating the story through a display of adequate pictures, directors who should have known better degraded the pictures to mere illustrations of the story. Plot and imagery fell asunder, and the latter was confined to the role of an accompaniment that added nothing. Many a film gave the impression of having been drawn from a novel, even if that novel did not exist.

The strange debilitation of the film sense affected cinematic techniques. Devices that up to 1924 had been developed to express definite meanings turned into meaningless routine matters from 1924 on. Having learned how to move a camera, the cameraman let it run wild on every occasion.[21] Close-ups became a habit. Directors would not even take the trouble to vary them, but would use standardized sets of close-ups to render commonplace events that were quite understandable without any such insertions. Whenever the leading character of a film mounted a train, the audience could count on being informed of his departure by fragments of the locomotive and slowly revolving wheels. In SHATTERED, close shots of that kind had had a structural function [22]; in these films, they were ready-made ornaments—products of an absent-mindedness that also accounted for the negligent handling of many details. The sumptuous screen lobbies of de luxe hotels recalled real lobbies but vaguely, and when the whole of a building and one of its parts were shown, that part seemed to belong to another building.

The mechanization of all editing procedures was conspicuous. In the case of night-club episodes, no film-maker could resist the temptation of illustrating ecstasy at its height through a cliché juxtaposition of performing legs, giant saxophone tubes and staggering torsos. Many films referred to the first World War: even the remotest reference to it sufficed to provoke the sudden appearance of barbed-wire fences, marching columns and shell-bursts—stock material cut in automatically. Fixed types of transitions predominated. One of them connected two different objects by inserting details of them in close-up. If, for instance, the scene was to shift from an

[21] See, for instance, "Die entfesselte Kamera," *Ufa-Magazin,* March 25–31, 1927. For the run-of-the-mill techniques of the period, see Kracauer, "Der heutige Film und sein Publikum," *Frankfurter Zeitung,* Nov. 30, 1928.

[22] Cf. p. 103.

elegant gentleman to a poor woman, the camera first focused upon the gentleman, then tilted down to his shoes, stopped there until the shoes had transformed themselves into those of the woman, and finally tilted up again to make the woman appear. Most Ufa comedies included picture units that paralleled the behavior of some actor to that of a pet animal. When a glamour girl was all sunshine, her Pekingese would be in high spirits as well; when the Pekingese became morose, one could be fairly sure that the subsequent shot would show big tears gliding down the girl's cheeks.

There was no lack of grade-A films produced with all the craftsmanship of which the German studios were capable, but most of them dealt with unimportant subjects or drained important subjects of their significance. What made these elite products seem different from the standardized average output was mainly their technical perfection—that consummate grand-style manner in which they handled nothing as if it were something. They simulated content. It was through this very pretentiousness that they testified to the existing paralysis.

Since THE LAST LAUGH had been a world success, Carl Mayer and F. W. Murnau continued collaborating; the outcome was TARTUFFE (1925), an Ufa superproduction, in which the two artists paid tribute to the grand-style manner [Illus. 26]. The paralysis was all-pervading. Mayer seemed aware of its contagious power, and, as if he felt that the indifference around and in him would do away with any immediacy of thought and emotion and thus engender a deep and general hypocrisy, he tried in TARTUFFE to emphasize hypocrisy as the basic vice of contemporary society. This he did by means of a story framing his screen version of Molière's comedy. The film opens with a prologue showing a wealthy old gentleman in the clutches of his housekeeper who, another Tartuffe, courts him brazenly. To open the old fool's eyes, his grandson invites him and the housekeeper to a screening of *Tartuffe* he has been clever enough to prearrange. Here the prologue ends, and *Tartuffe* commences. Like the play in *Hamlet*, this film within a film fulfills an enlightening mission: in the epilogue the female legacy-hunter is ousted. But elaborate production snowed under what Mayer had to impart. The critics dismissed the modern framing story as an unnecessary addition. The rendering of Molière culminated in moments of accomplished acting and such decorative finesse as "the lace négligé in the final bedroom scene, the pattern of the bed covering, the porcelain clock on the fireplace," and so forth.[23] It was a slick theatrical performance. Much as the camera hovered about, it subordinated itself always to Jannings and the other players instead of using them for purposes of its own.[24] This TARTUFFE, far from bringing home hypocrisy to the audience, was itself Tartuffish, for it flattered an audience anxious to leave things in the depths untouched.

Before going to Hollywood, Murnau staged another Ufa superproduction: FAUST (1926). Ufa seemed determined to make this film a cultural monument. Hans Kyser's script exploited Marlowe and Goethe and German folk sagas, and Gerhart Hauptmann, Germany's foremost poet, composed the film titles. Technical ingenuity was lavished on angelic apparitions and devilish conjuring tricks. Karl Freund's camera rushed on a roller coaster of his own invention through a vast, studio-built landscape filled with towns, woods and villages, and the views thus obtained enabled the spectators to participate in the aerial trip Mephistopheles undertook with the rejuvenated Faust. Their flight was a celestial sensation. But neither the roller coaster nor Gerhart Hauptmann could compensate for the futility of a film which misrepresented, if not ignored, all significant motifs inherent in its subject-matter.[25] The metaphysical conflict between good and evil was thoroughly vulgarized, and the drawn-out love story between Faust and Margarete induced the critic of the *National Board of Review Magazine* to remark: "We find ourselves descending from the masculine version of Marlowe and the philosophical concept of Goethe to the level of the libretto which inspired Gounod to write his opera." [26] FAUST was not so much a cultural monument as a monumental display of artifices capitalizing on the prestige of national culture. The obsolete theatrical poses to which the actors resorted betrayed the falsity of the whole. While the film had considerable success abroad, it met with indifference in Germany itself. The Germans of the time did not take to Faustian

[23] Quoted from Rotha, *Film Till Now*, p. 198. Cf. Weinberg, *Scrapbooks*, 1927; Zaddach, *Der literarische Film*, pp. 59–60; *Film Society Programme*, April 1, 1928.

[24] Cf. "Tartuffe, the Hypocrite," *National Board of Review Magazine*, May 1928, p. 6.

[25] Program brochure to the film; Rotha, *Film Till Now*, p. 198; Vincent, *Histoire de l'Art Cinématographique*, p. 152; "Die entfesselte Kamera," *Ufa-Magazin*, March 25–31, 1927; *Cinéa-Ciné*, March 15, 1927, pp. 19–20.

[26] "Faust," *National Board of Review Magazine*, Nov. 1926, p. 10. See also Potamkin, "The Rise and Fall of the German Film," *Cinema*, April 1930, p. 59.

problems, and moreover resented any interference with their traditional notions of the classics.[27]

Outstanding instances of grand-style manner were the three films Fritz Lang produced during the stabilized period. They dealt with thrilling adventures and technical fantasies symptomatic of the then current machine cult. The first of them was METROPOLIS, an Ufa production released at the beginning of 1927. Lang relates that he conceived the idea of this internationally known film when from shipboard he saw New York for the first time—a nocturnal New York glittering with myriad lights.[28] The city built in his film is a sort of super New York, realized on the screen with the aid of the so-called Shuftan process, an ingenious mirror device permitting the substitution of little models for giant structures.[29] This screen metropolis of the future consists of a lower and an upper city. The latter—a grandiose street of skyscrapers alive with an incessant stream of air taxis and cars—is the abode of big-business owners, high-ranking employees and pleasure-hunting gilded youth. In the lower city, shut off from daylight, the workers tend monstrous machines. They are slaves rather than workers. The film elaborates upon their rebellion against the master class in the upper world, and ends with the reconciliation of the two classes.

However, what is important here is not so much the plot as the preponderance of surface features in its development. In the brilliant laboratory episode, the creation of a robot is detailed with a technical exactitude that is not at all required to further the action. The office of the big boss, the vision of the Tower of Babel, the machinery and the arrangement of the masses: all illustrate Lang's penchant for pompous ornamentation.[30] In NIBELUNGEN, his decorative style was rich in meaning; in METROPOLIS, the decorative not only appears as an end in itself, but even belies certain points made through the plot. It makes sense that, on their way to and from the machines, the workers form ornamental groups; but it is nonsensical to force them into such groups while they are listening to a comforting speech from the girl Maria during their leisure time. In his exclusive concern with ornamentation, Lang goes so far as to com-

[27] Jacobs, *American Film*, p. 310; "Was is los?" *Ufa-Magazin*, Feb. 4–10, 1927; "Erläuterungen," *Film-Photos*, p. 53.

[28] Information offered by Mr. Lang.

[29] Information offered by Mr. Shuftan.

[30] Cf. Rotha, *Celluloid*, pp. 230–32; "Die entfesselte Kamera," *Ufa-Magazin*, March 25–31, 1927; Jahier, "42 Ans de Cinéma," *Le Rôle intellectuel du Cinéma*, p. 62.

pose decorative patterns from the masses who are desperately trying to escape the inundation of the lower city. Cinematically an incomparable achievement, this inundation sequence is humanly a shocking failure [Illus. 28]. METROPOLIS impressed the German public. The Americans relished its technical excellence; the English remained aloof; the French were stirred by a film which seemed to them a blend of Wagner and Krupp, and on the whole an alarming sign of Germany's vitality.[31]

Lang's subsequent film, the mystery thriller SPIONE (THE SPY, 1928), shared two traits with his DR. MABUSE. It featured a master spy who, like Mabuse, led several different lives: besides the spy, he was also the president of a bank and a music-hall clown. And exactly like DR. MABUSE, this new film refrained from conferring moral superiority upon the representatives of the law.[32] Espionage and counterespionage were on the same level—two gangs fighting each other in a chaotic world. Yet there was one important difference: while Dr. Mabuse had incarnated the tyrant who takes advantage of the chaos around him, the master spy indulged in the spy business for the sole purpose, it seemed, of spying. He was a formalized Mabuse devoted to meaningless activities. By emphasizing this figure, the film reflected the neutrality prevalent during that period —a neutrality which also manifested itself in the absence of any distinction between legal and illegal pursuits and in a prodigal abundance of disguises. No character was what he appeared to be. This constant change of identities was appropriate to denote a state of mind in which the paralysis of the self interfered with any attempt at self-identification. As if to fill the void, Lang piled up sensations which conveyed no meaning. His imaginative virtuosity in shaping them reached its climax with a train wreck in a tunnel. Since it proved impossible to stage the catastrophe in life-size proportions, he gave the impression of it through confused mental images of the persons involved in this shock situation.

THE SPY would have been a true forerunner of the Hitchcock thrillers if Lang had not fashioned it after the pompous manner of METROPOLIS, so that empty sensations took on the air of substantial revelations. Virtuosity alienated from content posed as art. In accordance with this pretense, Ufa issued a volume that was a

[31] While H. G. Wells damned METROPOLIS as "quite the silliest film" (Rotha, *Film Till Now*, p. 194), Conan Doyle was enthusiastic about it (cf. "Was is los?" *Ufa-Magazin*, April 15–21, 1927). For further comment on METROPOLIS, see p. 162 ff.

[32] Cf. p. 83.

triumph of bookbinding though it contained nothing but the Thea von Harbou novel from which THE SPY had been made.[33]

In his third film, DIE FRAU IM MOND (THE GIRL IN THE MOON, 1929), Lang imagined a rocket projectile carrying passengers to the moon. The cosmic enterprise was staged with a surprising veracity of vision; the plot was pitiable for its emotional shortcomings. These were so obvious that they discredited many an illusion Lang tried to create by showy virtuosity. The lunar landscape smelled distinctly of Ufa's Neubabelsberg studios.[34]

Other films in grand-style manner masked their insignificance by assuming the character of tragedies. It was easy: you had only to introduce some unlucky incident and make it appear a fateful event. In Ufa's Henny Porten film ZUFLUCHT (REFUGE, 1928), a young man who had once run away from his bourgeois parents to join the proletariat returns to his native town, completely disillusioned. A poor girl there takes care of the broken ex-revolutionary, and his parents are finally willing to accept him and the pregnant girl. Happiness seems close at hand, but Ufa, inexorable, frustrates it. At the very last moment the young man dies a death designed to impress tragedy upon the audience.[35] Since he had been a revolutionary, Ufa may also have considered his death morally justified. In cases in which a tragic outcome was not held opportune, the films in grand-style manner frequently relied on the spell of beautiful settings to conceal their emptiness. Bergner in DONA JUANA (1928) was seen before the fountains of Granada and on the roads Don Quixote had trodden. It was all trappings.

Even the documentaries inclined to be grandiloquent. The Ufa *Kulturfilm* NATUR UND LIEBE (NATURE AND LOVE) combined with its scenes of sex life monumental visions of mankind's birth and

[33] Program brochure to the film; Rotha, *Film Till Now*, p. 193, and *Celluloid*, p. 223; Herring, "Reasons of Rhyme," *Close Up*, Oct. 1929, pp. 280–81.

[34] Rotha, *Celluloid*, pp. 232–37; Dreyfus, "La Femme sur la Lune," *La Revue du Cinéma*, May 1930, pp. 62–63; "Frau im Mond," *Close Up*, Nov. 1929, pp. 443–44; Jahier, "42 Ans de Cinéma," *Le Rôle intellectuel du Cinéma*, p. 62; Arnheim, *Film als Kunst*, p. 180.

[35] Kracauer, "Der heutige Film und sein Publikum," *Frankfurter Zeitung*, Dec. 1, 1928. See also "Zuflucht," *Ufa-Leih*.—In this context, several costume films more or less affected by the predominant grand-style manner should at least be mentioned: MANON LESCAUT, 1926 (cf. Rotha, *Film Till Now*, pp. 200–1, and *Illustrierter Film-Kurier*); DER ROSENKAVALIER, 1926 (cf. Kalbus, *Deutsche Filmkunst*, I, 81); MARTIN LUTHER, 1928 (cf. "Martin Luther," *National Board of Review Magazine*, Oct. 1928, p. 4, and Blakeston, "Snap," *Close Up*, May 1929, pp. 41–42); SCHINDERHANNES, 1928 (Rotha, *ibid.*, p. 206, and Hellmund-Waldow, "Alraune and Schinderhannes," *Close Up*, March 1928, pp. 45–48); NAPOLEON AUF ST. HELENA, 1929 (program to this film).

rise.[36] Similarly, the *Kulturfilm* WUNDER DER SCHÖPFUNG (MIRACLES OF CREATION, 1925) not only pictured present-day miracles, but foreshadowed astronomical events of the future, including the wholesale death of our universe. According to the prospectus to this latter film, Ufa was convinced that the sight of such astronomical events would induce any thinking spectator to become aware of the utter unimportance of his ephemeral existence.[37] In other words, the tragic destiny of the cosmos was exhibited to deflect the spectator's attention from the problems of everyday life. Grand-style manner in such instances as this helped to stupefy social consciousness.

[36] Kracauer, "Der heutige Film und sein Publikum," *Frankfurter Zeitung*, Nov. 30, 1928.

[37] *Ufa Verleih-Programme*, 1924/25, p. 102.

13. THE PROSTITUTE AND THE ADOLESCENT

THE second group of films that appeared during the stabilized era allows one to specify the psychological contents then paralyzed. Having no direct outlet, they made themselves known in a devious and distorted way. A number of films of this group divulged their messages after the manner of dreams; it is as if they were the confessions of someone talking in his sleep.

A few films, stragglers of a bygone era, reveal that the old psychological unrest continued to smolder in the collective soul. In 1926, Henrik Galeen staged a second STUDENT VON PRAG (THE STUDENT OF PRAGUE), which differed thematically from the first only in that it put more emphasis on the psychological significance of the plot. This beautiful, if in some respects questionable, version of Wegener's prewar film deliberately interpreted Baldwin's fight with his double as a fight with his other self.[1] The film was a big success in Germany; it seemed to make the Germans realize their own duality, which during the stabilized period was deepened by the latent conflict between republican institutions and paralyzed authoritarian dispositions. Galeen's picture, which was full of E. T. A. Hoffmann reminiscences, sensitized these dispositions and all the impulses and longings connected with them. It may have been the story's inherent material that caused the Nazis to release another STUDENT OF PRAGUE in 1936.

Expert in fantastic horror films, Galeen also made ALRAUNE (UNHOLY LOVE, 1928), which was based upon a novel by H. H. Ewers. A scientist (Paul Wegener), experimenting in artificial impregnation, creates a human being: Alraune, daughter of a hanged criminal and a prostitute. This creature, portrayed by Brigitte Helm as a somnambulant vamp with seductive and empty features, ruins

[1] "The Man Who Cheated Life," *National Board of Review Magazine*, Feb. 1929, pp. 10–11; H. D., "Conrad Veidt, The Student of Prague," *Close Up*, Sept. 1927, pp. 36–43; Blakeston, "An Epic—Please!" *ibid.*, p. 65; Rotha, *Film Till Now*, pp. 202–3, 285; *Illustrierter Film-Kurier* (synopsis of the film); Wesse, *Grossmacht Film*, pp. 127–28.

all those who are in love with her, and at the end destroys herself.[2] Alraune's family resemblance to Homunculus is apparent. In her case, too, abnormal origins are called upon to account for inner frustration and its devastating consequences. The story aroused sufficient interest to be made into a talkie a few years later. This indicates that among the paralyzed psychological processes those to which the film referred were of consequence.

Several films remotely akin to the instinct and peasant dramas of the postwar years glorified nature—to be more precise, the interrelationship between human nature and external nature. Regardless of whether they rendered storms or frosts, farmers or fishermen, they placed the laws of nature—an eternally unchanging nature—above the decrees of autonomous reason. Their sporadic appearance testified to the existence of a romanticizing tendency which had been strengthened by suffering resulting from the streamlining of all working processes. This tendency, hostile to the intellect as such, turned not only against a rationalism which ignored the friendly forces of nature, but also against the ever-repeated attempts of reason to defeat nature's destructive forces manifesting themselves through tyranny. Widespread as such an anti-intellectualism was, it expressed itself not so much on the screen as in philosophy and literature—which means that it was actually prevented from achieving full expression in that period.

Among the films subordinating reason to nature, Fritz Wendhausen's DER SOHN DER HAGAR (OUT OF THE MIST, 1927) ranked high because of its magnificent pictures of snowy woods, spring scenery and old-fashioned interiors. It was a romance elaborating upon the return of a handsome young man to his native mountain village. He arrives from faraway "large cities," and becomes involved in passions springing up in a wayside inn and a sawmill.[3] The ties between the villagers and their land are so indissoluble that he appears as an intruder up to the end. In her review of the film, Miss Lejeune states that "every achieved action, every enduring motive springs from the life of the soil . . . while the foreign emotions remain unfulfilled." [4] The affiliation of this cult of the soil with

[2] Cf. Hellmund-Waldow, "Alraune and Schinderhannes," *Close Up,* March 1928, pp. 49–50; etc. In a similar vein was Wiene's ORLAC'S HÄNDE (THE HANDS OF ORLAC, 1925); cf. *Film Society Programme*, Oct. 24, 1926.

[3] "Films of the Month: Out of the Mist," *Close Up*, Oct. 1927, p. 85.

[4] Lejeune, *Cinema*, p. 234. See also Rotha, *Film Till Now*, p. 206. For other films of this kind, see Martini, "Nature and Human Fate," *Close Up,* Nov. 1927, pp. 10–14; *Das grosse Bilderbuch*, 1925, p. 375; etc.

authoritarian behavior was to be revealed by the blood-and-soil literature of the Nazis.

Dr. Arnold Fanck continued his series of mountain films with the already-mentioned HOLY MOUNTAIN and a rather insignificant comedy.[5] The yield was slight. Under the sun of Locarno, the heroic idealism of the mountain climbers seemed to melt away like the snow in the valleys. Yet it survived and, as prosperity drew to a close, again attained the heights in DIE WEISSE HÖLLE VON PIZ PALÜ (THE WHITE HELL OF PITZ PALÜ, 1929), in which Ernst Udet's daredevil flights matched the stunt ascensions. Fanck made this cinematically fascinating film with the aid of G. W. Pabst, who probably did his best to cut down emotional exuberance.[6] However, sentimentality was inseparable from that variety of idealism.

The national films of the stabilized period were also affected by the general apathy. In a number of them patriotic fervor seemed suspended. A Bismarck film, released in 1926, was a purely matter-of-fact biography.[7] DER WELTKRIEG (WORLD WAR, 1927)—an Ufa documentary in three parts utilizing stock candid-camera work —resulted from the express design of "presenting the historic facts with incontestable objectivity." [8] This film included an important innovation: maps illustrating battle arrays and army evolutions after the manner of animated cartoons. Sven Noldan, their creator, called them a means of giving the illusion of phenomena not to be found in camera reality.[9] He was also to make the maps for the Nazi war films BAPTISM OF FIRE and VICTORY IN THE WEST, but in these films their propaganda function of symbolizing Nazi Germany's irresistible military might was to overshadow their character as objective statements. (It is, by the way, not surprising that Léon Poirier's war documentary VERDUN, 1928, rivaled WORLD WAR in neutrality: to some extent, the Treaty of Locarno determined the outlook of both the French and the German partner.) THE EMDEN

[5] Cf. p. 112.—For THE HOLY MOUNTAIN, see Kalbus, *Deutsche Filmkunst,* I, 92; Weinberg, *Scrapbooks,* 1927; for the comedy, DER GROSSE SPRUNG (THE BIG JUMP, 1927), Kalbus, *ibid.,* and *Illustrierter Film-Kurier.* Fanck also wrote the script of another mountain film, DER KAMPF UMS MATTERHORN (STRUGGLE FOR THE MATTERHORN, 1928).

[6] Rotha, *Celluloid,* pp. 32–33; "The White Hell of Piz Palu," *Close Up,* Dec. 1929, p. 543.

[7] For BISMARCK, see Kalbus, *Deutsche Filmkunst,* I, 57.

[8] Quoted from Krieger, "Wozu ein Weltkriegsfilm?" *Ufa-Magazin* (Sondernummer: Der Weltkrieg). See also *Illustrierter Film-Kurier.*

[9] Noldan, "Die Darstellung der Schlachten," *Ufa-Magazin* (Sondernummer: Der Weltkrieg).

(1926) and U-9 WEDDIGEN (1927), two films of fiction extolling war feats of the German navy, were no less eager to seem impartial. An American correspondent who attended the première of U-9 WEDDIGEN during a Berlin *Stahlhelm* convention praised it for avoiding nationalistic coloring.[10]

This reserve was not general. The Fridericus films of the period and several kindred films similarly exploiting top figures of Prussian history indulged in an obtrusive patriotism.[11] However, their patriotism had an outright cliché character which, exactly like the neutrality of WORLD WAR or EMDEN, suggested the existing paralysis of nationalistic passions. As a matter of fact, the public of the Dawes Plan era considered these patriotic cut-to-pattern films somewhat antiquated reminiscences. Two of them— KÖNIGIN LUISE (QUEEN LUISE, 1927) and WATERLOO (1929)—were made by Karl Grune.

The direction Grune took after his memorable THE STREET is revealing. He approached vital problems from different angles in a cinematically interesting way. His ARABELLA (1925) was a melodramatic survey of human life seen through the eyes of a horse; his EIFERSUCHT (JEALOUSY, 1925) transferred the main motif of WARNING SHADOWS into realistic surroundings [12] ; his AM RANDE DER WELT (AT THE EDGE OF THE WORLD, 1927) treated an "unconvincing pacifist theme" in the form of a saga set against an impressive landscape.[13] Then, as if overwhelmed by disillusion, he renounced any emotional directness, and fell back on the conventionalism of historical costume films. WATERLOO, in which he adopted Abel Gance's idea of projecting simultaneous events on three screens, concentrated upon Blücher's triumph over Napoleon; it was a Blücher played by Otto Gebühr, alias Frederick the Great.[14] As has been stated in an earlier chapter, the appearance of some Frederick would be needed to release the philistine in THE STREET from the sadness of his plush parlor: Grune's development was logical. It was also the outcome of inner exhaustion and as such once more pointed to the paralysis behind these patriotic films.

[10] Quoted from Weinberg, *Scrapbooks*, 1927. For THE EMDEN, see Bryher, "The War from Three Angles," *Close Up*, July 1927, p. 20.

[11] Kalbus, *Deutsche Filmkunst*, I, 56–57.

[12] For QUEEN LUISE and ARABELLA, see programs to these films; for JEALOUSY, Vincent, *Histoire de l'Art Cinématographique*, p. 150, and *Illustrierter Film-Kurier*.

[13] Quoted from Rotha, *Film Till Now*, pp. 201–2. See also D. L. H., "Films in the Provinces," *Close Up*, June 1929, p. 56; "Wie ein Film entsteht," *Ufa-Magazin*, April 29–May 5, 1927. According to Rotha the script was by Carl Mayer.

[14] Vincent, *Histoire de l'Art Cinématographique*, p. 150.

Much pertinent information can be derived from a series of films which may be called "street" films, because they resumed the theme Grune had introduced in THE STREET. Their concern with the street was so intense that they rarely failed to include the word, or a synonym, in their titles.

On the surface, these films were nothing but derivatives of Grune's film: they, too, featured a rebellious individual who would break away from home and security, follow his passions on the street and at the end again submit to the exigencies of conventional life. However, what seemed a mere repetition of Grune's story in fact differed from it essentially. The street in the street films was no longer the dreadful jungle it appeared in THE STREET of 1923; it was a region harboring virtues that had deserted bourgeois society. To be sure, the outcast as the "keeper of the flame" was not at all a novelty on the stage, but on the German screen this figure became an institution only during the stabilized period. In Pabst's DIE FREUDLOSE GASSE (THE JOYLESS STREET, 1925), which will be discussed later,[15] the sole character manifesting true inner grandeur was a girl with all the earmarks of a prostitute. Abandoned by her lover for a wealthy match, she kills a socialite who might have thwarted his marriage project, and then confesses her crime before the judge to clear her lover from suspicion of being himself the murderer.

While this girl was only of episodic importance, a character of similar magnanimity played the leading part in Bruno Rahn's impressive and successful DIRNENTRAGÖDIE (TRAGEDY OF THE STREET, 1927): she was an elderly, worn-out prostitute. Walking her beat, she stumbles upon a drunken young man—a bourgeois offspring who, after a quarrel with his parents, has left home for the street. She takes him to her room, and is foolish enough to believe him in love with her. During her absence—she goes out to invest her savings in a confectionery shop, so as to become worthy of him—her *souteneur* introduces him to Clarissa, a pretty young streetwalker, for whom he abandons the old prostitute. She is wounded deeply; but what grieves this loving heart most is not so much her own misery as the thought that life with Clarissa may spoil the boy's whole future. In her despair, she incites her *souteneur* to kill the girl. Detectives track down the murderer, and the prostitute herself commits suicide. On the door of the shabby rooming-house a signboard reads "Room to Let." Back home, the boy performs the well-known

[15] Cf. p. 167 ff.

gesture: he sobs, his head sheltered in his mother's lap.[16] Asta Nielsen, emerging from the spheres of Ibsen and Strindberg, portrayed the prostitute incomparably: not a realistic one, but that imaginary figure of an outcast who has discarded social conventions because of her abundance of love, and now, through her mere existence, defies the questionable laws of a hypocritical society [17] [Illus. 29].

Joe May's ASPHALT (1929)—one of the films Erich Pommer suggested and supervised after his return from America—surpassed TRAGEDY OF THE STREET in explicitness. The boy who in ASPHALT risks his professional honor in a love adventure with a thievish tart is a traffic cop and moreover the son of a police sergeant—Crown Prince Frederick rebelling against, and finally submitting to, his father. The act of submission itself acquires new meaning in this film. When towards the end the traffic cop is indicted for having murdered a man in the tart's flat, the girl volunteers a confession of her own complicity that exonerates him. She is marched off to the prison. But the young crown prince of the police follows her with his eyes, and his gaze implies a promise of loyalty and ensuing marriage.[18] Here the street penetrates the bourgeois parlor—a penetration which also marks the end of DIE CARMEN VON ST.-PAULI (CARMEN OF ST. PAUL, 1928), another of this series.[19] In the street films, two dimensions of life were interrelated which in Grune's THE STREET had been incompatible with each other.

The imagery of the street films reveals that in the Germany of the time the street exerted an irresistible attraction. Paul Rotha remarks of Rahn's TRAGEDY OF THE STREET: "Throughout, all things led back to the street; its pavements with the hurrying, soliciting feet; its dark corners and angles; its light under the sentinel lamp-posts." [20] The street in this film, Rotha adds, was mainly characterized by the motif of "the feet that walk over its stones"—a motif traceable to that close shot which in the Grune

[16] Herring, "La Tragédie de la Rue," *Close Up*, July 1928, pp. 31–40; Buchner, *Im Banne des Films*, pp. 120–21; Bardèche and Brasillach, *History of Motion Pictures*, p. 254.

[17] Asta Nielsen was also featured in HEDDA GABLER (1925) and LASTER DER MENSCHHEIT (LUSTS OF MANKIND, 1927). For the latter film, see Blakeston, "Lusts of Mankind," *Close Up*, Nov. 1928, pp. 38–41. Jahier speaks of "l'apparition baudelairienne d'Asta Nielsen" in THE JOYLESS STREET ("42 Ans de Cinéma," *Le Rôle intellectuel du Cinéma*, p. 63). See also Mungenast, *Asta Nielsen*.

[18] Synopsis of film in *Illustrierter Film-Kurier*. Cf. Gregor, *Zeitalter des Films*, pp. 209–10.

[19] Synopsis of film in *Illustrierter Film-Kurier*.

[20] Rotha, *Film Till Now*, p. 206.

film showed the philistine's legs following a wavy line on the pavement. Rahn's film opens with an incident photographed at the level of a dog's eyes: the feet of a man follow those of a girl along a sidewalk, then upstairs, and then into a room. It is as if the feet were no less expressive than the faces. Clarissa's high heels are seen moving uptown, and later the heavy feet of the *souteneur* pursue her light ones like a threat. In ASPHALT, the pavement itself is a central motif. The prologue to this film illustrates, after the manner of a documentary, how asphalt is produced and how it voraciously swallows the open land to pave the way for city traffic—that thundering chaos mastered, as in THE STREET, by the magic gestures of the policeman. Shots featuring the union of asphalt and traffic also form the epilogue of the action proper. The emphasis put on the asphalt goes hand in hand with the insertion of street pictures at every dramatic high point. They herald, for example, a significant love scene between the traffic cop and the tart. Such street pictures were essential components of all street films. In Grune's film, they had helped objectify the horrors of anarchy; in the street films, they denoted the hope of genuine love.

TRAGEDY OF THE STREET and ASPHALT radiated a warmth rarely to be found during the stabilized period. This and their pictorial sensitivity—the petty-bourgeois home of the police family in ASPHALT, for instance, is portrayed absorbingly [21]—suggest that in those street films the paralyzed inner attitudes rose to the surface. But they were able to pierce the cover of neutrality only by manifesting themselves in the form of dreams. TRAGEDY OF THE STREET and the other street films are dreamlike complexes of images constituting a sort of secret code. By glorifying what Potamkin calls " '*die Strasse*' of brothels," the street films figuratively express discontent with the stabilized republican regime.[22] Life, they seem to say, is not worth while within the boundaries of the "system"; it comes into its own only outside the rotten bourgeois world. That the center of life is the street—a quarter peopled not with proletarians, but with outcasts—indicates that the discontented are far from being socialist-minded. Love in the street stands for ideals averse to Locarno, Weimar and Moscow.

During the postwar period, the Grune film emphasized the

[21] Cf. Balázs, *Der Geist des Films*, p. 71.

[22] Potamkin, "Pabst and the Social Film," *Hound & Horn*, Jan.–March 1933, p. 293.

philistine's return to his middle-class home—a resumption of authoritarian behavior. The street films emphasize desertion of the home, but still in the interest of authoritarian behavior. The bourgeois runaway whose rebellion was once nothing but a futile escapade now is engaged in an escape that amounts to an antidemocratic, antirevolutionary rebellion. (From 1933 on, such Nazi films as HITLERJUNGE QUEX and UM DAS MENSCHENRECHT are to present the communists and leftist intellectuals as libertines given to orgies with loose girls. However, these girls have nothing in common with the ideal prostitutes who under the Republic lured rebels predestined to become Nazis.) In most street films, the rebellion against the "system" is followed by a submission to it which, instead of putting a definite end to the rebellion, marks it as an event of far-reaching consequence. In fact, these films foreshadow the thorough change of all values then prevalent by implying that the bonds between the prostitute and her bourgeois lover will survive the latter's submission.

The street films were no isolated phenomenon. Like them, the many youth films of the period—films featuring children or adolescents—had the character of dreams arising from the paralyzed layers of the collective mind. On the whole, Potamkin's statement that "the German is interested in children, not in a child" proves correct. DIE RÄUBERBANDE (THE ROBBER BAND, 1928) dealt with the play life of a boys' gang; DER KAMPF DER TERTIA (1929), with a fine understanding of pre-adolescent emotions, pictured the Homeric fight boys of a school community put up to prevent the seizure and extermination of stray cats [Illus. 30].[23] It occasionally happened, though, that the action centered around an individual youngster. In DIE UNEHELICHEN (CHILDREN OF NO IMPORTANCE, 1926), for instance, two little children growing up in a true Zille milieu were seen suffering under a ruthless father.[24]

Youth films devoted to the inner difficulties of the eighteen-year-old predominated. Descending from the expressionist son-father dramas, they paralleled the street films in that they stressed the right to rebel. These films sided with juvenile insurgence against the

[23] Quoted from Potamkin, "The Rise and Fall of the German Film," *Cinema*, April 1930, p. 57. For the two films, see Potamkin, "Kino and Lichtspiel," *Close Up*, Nov. 1929, p. 394; for DER KAMPF DER TERTIA, Bryher, "A German School Film," *Close Up*, Feb. 1930, pp. 129–32.

[24] Kalbus, *Deutsche Filmkunst*, I, 131; Weinberg, *Scrapbooks*, 1928.

rule of insensate adults. Most of them were loose variations of Wedekind's *The Awakening of Spring* (*Frühling's Erwachen*), which itself was made into a film by Richard Oswald (1929). Robert Land's PRIMANERLIEBE (1927) stood out among these studies in adolescence. In it, a youthful college boy is so terrorized by the severity of his guardian and his teachers that only one escape seems open to him: suicide. When he calls on the girl he loves to bid her farewell, he finds her on the point of falling prey to an unscrupulous seducer. He shoots the man with the bullet designed to kill himself. During the court proceedings, all his hidden motives and intentions come to the fore, and it dawns upon the guardian and the teachers that their rigorous discipline has been a grave mistake. They will undoubtedly try to mitigate it.[25] Ufa's DER KAMPF DES DONALD WESTHOF (THE TRIAL OF DONALD WESTHOF, 1928) echoed this film without matching it.[26]

In DER GEIGER VON FLORENZ (THE VIOLINIST OF FLORENCE, 1926), another film of adolescence, Elisabeth Bergner plays a half-grown girl jealous of the love with which her father surrounds her young stepmother. Close shots render her smallest gestures and actions, so as to impress them upon the spectator as symptoms of her emotions. It is an all but psychoanalytical affair, made still more interesting by Bergner's boyish appearance. Strolling along Italian roads in boy's clothing, she looks half lad, half girl.[27] The androgynous character she created found a response in Germany which may have been intensified by the existing inner paralysis. Psychological frustration and sexual ambiguity reinforce each other. Bergner in her subsequent films was to turn from the girlish boy to the similarly complex child-woman—a figure of limited range, brought to perfection in such films of hers as FRÄULEIN ELSE (1929) and ARIANE (1931).[28]

The youth films begin to emerge immediately after the stabilization of the mark, and from then on remain popular throughout the

[25] For THE AWAKENING OF SPRING, see *Illustrierter Film-Kurier*; for PRIMANERLIEBE, Weinberg, *Scrapbooks*, 1928.

[26] Cf. Weinberg, *ibid.* Another youth film was JUNGES BLUT, 1928 (French title: PREMIER AMOUR—PREMIER DOULEUR); cf. "Les Présentations de l'Alliance Cinématographique Europèene, *Cinéa-Ciné*, April 1, 1927, p. 15.

[27] Program to the film; Rotha, *Film Till Now*, pp. 195–96; *Film Society Programme*, March 8, 1931; "Comment and Review," *Close Up*, Feb. 1928, pp. 65–71; Gregor, *Zeitalter des Films*, pp. 212–16.

[28] For FRÄULEIN ELSE, see program brochure to the film. Rotha, *Film Till Now*, p. 196, briefly appraises the Bergner films, including LIEBE (French title, L'HISTOIRE DES TREIZE, 1927) and DONA JUANA (1928). For comment on ARIANE, see p. 255 f.

republican era. It therefore seems justifiable to trace them to the paralysis of the retrogressive tendencies during that period. Since these tendencies are prevented from asserting themselves within the "system," they try to find an outlet by forcing imagination back to the time of premanhood when immaturity is still legitimate. The Germans under the Republic are homesick for youth—which accounts for the genuine tenderness with which their youth films dwell upon the inherent conflicts of adolescence. (Even though the retrogressive tendencies are released under Hitler, the Nazi films continue to feature juvenile life; however, they do so not to symbolize the desire for retrogression, but to advertise youth as a pillar of the Nazi world.)

In their concern with the aims of rebellion, the youth films go beyond the street films. They do not confine themselves to sympathizing with the rebellious adolescents; they overtly turn against the adult tyrants and their authoritative discipline. Authority declaring itself omnipotent is here attacked with a directness never before attempted. This repudiation of absolute authority has two distinct meanings. First, notwithstanding the democratic constitution of the existing regime, the autocratic adults are made to appear its representatives. This is, for instance, the way they affect the youth in PRIMANERLIEBE. By stigmatizing them and simultaneously holding out the prospect of their inner change, the youth films assume the function of the street films: they express discontent with the regime and forecast its decomposition. Second, the repudiation of absolute authority means just that and nothing more. But the youth films have the character of dreams, and in dreams opposition to an attitude is often tantamount to its acceptance. Not unlike the old expressionist tyrant films, which themselves were dreamlike projections of an agitated soul, the youth films affirm fixation to authoritarian behavior precisely by stressing rebellion against it. Young rebels frequently develop into old tyrants who, the more fanatical they were as rebels, the more relentless they are as tyrants. Significantly, none of the films offers a definition of freedom that would annul the paradoxical interrelationship between tyrant and rebel.

One film was more explicit than all others: METROPOLIS. In it, the paralyzed collective mind seemed to be talking with unusual clarity in its sleep. This is more than a metaphor: owing to a fortunate combination of receptivity and confusion, Lang's script writer, Thea von Harbou, was not only sensitive to all undercurrents of the time, but indiscriminately passed on whatever happened to haunt her imagination.[29] METROPOLIS was rich in subterranean content that, like contraband, had crossed the borders of consciousness without being questioned.

Freder, son of the mammoth industrialist who controls the whole of Metropolis, is true to type: he rebels against his father and joins the workers in the lower city. There he immediately becomes a devotee of Maria, the great comforter of the oppressed. A saint rather than a socialist agitator, this young girl delivers a speech to the workers in which she declares that they can be redeemed only if the heart mediates between hand and brain. And she exhorts her listeners to be patient: soon the mediator will come. The industrialist, having secretly attended this meeting, deems the interference of the heart so dangerous that he entrusts an inventor with the creation of a robot looking exactly like Maria. This robot-Maria is to incite riots and furnish the industrialist with a pretext to crush the workers' rebellious spirit. He is not the first German screen tyrant to use such methods; Homunculus had introduced them much earlier.[30] Stirred by the robot, the workers destroy their torturers, the machines, and release flood waters which then threaten to drown their own children. If it were not for Freder and the genuine Maria, who intervene at the last moment, all would be doomed. Of course, this elemental outburst has by far surpassed the petty little uprising for which the industrialist arranged. In the final scene, he is shown standing between Freder and Maria, and the workers approach, led by their foreman. Upon Freder's suggestion, his father shakes hands with the foreman, and Maria happily consecrates this symbolic alliance between labor and capital [Illus. 27].

On the surface, it seems that Freder has converted his father; in reality, the industrialist has outwitted his son. The concession he makes amounts to a policy of appeasement that not only prevents the workers from winning their cause, but enables him to tighten his grip on them. His robot stratagem was a blunder inasmuch as it rested upon insufficient knowledge of the mentality of the masses. By yielding to Freder, the industrialist achieves intimate contact with the workers, and thus is in a position to influence their mentality. He allows the heart to speak—a heart accessible to his insinuations.

In fact, Maria's demand that the heart mediate between hand

[29] For the mixture of story ingredients in METROPOLIS, see article by Willy Haas on this film (*Kinematograph*, Jan. 11, 1927), quoted by Zaddach, *Der literarische Film*, p. 62.

[30] Cf. p. 32.

and brain could well have been formulated by Goebbels. He, too, appealed to the heart—in the interest of totalitarian propaganda. At the Nuremberg Party Convention of 1934, he praised the "art" of propaganda as follows: "May the shining flame of our enthusiasm never be extinguished. This flame alone gives light and warmth to the creative art of modern political propaganda. Rising from the depths of the people, this art must always descend back to it and find its power there. Power based on guns may be a good thing; it is, however, better and more gratifying to win the heart of a people and to keep it." [31] The pictorial structure of the final scene confirms the analogy between the industrialist and Goebbels. If in this scene the heart really triumphed over tyrannical power, its triumph would dispose of the all-devouring decorative scheme that in the rest of METROPOLIS marks the industrialist's claim to omnipotence. Artist that he was, Lang could not possibly overlook the antagonism between the breakthrough of intrinsic human emotions and his ornamental patterns. Nevertheless, he maintains these patterns up to the very end: the workers advance in the form of a wedge-shaped, strictly symmetrical procession which points towards the industrialist standing on the portal steps of the cathedral. The whole composition denotes that the industrialist acknowledges the heart for the purpose of manipulating it; that he does not give up his power, but will expand it over a realm not yet annexed—the realm of the collective soul. Freder's rebellion results in the establishment of totalitarian authority, and he considers this result a victory.

Freder's pertinent reaction corroborates what has been said about the way in which the street films as well as the youth films anticipate the change of the "system." Now it can no longer be doubted that the "new order" both series foreshadow is expected to feed upon that love with which Asta Nielsen's prostitute overflows, and to substitute totalitarian discipline for the obsolete mechanical one. In the case of METROPOLIS, Goebbels' own words bear out the conclusions drawn from this film. Lang relates that immediately after Hitler's rise to power Goebbels sent for him: ". . . he told me that, many years before, he and the Führer had seen my picture *Metropolis* in a small town, and Hitler had said at that time that he wanted me to make the Nazi pictures." [32]

[31] Cf. p. 299 f.

[32] "Fritz Lang," *New York World Telegram*, June 11, 1941.

14. THE NEW REALISM

DURING the stabilized era, along with those two groups of films which testify to the state of paralysis and shed light on the paralyzed psychological content, appears a third group still more characteristic. The films of this group reveal the workings of the paralyzed collective soul. They elucidate the ways in which the collective soul reacted to the existing situation.

The most important films of this group were animated by the spirit of "New Objectivity" (*Neue Sachlichkeit*) which during the stabilized period manifested itself in the sphere of real life as well as in the sphere of art. This spirit also materialized in other countries, but it was in Germany that "the *neue Sachlichkeit* first became self-conscious, and . . . is strongest relatively and intrinsically." [1] In 1924, Gustav Hartlaub, director of the Mannheim Museum, coined the term "*Neue Sachlichkeit*" to define the new realism in painting. "It was related," he says of this realism, "to the general contemporary feeling in Germany of resignation and cynicism after a period of exuberant hopes (which had found an outlet in expressionism). Cynicism and resignation are the negative side of the *Neue Sachlichkeit;* the positive side expresses itself in the enthusiasm for the immediate reality as a result of the desire to take things entirely objectively on a material basis without immediately investing them with ideal implications." [2] Hartlaub and, somewhat later, Fritz Schmalenbach both emphasize disillusionment as an emotional source of the new current.[3]

In other words, New Objectivity marks a state of paralysis. Cynicism, resignation, disillusionment: these tendencies point to a mentality disinclined to commit itself in any direction. The main

[1] Barr, "Otto Dix," *The Arts*, Jan. 1931, p. 237.

[2] Letter from Hartlaub, quoted by Barr, *ibid.*, p. 236, footnote.

[3] Schmalenbach, "The Term *Neue Sachlichkeit*," *Art Bulletin*, Sept. 1940, pp. 161, 163–64; Hartlaub, "Zur Einführung," *Die neue Sachlichkeit* . . , Sächsischer Kunstverein Dresden, 18 Oct.–22 Nov. 1925, pp. 3–4.

feature of the new realism is its reluctance to ask questions, to take sides. Reality is portrayed not so as to make facts yield their implications, but to drown all implications in an ocean of facts, as in the Ufa *Kulturfilme.* "We have lost the power of faith," August Ruegg confesses in 1926, "and, since the wheels of the world-mechanism seem to continue to move on their own impetus, we accustom ourselves to living on without trust or a feeling of responsibility. . . . One slides along either elegantly or wearily and lets the others slide along in a similar manner." [4] This is the language of a paralyzed mind.

A position of complete disillusionment is extremely difficult to maintain. Hartlaub himself differentiates between two wings of New Objectivity: a romanticizing right wing and a left wing "bearing a socialist flavor." [5] This socialist flavor was found in many paintings, architectural structures, and so forth, which showed themselves infatuated with technological concepts and forms; their whole appearance revealed them to be inspired by a belief in the social mission of modern technology. They breathed, or seemed to breathe, socialist optimism. Meyer Schapiro is doubtless right in identifying this optimism as "the reformist illusion, which was especially widespread in the brief period of post-war prosperity . . . , that the technological advance, in raising the living standards of the people, in lowering the costs of housing and other necessities, would resolve the conflict of classes, or at any rate form in the technicians habits of efficient, economic planning, conducive to a peaceful transition to socialism." [6] The illusion consisted in attributing to technological advance the power of bringing about changes that can be attained only by organized political effort. Technical progress may serve any master. This accounts for the ambiguity inherent in the socialist-flavored products of New Objectivity. The architecture of this style was echoed throughout fascist Italy; in Germany itself it often seemed strangely hollow, thus disavowing its socialist implications.

Since the German screen adopted this equivocal realism, one is safe in assuming that from a psychological point of view the socialist attitudes of the time had by no means the character of primary impulses. They were much weaker than the authoritarian dispositions had ever been; in fact, they could develop only because these

[4] Ruegg, "Vom grossen Unbehagen unserer Zeit," quoted by Samuel and Thomas, *Expressionism in German Life*, p. 174.

[5] Hartlaub, "Zur Einführung," *ibid.*, and letter from Hartlaub, quoted by Barr, "Otto Dix," *The Arts,* Jan. 1931, p. 236, footnote.

[6] Schapiro, "Nature of Abstract Art," *Marxist Quarterly,* Jan.–March 1937, p. 97.

authoritarian dispositions were actually paralyzed. Resting upon frozen ground, they were surface excitements and as such incapable of upsetting the essential indifference of the *Neue Sachlichkeit*. (The "reformist illusion" reflected the state of inner paralysis inasmuch as it completely overlooked the part passions and decisions play in any social evolution.) This psychological situation was of course open to changes. The authoritarian dispositions might awaken from their paralysis and then do away with all liberal and socialist tendencies; or the latter might gain momentum and increasingly absorb those paralyzed dispositions.

The Austrian G. W. Pabst was prominent among the directors cultivating the new realism. He came to the cinema from the theater, which he had left because of his doubts as to its artistic future. He was a late arrival in the studios; it was only at the end of the postwar period that he made his first film, Der Schatz (The Treasure, 1924), a legend of love and greed clumsily unfolding within medieval décors. This dull and impersonal product demonstrated that Pabst felt himself a stranger in a period bent on externalizing inner conflicts and longings without any regard for the given facts. Pabst was a realist. He once said in a conversation: "What need is there for romantic treatment? Real life is too romantic, too ghastly." [7]

Real life was his true concern. He began to penetrate it in Die freudlose Gasse (The Joyless Street, 1925), an adaptation of a novel by Hugo Bettauer which had been serialized in Vienna's leading newspaper, *Neue Freie Presse*. The film, which soon won fame in Germany and abroad, pictured Vienna during the inflation, with special emphasis on the pauperization of the middle class. Pabst's unhesitating realism in rendering this decline shocked his contemporaries. England prohibited public showings of the film. The versions released in Italy, France, Austria, and elsewhere were considerably mutilated.[8]

The Joyless Street contrasts tough profiteers and destitute middle-class people; expensive restaurants sparkling with light and dim-lit homes visited by hunger; noisy effervescence and silent withdrawal into sadness. Surrounded by sadness, the elderly councillor Rumfort sees his savings vanish and finally faces starvation. He would be lost if it were not for his daughter—Garbo in her first important role—who succeeds in getting a dubious job as a night-

[7] Quoted from Bryher, "G. W. Pabst. A Survey," *Close Up*, Dec. 1927, p. 60.
[8] Cf. Rotha, *Film Till Now*, p. 37.

club dancer. The ruin of this bourgeois family is portrayed with a social consciousness that transforms it into a typical case. One series of episodes shows the profiteers and their parasites trading stocks, making love to spectacular women and snatching all the joys that money can buy. Another series details the lot of those on the losing side. In their fight for survival a few of them are tragically hampered by inherited decency. Rumfort suffers for the stubbornness with which he shrinks from the slightest concession. Asta Nielsen as the kept woman demonstrates that uncompromising love is likely to perish in a society in which marketable goods supplant the essentials.[9] However, she is an outsider, emotionally and socially. Most middle-class characters proper try to compromise, or simply yield to the powers of corruption. Pabst's film of the inflation elaborates upon the interrelationship between the enforced economic decay of the middle class and the selling-out of its moral values. What he exhibits—for the first time from the angle of a realistic observer—is the feverish finale of that postwar world which, while it still existed, expressed its inmost preoccupations through screen fantasies wavering between the images of tyranny and chaos.

The ghastliness of this world is displayed in scenes that seem to record unstaged events. Everyday life of the time unveils itself in the episode of the "joyless street": a crowd on the verge of despair queues up before the butcher's shop, and, accompanied by his grim white dog, Werner Krauss as the brutal butcher walks off to fetch a policeman [Illus. 31]. In this effective scene nothing is stylized; rather, it springs from the desire to watch the course events take of their own accord. Pabst "let his characters unfold their plight without the inquisitional rack." [10] A convincing proof of his innate realism is the short scene in which Garbo hangs the new fur coat given her in some questionable shop close to her threadbare old coat. For a moment the two coats are seen hanging side by side. In any of Carl Mayer's postwar films, this shot would have had to symbolize the change of Garbo's condition; in the Pabst film, it just shows the two coats in a chance combination which may, or may not, convey a symbolic meaning [Illus. 32]. Instead of arranging significant pictorial compositions, Pabst arranges real-life material with veracity as his sole object. His is the spirit of a photographer. What Iris

[9] Cf. p. 157. For the film in general, see also Rotha, *Film Till Now,* esp. p. 185; *Film Society Programme,* Jan. 16, 1927.

[10] Potamkin, "Pabst and the Social Film," *Hound & Horn,* Jan.–March 1933, p. 294.

Barry says about his LOVE OF JEANNE NEY also applies to THE JOYLESS STREET: "Pabst's work here is in no sense picturesque, it is photographic. His settings and his individual scenes are quite as carefully composed as those of the more obviously artistic German films, but the craftsmanship is less apparent, the spectator is led to feel 'how true' rather than 'how beautiful.' "[11] Compared to the open universe into which THE JOYLESS STREET embarks, the world of VARIETY is rather an indoor affair.

It was a strange coincidence that, shortly before the Pabst film, an American film about the German inflation appeared: D. W. Griffith's ISN'T LIFE WONDERFUL? Griffith, the great pioneer of the cinema, had been eager for genuine local color; he had shot the exteriors in Germany, and entrusted several native actors with important roles. His plot differed from Pabst's in that it featured, instead of a German middle-class family, a group of Polish refugees, the Poles being more popular with the American public than the Germans. Nevertheless, the two films had traits in common. Particularly striking was the similarity in their treatment of everyday life under the inflation: like THE JOYLESS STREET, the American film focused upon a queue of despondent people besieging a butcher's shop. Pabst may well have been influenced by the emphasis Griffith put on this sequence, and also by the realism with which he handled the backgrounds and all the fleeting moments of life. Griffith's realism was as naïve as the message it served to impart. The pacifist credo inherent in his film manifested itself plainly through the reasoning of one of the leading characters—a German worker grieved over his wife's suffering under the famine. This worker, having knocked down a man to rob him of his potatoes, emphatically harangues the audience: "Yes, beasts we are; beasts they have made us. Years of war—beasts they have made us." In addition, Griffith preached "the triumph of love over hardship," answering the question "Isn't life wonderful?" in the affirmative. The young Polish couple whom he makes the standard-bearers of his invincible optimism pass through the horrors of the German postwar world without being seriously afflicted, and at the end find happiness in a tiny wooden cottage.[12]

While Griffith in his ill-founded reformist zeal does not confine

[11] Barry, *Program Notes*, Series III, program 8.

[12] Cf. Jacobs, *American Film*, p. 393; "Isn't Life Wonderful?" *Exceptional Photoplays*, Dec.–Jan. 1925, p. 5.

himself to presenting life as it is, Pabst seems to have no other ambition. With a profound sense of fact he exhibits the predicament of the middle class and the moral confusion of the time. But although his pictorial statements never go so far as to suggest a line of conduct, a solution after the manner of Griffith, they undeniably point to the relation between individual suffering and social injustice. At any rate, this was the impression they made upon many intellectuals; to them, Pabst's realism appeared a moral protest, if not a socialist manifestation.

On the other hand, THE JOYLESS STREET inclines toward melodrama.[13] Theoretically, Pabst could have yielded to this tendency for the purpose of making his realism acceptable. But his marked interest in melodramatic motifs indicates that their insertion is not due merely to such practical considerations. The longish episode featuring Asta Nielsen disavows his realistic designs and radiates his infatuation with this improbable figure. As Stroheim's famous GREED (1924) proves, melodrama need not drain realism of its inner weight. But in THE JOYLESS STREET it tends to do precisely this. At the very moment when, according to Pabst's own premises, Rumfort and his daughter are bound to become full-fledged victims of the inflation, a beautiful lieutenant of the American Red Cross emerges as *deus ex machina*, and instantly makes these two people happy. Pabst is sufficiently courageous to detail the ghastliness of social misery, but he does not mind cutting short the conclusions that might be drawn from his report. His weakness for melodrama counterbalances those implications of his realism which a generation not yet accustomed to the free display of camera reality too readily took for granted.

After an unimportant film, MAN SPIELT NICHT MIT DER LIEBE (DON'T PLAY WITH LOVE, 1926), Pabst staged GEHEIMNISSE EINER SEELE (SECRETS OF A SOUL, 1926)—a neat account of a psychoanalytical case drawn up with the assistance of two collaborators of Freud, Dr. Hanns Sachs and the late Dr. Karl Abraham. A professor of chemistry (Werner Krauss) learns that his wife's cousin, a handsome fellow, has announced his return from India. The three were playmates in their childhood. Under the impact of this news and certain other occurrences, the professor is anguished by a dream

[13] Potamkin, "Pabst and the Social Film," *Hound & Horn*, Jan.–March 1933, p. 294; Rotha, *Film Till Now*, p. 187.

in which reminiscences involving the cousin mingle with confused scenes denoting his longing for a child. The dream culminates in his attempt to stab his wife with a dagger. Next day, he is possessed by an inexplicable fear of touching knives, and this phobia makes him act in such a strange manner that his wife and the cousin are deeply disquieted. His own despair reaches its climax when, alone with his wife, he can hardly resist the compulsion to commit the murder anticipated in his dream. He flees from his home to his mother's place, and then consults a psychoanalyst who asks him to stay with his mother for the duration of the treatment.

Now the film summarizes a series of sessions dominated by the professor's narrative: Fragments of his dream alternate with various recollections, and from time to time the psychoanalyst is seen listening to the narrator or contributing explanations. Under his guidance, the elements of the jigsaw puzzle gradually arrange themselves into a comprehensible whole. In his childhood days the professor was jealous of his future wife's outspoken interest in her cousin; his jealousy engendered strong feelings of inferiority which after his marriage made him fall prey to a sort of psychological impotence; and the impotence on its part produced a guilty conscience that some day or other was bound to manifest itself in an irresponsible action. The treatment ends with the salutary shock he experiences in recognizing the subconscious forces that have held his mind in their grip. Freed from his inhibitions, a happy man, he returns home.[14]

The similarities between this film and Robison's WARNING SHADOWS, of 1922, are conspicuous.[15] Both are concerned with a mentally unbalanced character cured by means of psychoanalytical, or quasi-psychoanalytical, methods; both emphasize the fact that, prior to his recovery, this character acts in an immature way. Like the exuberant count in WARNING SHADOWS, Pabst's sober professor performs the gesture through which most males of the German screen express their immaturity: no sooner does he awaken from his nightmarish dream than he puts his head into his wife's protective lap. Another scene illustrates his retrogressive conduct even more strikingly. Having cut his meat into small pieces, his mother watches him ladle it with the spoon she has substituted for the dreadful knife—

[14] Cf. Rotha, *ibid.*, p. 186; Kalbus, *Deutsche Filmkunst*, I, 95–96; etc.

[15] See pp. 113 f.—Films in a similar vein were Grune's JEALOUSY (cf. p. 156) and the Ufa film LIEBESFEUER, both of 1925.

watches him as tenderly as if he were still her helpless little child. Yet what makes SECRETS OF A SOUL essentially different from WARNING SHADOWS is its unconcern for the significance of this retrogression. While Robison's expressive screen fantasy quivers with an excitement indicating the vital importance of the issues involved, Pabst's film maintains the coolness of an expert report on some psychoanalytical case. SECRETS OF A SOUL has rightly been called a "clever blend of a film of fiction and a documentary film." [16] In his zeal for documentary objectivity, Pabst adheres anxiously to matter-of-fact statements: no shot assumes a symbolic function, no passage implies that the professor's frustration may well mirror that of a multitude of Germans.

Two circumstances confirm the suspicion that this film which demonstrates how an individual can be relieved of his complexes is itself the product of a state of paralysis. First, at the film's very end the scene shifts to a mountain landscape, with the professor holding a brand-new baby in his arms. It is an epilogue which drags the whole plot into the sphere of melodrama, thus definitely nullifying its broader implications. Second, technical skill grows rampant. Pabst seems to have been interested not so much in his theme proper as in the opportunity it offers for testing certain cinematic devices—in particular those fit to externalize psychological processes [Illus. 33]. As a piece of artistry his film is remarkable. When, for instance, the professor in the course of his treatment remembers bits of his previous dream, these are no longer shown within their original surroundings, but are set against a white background so as to characterize them as stray recollections.[17] No doubt, Pabst is a consummate psychologist; however, his psychological finesse is grafted upon indifference to the primary events of inner life. Potamkin in his comment on SECRETS OF A SOUL is justified in saying of its director: "Psychologism became his preoccupation." [18]

Pabst's subsequent film was DIE LIEBE DER JEANNE NEY (THE LOVE OF JEANNE NEY, 1927), an Ufa production in which he turned from the secrets of the individual soul to those of a world in turmoil. He now resumed on a larger scale what he had begun in THE JOYLESS

[16] Quoted from Kalbus, *Deutsche Filmkunst*, I, 96.

[17] Cf. Rotha, *Film Till Now*, p. 186.

[18] Potamkin, "Pabst and the Social Film," *Hound & Horn*, Jan.–March 1933, p. 295.

STREET. This time, the plot, instead of involving a single European capital, encompassed virtually the whole of European postwar society, including Soviet Russia. That Ufa should acknowledge the existence of Bolsheviks and even treat them as human beings was not a miracle. Ufa simply thought it good business to capitalize on the Russian fashion inaugurated by Eisenstein's POTEMKIN and Pudovkin's MOTHER—films that had been the rage all over Germany. Naturally, many Germans praised them not so much for their revolutionary content as for their artistic novelty and national vigor.[19]

THE LOVE OF JEANNE NEY was based upon Ilya Ehrenburg's novel of the same title. At that time, Ehrenburg had not yet gained official prestige. A unique combination of Soviet journalist and European bohemian, he wrote books that fused brilliant, if superficial, satire with sentimental romance. His headquarters were in Paris, and he seemed emotionally attached to that Western civilization which he nevertheless accused of being utterly morbid. Ufa probably took to his novel because of its colorful plot and its tinge of melodrama. It is concerned with the love between Jeanne Ney, a French bourgeois girl, and the young Russian communist Andreas—a love that asserts itself in the Crimea during the civil war, and then develops into a great passion in Paris, the center of declining democracy. But wherever the two lovers meet, an unscrupulous adventurer, Khalibiev, intervenes and like a demon thwarts their fragile hopes. Khalibiev is a true incarnation of those evil forces which have their heyday in a period of transition, when all values are confused. Such a period is favorable both to horrible crimes and to heroic sacrifices. This may have encouraged Ehrenburg to indulge in black-and-white contrasts. In the Crimea, Andreas kills Jeanne's father for political reasons, but she immediately forgives him. In Paris, Jeanne finds employment in the detective agency of her uncle, a stingy bourgeois, whose blind daughter has all the traits of an angel devised by Victor Hugo or a naïve author in some pulp magazine. The relentless Khalibiev proposes to her, and simultaneously tries to lay hands on Jeanne—a Jeanne glowing with joy over her rendezvous with Andreas. Ehrenburg has contrived to make the communist party send Andreas on a mission to Paris. Now

[19] The Berlin première of POTEMKIN was on April 29, 1926. The film was selected as the best film of 1926 in Germany; see Weinberg, *Scrapbooks*, 1925–27. Grune praised POTEMKIN for being a truly national film; cf. Grune, "Was Karl Grune . . ," *Film-Photos*, p. 15.

the ultimate catastrophe sets in, with Khalibiev as its perpetrator. He breaks into the detective agency to steal a precious diamond; and when confronted by Jeanne's uncle, he murders him, and succeeds in turning all suspicions against her lover. Andreas is done for, and Jeanne is lost.

Of course, Ufa radically removed the moral and political poison this story contained.[20] In the film, Jeanne is spared the disgrace of loving the murderer of her father; it is Andreas' companion who kills him. In her attempt to rescue Andreas the Jeanne of the novel becomes Khalibiev's mistress; the screen Jeanne manages at the very last moment to shun his odious embraces. The scrupulous Ufa version does not allow her to sleep with Andreas in the cheap hotel room they share for a night, but forces the lovers to spend the night on separate chairs. This shameless bowdlerizing goes hand in hand with irresponsible optimism. Ehrenburg's terrible finale is superseded by a happy ending which assumes much the same structural function as the endings of the previous Pabst films. To make Andreas, the communist, acceptable, Ufa arbitrarily portrays him as a potential convert; upon Jeanne's suggestion he follows her into a Paris church where he kneels beside her before the altar. On the other hand, the film unhesitatingly goes beyond the novel in detailing communist agitation in France. The clandestine Paris press which prints subversive leaflets is a pure Ufa invention. Ufa may have taken pleasure in elaborating upon the embarrassments of a democracy.

Pabst was told to stage his picture "in the American style." [21] He tried to do so in the scenes that show Jeanne's uncle and his detectives recovering a diamond lost by an American millionaire—the very diamond which is to arouse Khalibiev's murderous instincts. However, these scenes with their insistence upon comic "gags" are nothing more than clever imitations and as such inferior to the rest of the film. In a remark to an interviewer, Pabst himself indicated the impossibility of Americanizing German pictures, "for the whole of our mentality is different. . . ." [22] While he felt uneasy about concessions to Hollywood, he readily yielded to the spirit of the Russian films. His scenes of the civil war are strongly influenced by Eisenstein and Pudovkin; he even repeats that typically Russian

[20] See Ehrenburg, "Protest gegen die Ufa," *Frankfurter Zeitung*, Feb. 29, 1928.
[21] Cf. p. 135.—Rotha, *Film Till Now*, p. 186.
[22] MacPherson, "Die Liebe der Jeanne Ney," *Close Up*, Dec. 1927, p. 18; Pabst, "Servitude et Grandeur d'Hollywood," *Le Rôle intellectuel du Cinéma*, pp. 251–55.

shot of a character taken from below eye-level so as to symbolize his arrogance or his lust for power.

Yet all this does not invalidate the originality of Pabst's achievement. His LOVE OF JEANNE NEY exceeds his JOYLESS STREET not only in scope of vision, but in the determination with which it records reality. In rendering it, Pabst proves as inventive as insatiable. The sequence of the Crimean civil war includes an orgy of anti-Bolshevist soldiery. "For this scene," Kenneth MacPherson reports in *Close Up*, "one hundred and twenty Russian officers . . . came in their own uniforms, working for twelve marks a day. Pabst supplied vodka and women, waited, and then calmly photographed" [23] [Illus. 34]. Similarly, Jeanne and Andreas are seen traversing a real Paris square—two passers-by lost in a chance crowd. Whenever Pabst cannot resort to quasi-documentary shots—but he relies on them as much as possible—he stages his scenes in such a manner that they nevertheless give the impression of being elicited from life itself. As in THE JOYLESS STREET, bits of reality seem to be picked up at random even in cases in which they serve to symbolize inner events. It appears a mere coincidence that, when in the Crimea Jeanne takes leave of Andreas, rain pours down and a throng of poor people separates the two lovers.

Pabst urged his cameraman, Fritz Arno Wagner, to stick to natural light values and make the camera rove about. "At Pabst's will," Paul Rotha comments on THE LOVE OF JEANNE NEY," Wagner's camera nosed into the corners and ran with the players. . . . Every curve, every angle, every approach of the lens was controlled by the material that it photographed for the expression of mood." [24] Rotha's remarks imply that in this film the traditional camera mobility of the German postwar screen changes its function. Carl Mayer unchained the camera to picture an imaginary universe swept by instincts, and even though E. A. Dupont in his VARIETY adopted the ubiquitous camera with a realistic design, he set up a world that was a stylized image of reality rather than its objective reflection. Unlike his predecessors, Pabst mobilizes the camera to photograph the casual configurations of real life. THE LOVE OF JEANNE NEY opens with a scene characterizing the scoundrel Khalibiev: from the tips of his shoes the camera glides along his legs to scattered newspapers, records cigarette stubs on the table, follows

[23] MacPherson, "Die Liebe der Jeanne Ney," *Close Up*, Dec. 1927, p. 21.
[24] Rotha, *Film Till Now*, p. 188.

his hand as it selects one stub, scrutinizes his face, and finally encompasses part of the dirty hotel room with Khalibiev lying on the sofa [Illus. 36].

A personal editing style supplements the camera movement. Pabst arranges the manifold shots in such a way that their very order reinforces the realistic illusion. Characteristically, even the smallest scene consists of a number of shots. Iris Barry remarks of that scene in which Khalibiev sells the list of Bolshevist agents to Jeanne's father: "It lasts about three minutes. . . . Though one is scarcely aware of a single shot, there are forty in this short scene—needless to say, the director cut and edited the film himself." [25] In combining these atomlike picture frames, Pabst goes the limit. Was he influenced by the emphasis Eisenstein and Pudovkin put on "montage"? The cuts in such screen epics as POTEMKIN and MOTHER have throughout the character of shocks calculated to transform the narrative into a dialectic process which ends with the triumph of the proletariat. But nothing of that kind holds true of THE LOVE OF JEANNE NEY; this film is far from spreading the Marxist doctrine, and moreover conceals rather than stresses its cuts. Nor was Pabst's editing technique the organic outcome of German screen traditions. Much as they cultivated the moving camera, Carl Mayer and Dupont were not yet in a position to realize all the effects that can be produced through cutting devices. For good reasons: they did not have to depend on such devices to render the self-sufficient world of their imagination. Pabst departs from them technically, because he ventures into the indefinite world of facts. His insistence upon cutting results from his keen concern with given reality. He utilizes tiny pictorial particles to capture the slightest impressions, and he fuses these particles into a finespun texture to mirror reality as a continuity.

This reality is postwar Europe in full disintegration. Its ghastliness unfolds in scenes which are unique not so much for their unhesitating frankness as for their insight into the symptoms of social morbidity. Such a symptom is, for instance, the mixture of cruelty and obscenity in Khalibiev. Surveying various strata of the population, the film sometimes assumes the character of a report on the diseases of European society. It is an infallible sign of Pabst's connoisseurship that this report time and again refers to the testimony of inanimate objects. He assigns to them about the same role as did

[25] Barry, *Program Notes*, Series III, program 3.

Carl Mayer in his instinct films, but while Mayer emphasized them as the landmarks of that mute region inhabited by his instinct-possessed characters, Pabst features objects because they help make up the kind of reality he wants to explore. In a decaying or transitional world, whose elements fall asunder, the objects rush out of their hiding-places and take on a life of their own. Behind Jeanne, who is detained by the victorious Bolsheviks, a broken mirror emerges and like a witness tells of glamour and destruction [Illus. 35]. The iron washbasin in the room that shelters Jeanne and Andreas for a few nocturnal hours testifies to the *tristesse* emanating from this background for futile sex adventures. Through their mere existence the objects corroborate what can be inferred from the events: that the world presented is a jungle peopled with beasts of prey. The film is a tacit accusation. It implies that all human values are doomed unless we change society radically.

But, as in THE JOYLESS STREET, Pabst permanently discredits his daring attitude. The imaginative way he satisfies Ufa's craving for melodrama confirms the strength of his own tendencies in this direction. He continues the tradition of the noble-minded prostitutes by making a Paris night-club girl bend her knees before the noble-minded blind angel; he dramatizes the first Paris meeting between Andreas and Jeanne by means of an extended traveling shot which transforms the lovers into a sort of Tristan and Isolde, and in other scenes pictures them as a pair of innocent children whom a malicious fairy wants to destroy. These evasive interludes neutralize the accusation inherent in his realism. Pabst, the neutral observer, obstructs Pabst, the moralist. It is noteworthy that his LOVE OF JEANNE NEY abounds in precise statements on ephemeral facts. If it holds true that only the mind's unconcern for definite meanings enables the innumerable phenomena of which reality consists to come to the fore, Pabst is an incomparable observer of these phenomena because he tends to shun essential questions. The veracity of his pictures—veracity should not be mistaken for truth—rests upon his neutrality.

This unwillingness to follow up vital issues also manifests itself through another quality of Pabst's cutting procedures: the accelerated succession of his picture elements. Whereas the Ukrainian film director Dovzhenko occasionally converts an important shot into a still so as to impress its meaning upon the mind, Pabst never allows the audience to watch any single phenomenon closely. "Every cut," he himself states, "is made on some movement. At the end of one cut somebody is moving, at the beginning of the adjoining one the movement is continued. The eye is thus so occupied in following these movements that it misses the cuts." [26] His interest in reality as a steady flow is symptomatic of his desire to withdraw from his advanced position.

In the last three films he made during the stabilized period, Pabst returned from the social scene to the "secrets of a soul." Thus he would no longer have to meddle in politics. This change of theme was a retreat; but it may also have been motivated by Pabst's genuine interest in psychology. All three films deal with the interrelationship between social and psychological processes—to be more precise, between social disintegration and sexual excesses. In ABWEGE (CRISIS, 1928), Brigitte Helm enacts a wealthy middle-class woman bored by everyday life with her husband. She establishes headquarters in a fashionable night-club and there joins a clique of people who like herself try to drown their disillusionment in debaucheries. The film would be negligible if it were not for the night-club scenes in which Pabst manages to evoke the impression that his characters are as they are because of the emptiness of the world they inhabit.[27] There is also the unforgettable figure of a big doll representing an ugly, worn-out roué. When early in the morning the clique invades Helm's bedroom to continue the nocturnal orgy in her company, the roué is seen lying on the floor, watching the exchange of stale caresses with the air of a cynical connoisseur. This doll incarnates the spirit of decomposition.

Pabst's subsequent film was DIE BÜCHSE DER PANDORA (PANDORA'S BOX, 1929), fashioned after Frank Wedekind's play about Lulu, a woman driven by insatiable sex lusts, who destroys all lives around her, and her own. In the pursuit of his basic designs, Pabst could not but feel attracted by the way in which Wedekind related the exuberance of instinctive life to the deterioration of our society. Contemporaries considered PANDORA'S BOX a failure. A failure it was, but not for the reason most critics advanced. They held that Pabst was fundamentally wrong in making a silent film from a liter-

[26] Quoted from MacPherson, "Die Liebe der Jeanne Ney," *Close Up*, Dec. 1927, p. 26.—For camera techniques in this Pabst film, see Balázs, *Der Geist des Films*, pp. 70, 73.

[27] Cf. Rotha, *Film Till Now*, pp. 188–89, 295; "Abwege (Crisis)," *Close Up*, Sept. 1928, pp. 72–75; Potamkin, "Pabst and the Social Film," *Hound & Horn*, Jan.–March 1933, p. 295.

ary play whose meaning depended mainly upon the fine points of its dialogue. However, the film's weakness resulted not so much from the impossibility of translating this dialogue into cinematic terms as from the abstract nature of the whole Wedekind play. It was a texture of arguments; its characters, instead of living on their own, served to illustrate principles. Pabst blundered in choosing a play that because of its expressive mood belonged to the fantastic postwar era rather than to the realistic stabilized period. The outcome of his misplaced endeavors was a film which, as Potamkin puts it, "is 'atmosphere' without content."[28]

Having founded his own film company—it turned out to be a very short-lived enterprise—Pabst produced TAGEBUCH EINER VERLORENEN (DIARY OF A LOST ONE, 1929), an adaptation of Margarete Böhme's well-known novel, the popularity of which among the philistines of the past generation rested upon the slightly pornographic frankness with which it recounted the private life of some prostitutes from a morally elevated point of view. The film transfers the Wedekind theme from the literary sphere to commonplace surroundings more in harmony with Pabst's realistic manner: the Lulu of PANDORA'S BOX becomes Thymian, a weak-minded pharmacist's easy-going daughter. Seduced by her father's assistant, a villain whom Fritz Rasp endows with all the traits of his Khalibiev, Thymian embarks upon a career which leads her straight into a brothel. Pabst harps on the immorality of her middle-class environment, so that the brothel almost appears to be a health resort. This twist, after the fashion of *Mrs. Warren's Profession*, makes the film resemble the street films—a resemblance increased by the emphasis on Thymian's melodramatic generosity. Here, as in the street films, the prostitute with the heart of gold testifies against bourgeois decadence. But to what end? Seemingly unconcerned about the possible implications of his criticism, Pabst elaborates upon the decadence itself. That he is well aware of its affinity to sadism follows from the extraordinary episode of the reformatory to which Thymian is sent. In this episode, a sadistic governess gets a thrill from striking out the rhythm in which the girls have to eat their soup or move about.[29]

[28] Potamkin, *ibid.*, p. 297. See also Kraszna-Krausz, "G. W. Pabst's 'Lulu,'" *Close Up*, April 1929, pp. 26–29; Rotha, *Film Till Now*, pp. 189–91; synopsis of the film in *Illustrierter Film-Kurier*.

[29] Arnheim, *Film als Kunst*, p. 103. See also Arnheim, *ibid.*, p. 73; Chavance, "Trois Pages d'un Journal," *La Revue du Cinéma*, June 1, 1930, pp. 53–54; synopsis of the film in *Illustrierter Film-Kurier*.

But Pabst, not content with merely describing her symbolic action, also indicates the particular kind of pleasure she derives from it. While upon her order the scantily clad girls perform exercises, this terrible female marks the tempo and simultaneously swings her head, until her whole body is involved in an oscillating movement that grows ever faster and then suddenly comes to a stop. Her conduct recalls that of the Tsarist officer in THE END OF ST. PETERSBURG who voluptuously watches his underling beat a captured revolutionary. Like Pudovkin, Pabst acknowledges the role sex plays within definite social contexts.

15. MONTAGE

IN the grip of the existing paralysis, the German film-makers cultivated a species of films presenting a cross section of some sphere of reality. These films were even more characteristic of the stabilized period than the Pabst films, for their neutrality was the logical result of the cross-section principle itself. They would have upset their own rules if they had sided with any of the pros and cons they surveyed. They were the purest expression of New Objectivity on the screen. Their such-is-life mood overwhelmed whatever socialist sentiments played about in them.

The first German film of that kind was DIE ABENTEUER EINES ZEHNMARKSCHEINS (THE ADVENTURES OF A TEN-MARK NOTE, 1926), produced by Karl Freund for Fox Europe. Béla Balázs wrote the original script; he himself called the film a "cross section." [1] This picture of Berlin during the inflation consists of a number of episodes which record the capricious travels of a ten-mark note continually changing hands. Guided by it, the film meanders through the maze of those years, picking up otherwise unrelated characters, and glancing over such locales as a factory, a night café, a pawnshop, the music room of a profiteer, an employment agency, a ragpicker's den and a hospital. According to Balázs, it is as if the plot "followed a thread that, connecting the dramatic junctions of the ways of Fate, leads across the texture of life." [2]

However, Balázs was not yet sufficiently bold, or indifferent, to substantiate his idea to the full. The documentary character of the cross-section pattern is blurred by its combination with a sentimental Berlin local drama concerning a worker and a factory girl. Like the Polish lovers in Griffith's ISN'T LIFE WONDERFUL?, these two finally achieve one of those wooden cabins that spread all over the outskirts of Berlin, and, to complete their happiness, the ten-mark note re-

[1] Balázs, "Der Film sucht seinen Stoff," *Die Abenteuer eines Zehnmarkscheins,* and Balázs, *Der Geist des Films,* p. 86.

[2] Balázs, "Der Film sucht seinen Stoff," *Die Abenteuer eines Zehnmarkscheins.*

turns to them. Its vagabondage not only serves to familiarize the audience with the infinite "texture of life," but also assumes the function of rounding out the local drama. That is, the succession of episodes results from two divergent tendencies, only one of which conforms to the cross-section principle, while the other obstructs it. This ambiguity of meaning explains why the allegedly purposeless adventures of the ten-mark note often give the impression of being concocted artificially. As if to reinforce the cross-section tendency, Berthold Viertel's staging imbues street life with especial significance. "There is a fascinating shot of the villain sitting in the window of a café. Trams, buses and passers-by are reflected in the plate-glass. The city is intent on doing something." [3] The thread intersecting various regions of social life is bound to lead through the street.

Street scenes predominate in the prototype of all true German cross-section films: BERLIN, DIE SYMPHONIE EINER GROSSSTADT (BERLIN, THE SYMPHONY OF A GREAT CITY, 1927). This most important film, a quota production of Fox Europe, was devised by Carl Mayer. About the time he stigmatized hypocrisy in his TARTUFFE, Mayer recognized that the moment had come for him to turn from the externalization of inner processes to the rendering of externals, from freely constructed plots to plots discovered in the given material. Paul Rotha, a close friend of Mayer until the latter's death, reports on this symptomatic change of attitude: "Mayer was tiring of the restriction and artificiality of the studios. All these films had been wholly studio-made. Mayer lost interest in 'fictional invention' and wanted his stories to 'grow from reality.' In 1925, standing amid the whirling traffic of the Ufa Palast am Zoo, he conceived the idea of a City Symphony. He saw 'a melody of pictures' and began to write the treatment of *Berlin*." [4] It does not lessen Mayer's profound originality that under the influence of the spirit of Locarno this idea asserted itself in France as well. Cavalcanti's documentary film of Paris, RIEN QUE LES HEURES, was released a few months before BERLIN.[5]

Like Mayer, the cameraman Karl Freund was tired of the studio

[3] Quoted from Blakeston, "The Adventures of a Ten-Mark Note," *Close Up*, Nov. 1928, pp. 59–60.

[4] Rotha, "It's in the Script," *World Film News*, Sept. 1938, p. 205.

[5] Cf. Rotha, *Documentary Film*, pp. 87–88; *Film Society Programme*, March 4, 1928.

and its artifices, so he enthusiastically espoused Mayer's project and set out to shoot Berlin scenes with the voracious appetite of a man starved for reality. "I wanted to show everything," he himself relates in a revealing interview in 1939. "Men getting up to go to work, eating breakfast, boarding trams or walking. My characters were drawn from all the walks of life. From the lowest laborer to the bank president." [6] Freund knew that to such ends he would have to rely on candid-camera work. Craftsman that he was, he hypersensitized the stock film which was then on the market, so as to cope with poor lighting conditions, and moreover invented several contrivances to hide the camera while shooting.[7] He would drive in a half-enclosed truck with slots in the sides for the lens or he would walk about with the camera in a box that looked like an innocent suitcase. No one ever suspected that he was taking pictures. Asked at the end of the above-mentioned interview whether he considered candid photography an art, Freund answered, glowing with zeal: "It is the only type of photography that is really art. Why? Because with it one is able to portray *life*. These big negatives, now, where people smirk and grimace and pose. . . . Bah! That's not photography. But a very fast lens. Shooting life. Realism. Ah, that is photography in its purest form. . . ." [8]

Walter Ruttmann, who up to then had excelled in abstract films, edited the immense amount of material assembled by Freund and several other photographers. His sense of optical music made Ruttmann seem the right man to produce "a melody of pictures." He worked in close collaboration with the young composer Edmund Meisel, known for his interesting score for POTEMKIN. Meisel dreamed of synchronizing Ruttmann's visual symphony with a symphonic composition which might even be performed independently of the film. The role he reserved for the music was bound to strengthen the formal tendency of the editing.[9]

Ruttmann's BERLIN is a cross section of a Berlin working day in late spring. Its opening sequence pictures the city at dawn: a night express arrives, and streets still void of human life seem the

[6] Evans, "Karl Freund, Candid Cinematographer," *Popular Photography*, Feb. 1939, p. 51.

[7] Evans, *ibid.*, pp. 51, 88–89; Blakeston, "Interview with Carl Freund," *Close Up*, Jan. 1929, pp. 60–61.

[8] Evans, *ibid.*, p. 89.

[9] *Film Society Programme*, March 4, 1928; Meisel, "Wie schreibt man Filmmusik," *Ufa-Magazin*, April 1–7, 1927. For Ruttmann's other films during that period, see *Film Society Programme*, May 8, 1927.

very counterpart of that limbo which the mind traverses between sleep and consciousness. Then the city awakens and stirs. Scores of workers set out for their factories; wheels begin to turn; telephone receivers are lifted off. The passage devoted to the morning hours is filled with glimpses of window-dressings and typical street incidents. Noon: the poor, the wealthy and the animals in the zoo are seen eating their lunch and enjoying a short respite. Work is resumed, and a bright afternoon sun shines over crowded café terraces, newspaper vendors, a woman drowning herself. Life resembles a roller coaster. As the day fades, the machine wheels stop, and the business of relaxation begins. A kaleidoscopic arrangement of shots surveys all kinds of sports, a fashion show, and a few instances of boys meeting girls or trying to meet them. The last sequence amounts to a pleasure drive through nocturnal Berlin, luminous with ruthless neon lights. An orchestra plays Beethoven; the legs of girl dancers perform; Chaplin's legs stumble across a screen; two lovers, or rather two pairs of legs, make for the nearest hotel; and finally a true pandemonium of legs breaks loose: the six-day race going on and on without interruption.

"The film as Ruttmann made it," Rotha reports, "was far from Mayer's conception. Its surface approach was what Mayer had tried to avoid. He and Ruttmann agreed to differ." [10] This accounts for Mayer's early withdrawal from the production of BERLIN. (His next enterprise—years before the appearance of river films in America and France—was a script narrating the story of the Danube. But this script was never produced.)

When Mayer criticized BERLIN for its "surface approach," he may well have had in mind Ruttmann's method of editing. This method is tantamount to a "surface approach," inasmuch as it relies on the formal qualities of the objects rather than on their meanings. Ruttmann emphasizes pure patterns of movement.[11] Machine parts in motion are shot and cut in such a manner that they turn into dynamic displays of an almost abstract character. These may symbolize what has been called the "tempo" of Berlin; but they are no longer related to machines and their functions. The editing also resorts to striking analogies between movements or forms.[12] Human legs walking on the pavement are followed by the legs of cows; a

[10] Rotha, "It's in the Script," *World Film News*, Sept. 1938, p. 205.

[11] Cf. *Film Society Programme*, Jan. 13, 1929.

[12] Balázs, *Der Geist des Films*, p. 59. For other devices in BERLIN, see Arnheim, *Film als Kunst*, p. 93, and Rotha, *Film Till Now*, p. 295.

sleeping man on a bench is associated with a sleeping elephant [Illus. 37]. In those cases in which Ruttmann furthers the pictorial development through specific content, he inclines to feature social contrasts. One picture unit connects a cavalcade in the Tiergarten with a group of women beating carpets; another juxtaposes hungry children in the street and opulent dishes in some restaurant. Yet these contrasts are not so much social protests as formal expedients. Like visual analogies, they serve to build up the cross section, and their structural function overshadows whatever significance they may convey.

In his use of "montage," Ruttmann seems to have been influenced by the Russians—to be more precise, by the Russian film director Dziga Vertov and his "Kino-eye" group.[13] Vertov, infatuated with every expression of real life, produced weekly newsreels of a special kind from the close of the Civil War on, and in about 1926 began to make feature-length films which still preserved a definite newsreel character. His intentions and Ruttmann's are much the same. Like Ruttmann, Vertov deems it essential to surprise life with the movie camera—the "Kino-eye." Like Ruttmann, he cuts his candid shots on the rhythmic movements inherent in them. Like Ruttmann, he is interested not in divulging news items, but in composing "optical music." His MAN WITH THE MOVIE CAMERA (1929) can be considered a lyric documentary.[14]

Notwithstanding such an identity of artistic intentions, Ruttmann's BERLIN carries a meaning that differs basically from the message Vertov's productions impart. This difference originates in a difference of given conditions: the two artists apply similar aesthetic principles to the rendering of dissimilar worlds. Vertov endeavors to live up to Lenin's early demand that "the production of new films, permeated with communist ideas, reflecting Soviet actuality, must begin with newsreels." [15] He is the son of a victorious revolution, and the life his camera surprises is Soviet life—a reality quivering with revolutionary energies that penetrate its every element. This reality has a significant shape of its own. Ruttmann, on

[13] Rotha, *Documentary Film,* p. 89; Potamkin, "The Rise and Fall of the German Film," *Cinema,* April 1930, p. 25.

[14] Vertov, "Dziga Vertov on Film Technique," prefaced by Moussinac, "Introduction," *Filmfront,* Jan. 28, 1935, pp. 7–9. For Vertov and "montage" in Russian films and in BERLIN, see Pudovkin, *Film Technique,* pp. 188–89; Richter, "Ur-Kino," *Neue Zürcher Zeitung,* April 2, 1940; Balázs, *Der Geist des Films,* pp. 57–58, 89, 94–95; Brody, "Paris hears Eisenstein," *Close Up,* April 1930, pp. 283–89.

[15] Quoted from Leyda, *Program Notes,* Series VII, program 2.

his part, focuses upon a society which has managed to evade revolution and now, under the stabilized Republic, is nothing but an unsubstantial conglomeration of parties and ideals. It is a shapeless reality, one that seems to be abandoned by all vital energies.

Ruttmann's film reflects this reality. The innumerable streets of BERLIN resemble the studio-built thoroughfare of Grune's THE STREET in yielding an impression of chaos. Symbols of chaos that first emerged in the postwar films are here resumed and supplemented by other pertinent symbols. Conspicuous in this respect is a unit of successive shots combining a roller coaster, a rotating spiral in a shop window and a revolving door [Illus. 38]. The many prostitutes among the passers-by also indicate that society has lost its balance. But no one any longer reacts vigorously against its chaotic condition. Another old motif called upon betrays the same lack of concern: the policeman who stops the traffic to guide a child safely across the street. Like the shots denoting chaos, this motif, which in earlier films served to emphasize authority as a redemption, is now simply part of the record—a fact among facts.

The excitement has gone. Indifference remains. That everybody is indifferent to his fellow men can be inferred from the formalization of social contrasts as well as from the repeated insertion of window-dressings with their monotonous rows of dolls and dummies. It is not as if these dummies were humanized; rather, human beings are forced into the sphere of the inanimate. They seem molecules in a stream of matter. In the Ufa brochure on contemporary *Kulturfilme*, one finds the following description of industrial documentaries: "Blast furnaces . . . emit . . . fire vapors, . . . white-hot iron pours into molds, material is torn, material is compressed, material is milled, material is polished, material becomes an expression of our time." [16] People in BERLIN assume the character of material not even polished. Used-up material is thrown away. To impress this sort of doom upon the audience, gutters and garbage cans appear in close-up, and as in THE STREET waste paper is seen littering the pavement. The life of society is a harsh, mechanical process [Illus. 39].

Only here can the difference between Ruttmann and Vertov be fully grasped: it is a difference of attitude. Vertov's continued survey of everyday life rests upon his unqualified acceptance of Soviet actuality. He himself is part of a revolutionary process which

[16] Cf. p. 142, and also "30 Kulturfilme," *Ufa-Leih.*

arouses passions and hopes. In his lyric enthusiasm, Vertov stresses formal rhythms but without seeming indifferent to content. His cross sections are "permeated with communist ideas" even when they picture only the beauty of abstract movements.

Had Ruttmann been prompted by Vertov's revolutionary convictions, he would have had to indict the inherent anarchy of Berlin life. He would have been forced to emphasize content rather than rhythm. His penchant for rhythmic "montage" reveals that he actually tends to avoid any critical comment on the reality with which he is faced. Vertov implies content; Ruttmann shuns it. This reluctance to appraise content is entirely consistent with his obvious delight in the "tempo" of Berlin and the *marche des machines*.[17] Tempo is a formal quality, and the socialist optimism that may manifest itself in the machine cult is nothing more than a vague "reformist illusion." Here is why Mayer called BERLIN a "surface approach." He did not object to formal editing as such; what he condemned was Ruttmann's formal attitude towards a reality that cried out for criticism, for interpretation. To be sure, Mayer was no revolutionary like Vertov; but he had a pronounced sense of the humane. It is hardly imaginable that he would have misused social contrasts as pictorial transitions, or recorded increasing mechanization without objectifying his horror of it.

Ruttmann's rhythmic "montage" is symptomatic of a withdrawal from basic decisions into ambiguous neutrality. This explains the difference between BERLIN and the street films. Whereas BERLIN refrains from idealizing the street, such films as ASPHALT and TRAGEDY OF THE STREET praise it as the refuge of true love and justified rebellion. These films are like dreams called forth by the paralyzed authoritarian dispositions for which no direct outlet is left. BERLIN is the product of the paralysis itself.

A few contemporary critics identified it as such. In 1928, I stated in *Frankfurter Zeitung*: "Ruttmann, instead of penetrating his immense subject-matter with a true understanding of its social, economic and political structure . . . , records thousands of details without connecting them, or at best connects them through fictitious transitions which are void of content. His film may be based upon the idea of Berlin as the city of tempo and work; but this is a formal idea which does not imply content either and perhaps for that very reason intoxicates the German petty bourgeoisie in real life and

[17] Rotha, *Film Till Now*, p. 283.

literature. This symphony fails to point out anything, because it does not uncover a single significant context." [18]

BERLIN inaugurated the vogue of cross-section, or "montage," films.[19] They could be produced at low cost; and they offered a gratifying opportunity of showing much and revealing nothing. Several films of that kind utilized stock material. One of them summarized the career of Henny Porten (1928); a second, similarly produced by Ufa, extracted love episodes from old movies (RUND UM DIE LIEBE, 1929); a third was the *Kulturfilm* DIE WUNDER DER WELT (MIRACLES OF THE UNIVERSE, 1929), a patchwork of various explorer films.[20]

Of greater interest were two cross-section films which, after the manner of BERLIN, reported actual life through an assemblage of documentary shots. In MARKT AM WITTENBERGPLATZ (STREET MARKETS IN BERLIN, 1929), Wilfried Basse used the stop-motion camera to condense the lengthy procedure of erecting tents and stands to a few seconds. It was neat and unpretentious pictorial reportage, a pleasing succession of such characteristic details as bargaining housewives, stout market women, glittering grapes, flower displays, horses, lazy onlookers and scattered debris. The whole amounted to a pointless statement on colorful surface phenomena. Its inherent neutrality is corroborated by Basse's indifference to the change of political atmosphere under Hitler. In 1934, as if nothing had happened, he released DEUTSCHLAND VON GESTERN UND HEUTE, a cross-section film of German cultural life which also refused "to penetrate beneath the skin." [21]

Shortly after this market film, another more important bit of reportage appeared: MENSCHEN AM SONNTAG (PEOPLE ON SUNDAY). Eugen Shuftan, Robert Siodmak, Edgar Ullmer, Billy Wilder, Fred Zinnemann and Moritz Seeler collaborated in the production of this late silent film. Its success may have been due to the con-

[18] Kracauer, "Der heutige Film und sein Publikum," *Frankfurter Zeitung*, Dec. 1, 1928, Rotha, *Documentary Film*, p. 161, comments on BERLIN in about the same way.

[19] Cf. Potamkin, "The Rise and Fall of the German Film," *Cinema*, April 1930, p. 25.

[20] Cf. Kraszna-Krausz, "The Querschnittfilm," *Close Up*, Nov. 1928, p. 27; "Rund um die Liebe," *Film-Magazin*, Jan. 27, 1929; Stenhouse, "The World on Film," *Close Up*, May 1930, pp. 417–18.

[21] Quoted from Rotha, *Documentary Film*, p. 121. For STREET MARKETS IN BERLIN, see *Film Society Programme*, May 4, 1930; Arnheim, *Film als Kunst*, p. 123; Balázs, *Der Geist des Films*, pp. 106–7.

vincing way it pictured a province of life rarely noticed until then. A salesgirl, a traveling salesman, an extra and a chauffeur are the film's main characters. On Sunday, they leave their dreary homes for one of the lakes near Berlin, and there are seen bathing, cooking, lying about on the beach, making futile contacts with each other and people like them. This is about all. But it is significant inasmuch as all the characters involved are lesser employees. At that time, the white-collar workers had turned into a political factor. They were wooed by the Nazis as well as the Social Democrats, and the whole domestic situation depended upon whether they would cling to their middle-class prejudices or acknowledge their common interests with the working class.

People on Sunday is one of the first films to draw attention to the plight of the "little man." In one sequence, a beach photographer is busy taking pictures which then appear within the film itself. They are inserted in such a way that it is as if the individuals photographed suddenly became motionless in the middle of an action.[22] As long as they move they are just average individuals; having come to a standstill, they appear to be ludicrous products of mere chance. While the stills in Dovzhenko's films serve to disclose the significance of some face or inanimate object, these snapshots seem designed to demonstrate how little substance is left to lower middle-class people. Along with shots of deserted Berlin streets and houses, they corroborate what has been said above of the spiritual vacuum in which the mass of employees actually lived.[23] However, this is the sole revelation to be elicited from a film which on the whole proves as noncommittal as the other cross-section films. Kraszna-Krausz states of it: "Melancholic observation. Not less, not more." [24] And Béla Balázs points out the "fanaticism for facts" animating People on Sunday and its like, and then comes to the conclusion: "They bury their meaning in an abundance of facts." [25]

[22] Arnheim, *Film als Kunst*, p. 140.

[23] Cf. p. 131 f.

[24] Kraszna-Krausz, "Production, Construction, Hobby," *Close Up*, April 1930, p. 318.

[25] Balázs, *Der Geist des Films*, p. 202.

16. BRIEF REVEILLE

The year 1928 marked a change. Politically, it was characterized by the Reichstag elections that resulted in an overwhelming victory for the so-called Marxist parties. Compared with the more than nine million votes for the Social Democrats, the number of Nazi votes was negligible. The republican regime seemed firmly established.[1] This political development was accompanied by an intellectual evolution: in the field of literature democratic, if not socialist, tendencies began to break through the crust of New Objectivity. People scrutinized their environment critically and regained the faculty of recollection. 1928 was a year of war novels which, headed by Remarque's *All Quiet on the Western Front*, expressed hatred of the war and concern for international rapprochement and similar desiderata.[2] At about the same time, leftist writers went in for books which disclosed social abuses and reactionary maneuvers. This kind of literature sold well. The public enjoyed social criticism. To all appearances a process of reorientation was under way.

At the end of the stabilized period, the screen tends to confirm this impression. Under the influence of Erich Pommer, even Ufa somewhat relinquished its grand-style manner and cut-to-pattern technique. Pommer, who had returned home from America, suggested and supervised the production of several films which he obviously intended to make into a synthesis of Hollywood and Neubabelsberg.[3] One of them was the street film ASPHALT; another was Hanns Schwarz's DIE WUNDERBARE LÜGE DER NINA PETROWNA (THE WONDERFUL LIE OF NINA PETROVNA, 1929), which vaguely recalled Hollywood's silent version of ANNA KARENINA. Nina, mistress of a Russian colonel, leaves him for one of his lieutenants, and finally kills herself to prevent the ruin of her lover's career. Laid

[1] Rosenberg, *Geschichte der Deutschen Republik*, pp. 217–18.

[2] Cf. Samuel and Thomas, *Expressionism in German Life*, p. 180.—Significantly, it was in 1928 that the cameraman Guido Seeber suggested the foundation of a national film library. See his article "Eine Staats-Kinothek," *Berliner Tageblatt*, Feb. 3, 1928, quoted by Ackerknecht, *Lichtspielfragen*, pp. 151–52.

[3] Rotha, *Film Till Now*, p. 182.

in a Russian garrison town, the film opens with a scene showing Brigitte Helm as Nina on a balcony; below her, the lieutenant (Francis Lederer) is passing by on horseback ahead of his men, and while he passes both gaze at each other for an endless moment. At the end, that balcony scene is repeated; but now Nina has already taken poison and the lieutenant is lost to her. The film involved a range of deep emotions genuinely motivated. It was an achievement which at least indicated that the existing paralysis was on the point of being broken up.[4]

This becomes the more obvious since Ufa, completely paralyzed under the "system," had excelled in misrepresenting emotions. In Joe May's HEIMKEHR (HOMECOMING, 1928), also a grade-A Pommer production, it continued to do so. The film is based upon Leonhard Frank's war novel *Karl und Anna*, which describes the flight of two German prisoners of war from a Siberian lead mine. Karl succeeds in reaching Germany before his friend Richard and is sheltered by Richard's wife Anna. Karl and Anna become intoxicated with each other. To picture their growing excitement, one scene of the film shows them restlessly turning about on beds separated only by a thin partition. What can be said in words is not always fit to be presented in pictures, for pictures, palpable as they are, sometimes fail to catch the implications of the words they illustrate. This grotesque scene is a misleading translation of the novel—a translation which under the pretense of rendering irresistible love exhibits mere sensuality.

HOMECOMING is interesting, though, for emphasizing the motif of the "feet that walk." It is not Karl who wanders home from the studio-built Siberian lead mine; it is his feet. Marching soldier boots change into slippers which in turn give way to foot-bandages that are finally superseded by the naked and dusty feet themselves.[5] The use made of this motif reveals the affinity between HOMECOMING and the dreamlike street films. With the paralysis drawing to its close, these dreams, stirred by the authoritarian dispositions, throbbed more and more distinctly below the surface.[6]

[4] Cf. Rotha, "Plastic Design," *Close Up*, Sept. 1929, pp. 228–30; etc.—Under Pommer's supervision, Schwarz also made UNGARISCHE RHAPSODIE (HUNGARIAN RHAPSODY, 1928).

[5] Motif mentioned by Balázs, *Der Geist des Films*, pp. 64–65.

[6] For HOMECOMING in general, see program to this film; "Homecoming," *National Board of Review Magazine*, Dec. 1928, pp. 7, 10; Kalbus, *Deutsche Filmkunst*, I, 75. In a similar vein was DR. BESSEL'S VERWANDLUNG (DR. BESSEL'S METAMORPHOSIS, 1927); cf. Zaddach, *Der literarische Film*, p. 72.—NARKOSE (NARCOSIS, 1929), based on a script by Balázs after a Stefan Zweig story, may also be mentioned in this context; cf. synopsis of film in *Illustrierter Film-Kurier*, and Balázs, *Der Geist des Films*, pp. 67, 74.

Simultaneously with THE WONDERFUL LIE OF NINA PETROVNA, a limited number of socialist-minded films appeared. That they could appear at all testifies to the relative strength of the intellectual leftist tendencies. To a certain extent these tendencies seemed to be enforced by favorable inner attitudes which profited by the paralysis of primary authoritarian impulses. The question was whether they were more than transitory moods.

The first leftist films did not run in movie theaters, but formed an integral part of Piscator's stage productions. During the stabilized period, the Berlin Piscator Theater served with its revolutionary plays as a sort of Grand Guignol for the rich, who enjoyed letting themselves be frightened by communism as long as they had no real fear of it. Since these plays were impregnated with belief in the dependence of the individual upon economic processes and class struggles, it was logical that Piscator should resort to bits of films, for they alone proved capable of evoking the social backgrounds from which the action proper was supposed to emerge. His *mise en scène* of Ernst Toller's play *Hoppla! Wir leben* (1927) included two film episodes which he had composed with the aid of Ruttmann. "The first episode is a War-time prologue to the play, which opens with the revolutionaries in prison. The prisoner-hero goes mad, and the progress of the external world during his seven-years' insanity (1920–1927) is seen in the second reel." [7] Assembled from stock material, these reels were projected onto a screen of transparent fabric, so that the actors could reappear immediately after the screening was over.

In 1928, the Popular Association for Film Art (*Volksverband für Filmkunst*) was founded "to fight reactionary trash on the one hand and, on the other, to develop artistically progressive films." [8] The sweeping success of the great Russian films made it seem a matter of course that true film art would have to be leftist-minded. Sponsored by Heinrich Mann, Pabst, Karl Freund, Piscator and others, this noncommercial association—counting democrats as well as communists among its ranks—organized groups of congenial moviegoers on a nation-wide scale and set out to familiarize them

[7] Quoted from *Film Society Programme*, Jan. 26, 1930. See also Freedley and Reeves, *History of the Theatre*, pp. 526, 531; Hellmund-Waldow, "Combinaison: Le Film et la Scène," *Close Up*, April 1928, pp. 24–27; Gregor, *Zeitalter des Films*, pp. 141–42.

[8] Quoted from Schwartzkopf, "Volkverband für Filmkunst," *Close Up*, May 1928, p. 71.

with superior films full of social criticism. The Association's opening performance provoked scandal by showing a cleverly cut newsreel: shots and scenes which had all been contained in old Ufa newsreels were here combined in such a manner that they suddenly lost their political innocence and assumed an inflammatory character. The police prohibited this devilish juggler's trick in utter disregard of the defendants' objection that the incriminating newsreel was nothing but an assemblage of unchanged Ufa material.[9]

One will remember the Ufa prospectus which defines the *Kulturfilm* as the mirror of a beautiful world, and in a survey of its beauties does not forget to mention "nimble-footed Chinese before palanquins."[10] The Popular Association antagonized Ufa by distributing SHANGHAI DOCUMENT, a Russian *Kulturfilm* in which those "nimble-footed Chinese" appeared as the victimized coolies they really were. However, in contrasting them with bathing and dancing whites characterized in a subtitle as the representatives of "European and American civilization," the film turned from truthful statement to biased accusations. An English admirer of Russian film art therefore calls SHANGHAI DOCUMENT "definitely propagandistic in the wrong sense of the term."[11] Yet the leading members of the Popular Association included the film in their program. A further sign of their lack of insight was their choice of DIE WUNDER DES FILMS (MIRACLES OF THE FILM), a neutral cross-section film overflowing with technological optimism.[12] The surface radicalism of this short-lived *Volksverband* did not testify to a serious change of the psychological situation.

In 1929, another progressive association cropped up: the German League for the Independent Film (*Deutsche Liga für unabhängigen Film*) which proposed to fight against the glorification of war and the encroachments of censorship. This League, a member of the Geneva International Film League, arranged showings of vanguard films and Russian films followed by discussions.[13] The soul of the enterprise was Hans Richter, one of the few truly incorruptible film artists of the left. In 1926, following the general tendency toward realism, he began to include eyes, faces, penguins, among his abstract

[9] Balázs, *Der Geist des Films,* p. 212. Cf. p. 297.

[10] Cf. p. 142.

[11] Quoted from Bryher, *Film Problems of Soviet Russia,* p. 125. Cf. program to SHANGHAI DOCUMENT; MacPherson, "A Document of Shanghai," *Close Up,* Dec. 1928, pp. 66–69; Balázs, *Der Geist des Films,* p. 97.

[12] Cf. Stenhouse, "Die Wunder des Films," *Close Up,* May 1929, pp. 89–91.

[13] Prospectus of the League, and information offered by Mr. Hans Richter.

lines and planes. His VORMITTAGSSPUK (GHOSTS BEFORE BREAKFAST, 1928), a charming short obviously influenced by René Clair and Fernand Léger, showed inanimate objects in full revolt against the conventional use we make of them. Bowlers mocking their possessors fly through the air, while a number of persons completely disappear behind a thin lamp post.[14]

At the time of this short, the film industry took a certain interest in vanguard productions: Ruttmann's BERLIN had been a success, and the desire for reorientation was widespread. So Richter made a few reels for insertion in commercial films in need of embellishment. One of these reels—it served as prologue for an insignificant Ufa film—was a cross section of life during the inflation.[15] Even though Richter came from abstract painting like Ruttmann, he repudiated the latter's formal transitions in favor of cutting procedures designed to bring about a true understanding of what inflation really meant. His ideal was to compose "film essays"—sagacious pictorial comments on socially interesting topics. But as for his League, it neither exerted noticeable influence nor did it long survive the *Volksverband.*

The existing vogue of social criticism may have stimulated the well-known film architect Ernö Metzner to compete with Richter in the field of unconventional nonfiction films. FREIE FAHRT (FREE TRIP, 1928), a propaganda film he made for the Social Democratic Party, was divided into two dissimilar parts. The first was a retrospect picturing the predicament of the workers under the Kaiser in splendid scenes shaped after the Russian manner; the second, devoted to current party activities, was hardly more than a pictorial manifesto which inevitably reflected the failings and inhibitions of the Social Democrats.[16]

Subsequent to this official screen eulogy, which was shown only at closed Party meetings, Metzner produced, staged and shot the experimental short ÜBERFALL (ACCIDENT, 1929), one of the most radical of German films despite its nonpolitical theme. It reports a minor street accident hardly worth a line in the local press. A petty bourgeois finds a coin on the street and stakes it in a dice game

[14] Balázs, *Der Geist des Films,* p. 124.

[15] Richter's INFLATION preluded DIE DAME MIT DER MASKE (THE LADY WITH THE MASK, 1928); cf. "Die Dame mit der Maske," *Ufa-Leih.* Other films by Richter are listed in his unpublished manuscript, "Avantgarde, History and Dates of the Only Independent Artistic Film Movement, 1921–1931."

[16] "Freie Fahrt," *Close Up,* Feb. 1929, pp. 97–99.

in an obscure tavern. He wins and leaves, followed by a thug who pursues him through a dark underpass and past ugly house façades. A prostitute pulls the frightened bourgeois inside a house and takes him up to her room. The man believes himself safe, but in reality he has only fallen into another trap. While he is all set to enjoy an amorous hour, the girl's *souteneur* appears, robs the visitor of his wallet and throws him out of the house. No sooner does the unfortunate collect himself, than he is knocked down by the thug from the tavern. In the last scene, his head bandaged, he is seen lying in a hospital bed, haunted by a feverish dream in which a circling coin is the leitmotiv.[17]

Unusual angles, distorting mirrors and other cinematic devices are used in rendering this sordid accident.[18] The result is a pictorial grotesque tending to color and deform objects and faces. This sabotage of the norm helps to mark Metzner's film as a protest against deep-rooted conventions [Illus. 40]. In ACCIDENT, all the characters and motifs of TRAGEDY OF THE STREET and ASPHALT reappear, but with basically changed meanings. ACCIDENT is a street film debunking those street films of the stabilized period. Unlike them, it neither glorifies the petty bourgeois as a rebel nor transforms the chaotic street into a haven for genuine love. The prostitute in this short remains a hard-boiled creature up to the very end. Ruttmann's BERLIN also pictures street figures realistically; but while Ruttmann retreats into the colorless neutrality of *Neue Sachlichkeit*, Metzner draws radical conclusions from his premises. ACCIDENT goes beyond BERLIN or any other film of the period in that it rebuffs the police, that reassuring symbol of authority on the German screen. When in the final scene the bedridden petty bourgeois is requested by a detective to identify his assailant, he silently shuts his eyes and again falls prey to his hallucination of the circling coin. The image of the coin is the answer to the policeman's request. ACCIDENT, that is, shows chaos without accepting submission to authority as the way out of it. Authoritarian dispositions are here repudiated emphatically. The truly heretic character of this film is confirmed by the censor's harsh reaction to it. Even though ACCIDENT deals with events far less crude than those of any Pabst

[17] MacPherson, "Überfall (Accident)," *Close Up*, April 1929, pp. 71–72. For Metzner's ACHTUNG, LIEBE—LEBENSGEFAHR (WHERE'S LOVE THERE'S DANGER, 1929), see "Achtung, Liebe—Lebensgefahr," *Close Up*, Nov. 1929, pp. 441–42.

[18] Rotha, *Film Till Now*, pp. 275–76. See also Hoffman, "Camera Problems," *Close Up*, July 1929, pp. 29–31.

film, it was prohibited for its allegedly "brutalizing and demoralizing effect."[19]

The same dissenting spirit manifested itself in the field of fictional films proper. Among them was an outright product of Red ideology: REVOLTE IM ERZIEHUNGSHAUS (REVOLT IN THE REFORMATORY, January, 1930), a screen version of Peter Martin Lampel's theatrical play of that title. It was an isolated attempt to make the screen as radical as the contemporary stage. The censor nipped this attempt in the bud, reducing to a tame drama of manners what was originally a violent attack against the sadistic regime of terror in German reformatories.[20]

For the rest, leftist inclinations materialized in three films, all of which appeared in 1929 and showed themselves strongly influenced by the Soviet cinema.[21] These films had an interesting trait in common: they were bathed in a dense atmosphere of sadness. One of them was Carl Junghans' SO IST DAS LEBEN (SUCH IS LIFE), an extraordinary piece of work achieved in Berlin and Prague under enormous financial difficulties. It featured a washerwoman portrayed by Vera Baranovskaia, the star of Pudovkin's MOTHER. Junghans (a Czech of German extraction) revealed the miserable life and death of this plain woman in a succession of episodes noteworthy for their realism as well as their social awareness. The banquet where the child falls asleep and the cobbler brings out his old gramophone is no less memorable than the funeral repast in a café resounding with the noise of a mechanical pianoforte. Although Junghans occasionally borrowed from Eisenstein—the gesticulating statue of a saint recalls Eisenstein's moving stone lion—his film was imbued with a mood of resignation not to be found in any Soviet production. Commenting on SUCH IS LIFE, Carl Vincent speaks of its "touching and smiling *tristesse*" in the face of human pain and decay.[22]

[19] Quoted from Metzner, "German Censor's Incomprehensible Ban," *Close Up*, May 1929, pp. 14–15.

[20] Berstl, ed., *25 Jahre Berliner Theater,* p. 99; Boehmer and Reitz, *Film in Wirtschaft und Recht*, p. 50; Petzet, *Verbotene Filme*, pp. 124–25; Stenhouse, "A Contemporary," *Close Up*, May 1930, p. 419. Lampel's theatrical play *Giftgas über Berlin* was also made into a film (GIFTGAS, 1929).

[21] MacPherson, "*Times* Is Not What They Was!" *Close Up,* Feb. 1929, p. 36, reports from Berlin: "The crowds during the first weeks of *Storm over Asia* were so dense that it was necessary to call out a special police control for those endeavoring to buy tickets." For the vogue of Soviet films, see also MacPherson, "As Is," *Close Up*, Aug. 1928, pp. 5–11.

[22] Vincent, *Histoire de l'Art Cinématographique*, p. 208. See also Bardèche and Brasillach, *History of Motion Pictures*, pp. 261–62; Arnheim, *Film als Kunst*, p. 122.

Leo Mittler's JENSEITS DER STRASSE (HARBOR DRIFT), which included beautiful Hamburg exteriors, was one of the first films to touch on the problem of unemployment. Crowds of unemployed fill the picture as background to the action proper. Apart from this timely thematic innovation, HARBOR DRIFT is a street film animated by much the same spirit as ACCIDENT. In it, a pearl necklace functions as did the coin in Metzner's short. A girl depraved by long unemployment watches an old beggar pick up the necklace on the street, and then lures the beggar's friend, a young unemployed worker, into stealing it for her. He fails and returns empty-handed; whereupon the girl leaves him for a well-to-do elderly gentleman. Haunted by the image of the glittering necklace, the demoralized worker sneaks back to the abandoned boat which serves his one-time friend as a shelter. There he and the beggar come to blows, and since the beggar reads murder in his assailant's mind, he flees with the pearls—flees in such panic that he falls in the water and drowns. Bubbles in the form of pearls appear and disappear on the surface of the water. At the end, we lose the worker in a crowd of unemployed. Contemporary German reviewers emphasized the Russian style of this film. Its variance with TRAGEDY OF THE STREET is as obvious as its gloominess.[23]

MUTTER KRAUSEN'S FAHRT INS GLÜCK (MOTHER KRAUSEN'S JOURNEY TO HAPPINESS), the most successful film of this group, was made by the former cameraman Piel Jutzi after a script Heinrich Zille wrote shortly before his death. Even though Zille's imagination as usual centered round his beloved Berlin slums and their human flotsam, the film differed considerably from the Zille films of 1925 and 1926. In them, studio-built proletarian surroundings had been the scene of developments that fed the social illusions of lower middle-class people; in this new and last authentic Zille film no such illusions were allowed to invalidate the veracity of its North Berlin milieu, brought to life with the help of numerous documentary shots.

This is a milieu characterized by abominable housing conditions. To augment her income as a news vendor, Mother Krausen has let her one room to a dubious tenant, while she herself, along with her grown-up children Paul and Erna, is camping in the kitchen. The tenant on his part keeps a prostitute and her child in his room. Since

[23] Prospectus to the film and synopsis (Museum of Modern Art Library, clipping files).

the young Krausens cannot avoid stumbling upon him, they are exposed to his evil influence. He seduces Erna and persuades Paul, who has wantonly dissipated his mother's earnings, to make up for this loss by participating in a burglary. Paul and the tenant break into a pawnshop, but the police interfere and come to fetch Paul at his mother's place. Her son led away as a criminal, Mother Krausen's whole universe goes to pieces. Taking the prostitute's child along—"What could life give to that child?"—she opens the gas pipe and departs on her journey to happiness.

The atmosphere of self-pity surrounding Mother Krausen's escape into death recalls the suicide of the café-owner in Carl Mayer's NEW YEAR'S EVE.[24] In fact, this last Zille film would be nothing but a modernized instinct drama did it not include a motif never before introduced on the German screen. The motif asserts itself in those parts of the film which elaborate upon the relation between Max and Erna. Max, a class-conscious young worker in love with Erna, furiously deserts her when he happens to find out about her liaison with the tenant. But, later on, his enlightened worker-friend succeeds in convincing him that all has been the seducer's rather than Erna's fault, and that he, Max, is behaving in a typically bourgeois way. Max, converted to socialist sex morals, repentantly returns to the girl. His conversion tends to reveal Mother Krausen as the petty-bourgeois heroine of a pseudo-tragedy. Two other episodes which also pierce her illusory world enhance the significance of this love affair. One of them satirizes the wedding party on the occasion of the tenant's marriage to the prostitute; the other pictures a workers' demonstration after the impressive manner of Pudovkin. The problem is whether or not Max's concept of happiness outbalances that of Mother Krausen. From the emphasis placed on her suicide only one conclusion can be drawn: that the film is intended not so much to play up socialist claims and hopes as to acknowledge them with melancholy. To be sure, Mother Krausen's notions are recognized as illusions; but even so they retain sufficient strength to overshadow the aspirations of the opposite camp.[25]

The sadness of these three films indicates that their underlying revolutionary inclinations are secondary attitudes rather than primary impulses. All three films seem to originate in a mind not too seriously concerned with emancipation. It is as if this mind were

[24] Cf. p. 99.

[25] Weiss, "Mutter Krausen's Fahrt ins Glück," *Close Up*, April 1930, pp. 318–21; Vincent, *Histoire de l'Art Cinématographique*, p. 163; Arnheim, *Film als Kunst*, p. 168.

ready at any moment to retreat from its vanguard position into noncommittal neutrality.

Even during 1928–1929—that short heyday of social criticism immediately preceding the break-up of the stabilized period—films typical of the existing paralysis predominated. They sometimes amounted to patterns of abysmal confusion. REFUGE, an Ufa film of 1928 already mentioned in other contexts,[26] included shots of proletarian quarters that seemed to be drawn from films by Pudovkin or Eisenstein, but although imbued with an revolutionary spirit, these shots in the Russian style served as background to an anti-revolutionary action that, of course, strictly contradicted their inherent meaning. The merely decorative use made of them must be traced to complete aloofness from content.

Not all contemporaries were insensitive to the persisting paralysis of the German screen. Potamkin spoke of "the German director's disregard of the subject-matter in films involving human experience." [27] At the end of 1928, surveying the current German screen output, I drew the following conclusions: "Lack of essence is the main characteristic of the entire stabilized production. . . . If the emptiness of our films, their shrinking from any human action, does not originate in a waning of substance, it can be explained only by obduracy [*Verstocktheit*]—that strange obduracy which from the end of the inflation on has prevailed in Germany and determined many public activities. It is as if during the years in which, along with the streamlining of big business, a social regrouping has taken place, German life has become heavily paralyzed. One is almost permitted to speak of its disease. . . . Is there a prescription for this? There is no prescription. Sincerity, the gift of observation, humanity—such things cannot be taught." [28]

Given certain conditions, a state of collective inner paralysis may occur anywhere. Prior to the outbreak of World War II, for instance, France had fallen into an apathy of that kind. Wherever the paralysis materializes, it gives rise to the same nondescript neutrality. But the meaning of this neutrality depends on the nature of the content paralyzed. It is not everywhere the same.

[26] Cf. p. 151.

[27] Quoted from Potamkin, "The Rise and Fall of the German Film," *Cinema*, April 1930, p. 57. See also Potamkin, "Kino and Lichtspiel," *Close Up*, Nov. 1929, p. 392.

[28] Kracauer, "Der heutige Film und sein Publikum," *Frankfurter Zeitung*, Nov. 30 and Dec. 1, 1928.

THE PRE-HITLER PERIOD
(1930–1933)

17. SONGS AND ILLUSIONS

WITH the New York stock market crash in the fall of 1929, the stabilized period came to a definite close. All loans to Germany were abruptly suspended. The ensuing shrinkage of German industry resulted in a sharp increase of unemployment, already widespread. Towards the end of the pre-Hitler period, as the last three years of the Republic may be called, Berlin resounded with demonstrations, and there rose to the surface sinister individuals reminiscent of medieval figures. Weeks before the Christmas of 1932, peddlers and beggars formed a compact lane on the sidewalks of Tauentzienstrasse. They offered toys and cleaning rags for sale, played harmoniums and drew strident tones from saw blades.

The economic crisis led to the collapse of the coalition between Social Democrats and bourgeois parties in the Reich. Brüning, appointed chancellor in March 1930, headed a purely bourgeois cabinet, though in Prussia the Social Democrats continued to hold office. Maintaining itself through reactionary emergency decrees (*Notverordnungen*), the Brüning regime was highly unpopular with the dejected masses, who resented it as the stronghold of capitalism and corruption. Hitler stole a march on the communists by captivating millions of unemployed, and at the same time successfully courted big business. The Reichstag elections of September 1930 brought a veritable landslide in favor of the Nazis. S. A. uniforms became ubiquitous; the noises of street assaults mingled with the dissonances of the musical saws.

Yet in spite of general discontent with the "system," the majority refused to vote for Hitler. Many of those who may have been stirred by his promises nevertheless preferred to stick to the traditional parties. In the Reichstag of 1930, the 150 Hitler and Hugenberg deputies were confronted with 220 Marxists and 200 Brüning followers. Shortly before his ultimate triumph, Hitler suffered a serious setback, and it is doubtful whether he would have won power at all if the Social Democrats had not been struck with apathy.[1]

[1] For the whole period, see Rosenberg, *Geschichte der Deutschen Republik*, pp. 222–38; Schwarzschild, *World in Trance*, esp. p. 319.

This strong ideological opposition to Hitler tends to suggest that a handful of fanatics and gangsters succeeded in subjugating the majority of the German people. Such a conclusion falls short of the facts. Instead of proving immune to Nazi indoctrination, the bulk of the Germans adjusted themselves to totalitarian rule with a readiness that could not be merely the outcome of propaganda and terror. Whereas Italian fascism was a sort of theatrical display, Hitlerism assumed aspects of a religion.

It is a puzzling spectacle: on the one hand, the Germans were reluctant to give Hitler the reins; on the other, they were quite willing to accept him. Such contradictory attitudes frequently spring from a conflict between the demands of reason and emotional urges. Since the Germans opposed Hitler on the political plane, their strange preparedness for the Nazi creed must have originated in psychological dispositions stronger than any ideological scruples. The films of the pre-Hitler period shed no small light on the psychological situation.

Before discussing them, some preliminary remarks are indispensable. First there was the transition from the silent to the talking films. In 1929, after having waged a fierce patent war, the two German companies in possession of all important sound-film patents fused into the Tobis-Klangfilm syndicate, which immediately began to fight competing American groups. A year later, representatives of the belligerents met in Paris and there reached an agreement fixing the distribution of international markets. During this transition period, the trade suffered somewhat. Thousands of musicians were fired; many small movie theaters disappeared because they were unable to finance conversion to sound. But the depression did not prevent the German sound-film industry from satisfying its export needs very effectively. It had the lead in Europe, and in other markets was surpassed only by Hollywood. In Germany itself, new *Kontingent* regulations, along with the centralization of all pertinent patents, stemmed the flood of American pictures. "The German sound film was left to its own development." [2]

When the first full-fledged talkies appeared—among them At-

[2] Quoted from Kraszna-Krausz, "A Season's Retrospect," *Close Up*, Sept. 1931, p. 227. See also Olimsky, *Filmwirtschaft*, pp. 63–66; Rotha, *Film Till Now*, p. 183; Boehmer and Reitz, *Film in Wirtschaft und Recht*, pp. 7–8; Jason, "Zahlen sehen uns an . . ," *25 Jahre Kinematograph*, pp. 67, 69–70; Kalbus, *Deutsche Filmkunst*, II, 10–11, 98–99.

LANTIC, made by E. A. Dupont in England, DIE NACHT GEHÖRT UNS, and MELODIE DES HERZENS (MELODY OF THE HEART), a Pommer production after the manner of his last silents—noted critics and film artists lived in fear that the introduction of sound might endanger the highly developed arts of camera movement and editing.[3] The cameraman Karl Hoffmann lamented in 1929, the year of the release of these films: "Poor camera! Alas! no more of your graceful movements, no more of your happy-go-lucky shifts? Are you again condemned to the same bondage and chains which you commenced breaking ten years ago?"[4] Even though Hoffmann proved to be too pessimistic—after a while, the camera began again to ramble about—those early apprehensions were by no means unfounded. Film-makers all over the world soon emphasized dialogue to such an extent that the visual track tended to degenerate into a mere accompaniment. To be sure, the new sphere of articulate reasoning enriched the screen; but this gain hardly compensated for the reduced significance of the visuals. While verbal statements more often than not express intentions, camera shots are likely to penetrate the unintentional. This is precisely what the mature silent films had done. They came upon levels below the dimension of consciousness, and since the spoken word had not yet assumed control, unconventional or even subversive images were allowed to slip in. But when dialogue took over, unfathomable imagery withered and intentional meanings prevailed. Need it be said that despite such changes the medium of the screen preserved its social significance? Talkies are as symptomatic of mass attitudes as silent films, although analysis of these attitudes is hampered rather than facilitated by the addition of spoken words.

On the whole, the Germans indulged less than the Americans in pure dialogue films. Both Pabst and Lang developed ingenious devices to perpetuate the leading role of the visuals.[5] This emphasis on pictorial values persisted throughout the Nazi era, as can best be exemplified by the striking contrast between German and American war newsreels: while the Nazis inserted long pictorial sequences

[3] Kalbus, *ibid.*, pp. 11–13, 38; synopsis of MELODY OF THE HEART in *Illustrierter Film-Kurier*.

[4] Hoffman, "Camera Problems," *Close Up*, July 1929, p. 31.

[5] The late Valerio Jahier, a distinguished French film writer, remarks of the German cinema: "This cinema has preserved its characteristics since the invention of sound, as may be seen in the films of Pabst and Fritz Lang, whether produced in Germany or abroad." Cf. Jahier, "42 ans de Cinéma," *Le Rôle intellectuel du Cinéma*, p. 71.

without any verbal comment, the Americans degraded the shots exhibited to scattered illustrations of some commentator's exuberant eloquence.

And finally, before examining the films themselves, the tightening of the censorship under Brüning must be mentioned. Pretending to strict neutrality, the Brüning administration more often than not yielded to Nazi claims and reactionary pressure groups. INS DRITTE REICH (1931), an electoral campaign film of the left, was banned for stigmatizing German business interests, the German judiciary and the National Socialist Party. The notorious Nazi demonstrations against ALL QUIET ON THE WESTERN FRONT in December 1930 induced the censors, who had originally admitted this film, to suspend its further screening under the rather tenuous pretext that it would endanger German prestige abroad. Thereupon leftist throngs disrupted the performances of the Fridericus film DAS FLÖTENKONZERT VON SANSSOUCI; but this time the censors remained unmoved.[6]

A multitude of German films gave no evidence of having been affected at all by the outbreak of the economic crisis. Along with the eternal mystery thrillers, Berlin local melodramas and military farces, several film types cultivated during the years of stabilization continued to flourish.[7] Among them were adaptations of French boulevard comedies as void of genuine life as their predecessors, and many *Kulturfilme* popularizing exotic countries and scientific matters.[8] Following the example of such anemic documentaries as BIS-

[6] Cf. Olimsky, *Filmwirtschaft*, p. 30; Boehmer and Reitz, *Film in Wirtschaft und Recht*, pp. 48, 52–54; Kraszna-Krausz, "A Letter on Censorship," *Close Up*, Feb. 1929, pp. 56–62; Altman, "La Censure contre le Cinéma," *La Revue du Cinéma*, Feb. 1, 1931, pp. 39–40.—Much pertinent material in Petzet, *Verbotene Filme*.

[7] For mystery thrillers, see Kalbus, *Deutsche Filmkunst*, II, 55–56, 85–86; Petzet, *Verbotene Filme*, pp. 14–16, 21–22; "Geheimdienst," *Filmwelt*, June 21, 1931; *Illustrierter Film-Kurier* (synopses of PANIK IN CHICAGO, 1931, and SCHUSS IM MORGENGRAUEN, 1932).—DAS EKEL (1931) with Max Adalbert, the brilliant Berlin comedian, may be mentioned as an instance of local melodrama; synopsis in *Illustrierter Film-Kurier*.—Kalbus, *ibid.*, pp. 91–92, lists a number of military farces. Particularly successful was DREI TAGE MITTELARREST (THREE DAYS IN THE GUARDHOUSE, 1930); cf. Kraszna-Krausz, "A Season's Retrospect," *Close Up*, Sept. 1931, p. 227, and Kalbus, *ibid.*, p. 92.

[8] Film comedies in French boulevard style were, for instance, NIE WIEDER LIEBE, 1931 (Kalbus, *ibid.*, p. 46, and Kracauer, "Courrier de Berlin," LA REVUE DU CINÉMA, Oct. 1, 1931, pp. 54–55); KOPFÜBER INS GLÜCK, 1931 (synopsis in *Illustrierter Film-Kurier*); DER FRECHDACHS, 1932 (synopsis in *Illustrierter Film-Kurier*).—For *Kulturfilme* of the time, see Ufa, *Kultur-Filme*, 1929–1933; *Film Society Programmes*, April 12, 1931, Jan. 31 and May 8, 1932; Weiss, "Achtung Australien! Achtung Asien!" *Close Up*, June 1931, p. 149; Bryher, "Notes on some Films," *ibid.*, June, 1932, pp. 198–99; Weiss, "Das keimende Leben," *ibid.*, Sept. 1932, pp. 207–8.

MARCK and WORLD WAR, Oswald's much-censored "1914" (1931) treated the causes of World War I with completely sham objectivity.[9] The tradition of diverting resentments which might threaten the existing regime to politically neutral issues was also kept alive. Outlets were easily found in cases of inhuman judicial procedures. One product of that kind was the Ufa film VORUNTERSUCHUNG (1931), in which Robert Siodmak cleverly dramatized the insufficiency of circumstantial evidence.[10]

The operetta profited more than any other escapist genre from the possibilities offered by sound. Now that music could be included, scores of musicals overflowing with songs cropped up. As early as 1930, Ufa helped to start the vogue by releasing DIE DREI VON DER TANKSTELLE (THE THREE OF THE FILLING STATION), a new type of operetta, which, it is true, failed to convince the New York public, but was a hit in most European countries. Staged by the Viennese Wilhelm Thiele under the supervision of Pommer, this film was a playful daydream woven of the materials of everyday life [Illus. 41]. Three careless young friends suddenly gone bankrupt buy a filling station with the proceeds of their car; there they devote themselves to flirting with a pretty girl who time and again turns up in her roadster—a dalliance which after some emotional confusion logically ends with one of the three rivals winning out. The refreshing idea of shifting the operetta paradise from its traditional locales to the open road was supported by the eccentric use made of music. Full of whims, the score constantly interfered with the half-rational plot, stirring characters and even objects to behave in a frolicsome manner. An unmotivated waltz invited workers clearing out the friends' unpaid-for furniture to transform themselves into dancers, and whenever the amorous roadster approached, its horn would emit a few bars which threaded the film with the stubbornness of a genuine leitmotiv.[11]

Most operettas followed the old recipes; from ZWEI HERZEN IM DREIVIERTELTAKT (TWO HEARTS IN WALTZ TIME, 1930) to Ludwig Berger's charming WALZERKRIEG (WAR OF THE WALTZES, 1933), they continued to sell the public standardized dreams of an

[9] Cf. Kalbus, *Deutsche Filmkunst*, II, 79–80.

[10] Bryher, "Berlin, April 1931," *Close Up*, June 1931, pp. 130–31; Arnheim, *Film als Kunst*, pp. 288–89. The film TÄTER GESUCHT (1931) was in a similar vein; cf. "Das Netz der Indizien," *Filmwelt*, March 22, 1931.

[11] Vincent, *Histoire de l'Art Cinématographique*, p. 164; Bardèche and Brasillach, *History of Motion Pictures*, p. 346; Kalbus, *Deutsche Filmkunst*, II, 25–26.

idyllic Vienna.[12] This lucrative speculation in romantic nostalgia reached its climax with Eric Charrell's DER KONGRESS TANZT (CONGRESS DANCES, 1931), a Pommer production which set the flirtations of a sweet Viennese girl against the stately background of the Viennese Congress of 1814.[13] Spectacular mass displays alternated with intimate tête-à-têtes involving the Tsar in person, and Metternich's diplomatic intrigues added a pleasing touch of high politics. Elaborate rather than light-winged, this superoperetta with its agreeable melodies and intelligent structural twists amounted to a compendium of all imaginable operetta motifs. Some of them set a fashion. Particularly frequent were imitations of that sequence of CONGRESS DANCES in which Lilian Harvey on her drive through the countryside passes various kinds of people who all take up the song she sings from her carriage.

The operetta was not the only film species which assigned a major role to music. No sooner did sound come true than the filmmakers hurried to capitalize on the popularity of famous singers. And even though the results could not have been worse, the public surrendered wholeheartedly. Films canning Tauber's glamorous voice were the vogue, and when Kiepura performed in a fishing boat with the panorama of Naples behind him, everybody was forcibly overwhelmed by such a blend of beauties.[14]

Unlike the *Kulturfilme* and operettas, cross-section films changed their character during the pre-Hitler years. They became vehicles of an over-all optimism alien to their previous moods. This new optimism vigorously asserted itself in Ruttmann's early sound experiment, DIE MELODIE DER WELT (WORLD MELODY, 1930), a cross-section film he made from materials put at his disposal by the Hamburg-Amerika Line. Cinematically, the film was an interesting piece of pioneering, for its rhythmic "montage" included not only variegated visual impressions but all kinds of sounds and musical strains. Thematically, this "montage" encompassed nothing less than the sum total of human activities and achievements: architectural

12 For TWO HEARTS IN WALTZ TIME, see Balázs, *Der Geist des Films*, p. 178; for WAR OF THE WALTZES, Kalbus, *Deutsche Filmkunst*, II, 33. Other operetta films of the time were LIEBESWALZER, 1930 (cf. Kalbus, *ibid.*, p. 25, and Arnheim, *Film als Kunst*, pp. 295–96); WALZERPARADIES, 1931 (synopsis in *Illustrierter Film-Kurier*); etc. See also Kalbus, *ibid.*, p. 26 ff.

13 Kalbus, *ibid.*, pp. 35–36.

14 Kalbus, *ibid.*, pp. 29–30, 32; Weiss, "The First Opera-Film," *Close Up*, Dec. 1932, pp. 242–45.

structures, typical modes of love, means of transportation, religious cults, the armies of the world, aspects of warfare, sports, entertainments and so on. According to Ruttmann's own comment on his film, the religious section "culminates in sumptuous mass demonstrations paying homage to diverse divinities. But the variety of personages worshiped by these devotees, who are addressing themselves now to Buddha, now to Jesus or Confucius, is a potential source of conflict, and as such leads to the subsequent part, 'The Army.' A martial bugle interrupts the sacred music, and soldiers of the whole world begin to file by," etc.[15]

Besides naïvely emphasizing the banality of thought in WORLD MELODY, this comment reveals the film's underlying principles. While BERLIN, neutral as it was, still dwelt upon the harshness of mechanized human relations, WORLD MELODY manifests a neutrality that is completely indiscriminating and implies wholesale acceptance of the universe. It is two different things to embrace the world in a spirit aware of the miracle of simple Leaves of Grass, and to embrace a world in which it does not matter whether "Jesus or Confucius" is adored, provided the crowds of the faithful are sumptuous. A French critic said of WORLD MELODY: "In my opinion, it would have been more valuable to deal only with one or another of the subjects presented." [16] This remark points at the basic weakness of Ruttmann's cosmic hymn. His "world melody" is void of content, because his concern with the whole of the world leads him to disregard the specific content of each of the assembled melodies.

DAS LIED VOM LEBEN (SONG OF LIFE, 1931), which was released only after embittered fights with the board of censors, followed a similar pattern. It was a typical cross-section film. Made by the Russian theater director Alexis Granovsky, who had moved from Moscow to Berlin, this Tobis production grew out of a daring documentary of a Caesarian operation. The film consists of loosely connected episodes which, with the aid of Walter Mehring's pleasing songs, elaborate upon such generalities as love, marriage and birth. In the opening sequence, a young girl attends a dinner in honor of

[15] Quoted from Ruttmann, "La Symphonie du Monde," *La Revue du Cinéma,* March 1, 1930, p. 44. Cf. Vincent, *Histoire de l'Art Cinématographique,* p. 169; Jahier, "42 Ans de Cinéma," *Le Rôle intellectuel du Cinéma,* p. 65.

[16] Quoted from Chevalley, "Mickey Virtuose—La Mélodie du Monde," *Close Up,* Jan. 1930, p. 72.—*Film Society Programme,* Dec. 14, 1930, expresses a more positive opinion.

her engagement to an elderly roué, who wants to introduce her to his friends. Veritable fireworks of cinematic devices transform the betrothal party into a macabre gathering designed to symbolize the depraved generation of yesterday. In her dread of this company the girl runs away. She makes an attempt to drown herself in the sea, and then falls in love with her rescuer, a young marine engineer. The passage picturing her rekindled desire for life and the couple's honeymoon on a southern coast is an ambitious piece of film poetry. Now the Caesarian operation takes place. This remarkable episode emphasizes the contrast between the surgeons' white coats and their black rubber gloves—a contrast which effectively intimates that the girl hovers between life and death. A son is born, and his arrival gives rise to scenes idealizing the mother-child relationship. At the very end, the grown-up boy is seen going away to the sea from which his father came and to which his mother tried to escape.

The emphasis this film puts on images of the sea is symptomatic of an attitude which finds its verbal expression in the following scene: after having rescued the girl, the marine engineer takes her up in a crane, and as they float through the sky, "the man and the girl and a third person, who might be a doctor or a philosopher or a prophet, look down upon life while a voice sings of the glory of work and the doctor proclaims the gospel of vitality: the will to live, to produce, to progress" [17] [Illus. 42]. Symbolic scenes of this kind recur. An aftermath of popular postwar thought, the film does not differentiate between various forms of life, but extols life in every form. This accounts for the omnipresence of the sea: it is as grandiose and inarticulate as the film's underlying conception of life. SONG OF LIFE parallels WORLD MELODY in the vagueness of its enthusiasm.[18]

[17] Quoted from Hamilton, "Das Lied vom Leben," *National Board of Review Magazine*, Nov. 1931, p. 8. See also synopsis in *Illustrierter Film-Kurier*; Bryher, "Berlin, April 1931," *Close Up*, June 1931, p. 132; Arnheim, *Film als Kunst*, pp. 91, 254–56, 288, 290, 298. For Granovsky's DIE KOFFER DES HERRN O. F. (THE LUGGAGE OF MR. O. F., 1931), see Kraszna-Krausz, "Four Films from Germany," *Close Up*, March, 1932, p. 45.

[18] That this was the same vague enthusiasm that manifested itself in the abstract films of the time seems the more probable as Ruttmann, the creator of WORLD MELODY, went on to cultivate the field of objectless art. His WEEK END (1930) was nothing but a short sound track recording the manifold noises of a working day and a Sunday in the countryside; his IN DER NACHT (1931) translated Schumann's music of that title into terms of abstract visual configurations. Oskar Fischinger, a disciple of Ruttmann, specialized in similar illustrations of musical scores and in addition made advertising films from abstract patterns. It may also be mentioned that during those years Hans Richter maintained his standing as a vanguard artist and Lotte Reiniger

The turn of cross-section films from New Objectivity to hymnic optimism indicates an important change. During the years of stabilization the reluctant neutrality of these films had testified to inner discontent with the well-established "system"; one is therefore safe in assuming that their overflowing cheerfulness during the years of crisis reflected a reverse attitude: the desire to believe that all was well. It was as if, now that economic depression threatened to upset the existing order of things, people were possessed by the fear of a catastrophe and in consequence cherished all kinds of illusions about the survival of their world.

Scores of films—mostly comedies interspersed with songs—fed such hopes. Animated by the very optimism which enlivened WORLD MELODY and SONG OF LIFE, they maintained neutrality in the interest of the *status quo.* Their surprising preponderance was an infallible sign of widespread despair.

Many of these products were calculated to put the unemployed at ease. Lupu Pick's GASSENHAUER (1931), for instance, featured a band of jobless musicians who successfully defy misery by playing in somber backyards a street song which eventually becomes popular. The film with its familiar Zille figures recalled René Clair's SOUS LES TOITS DE PARIS as well as Balázs' ADVENTURES OF A TEN-MARK NOTE. It was, incidentally, Pick's first and last talkie; he died shortly after its completion.[19] Another film gaily invited the hard-pressed unemployed to place confidence in a mirage of resettlement schemes, tent colonies and the like.[20] The title of the film, DIE DREI VON DER

went on issuing her familiar type of silhouette films. For Ruttmann films of the period, see Hamson, "Une Nouvelle Œuvre de Ruttmann," *La Revue du Cinéma,* July 1, 1930, pp. 70–71; *Film Society Programme,* Dec. 6, 1931; *Film Index,* p. 642a; Kracauer, "Courrier de Berlin," *La Revue du Cinéma,* Aug. 1, 1931, pp. 64–65. For Fischinger films, see Weinberg, "Complete List of Films by Oskar Fischinger, typewritten note, Museum of Modern Art Library, clipping files; Vincent, *Histoire de l'Art Cinématographique,* p. 160; *Film Society Programme,* Jan. 10, 1932. Richter's first sound film was a burlesque of a fair, ALLES DREHT SICH, ALLES BEWEGT SICH (EVERYTHING REVOLVES, 1929). Weinberg, *An Index to . . . Hans Richter,* pp. 9–15, takes stock of Richter's creative work. For Lotte Reiniger, see Bryher, "Notes on Some Films," *Close Up,* Sept. 1932, p. 198; *Film Society Programmes,* Oct. 19 and Dec. 14, 1930, March 8, 1931, Oct. 30, 1932. The Film Society, London, also showed, and briefly commented on, Moholy-Nagy's abstract film SCHWARTZ—WEISS—GRAU, 1932 (*Film Society Programme,* Nov. 20, 1932). Mr. Richter's unpublished manuscript "Avantgarde . . ." is rich in pertinent information.

19 Arnheim, *Film als Kunst,* pp. 203, 249; "Gassenhauer," *Filmwelt,* April 5, 1931. A sort of Zille film was also MIETER SCHULZE GEGEN ALLE (1932). Kalbus, *Deutsche Filmkunst,* II, 38–39, emphasizes the optimism underlying this film.

20 Cf. Kracauer, "'Kuhle Wampe' verboten!" *Frankfurter Zeitung,* April 5, 1932.

STEMPELSTELLE (1932), was an outright plagiarism of Thiele's earlier DIE DREI VON DER TANKSTELLE.

A favored expedient consisted in pretending that the underprivileged themselves were fully satisfied with their lot. In the Ufa comedy EIN BLONDER TRAUM (BLOND DREAM, 1932), poverty forces two window washers and a girl acting as a living projectile in a tent show to seek shelter in old railway cars on a meadow. Do they complain of their predicament? The song expressing the feelings of these enviable creatures includes the following words: "We are paying rent no longer, we have made our home in the heart of nature, and even if our nest were smaller, it really would not matter." [21]

Since most people prefer bigger nests, a series of films devoted themselves to success stories. An interesting contribution was made by Ufa with MENSCH OHNE NAMEN (THE MAN WITHOUT A NAME, 1932).[22] In it, Werner Krauss portrays a German industrialist who contracts amnesia while a prisoner of war in Russia. Years after the war, he regains his memory, returns to Berlin, and there learns that the authorities have proclaimed him dead. The scene in which a clerk climbs a giant ladder between rows of file cases and from its top shouts down to him that he no longer exists impressively illustrates the nightmarish workings of bureaucracy [Illus. 43]. To complete the ex-industrialist's misfortune, both his wife and his friend fail to recognize him. His downfall unintentionally mirrors that of the middle class during these years of crisis. The film now develops in a direction strangely reminiscent of the Zille film SLUMS OF BERLIN.[23] The man, who of course plans to commit the customary suicide, is taken care of by an obscure sales agent and a jobless stenographer, and with their help re-embarks upon a promising career. He assumes a new name after having been refused the right to his old one, successfully promotes an invention of his, and in his upward flight differs from the engineer in SLUMS OF BERLIN only in that he marries the poor stenographer instead of an upper middle-class girl. Times were bad for stenographers, and something had to be done in their favor.

Times were indeed so bad that even qualified specialists could not count on re-employment once they had been dismissed. Most

[21] Synopsis with song texts in *Illustrierter Film-Kurier*. Kalbus, *Deutsche Filmkunst*, II, 46.

[22] Synopsis in *Illustrierter Film-Kurier*. Kalbus, *ibid.*, p. 56.

[23] Cf. p. 143 f.

success films therefore emphasized luck rather than capability as the true source of brilliant careers. Characteristically, such film titles as DAS GELD LIEGT AUF DER STRASSE (MONEY LIES ON THE STREET), MORGEN GEHT'S UNS GUT (TOMORROW WE'LL BE FINE), and ES WIRD SCHON WIEDER BESSER (THINGS WILL BE BETTER AGAIN) were then quite common. And no matter how improbable the films themselves proved to be, the audience readily swallowed them provided that they lived up to their titles. Luck as the vehicle of success: the Germans must have been on the verge of hopelessness to accept a notion so utterly alien to their traditions.

Lesser employees and lower middle-class people were the declared favorites of Fortuna in all these films. Representative of the whole trend, which reached its artistic climax with Erich Engel's witty comedies, was DIE PRIVATSEKRETÄRIN (THE PRIVATE SECRETARY, 1931), an easy-going film whose tremendous popularity established Wilhelm Thiele's mastership of attractive concoctions. A sprightly small-town girl (Renate Müller) manages to get a job in a Berlin bank, and while working overtime one evening is approached by her big boss, whom she imagines to be just another office worker. They go out for the evening together, and the predictable result is her promotion to the position of banker's wife.[24]

In the Ufa film DIE GRÄFIN VON MONTE CHRISTO (COUNTESS OF MONTE CRISTO, 1932), this sort of daydreaming developed into a veritable fairy tale drawn from everyday life. Brigitte Helm as a film extra is cast in the role of a lady traveling in a fashionable car. Night-shooting begins; but instead of pulling up by the entrance of the studio-built hotel front, Helm and her girl friend drive ahead until they land in a real de luxe hotel, where the pseudo-lady is received as a guest of distinction because of the name "Countess of Monte Cristo" on her empty trunks. An amusing intrigue involving an unpleasant hotel thief and a noble gentleman crook enables her for a short time to keep up appearances and lead the life she has craved—a life considerably enriched by the gentleman crook's infatuation with her. One fine day, the police enter the scene; they arrest the loving crook and would doubtless have put an end to the false countess' shenanigans if it were not for Ufa's desire to kindle hopes in the hearts of poor film extras. Helm's escapade becomes a front-page story, and with their flair for publicity the studio execu-

[24] Kalbus, *Deutsche Filmkunst,* II, 54. For a similar film, DOLLY MACHT KARRIERE (DOLLY'S CAREER, 1930), see Weiss, "A Starring Vehicle," *Close Up,* Nov. 1930, pp. 334–35.

tives not only refrain from persecuting her, but have her sign an advantageous contract; proving conclusively what all these screen opiates tended to demonstrate: that everyday life itself is a fairy tale.

But how to endear oneself to a benevolent fairy? Here Hans Albers came in. This film actor, who once had portrayed adulterers and well-dressed rogues, suddenly turned into Germany's No. 1 screen favorite, the incarnation of Prince Charming. Pommer starred him in four Ufa films, and except for the last one, F. P. 1 ANTWORTET NICHT (F. P. 1 DOES NOT ANSWER, 1932), in which sentimental resignation prevailed, Albers invariably was a glorious victor—whether he played the crazy captain of an operetta cruiser in BOMBEN AUF MONTE CARLO (MONTE CARLO MADNESS, 1931), an amorous clown in QUICK (1932), or a simple telegraphist in DER SIEGER (THE VICTOR, 1932).[25] He quivered with radiant vitality, was extremely aggressive and like a born buccaneer seized any opportunity within his reach. But whatever his undertaking, whether attacking enemies or courting girls, it all was done in an unpremeditated way—as if he were driven by changing moods and circumstances rather than by the steadfast will to realize a project. In fact, he was the reverse of a schemer. And since he did not even care too much about luck, Fortuna on her part pursued him with the persistence of a loving woman and lent him a helping hand whenever he stumbled into one of the many pitfalls prepared for him. Of course, he took the hand she offered and then rushed on, as heedless as ever. Each Albers film filled the houses in proletarian quarters as well as on Kurfürstendamm. This human dynamo with the heart of gold embodied on the screen what everyone wished to be in life [Illus. 44].

[25] For films featuring Albers, see Kalbus, *Deutsche Filmkunst*, II, 38, 53, 59. Cf. synopses in *Illustrierter Film-Kurier*; program to MONTE CARLO MADNESS.

18. MURDERER AMONG US

DESPITE all efforts to maintain neutrality for the sake of the *status quo*, the façade of New Objectivity began to crumble after 1930. This is corroborated by the disappearance of those street and youth films which during the stabilized period had served the paralyzed authoritarian dispositions as a dreamlike outlet. Such screen dreams were no longer needed, for now that the paralysis had subsided, all kinds of leanings, authoritarian or otherwise, were at liberty to manifest themselves. As in the postwar period, the German screen became a battleground of conflicting inner tendencies.

In 1930, Potamkin wrote: "There are indications in Germany that the serious-minded will force the German cinema out of its lethargy and studio-impasse to a treatment of important subject-matter. Germany is approaching a political crisis, and with it an intellectual and aesthetic crisis. . . ."[1] He who undergoes a crisis is bound to weigh all pros and cons before determining his line of conduct. This was precisely what the Germans did—judging by two important films, THE BLUE ANGEL and M, which can be considered statements on the psychological situation of the time. Both pictures penetrated depths of the collective soul which in such films as SONG OF LIFE and PRIVATE SECRETARY were completely ignored. It is true that during the years of stabilization Pabst and Ruttmann, too, had attempted to uncover subterranean layers of contemporary reality. But while they had eluded the significance of their films by means of melodrama or sustained detachment, THE BLUE ANGEL as well as M breathed a strong sense of responsibility for all that was exposed in them. They were products of a mind freed from that "lethargy" to which Potamkin alludes.

DER BLAUE ENGEL (THE BLUE ANGEL, 1930) was an Ufa film based upon Heinrich Mann's prewar novel *Professor Unrath*, which along with other novels by the same author stigmatized the peculiar vices of German bourgeois society. Any nation depends upon critical

[1] Potamkin, "The Rise and Fall of the German Film," *Cinema*, April 1930, p. 59.

introspection as a means of self-preservation, and it is the lasting merit of Heinrich Mann that he tried to develop a German variety of that social-minded literature which flourished in England and France for many decades. Had a strange acrimony not narrowed his views, he might have exerted more influence than he actually did.

Emil Jannings enacts the film's main character, a bearded high-school professor in a small seaport town. This middle-aged bachelor violently antagonizes his pupils, who are quick to sense the many inhibitions behind his petty-tyrannical manner [Illus. 45]. When he learns that the boys frequent the dressing room of Lola Lola, star of a little company of artists performing in the tavern The Blue Angel, he decides to settle accounts with that vicious siren. Driven by moral indignation and ill-concealed sex jealousy, the foolish professor ventures into her den; but instead of putting an end to the juvenile excesses, he himself succumbs to the charms of Lola Lola, alias Marlene Dietrich—so much so that he shares her bedroom and then proposes to her. The consequence is that he has to leave the school. What does it matter? During his wedding party, having fallen into a state of euphoria, he succeeds in impressing the artists with a wonderful imitation of cockcrowing. But this high point of his career as a free man is also the beginning of his downfall. While the troop travels from town to town, Lola Lola not only makes him drudge for her, but agrees to the manager's suggestion that her husband produce his funny cockcrowing on the stage. His humiliation reaches its climax when the artists return to The Blue Angel in the hope of stirring up a sensation with the ex-professor. Their hope proves justified: the whole town rushes in, eager to listen to their fellow-citizen's cock-a-doodle-doo. Asked to perform, he launches into a terrific crowing, walks off the stage and, incessantly roaring, begins to strangle Lola Lola. The personnel overpower the raging madman and eventually leave him to himself. Then he seems to awaken from the nightmare of his recent existence. Like a mortally wounded animal seeking shelter in its lair, he sneaks back to the old school, enters his classroom, and there passes away.

Pommer, bent on promoting artistic German talkies, engaged Joseph von Sternberg to direct the film. A native of Austria, this brilliant Hollywood director had proved in UNDERWORLD and THE LAST COMMAND that he was master of the art of rendering milieus so that they amplified imperceptible emotions. In THE BLUE ANGEL, faraway foghorns sound from the harbor as Jannings walks through nocturnal streets to the tavern. When, on the point of leaving school for good, he sits, lonely, at his desk, a traveling shot encompasses the empty classroom with the tender slowness of a last embrace. This shot re-emerges at the film's very end, and now serves as an obituary impressively summarizing the story of the dead man whose head has sunk on the desk. The narrow interiors of The Blue Angel are endowed with a power of expression rarely even aspired to during the stabilized period. There is a promiscuous mingling of architectural fragments, characters and nondescript objects. Lola Lola sings her famous song on a miniature stage so overstuffed with props that she herself seems part of the décor. Jannings fights his way to the dressing room through a maze of fishing nets, and somewhat later appears in the company of a wooden caryatid, which supports the tiny gallery from which he glares at his idol. As in Carl Mayer's postwar films, the persistent interference of mute objects reveals the whole milieu as a scene of loosened instincts. Perfect conductors, these objects transmit Jannings' delayed passion as well as the waves of sexual excitement emanating from Lola Lola.

The film's international success—soon after its release, a Paris night-club opened under the name "The Blue Angel"—can be traced to two major reasons, the first of which was decidedly Marlene Dietrich. Her Lola Lola was a new incarnation of sex. This petty bourgeois Berlin tart, with her provocative legs and easy manners, showed an impassivity which incited one to grope for the secret behind her callous egoism and cool insolence [Illus. 46]. That such a secret existed was also intimated by her veiled voice which, when she sang about her interest in love-making and nothing else, vibrated with nostalgic reminiscences and smoldering hopes. Of course, the impassivity never subsided, and perhaps there was no secret at all. The other reason for the film's success was its outright sadism. The masses are irresistibly attracted by the spectacle of torture and humiliation, and Sternberg deepened this sadistic tendency by making Lola Lola destroy not only Jannings himself but his entire environment. A running motif in the film is the old church-clock which chimes a popular German tune devoted to the praise of loyalty and honesty (*Üb' immer Treu und Redlichkeit . . .*)—a tune expressive of Jannings' inherited beliefs. In the concluding passage, immediately after Lola Lola's song has faded away, this tune is heard for the last time as the camera shows the dead Jannings. Lola

Lola has killed him, and in addition her song has defeated the chimes.[2]

Besides being a sex story or a study in sadism, Sternberg's film vigorously resumes postwar traditions, marking the definite end of the paralysis. The Blue Angel can be considered a variation on Karl Grune's The Street. Like the philistine from the plush parlor, Jannings' professor is representative of the middle class; like the philistine, he rebels against the conventions by exchanging school for The Blue Angel, counterpart of the street; and exactly like the philistine, this would-be rebel again submits—not, it is true, to the old middle-class standards, but to powers far worse than those from which he escaped. It is significant that he increasingly appears to be the victim of the manager rather than Lola Lola's personal slave. Love has gone, indiscriminate surrender remains. The philistine in The Street, the café-owner in New Year's Eve, the hotel porter in The Last Laugh and the professor in Sternberg's film all seem shaped after one and the same model. This archetypal character, instead of becoming adult, engages in a process of retrogression effected with ostentatious self-pity. The Blue Angel poses anew the problem of German immaturity and moreover elaborates its consequences as manifested in the conduct of the boys and artists, who like the professor are middle-class offspring. Their sadistic cruelty results from the very immaturity which forces their victim into submission. It is as if the film implied a warning, for these screen figures anticipate what will happen in real life a few years later. The boys are born Hitler youths, and the cockcrowing device is a modest contribution to a group of similar, if more ingenious, contrivances much used in Nazi concentration camps.

Two characters stand off from these events: the clown of the artists' company, a mute figure constantly observing his temporary colleague, and the school beadle who is present at the professor's death and somehow recalls the night-watchman in The Last Laugh. He does not talk either. These two witness, but do not participate. Whatever they may feel, they refrain from interference. Their silent resignation foreshadows the passivity of many people under totalitarian rule.

Fritz Lang told me that in 1930, before M went into production, a short notice appeared in the press, announcing the tentative title

[2] Cf. Kalbus, *Deutsche Filmkunst*, II, 16; Vincent, *Histoire de l'Art Cinématographique*, p. 163.

of his new film, *Mörder unter uns* (*Murderer Among Us*). Soon he received numerous threatening letters and, still worse, was bluntly refused permission to use the Staaken studio for his film. "But why this incomprehensible conspiracy against a film about the Düsseldorf child-murderer Kürten?" he asked the studio manager in despair. "*Ach*, I see," the manager said. He beamed with relief and immediately surrendered the keys of Staaken. Lang, too, understood; while arguing with the man, he had seized his lapel and caught a glimpse of the Nazi insignia on its reverse. "Murderer among us": the Party feared to be compromised. On that day, Lang added, he came of age politically.

M opens with the case of Elsie, a schoolgirl who disappears and after a while is found slain in the woods. Since her murder is preceded and followed by similar crimes, the city lives through a veritable nightmare. The police work feverishly to track down the child-murderer, but succeed only in disturbing the underworld. The city's leading criminals therefore decide to ferret out the monster themselves. For once, their interests coincide with those of the law. Here Thea von Harbou borrows a motif from Brecht's *Dreigroschenoper* [3]: the gang of criminals enlists the help of a beggars' union, converting its membership into a network of unobtrusive scouts. Even though the police meanwhile identify the murderer as a former inmate of a lunatic asylum, the criminals with the aid of a blind beggar steal a march on the detectives. At night, they break into the office building in which the fugitive has taken refuge, pull him out of a lumber room beneath the roof, and then drag him to a deserted factory, where they improvise a "kangaroo court," which eventually pronounces his death sentence. The police appear in time to hand him over to the authorities.

Released in 1931, this Nero production found enthusiastic response everywhere. It was not only Lang's first talkie, but his first important film after the pretentious duds he had made during the stabilized period. M again reaches the level of his earlier films, DESTINY and NIBELUNGEN, and moreover surpasses them in virtuosity. To increase the film's documentary value, pictorial reports on current police procedures are inserted in such a skillful way that they appear to be part of the action. Ingenious cutting interweaves the milieus of the police and the underworld: while the gang leaders discuss their plans, police experts, too, sit in conference, and these

[3] Cf. p. 236.

two meetings are paralleled by constant shifts of scene which hinge on subtle association. The comic touch inherent in the cooperation between the lawless and the law materializes on various occasions. Witnesses refuse to agree upon the simplest facts; innocent citizens indict each other fiercely. Set against these gay interludes, the episodes concentrating upon the murders seem even more horrifying.

Lang's imaginative use of sound to intensify dread and terror is unparalleled in the history of the talkies. Elsie's mother, after having waited for hours, steps out of her flat and desperately shouts the child's name. While her "Elsie!" sounds, the following pictures pass across the screen: the empty stairwell [Illus. 47]; the empty attic; Elsie's unused plate on the kitchen table; a remote patch of grass with her ball lying on it; a balloon catching in telegraph wires —the very balloon which the murderer had bought from the blind beggar to win her confidence. Like a pedal point, the cry "Elsie!" underlies these otherwise unconnected shots, fusing them into a sinister narrative. Whenever the murderer is possessed by the lust for killing, he whistles a few bars of a melody by Grieg. His whistling threads the film, an ominous foreboding of his appearance. A little girl is seen walking along: as she stops in front of a shop window, the weird Grieg melody approaches her, and suddenly the bright afternoon street seems clouded by threatening shadows. Later on, the whistling reaches the ears of the blind beggar for a second time and thus brings about the murderer's own doom. Another fatal sound is produced by his vain effort to remove, with his jackknife, the lock of the door which has slammed behind him after his flight into the lumber room. When the criminals pass along the top floor of the office building, this jarring noise reminiscent of the prolonged gnawing of a rat, betrays his presence.[4]

The film's true center is the murderer himself. Peter Lorre portrays him incomparably as a somewhat infantile petty bourgeois who eats apples on the street and could not possibly be suspected of killing a fly. His landlady, when questioned by the police, describes this tenant of hers as a quiet and proper person. He is fat and looks effeminate rather than resolute. A brilliant pictorial device serves to characterize his morbid propensities. On three different occasions, scores of inanimate objects, much more obtrusive than in THE BLUE ANGEL, surround the murderer; they seem on the point of engulfing

[4] Arnheim, *Film als Kunst,* pp. 230, 252, 300, comments on several devices in M. Cf. Hamilton, "M," *National Board of Review Magazine,* March 1933, pp. 8–11.

him. Standing before a cutlery shop, he is photographed in such a way that his face appears within a rhomboid reflection of sparkling knives [Illus. 48]. Sitting on a café terrace behind an ivy-covered trellis, with only his cheeks gleaming through the foliage, he suggests a beast of prey lurking in the jungle. Finally, trapped in the lumber room, he is hardly distinguishable from the tangled debris in which he tries to evade his captors. Since in many German films the predominance of mute objects symbolizes the ascendancy of irrational powers, these three shots can be assumed to define the murderer as a prisoner of uncontrollable instincts. Evil urges overwhelm him in exactly the same manner in which multiple objects close in on his screen image.

This is corroborated by his own testimony before the "kangaroo court," an episode opening with a couple of shots which render perfectly the shock he experiences at that moment. Three criminals, insensitive to the murderer's frantic protests, push, drag and kick him forward. He lands on the floor. As he begins to look about, the close-up of his face—a face distorted with rage and fear—abruptly gives way to a long shot surveying the group of criminals, beggars and street women in front of him [Illus. 49]. The impression of shock results from the terrifying contrast between the wretched creature on the floor and this immovable group which, arranged in Lang's best monumental style, watches him in stony silence. It is as if the murderer has unexpectedly collided with a human wall. Then, in an attempt to justify himself, he accounts for his crimes in this way: I am always forced to move along the streets, and always someone is behind me. It is I. I sometimes feel I am myself behind me, and yet I cannot escape. . . . I want to run away—I must run away. The specters are always pursuing me—unless I do it. And afterwards, standing before a poster, I read what I have done. Have I done this? But I don't know anything about it. I loathe it—I must —loathe it—must—I can no longer . . .

Along with the implications of the pictorial texture, this confession makes it clear that the murderer belongs to an old family of German screen characters. He resembles Baldwin in THE STUDENT OF PRAGUE, who also succumbs to the spell of his devilish other self; and he is a direct offspring of the somnambulist Cesare. Like Cesare, he lives under the compulsion to kill. But while the somnambulist unconsciously surrenders to Dr. Caligari's superior will power, the child-murderer submits to his own pathological impulses and in addition is fully aware of this enforced submission. The way he acknowledges it reveals his affinity with all those characters whose ancestor is the philistine in THE STREET. The murderer is the link between two screen families; in him, the tendencies embodied by the philistine and the somnambulist finally fuse with each other. He is not simply a fortuitous compound of the habitual killer and the submissive petty bourgeois; according to his confession, this modernized Cesare is a killer because of his submission to the imaginary Caligari within him. His physical appearance sustains the impression of his complete immaturity—an immaturity which also accounts for the rampant growth of his murderous instincts.

In its exploration of this character, who is not so much a retrogressive rebel as a product of retrogression, M confirms the moral of THE BLUE ANGEL: that in the wake of retrogression terrible outbursts of sadism are inevitable. Both films bear upon the psychological situation of those crucial years and both anticipate what was to happen on a large scale unless people could free themselves from the specters pursuing them. The pattern had not yet become set. In the street scenes of M, such familiar symbols as the rotating spiral in an optician's shop and the policeman guiding a child across the street are resuscitated.[5] The combination of these motifs with that of a puppet incessantly hopping up and down reveals the film's wavering between the notions of anarchy and authority.

[5] Cf. comment on the imagery of BERLIN, p. 186.

19. TIMID HERESIES

A BATTLEGROUND of conflicting inner tendencies, the German screen of the pre-Hitler period was dominated by two major groups of films. One of them testified to the existence of antiauthoritarian dispositions. It included films concerned with humanization and peaceful progress; they sometimes went so far as to manifest outspoken leftist leanings.

Among the films of this first group two were conspicuous for implying that the retrogressive processes emphasized in THE BLUE ANGEL and M might well be averted under the *status quo*. BERLIN-ALEXANDERPLATZ (1931), made by Piel Jutzi after Alfred Döblin's famous novel of that title, tacitly opposed the pessimistic outlook of Sternberg and Lang. It was an underworld drama with many documentary shots in the manner of Ruttmann's BERLIN, which occasionally developed into a pictorial thicket arresting the action. The film's main character is Franz Biberkopf, a true Zille figure splendidly enacted by Heinrich George. After serving a prison term for manslaughter, he turns to peddling on Alexanderplatz and is perfectly happy with his girl until Reinhold, the boss of a gang of criminals, appears. This anemic-looking rogue talks the somewhat slow-witted Biberkopf into joining the gang. But soon the new member's innate honesty interferes so seriously with the activities of the criminals that they throw him out of a car going at full speed. There he lies. Months later, his right arm amputated, he returns to Reinhold—not to take revenge, but to offer full cooperation. Biberkopf has become an embittered cripple who despairs of making an honest living. His share from well-planned burglaries allows him to enjoy a comfortable existence in the company of his new girl, Mieze. But his luck does not last long. Reinhold, intent on possessing Mieze, lures her into the woods, and when she does not yield to his desire, he murders her in a fit of cold rage. A sample of genuine film-making is the scene in which singing boy-scouts pass along the highway immediately before the murderer re-emerges from the bushes and speeds away in his car. The police capture Reinhold in time to prevent Biberkopf from killing him; whereupon Biberkopf, left to himself, again takes to honesty and peddling.[1] At the film's very end, he is seen on Alexanderplatz, hawking a sort of tumbler puppet with the words: This puppet always bobs up again. Why does it always bob up again? Because it has metal in the right place.

The moral is obvious: he whose heart is in the right place surmounts any crisis without being corrupted. This is exemplified by Biberkopf's own development. When profound resentment prompts him to make common cause with Reinhold, he seems on the point of following the pattern set by the child-murderer and his predecessors. But unlike them, he succeeds in exorcising the evil spirits. Biberkopf himself is a tumbler figure. Vaguely reminiscent of the count in WARNING SHADOWS, he tends to prove that during the pre-Hitler period the image of submission was by no means sacrosanct.

The problem is whether or not his metamorphosis goes far enough to turn the audience against this image. The first time Biberkopf peddles on Alexanderplatz, he asks several S.A. men in the crowd around him to come nearer—asks them as kindly as if they were nondescript bystanders. This incident, unimportant in itself, illustrates strikingly the narrow scope of his tumbler attitude. To be sure, his heart is in the right place; but where other people have theirs does not concern him. Let social conditions be what they will, if only he can carry on, a decent peddler. Biberkopf has turned adult in a limited personal sense; his main characteristic is a blend of private honesty and political indifference. It would be inconceivable for any such Biberkopf to stem the mounting flood of retrogression, even if he has overcome retrogression within himself.

Although Biberkopf's change from a potential child-murderer into a half-mature character proves of little consequence, it discounts the leader principle proclaimed by the Nazis. To some extent, BERLIN-ALEXANDERPLATZ fostered belief in a positive evolution of the existing republican regime. Another faint suggestion of democratic mentality was Gerhart Lamprecht's charming and very successful child-film EMIL UND DIE DETEKTIVE (1931), fashioned after a popular novel by Erich Kästner; at least, this Ufa production in-

[1] A kindred film was STÜRME DER LEIDENSCHAFT (1932?) with Jannings as a criminal betrayed by his girl and his chums. Cf. "Stürme der Leidenschaft," *Filmwelt*, Dec. 27, 1931.

cluded nothing that would have justified the sinister forebodings in M and THE BLUE ANGEL. Emil is a small-town boy whose mother sends him to Berlin on an important mission: he is to deliver money to his grandmother. On the train, a thief robs the boy of his precious envelope. No sooner do they arrive than Emil starts pursuing the thief—a pursuit which, owing to the cooperation of a gang of Berlin urchins, develops into a veritable children's crusade. Passionate detectives, the children establish headquarters in a vacant lot opposite the criminal's hotel and, with a truly German gift for organization, even think of assigning one of their number to take charge of telephone messages. Their activities assume proportions which cause the police to intervene, and since the thief turns out to be a long-sought bank robber, the youths receive the 1000-mark reward offered for his capture. When Emil returns home in the company of his new friends, the whole town assembles on the airfield to hail the conquering heroes.

The literary figure of the detective is closely related to democratic institutions.[2] Through its praise of juvenile sleuthing EMIL UND DIE DETEKTIVE therefore suggests a certain democratization of German everyday life. This inference is bolstered by the independent and self-disciplined conduct of the boys as well as by the use made of candid-camera work. Neat and unpretentious documentary shots of Berlin street scenes portray the German capital as a city in which civil liberties flourish. The bright atmosphere pervading these passages contrasts with the darkness which invariably surrounds Fritz Rasp as the thief. He wears a black coat and has all the traits of the bogey in nursery tales. When he falls asleep in his hotel room, Emil in the uniform of a bellboy emerges from under the bed and looks around for the stolen money—a courageous youngster engulfed by menacing shadows. Light once for all defeats darkness in that magnificent sequence in which the thief is eventually cornered. Under a radiant morning sun, which seems to scoff at his eerie blackness, this Pied Piper in reverse tries in vain to escape the ever-increasing crowd of children who pursue and besiege him [Illus. 50].

No doubt the triumph of clarity helps to express what can be considered the film's democratic spirit. Yet this spirit evades definition. Instead of crystallizing in some tangible conviction, it remains a mood, just strong enough to neutralize the patriarchal tendencies which try to assert themselves in sundry scenes of the film. Since this

[2] Cf. p. 19 f.

mood is rather indistinct—it also results from the tender concern with politically ambiguous childhood events—the conclusion that the democratic attitudes behind the film lack vitality seems unavoidable.

Other films of the first pre-Hitler group were more explicit. Overtly they tackled the basic problem of authority. Unlike the youth films of the stabilized period—screen dreams in which sympathy for authority had been disguised as protest against authority—these films were quite candid in criticizing authoritarian behavior.

Outstanding among them was MÄDCHEN IN UNIFORM (1931), produced by Deutsche Film Gemeinschaft, an independent cooperative. It was drawn from Christa Winsloe's play *Gestern und Heute*. Leontine Sagan directed the film under the guidance of Carl Froelich, one of the most experienced directors of the German cinema.

MÄDCHEN IN UNIFORM, with an exclusively female cast, pictures life in a Potsdam boarding-school for the daughters of poor officers, who belong nevertheless to the aristocracy. In rendering this milieu, the film exposes the devastating effects of Prussianism upon a sensitive young girl. The headmistress of the school is the "spirit of Potsdam" incarnate. Another Frederick the Great, she moves along with a cane and proclaims orders of the day which recall the glorious times of the Seven Years' War [Illus. 51]. For instance, when annoyed by complaints of scarce food, she decrees: "Through discipline and hunger, hunger and discipline, we shall rise again." While the girls on the whole manage to put up with the hardship inflicted upon them, Manuela, a newcomer, suffers intensely under a rule alien to her tender and imaginative nature. She craves helpful understanding and finds ruthless efficiency. Only one teacher is sympathetic: Fräulein von Bernburg. This woman, whose beauty has begun to fade under the strain of resignation, is not yet resigned enough to give up advocating a more considerate education. "I cannot stand the way you transform the children into frightened creatures," she says to the headmistress in a fit of insubordination which enrages the latter. Manuela senses Fräulein von Bernburg's unavowed affection for her and responds to it with a passion involving her suppressed desire for love. After a theatrical performance in honor of the headmistress' anniversary—a day of harmless saturnalia and light spirits—this pent-up passion explodes. The girl is overjoyed with her success as an actress, and watered punch does the rest. In a state of frenzy, she blurts out her inmost feelings for the beloved teacher and then swoons.

The consequences are terrible: by order of the scandalized headmistress no one is allowed to speak to the culprit. Fräulein von Bernburg disregards this interdict, but succeeds only in increasing the girl's anguish. Manuela believes herself deserted by the woman she idolizes and attempts to commit suicide. She is on the point of throwing herself from the top of the staircase, when the girls arrive and pull her back from outside the railing. Attracted by the unusual tumult, the headmistress approaches energetically—every inch a Fridericus ready to crush a revolt. They tell her what has happened, and it is as if she were suddenly stripped of her authority. An old, stooped woman, she retreats under the accusing stares of the girls and silently disappears in the dark corridor.

The film owes part of its fame to the acting. Hertha Thiele's Manuela is a unique compound of sweet innocence, illusory fears and confused emotions. While she embodies youth in its utter vulnerability, Dorothea Wieck as Fräulein von Bernburg still glows with a youth that is irretrievably departing. Each gesture of hers tells of lost battles, buried hopes and sublimated desires. The *mise en scène*, mellow rather than daring, excels in delicate shades. Potsdam is masterfully characterized through such simple leitmotivs as the statue of a soldier, the soldierlike steeple of the parish church and the remote blare of the garrison bugles. Towards the end of the film, a stately princess crowned by an enormous plumed hat reviews the girls; the irony in the rendering of her shallow benevolence could not be subtler. Perhaps the most perfect sample of effective unobtrusiveness is the repeated insertion of the school's beautiful old staircase hall. The first views serve to familiarize us with it. When it re-emerges in the middle of the film, the girls amuse themselves by throwing objects from the top of the stairs, and then, shuddering, express their horror of the abyss beneath them. These two series of shots enable the audience to grasp the significance of the final staircase scene in which Manuela, her mind bent on suicide, walks upstairs: her appearance at the top immediately evokes the image of the shuddering girls [Illus. 52]. To round out Manuela's own image, the symbolic power of light is explored in much the same manner as in EMIL UND DIE DETEKTIVE. Throughout the film, her luminous face appears against bright backgrounds, so that it seems all but one with them. This transparence makes Manuela particularly touching.

MÄDCHEN IN UNIFORM enjoyed immense popularity. In Germany, it was considered the best film of the year; in America, the reviewers were enthusiastic.[3] The National Board praised the picture as "one of the most human films that has been made anywhere" [4]; the *New York Herald Tribune* called it "the drama of the need for tenderness and sympathy as opposed to the harshness of a tyrannical system of boarding school domination." [5] It was again Potamkin who went beyond such easy generalizations. He identified the film as a specifically German document and criticized it for its timidity. "*Mädchen in Uniform* . . . is sincere but cautious, does not venture upon its own terrain, but preserves a respectable distance from its own social implications." [6]

This criticism holds. What on the surface appears to be a wholesale attack against rigid Prussian discipline is in the final analysis nothing but a plea for its humanization. It is true that the headmistress indicts Fräulein von Bernburg for fomenting unrest among the girls and terms her a rebel. But this strange rebel is so loyal to the system which has broken her that in her last talk with Manuela she makes an effort to convince the trembling girl of the headmistress' good intentions. She does not want to do away with the "spirit of Potsdam"; she merely fights its excesses. One is tempted to suspect that her understanding, if not motherly, attitude toward the girls originates in patriarchal notions inseparable from the authoritarian regime. Fräulein von Bernburg is a heretic who never dreams of exchanging the traditions she shares with the headmistress for a "new order."

In the whole film, there is no hint of the possibility that authoritarian behavior might be superseded by democratic behavior. This accounts for Potamkin's conjecture: "The film does not fail to leave a sense of faith in the princess, the benefactress, who had she but known would have changed all that oppression of arbitrary discipline —there is still a nostalgia for the nobility." [7] The final scene, it is true, elaborates upon the symbolic defeat of the headmistress: Prussianism seems definitely done for when she moves back through the dark corridor, leaving the bright foreground to Fräulein von Bernburg and the girls. Yet at its end this very scene invalidates

[3] Kraszna-Krausz, "Four Films from Germany," *Close Up*, March 1932, p. 39. See also Jahier, "42 Ans de Cinéma," *Le Rôle intellectuel du Cinéma*, pp. 67–68.

[4] "Mädchen in Uniform," *National Board of Review Magazine*, Sept.–Oct. 1932, p. 10.

[5] Watts, "Mädchen in Uniform," *New York Herald Tribune*, Sept. 21, 1932.

[6] Potamkin, "Pabst and the Social Film," *Hound & Horn*, Jan.–March 1933, p. 305.

[7] Potamkin, *ibid.*, p. 305.

the impression that the headmistress has abdicated. As the shadows envelop her, the garrison bugles blare again. They have the last word in the film. The resumption of this motif at such an important moment unmistakably reveals that the principle of authority has not been shaken. The headmistress will continue to wield the scepter. And any possible softening of authoritarian discipline would only be in the interest of its preservation.[8]

Simultaneously with MÄDCHEN IN UNIFORM appeared another film raising similar issues: DER HAUPTMANN VON KÖPENICK (THE CAPTAIN OF KÖPENICK, 1931). It was fashioned by Richard Oswald after Carl Zuckmayer's 1928 play of the same title—a play built around the true story of the famous cobbler Wilhelm Voigt, who made the world of 1906 realize the absurdities of Prussian militarism. On the screen, the actor Max Adalbert portrayed this character with a vernacular authenticity that undoubtedly contributed to the film's success in Germany and abroad.

Following the play closely, the film goes far in its criticism of Prussian police methods under the Kaiser. The police, not content with refusing a passport to the old jailbird Voigt, expel him from every town as an undesirable unemployed. It is a vicious circle, as he himself recognizes: if he had a job, the authorities would give him a passport, but since he has none, he cannot get a job. The passport becomes his obsession (an obsession millions of Europeans persecuted under Hitler would find quite understandable). In his despair, the ingenious cobbler finally decides to capitalize on the spell any officer's uniform casts over German soldiers and civilians alike. He buys a worn-out uniform and dons it in a men's room from which he emerges as a demigod. His disguise is more than transparent; but who would dare to scrutinize a magic phenomenon? The self-appointed captain marches two squads of soldiers whom he meets on the street to the town hall of Köpenick, arrests the dazed top officials "by order of his Majesty," without encountering the slightest doubt of his right to do so, and then asks for the passport office, the real objective of his military expedition. Alas, there is no passport office in Köpenick. Voigt throws in the sponge and slips away. But the story of his exploit leaks out, and the whole world laughs at the

[8] Hertha Thiele and Dorothea Wieck again co-starred in Wysbar's ANNA UND ELISABETH (1933); cf. *Film Society Programme*, Nov. 19, 1933. Leontine Sagan directed, in England, MEN OF TOMORROW (1932), but this film about Oxford students was only a weak aftermath of her MÄDCHEN IN UNIFORM.

"captain of Köpenick." The film emphasizes particularly the authentic fact that the Kaiser, too, had a good laugh. At the end, the cobbler surrenders to the police. He is soon pardoned and granted the coveted passport—by order of his Majesty.

An uncertain blend of satire and comedy, this film is even more ambiguous than MÄDCHEN IN UNIFORM. It ridicules German awe of the uniform and at the same time justifies Prussian militarism as such. For the Kaiser's laughter as well as his indulgent pardon reduces the whole chain of absurdities to minor shortcomings of a sound and strong regime, which can well afford to tolerate them. One sequence, moreover, suggests that these shortcomings spring from the very *Weltanschauung* which is also the source of Prussia's power. Voigt, shocked by a new order of expulsion, shows it to his warm-hearted brother-in-law Friedrich, who has tried hard to rehabilitate him. Friedrich is a town clerk imbued with pride of the fatherland, the army, the Kaiser. He considers ill luck what the other resents as a flagrant injustice. Their discussion develops into a clash of two concepts of authority, and as Voigt freely voices his exasperation, Friedrich retorts: I refuse, and I am not even allowed to listen to you. We are governed by justice. And when you are crushed, you just have to submit to it. You have to keep quiet. Then you will still belong to us.

This outburst of a born authoritarian is recorded without a shadow of irony. In addition, the film tends to prove that Voigt lives up to Friedrich's tenets. Towards the end, when examined by the police, he declares that his desire to be buried in native soil kept him from crossing the borders to safety. This unwilling rebel still ardently wants to "belong." That in the core of his soul he is as militaristic-minded as his brother-in-law follows conclusively from the very last scene, which resumes the motif of the film's opening shots: a column of soldiers moving along to the sound of a military band. Voigt, now a free man with a passport, comes upon the soldiers and, his feet electrified, marches off in their company. The Friedrichs win out.

One more film dealing with the problem of militarism was KADETTEN (CADETS, 1931), a military-academy romance laid in Lichterfelde, the cradle of the Prussian officers' corps. While MÄDCHEN IN UNIFORM honestly exposed the deficiencies of authoritarian discipline, CADETS carefully concealed them. In this spineless grade-B production, the German West Point is passed off as a privileged boarding-school, whose director has all the traits of a soft-pedaling humanitarian—at least, the headmistress of MÄDCHEN IN UNIFORM would have despised him as such. It was all idle whitewash. But, as has been remarked earlier, many people wished to believe that in spite of the crisis all was going well.[9] Of course, their escapism only benefited the authoritarian-minded.

Strong antimilitaristic feelings manifested themselves in Max Ophuls' delightful LIEBELEI, a Viennese film drawn from the famous Schnitzler play of that title, which had been several times transferred to the screen. This last version was released in Berlin as late as March 16, 1933. It contrasts in a very touching way the tenderness of a love story with the severity of the military code of honor. A young lieutenant in love with a sweet Viennese girl is called to account by a baron who believes him to be the lover of the baroness. In reality, the lieutenant has broken off this liaison some time before. Nevertheless the code requires a duel. The lieutenant is killed in it and his girl throws herself out of the window in a fit of despair.

In rendering this terrible triumph of conventional prejudices, the film persistently points at their obsolescence and moral inadequacy. When the lieutenant's friend, himself an officer, refuses to second in a duel provoked by a dead affair, his colonel tells him bluntly that he will have to leave the army; whereupon the officer expresses his readiness to start a new life on a Brazilian coffee plantation. The significance of this showdown is enhanced by the splendor of the love episodes proper. They glow with genuine emotion. In the middle of the film, the lieutenant and the girl drive in a horse-drawn sled through snowy woods, each assuring the other: "I swear that I love you." At the end, after the girl has committed suicide, their love survives in an epilogue formed by two shots: the first pans through the girl's familiar room, while her voice whispers: "I swear . . ."; the second, evoking the image of the snowy woods, is accompanied by the words: ". . . that I love you." The code of honor appears the more odious as it is instrumental in destroying a love of such intensity.

Considering the implications of LIEBELEI, its release at the hour of Hitler's ultimate triumph may seem to have been ill-timed. But the public enjoyed the film solely as a love story bathed in the enchanting atmosphere of Imperial Vienna, which would have been unimaginable without its lieutenants. From this angle, the duel was nothing but a remote event designed to add the touch of tragedy which many Germans consider an infallible sign of emotional depth.

[9] Cf. p. 211.

20. FOR A BETTER WORLD

IT is noteworthy that those films of the first pre-Hitler group which overtly indulged in social criticism belonged among the top-ranking artistic achievements of the time. Aesthetic quality and leftist sympathies seemed to coincide.

Pabst again took the lead. In the three important films he made during the pre-Hitler years, his preoccupation with social problems outweighed the melodramatic inclinations characteristic of his New Objectivity period. Potamkin traces this change of Pabst's impressionable mind to the change of external conditions: "The sharpening conflict in Germany, the polarization of the forces, would naturally touch a man like Pabst. It would intensify and direct his social suspicions and tend to dissipate from his concern the shallow complacencies of the ladies and gentlemen of euphemy." [1]

The first of those three films was WESTFRONT 1918 (1930), a Nero production which appeared almost simultaneously with the Remarque film ALL QUIET ON THE WESTERN FRONT. Fashioned after Ernst Johannsen's war novel, *Four of the Infantry* (*Vier von der Infanterie*), it dealt with trench warfare in the last stages of World War I. On a stagnant front, a German lieutenant and his men try to hold their position against French attacks, and that is all. The battle flares up and subsides; hours of desperate action alternate with periods of complete lull. One day, a crowded dugout is hit by a shell, and but for the efforts of the rest of the group the men buried in it would have died of suffocation. In another sequence, a student-soldier volunteers to slip back to headquarters and on this occasion spends the first love night of his life with a French girl. Returning to the front, he meets his friend Karl going off on leave. But the war is inescapable: back home, Karl sees the queues before food shops and surprises his young wife in the company of a butcher boy, who has

[1] Potamkin, "Pabst and the Social Film," *Hound & Horn*, Jan.–March 1933, p. 296.

bought her favors with extra rations of meat. "One should not leave a wife alone for so long," Karl's mother says to her son. He dimly realizes that the war is behind it all—the war which goes on and on. When he rejoins his comrades, they tell him that the student has been slain by a French colonial soldier who, himself wounded, is heard screaming from no-man's land. Karl, seeking death, engages in a reconnoitering mission which takes him past the student's corpse; a cramped hand juts out from a muddy pool. Then the French make a tank attack in overwhelming strength. The treacherous calm following the attack is suddenly interrupted by a horrible roar. The German lieutenant shouts: "Hurrah, hurrah!" He has gone mad; his head resembles a death's-head. They drag him to a ruined church hastily converted into a field hospital. The dark nave is filled with moans and agonized cries [Illus. 53]. A French and a German soldier, lying side by side, grope for each other's hands and murmur something like forgiveness or "Never again war." There is no chloroform left for amputations. Karl dies, enraptured by a vision of his wife.

In its analysis of WESTFRONT 1918 the London Film Society mentions the film's "striking similarities to the doctrine of the New Objectivity." [2] This remark points at one of Pabst's basic intentions: in his new war picture as well as in his previous films he endeavors to render the commonplace in real life with photographic veracity. Many shots betray the unconscious cruelty of the candid camera. Helmets and fragments of corpses form a weird still life; somewhere behind the front lines, several privates carry scores of wooden crosses destined to adorn soldier graves. As always, Pabst manages to avoid cheap symbolism. The undamaged statue of Christ in the ruined church is made to appear a casual fact which only incidentally conveys a symbolic meaning. Throughout the film war seems experienced rather than staged.

To deepen this experience much use is made of traveling shots. They are produced by a camera which may travel long distances to capture the whole of some scenery or action. Pabst, eager to preserve the essential virtues of the silent film, now relied frequently on shots of this kind. He had to, for early sound technique did not yet allow him to resume his favorite method of swift cutting. One traveling shot follows the student on his way to headquarters; he falls down, rises again and then runs past the battered trunk of a lone tree which stands erect in the void. Similarly, the camera roams through the

[2] *Film Society Programme,* Dec. 6, 1931.

church, catching glimpses of the delirious Karl and a singing soldier who in his mental confusion keeps one of his arms hanging in mid-air.[3]

This "least showman-like of war-films" is neither picturesque nor rich in suspense.[4] A drab gray predominates and certain motifs reassert themselves insistently. Through such devices Pabst succeeds in impressing the dreary monotony of trench warfare upon the audience. One of the often-repeated pictures is the barren stretch of land before the German front lines. Its vegetation consists of torn barbed-wire fences, cut off from the sky by clouds of smoke or impenetrable fog. When for once the fog dissolves, rows of tanks emerge from the vacuum and successively fill the picture frame. The barren field is the landscape of death, and its permanent appearance only reflects what those caught in the gray limbo endure. The pandemonium of battle noises joins in, deepening these impressions. Inarticulate outbursts of panic and madness mingle with the ack-ack of machine guns and the whizz of bombs—a terrible cacophony which at intervals is drowned out by the long-lasting, deafening sound of an artillery barrage.[5]

The film's international prestige success resulted no less from its message than from its artistic merit. In an article comparing Pabst with Dovzhenko, John C. Moore comments on the hospital sequence: "In his final scenes Pabst makes one last desperate effort to convey to us not only the horror of war, but its futility and its gross stupidity as well. . . ."[6] WESTFRONT 1918 is an outright pacifist document and as such goes beyond the scope of New Objectivity. Its fundamental weakness consists in not transgressing the limits of pacifism itself. The film tends to demonstrate that war is intrinsically monstrous and senseless; but this indictment of war is not supported by the slightest hint of its causes, let alone any insight into them. Silence spreads where it would be natural to ask questions. While Dovzhenko in his grandiose ARSENAL (1929) reveals the Ukrainian Civil War to be an inevitable explosion of pent-up class hatred, Pabst in his World War film confines himself to expressing his abhorrence of war in general.

Potamkin, seduced by Pabst, the artist, tries to justify Pabst, the

[3] Cf. Spottiswoode, *A Grammar of the Film*, p. 241.

[4] Quoted from Potamkin, "Pabst and the Social Film," *Hound & Horn*, Jan.–March 1933, p. 298.

[5] Spottiswoode, *A Grammar of the Film*, p. 80.

[6] Moore, "Pabst—Dovjenko—A Comparison," *Close Up*, Sept. 1932, p. 180.

humanitarian, by contending that the pacifism of Westfront 1918 "is on its way to an acute attack upon the warmakers." But this appraisal sounds somewhat optimistic; in fact, Pabst's artistic brilliance, instead of compensating for the absence of pertinent arguments, makes his lack of reasoning all the more obvious. Except for stray pacifist remarks in the hospital sequence, the whole of Westfront 1918 amounts to a noncommittal survey of war horrors. Their exhibition is a favorite weapon of the many pacifists who indulge in the belief that the mere sight of such horrors suffices to deter people from war.

The Nazis were quick in discrediting this pacifist "argument." Hans Zöberlein's Stosstrupp 1917 (Shock Troop 1917), a World War film produced soon after Hitler's rise to power, seems to have been a deliberate answer to Westfront 1918; at least, the two films resemble each other strikingly. Zöberlein renders the horrors of trench warfare with a realistic objectivity equaling, if not exceeding, Pabst's and, exactly like Pabst, elaborates upon the despondency of the soldiers. There is not a single note of exceptional bravery or heroism in his film. Nevertheless he manages to exclude any pacifist implications by interpreting the last stages of World War I as a struggle for Germany's survival. In other words, the display of war horrors, Pabst's main "argument," is not an effective instrument against war. The Nazi film points up the unreliable vagueness of the Pabst film.

Pre-Hitler pacifism found another outlet in Victor Trivas' Niemandsland (Hell on Earth, 1931), a fantastic war film based upon an idea by Leonhard Frank. Five soldiers of different nations—a German carpenter, a Frenchman, a British officer, a Jewish tailor and a Negro singer—get lost between the front lines and seek shelter in an abandoned trench under a ruined building. While the war around them draws ever closer, they change from "enemies" into comrades who learn to understand and respect each other. A fraternal spirit animates this human oasis in no-man's land. The whole film is an attempt to defame war by contrasting it with a community which has all the traits of the lamasery of Shangri-La. The attempt is thoroughly abortive, for Hell on Earth disregards the different causes of wars in much the same way as Westfront 1918, and in addition blurs the image of peace conveyed by the community of the five soldiers. Since this community results from the acute pressure of catastrophic events, it is nothing but an emergency brotherhood. Many European refugees, experienced in such temporary fraternities, know about the quick transition from brotherliness to loneliness. This aesthetically interesting film opposes the inadequate dream of a terrestrial paradise to a shadowy notion of "hell on earth." Particularly evasive is the symbolic concluding scene in which the five are forced out of their refuge by the approaching battle. "The last we see of them," Shelley Hamilton writes, "is five figures side by side against the sky, tramping down the wire entanglements that block their way, stepping forward together."[7] From no-man's land they move towards never-never land, and the war continues. The German militarists did not have to fear the German pacifists.

After a silly provincial comedy, SKANDAL UM EVA (THE EVA SCANDAL, 1930),[8] Pabst made DIE DREIGROSCHENOPER (THE BEGGAR'S OPERA, 1931), a Warner-Tobis picture drawn from Brecht-Weill's successful play of that title, which itself was based upon John Gay's old *Beggar's Opera.* The film version, originally influenced by Brecht, differed much from the play, but on the whole preserved its social satire, genuine lyricism and revolutionary coloring. Kurt Weill adjusted his songs to the exigencies of the screen.

The plot, laid in an imaginary London of the end of the nineteenth century, features three rogues: Mackie Messer, the leader of a gang of criminals, Peachum, the king of the beggars, and Tiger Brown, the police commissioner.[9] Mackie, upon leaving the brothel which harbors his mistress Jenny, meets Peachum's daughter Polly on the street. After a few dances in a café he decides to marry her and orders his underlings to make proper arrangements for the wedding. Many London shops are plundered that night. The sumptuous wedding party takes place in a deserted underground warehouse, with the corrupt police commissioner as the guest of honor. Tiger Brown benevolently overlooks the crimes of his old friend Mackie. Peachum on his part is so infuriated over Polly's marriage that he threatens

[7] Hamilton, "Hell on Earth," *National Board of Review Magazine,* April 1933, p. 9. Cf. Kraszna-Krausz, "Four Films from Germany," *Close Up,* March 1932, pp. 44–45.

[8] Cf. Potamkin, "Pabst and the Social Film," *Hound & Horn,* Jan.–March 1933, p. 298. Potamkin decidedly overestimated this film. For a more critical comment, see "Skandal um Eva," *Close Up,* Sept. 1930, pp. 221–22.

[9] Cf. Rotha, *Celluloid,* p. 109. Barry, "The Beggar's Opera," *National Board of Review Magazine,* June 1931, pp. 11–13.

to disturb the imminent coronation of the Queen by a beggars' demonstration unless the police commissioner sends Mackie to the gallows. Unfortunately, the police commissioner cannot risk imperiling the coronation. Mackie hides in the brothel. It does not help him much, for his jealous mistress, Jenny, turns informer. Even though Mackie is captured, Peachum in his distrust of Tiger Brown's promises mobilizes the beggars. Meanwhile Polly embarks upon an amazing career. With the gang members as her associates, she opens a bank, arguing that lawful robberies pay better than illegal activities. This whole banking farce has been added in the film. No sooner does Peachum learn of his daughter's prosperous enterprise than he wants to have a share in it. He implores the beggars not to interrupt the royal procession, but they refuse to listen to him. While they march on, Mackie escapes from prison with the aid of Jenny, whose love surpasses her jealousy—she is a late descendant of the German stage and screen prostitutes. The beggars' demonstration causes the downfall of both Peachum and Tiger Brown. Yet Mackie cares sufficiently for the two to admit them as partners in Polly's bank. A new financial empire is in the making, and the three rogues become pillars of society.

Since this essentially theatrical plot could not well be made into a realistic film, Pabst reversed his usual method of approach: instead of penetrating our existing world, he built up an unreal universe. The whole film is bathed in a "queer, fantastic atmosphere," greatly intensified by Andrej Andrejew's settings.[10] In discussing them, Rotha mentions the "incredibly steep and very long flight of narrow wooden steps" in the underground warehouse and also praises "the late-Victorian brothel with its paper-patterned windows and antimacassars, its multitude of useless ornaments and its giant negress statues standing about the room."[11] To enhance the bizarre character of these interiors, the illusionary possibilities of glass are thoroughly utilized. The numerous screens of glass in the café which serves as background to Mackie's short courtship apparently have no function other than to transform the crowded and smoky room into a confusing maze [Illus. 54]. Later Mackie is seen entering the brothel behind a glass partition which surrounds him with a furtive halo.

The characters of this film appear as true products of their

[10] Quoted from Rotha, *Celluloid*, p. 111.
[11] *Ibid.*, pp. 111–12.

milieu. On his way to the docks, where a ballad singer is performing, Mackie walks past a row of prostitutes and pimps who lean motionless against the houses; it is as if the houses exuded them. The ballad singer emerges at regular intervals, and since his songs comment on the action, the action itself assumes the air of a ballad. All seems to be dreamed. This impression is also strengthened by F. A. Wagner's camera work. Owing to an uninterrupted succession of pan and traveling shots, the scenery never comes to a standstill. The movements of the brothel room resemble those of a ship's cabin. Normal stability is upset and a hovering phantom world arises.[12]

Although Pabst establishes this world with undeniable mastery, his rendering of DREIGROSCHENOPER is less adequate than the Berlin stage production of 1928. While the theatrical *mise en scène* isolated the episodes of the play, so as to stress its wanton, kaleidoscopic character, the screen treatment eliminates all caesuras in the interest of a coherent whole. Motifs originally intended to produce effects of light improvisation are woven into an elaborate texture, as compact and decorative as tapestry. Its heavy beauty muffles the clang of satire. The film is the tour de force of an artist not too familiar with spheres beyond the realm of what he himself once called "real life."

In contending that this Pabst film "is a further step in his progress towards social conclusiveness," Potamkin thinks in particular of the beggars' demonstration.[13] It is the one sequence of the film in which deadly earnestness disperses all jests. For once, reality breaks through. And as if the touch of it restored Pabst's artistic freedom, he is able in this brief sequence to mirror the irresistible impact of revolutionized masses. The beggars, marching through narrow, dim streets, not only ignore their own leader's attempt to force them back, but continue to advance when they reach the bright thoroughfare in expectation of the royal cortege. The police cannot stop their forward thrust; the horse guards try in vain to keep them away from the carriage of the Queen. For a memorable moment, all life is arrested. Fully exposed to the light which increases their ugliness, the beggars stare at the white-clad Queen, who makes an effort to endure the threatening gaze of these sinister figures. Then she surrenders. She hides her face behind her bouquet, and the magic spell fades away. The royal procession moves on, and the beggars return to the

[12] Cf. Arnheim, *Film als Kunst*, pp. 125–26.

[13] Potamkin, "Pabst and the Social Film," *Hound & Horn*, Jan.–March 1933, p. 300.

darkness from which they came. Potamkin defines this passage as "a very stirring approximation of the revolutionary march." [14]

Except for the beggars' demonstration, the film mingled sincere enlightenment and frivolous bluff after the manner of the play. It was an iridescent spectacle which both antagonized and amused bourgeois audiences. Its fair success indicates not so much a turn towards the left as an unbalanced wavering of viewpoints and attitudes during those years of crisis.

Pabst himself seemed unwavering. At about this time, he assumed social responsibilities, succeeding the late Lupu Pick as president of Dacho, the top organization of German film workers.[15] His "progress towards social conclusiveness" culminated in KAMERADSCHAFT (COMRADESHIP, 1931), a Nero picture suggested by the leftist writer Karl Otten. It is based upon an actual French mining disaster that occurred more than a decade before World War I in Courrières, near the German border. The event was interesting for a particular reason: German miners had come to the aid of their French comrades. In the film, Pabst heightened the significance of the story by making it take place shortly after Versailles.[16]

The film's introductory section exposes economic and political conditions in the mining district. Under the pressure of unemployment scores of German miners try their luck across the border, but since the nearby French mine has no jobs to offer, they return home empty-handed. Occasional outbursts of French chauvinism increase the tension. In a restaurant of the French coal town, Françoise, a native girl, offends three German miners by flatly refusing to dance with one of them. The catastrophe in the French mine and the ensuing panic of the town are rendered in episodes reminiscent of Zola's *Germinal.*

News of the disaster quickly reaches a gang of German miners busily scrubbing themselves in an enormous washroom. This sequence is the turning point of the film, for, after a heated discussion in which much pent-up resentment against the French explodes, the miners decide to volunteer in the rescue action. The director of the mine reluctantly grants them permission, and off they go. Deep down in the pit, the three miners who have been offended by Françoise head

[14] *Ibid.*
[15] *Ibid.*, p. 304.
[16] *Ibid.*, p. 301.

in the same direction. They remove the iron fence which since Versailles has marked the boundary between the French and German shafts, and then join the rescuers [Illus. 55].

Nightmarish scenes of anguish and heroism unfold amidst splintered wooden supports, pools of water and overhanging rock. As masses of stone crash with the thundering noise of a bombardment, a young French miner on the verge of being suffocated believes himself back in the war. Protected by a gas mask, one of the Germans approaches the raving Frenchman, who summons up his last strength to fend off this imaginary enemy. His hallucination materializes in a very short scene in which the two transform themselves into soldiers desperately trying to kill each other. Only after knocking the Frenchman down is the German able to drag him to safety. The wounded German miners are taken care of in a French hospital. When they depart, the whole town escorts them back to the border. There a brief stop is made, and words of farewell seal the bonds of mutual sympathy. Spokesmen of the two miner groups spontaneously condemn the war, extol the fraternity of all workers and insist upon unity between Germany and France. In the concluding scene, an acid epilogue, the miners' outlook is contrasted with the actual situation. One French and one German official, separated by a new iron fence in the shafts, exchange protocols ratifying the re-establishment of the frontier. Versailles wins out. The strictly symmetrical gestures of both officials satirize this victory of bureaucratic wisdom.

With COMRADESHIP, Pabst again came into his own. His innate sense of reality strikingly reasserts itself in the washroom episode. An all-pervading spray envelops the naked miners as well as the rows of clothes which hang down from a distant ceiling; it is as if a weird mass of animal carcasses loomed high above the faintly gleaming group of lathered human bodies.[17] Nothing seems staged in this episode; rather, the audience is let into one of the arcana of everyday life [Illus. 56]. The studio-built mine gives a complete illusion of subterranean rock. Ernö Metzner, who made the settings, remarked that candid shots of a real mining disaster would scarcely have produced a convincing impression of it. "In this instance nature could not be used as a model for the studio." [18] Dreadful reality is insepa-

[17] Grune's miner film, EXPLOSION (1923), seems to have included a similar scene; cf. Balázs, *Der sichtbare Mensch*, pp. 101–2.

[18] Metzner, "A Mining Film," *Close Up*, March 1932, p. 4.

rable from the halo with which our imagination surrounds it. One of the traveling shots exploring the mine glides from a conglomerate of broken beams and uprights to a somber stretch of stone suddenly illuminated by an inexplicable light.[19]

Even minor details carry special weight in the film. After the explosion, the panic-stricken townspeople hurry towards the mine, except for an isolated tailor who is standing indifferently before his shop window containing only a single male dummy. A close shot reveals the similarity of both figures, intimating that the tailor is equally void of life. To shape proletarian mass scenes without borrowing from the Russians was apparently impossible in those days. When a frantic crowd attempts to storm the gate of the French mine, the watchman's frightened face is seen encircled by the bare arms of his fanatic assailants. This close-up might well have figured in any Pudovkin film.[20]

Pabst's mining film marks a progress in theoretical thought; for he now tries to make his pacifism invulnerable by endorsing the socialist doctrine. Comradeship advocates the international solidarity of the workers, characterizing them as the pioneers of a society in which national egoism, this eternal source of wars, will be abolished. It is the German miners, not their superiors, who conceive the idea of the rescue action. The scene in which they urge the director to consent is the more revealing as it illustrates the omnipotence of authoritarian rule in the German mine. Throughout the interview, which is laid in the decorative staircase hall of the administration building, the miners remain on the ground floor, while the director talks to them from the height of a landing. It is as if he stood on a balcony, and in addition the camera angles are chosen in such a way that they accentuate his position. Not content with stigmatizing the phenomenon of nationalism, Pabst interprets it in a socialist sense. The passages dealing with the management of the French and the German mine subtly imply the alliance between capitalists and nationalists. This is also the meaning of the symbolic epilogue, which, however, was frequently mistaken for a German protest against Versailles. Perhaps, Pabst failed to make himself clear because of his unfamiliarity with symbolic language.

That the socialist pacifism of Comradeship was better founded

[19] Cf. Spottiswoode, *A Grammar of the Film*, pp. 240–41.

[20] Cf. Potamkin, "Pabst and the Social Film," *Hound & Horn*, Jan.–March 1933, p. 301.

than the humanitarian pacifism of WESTFRONT 1918 does not justify the assumption that it was more substantial. Under the Republic, the German socialists, especially the Social Democrats, proved increasingly unable to grasp the significance of what happened around them. Misguided by conventionalized Marxist concepts, they overlooked the importance of the middle class as well as the ramified mental roots of the existing national aspirations. They had no psychological insight; it never occurred to them that their simplistic frame of reference was inadequate to explain the turn of the petty-bourgeoisie towards the right or the attraction the Nazi creed exerted on German youth. Pabst adopted the socialist ideas of class solidarity and pacifism at a time when these ideas had degenerated into anemic abstractions and as a consequence the Social Democrats could not be expected to cope with the actual situation. In fact, as if the dead weight of an outworn ideology had exhausted them, the Social Democrats watched the Nazi movement grow and grow without stirring from their apathy. COMRADESHIP reflects this exhaustion. Exceptional though it is, the film does not include a single motif which would have challenged the traditional notions of life in the radical manner of Metzner's ACCIDENT or Jutzi's MOTHER KRAUSEN'S JOURNEY TO HAPPINESS. Pabst penetrates reality visually, but leaves its intellectual core shrouded.

The film was praised by the reviewers and shunned by the public. In Neukölln, one of Berlin's proletarian quarters, it ran before empty seats, while some dull comedy in the immediate neighborhood attracted huge crowds.[21] Nothing could be more symptomatic of the workers' inertia. Pabst himself abandoned the cause he had advocated so ardently. ATLANTIDE (ATLANTIS, 1932), his last German pre-Hitler film, was an outright retrogression from "social conclusiveness" into pure escapism. The English film critic Bryher comments on this screen version of Pierre Benoît's fantastic desert novel in an article devoted to several films she saw in Berlin in the summer of 1932: "It is never done in a Hollywood manner, and the atmosphere of the desert is absolutely authentic. But I could not read a Victorian novel at this time of crisis. . . ." [22]

During the following years, Pabst established headquarters in

[21] Information offered by Mr. Jean Oser, New York. See also Kraszna-Krausz, "Four Films from Germany," *Close Up*, March 1932, p. 42.

[22] Bryher, "Notes on Some Films," *Close Up*, Sept. 1932, p. 199. Cf. Jahier, "42 Ans de Cinéma," *Le Rôle intellectuel du Cinéma*, p. 70.

Paris. There he started with DON QUIXOTE (1933), which was beautifully photographed, very boring and perhaps halfway sincere, and then directed or supervised one melodrama after another. At the outbreak of World War II he returned to Nazi Germany. And that was that.

"Berlin is too unsettled, too fearful of the coming winter, to care much for cinema," Bryher notes in her above-mentioned article. "The atmosphere in the streets is only to be compared with that of any large city in 1914–1918. After two or three days, the visitor wonders why revolution does not happen, not that there is any specific thing to provoke it apparent to the eyes, but outbreak against this odd insecure heaviness is to be preferred than waiting for a storm that has sometime got to burst." And she adds: "The film that interests Berlin most at this moment is *Kuhle Wampe*." [23]

KUHLE WAMPE (1932), shown in America under the title WHITHER GERMANY?, was the first, and last, German film which overtly expressed a communist viewpoint. Bert Brecht and Ottwalt did the script; the music was by Hanns Eisler. Thousands of members of such leftist organizations as the Labor Sports Union, a Workers' Theatre Unit and the Workers' Chorus of Greater Berlin volunteered for the mass scenes.[24] It was a true free-lance film, produced under the greatest of difficulties. "About half way through the film the company whose sound installation was being used objected on political grounds. They could not begin the picture over again from the beginning and therefore much of the money . . . went . . . into lawsuits." [25]

The first section of this film about the unemployed details a typical situation in a worker's family wrecked by the economic crisis. The father, long jobless, is discouraged and embittered; the backward-minded mother stubbornly quotes the saying that any able individual is bound to make headway in life. Their daughter Anni (Hertha Thiele), the only working member of the family, braces herself against the morbid atmosphere at home, while the son finally succumbs to it. Unemployed, he lives on his dole. After one of his fruitless job hunts he learns from his father that the dole will be cut by a new "emergency decree." The father goes off to his tavern;

[23] Bryher, "Notes on Some Films," *Close Up*, Sept. 1932, p. 196.
[24] *Film Forum*, Program 3, March 19, 1933.
[25] Bryher, "Notes on Some Films," *Close Up*, Sept. 1932, p. 198.

whereupon the son, in a state of utter despondency, throws himself out of the window. "One less unemployed," comments a woman on the street. Since the family can no longer pay rent, they are ordered to move out. Anni implores the authorities to revoke this order, but they insist upon the eviction.

The second section is laid in "Kuhle Wampe," a tent colony of the unemployed on the outskirts of Berlin. The family has been taken to this shelter by Fritz, a young mechanic and Anni's lover. When Anni tells him that she is going to have a child, Fritz in his desire to shun responsibilities tries to persuade her of the necessity of an abortion. Here Brecht borrows the motif of conversion from MOTHER KRAUSEN'S JOURNEY TO HAPPINESS: impressed by the arguments of a class-conscious worker-friend, Fritz reluctantly decides to face the music.[26] His proposal to Anni results in a betrothal party which, considering the scanty living standards of the tent colonists, is surprisingly opulent. Anni's parents and other elder people empty plates and bowls with gluttonous greed, show their feelings in hilarious shouting and singing, and at the end get hopelessly drunk. The idea is obviously to characterize the old generation of workers as a lot of philistines who have no more fight in them and drown their resignation in mean excesses. Anni is determined not to sink into the swamp that threatens to engulf her. As Fritz admits that he feels he is being victimized by their engagement, she immediately breaks it off and also parts with her parents to live a life of her own in Berlin.

In the third and last section, a mood of hope supersedes the gloominess. Having joined the workers' sports movement, Anni attends a sport festival held by the radical labor unions. There she again meets Fritz, who meanwhile has lost his job. Even though the two avoid talking about themselves, it is made unmistakably clear that they still love each other and will become reconciled on a sounder basis. But this private idyll is overshadowed by the display of collective life. Candid-camera work zealously records an uninterrupted succession of athletic contests, speaking choruses and open-air theatrical performances [Illus. 57]. The whole festival breathes a youthful optimism which expresses itself in the words of the concluding song: "Forward, never relax . . . don't be resigned, but determine to alter and better the world." The film ends in a commuters' train crowded with middle-class people and returning young

[26] Cf. p. 198.

athletes. English reviewers have praised this final episode for its cinematic rendition of such abstract subject-matter as a discussion on economics. One traveler, a shopkeeper or the like, starts arguing about a newspaper item reporting the burning of several million pounds of coffee in Brazil, and the ensuing controversy develops into a clash of opinions intended to reveal the antagonism between proletarian and bourgeois mentality. Whenever the workers draw revolutionary inferences from economic facts, their opponents turn nationalistic or take refuge in nebulous generalities. At the station, the young disperse, singing "Forward, never relax. . . ."[27]

Of course, the board of censors banned the film, on the pretext that it vilified (1) the President of the Reich, (2) the administration of justice, and (3) religion. The first charge referred to the passage in which an "emergency decree" issued by Hindenburg appears as the cause of the son's suicide; the second bore on the attack against current methods of eviction and Fritz's indifference to the illegality of abortion; the third was exacted from some shots of naked youths who plunge into the water while the church bells ring. Along with other critics, I opposed an interdict based upon such questionable arguments.[28] Finally the film was admitted, with a number of cuts tending to neutralize its political significance.

The young Bulgarian S. Th. Dudow who directed KUHLE WAMPE had learned from the Russians to characterize social situations through well-chosen faces and suggestive camera angles. A convincing proof of his talent is the opening sequence which pictures a group of unemployed, among them the son, in search of jobs. Near a triangular vacant lot, whose sadness reflects theirs, the young workers linger with their bicycles waiting for the newsboy with the latest papers. Then, after an expert glance through the ads, the group starts moving. They bicycle past "No help wanted" signboards, enter a factory gateway without alighting and reemerge instantly, repeat this vain attempt several times, and wheel on and on, never separating and always increasing in speed. It is rare that the intangible spirit of a whole epoch is crystallized in such clear-cut images. This sequence with its telling details of rotating wheels and noncommittal house façades gives a concise idea of what German life was like during the crucial pre-Hitler days. In other

[27] *Film Society Programme*, Dec. 11, 1932. Kracauer, "'Kuhle Wampe' verboten!" *Frankfurter Zeitung*, April 5, 1932.

[28] Kracauer, *ibid.* Cf. also Boehmer and Reitz, *Film in Wirtshaft und Recht*, pp. 51, 53, 59–60.

places, Dudow's lack of experience becomes obvious. The pictorial report of the sport festival is unnecessarily long, and the introductory shots of each section are assembled in too absent-minded a fashion to set the tone effectively.

The film's underlying radicalism manifests itself in the unusual construction of the plot. That the son kills himself in the first section practically defies all German screen traditions. Dudow once told me that, while preparing KUHLE WAMPE, he was urged by his producer and several advisers to shift this suicide episode to the film's finale so as to re-establish the natural order of things. In fact, since the early days of the German cinema nearly all important films have ended with an act of submission, and the suicide so frequent in them is nothing but the most extreme and dramatic form of this act. In displacing the suicide motif, KUHLE WAMPE disavows psychological retrogression. This is confirmed by the relation between the son's suicide and the song which exhorts youth: "Don't be resigned, but determine to alter and better the world." Significantly, the song is reiterated at the very end, the normal place for suicides. Through these words as well as their position the film explicitly repudiates the submissive impulses which drive the son to his death.

The same revolutionary attitude is apparent in the love affair between Anni and Fritz. Perhaps misled by the many cuts, an American reviewer remarked of it: "It is one of the chief defects of the picture that its author . . . has been unable to show the proper connection between the amorous difficulties of his heroine and the problems of the despairing unemployed. . . ." [29] But even in the mutilated version the development of the love story has a distinct bearing on the situation of the worker class. Anni precedes Fritz in liberating herself, and Fritz finds his way back to her as soon as he, too, becomes sufficiently adult—that is, class-conscious in this context—to suppress his bourgeois inclinations. What holds true of the two lovers, the film suggests, also applies to the workers in general: their freedom is the result of self-emancipation, their happiness depends on their maturity.

Although undeniably genuine, this radical attitude lacks flair and experience on the political plane. It is an intellectual radicalism, unable to cope with reality. The gravest blunder committed in KUHLE WAMPE is its gross attack against the petty-bourgeois mentality of the old workers—an attack obviously designed to stigmatize

[29] Watts, "Kuhle Wampe," *New York Herald Tribune*, April 25, 1933.

social democratic behavior. At a time when the menace of Nazi domination was felt throughout Germany, it would have been better strategy to emphasize the solidarity of the worker masses instead of criticizing a large portion of them. In addition, this criticism is spiteful rather than solicitous. Like any reactionary film, KUHLE WAMPE in its depiction of the betrothal party goes so far as to ridicule the bad table manners of the older generation. Such a petty insinuation was bound to increase retrogressive obduracy on the part of the offended unemployed; that is, it counteracted the film's own effort to break up retrogression. In the last section, communistic youth is introduced as the vanguard of revolution, the true antagonist of the powers of darkness. And what are these pioneers doing? They indulge in athletic games and sing songs full of a militant spirit and grandiose promise. But since sport festivals are held by people of all colors, this one does not prove the particular strength of the Reds. Nor do the songs carry enough weight to warrant the belief in a redemption of the unemployed, whose misery is so impressively pictured in the first section. Compared with the display of their hardships, the "Forward, never relax . . ." sounds merely rhetorical.

Nevertheless, hope might have outbalanced suffering, had the demoralized old workers been contrasted not only with youth groups but also with groups of their own age. The film invalidates its cause by expressing differences of attitude through differences between generations. The optimism typical of radical youth is in itself no guarantee for the future. It is true that during the discussion on economics the young athletes live up to the standards of Marxian propagandists of any age. But their line of argument is the party line, and after asserting it they immediately resume the song which marks them as youths. KUHLE WAMPE is not free from glorifying youth as such, and to some extent its young revolutionaries resemble those youthful rebels who in numerous German films of the opposite camp are finally ready to submit or to enforce submission. This resemblance is by no means accidental. Towards the end of the pre-Hitler period many anguished young unemployed were so unbalanced that one evening they would be swayed by a communistic spokesman and the next succumb to a Nazi agitator's harangue.[30]

[30] Most of this analysis is drawn from my article "'Kuhle Wampe' verboten!" *Frankfurter Zeitung*, April 5, 1932.

When what remained of the German Republic was about to collapse, Fritz Lang made DAS TESTAMENT DES DR. MABUSE (THE LAST WILL OF DR. MABUSE), a sort of last-ditch stand against impending disaster. But the curtain fell before this Nero production could be released, and no sooner did the Nazis take over than Dr. Goebbels banned it. In his subsequent talk with Lang he expressed his delight in METROPOLIS, without so much as mentioning his disapproval of the new Mabuse film; whereupon Lang deemed it wise to leave Germany.[31] An uncut print of the film's French version, made simultaneously with the German original, was smuggled across the border and edited in France.

In 1943, when the film reached New York audiences, Lang wrote a "Screen Foreword," expounding his original intentions: "This film was made as an allegory to show Hitler's processes of terrorism. Slogans and doctrines of the Third Reich have been put into the mouths of criminals in the film. Thus I hoped to expose the masked Nazi theory of the necessity to deliberately destroy everything which is precious to a people. . . . Then, when everything collapsed and they were thrown into utter despair, they would try to find help in the 'new order.' "[32]

Even though this self-interpretation smacks of hindsight, it is nevertheless true that the film foreshadows Nazi practices. The noted psychiatrist Baum, its main character, is under the hypnotic influence of Dr. Mabuse, who, it will be remembered, went mad at the end of Lang's first Mabuse film, of 1922.[33] In the sequel, this early screen tyrant reappears as an inmate of Baum's lunatic asylum, covering innumerable sheets of paper with detailed instructions for attacks on railways, chemical factories, the currency system and so on. His writings form a manual of crime and destruction, governed by a maxim which strikes a familiar note: "Mankind must be thrown into an abyss of terror." Baum, possessed by what he calls the genius of Mabuse, leads a double life like Dr. Caligari: while playing the role of the psychiatrist, he also heads an underworld organization through which he painstakingly carries out the madman's scrawled instructions. From murder to forgery his gang covers

[31] "Fritz Lang," *New York World Telegram,* June 11, 1941. Cf. *Film Society Programme,* May 6, 1934. See also p. 164. Lang left Germany for France, where he made LILIOM (1935). For Lang's whole development, see Weinberg, *An Index to . . . Fritz Lang.*

[32] Lang, "Screen Forward," program to the film, World Theatre, New York, March 19, 1943.

[33] Cf. p. 82.

the whole field of criminal activities. After Mabuse's death, this paranoiac aspirant to world domination believes himself a reincarnation of his idol. He is tracked down by Chief Inspector Lohmann, the same screen sleuth who established the identity of the child-murderer in M. A systematic-minded and shrewd police officer, Lohmann represents the German version of the Anglo-Saxon detective. When he finally solves the case, Baum flees into the former cell of Mabuse, where his own madness becomes manifest.

The film is inferior to M. In it, Lang accumulates mere thrills, elaborating upon them zealously. Whenever Baum feels swayed by Mabuse, the latter's ghostly apparition emerges with clocklike punctuality. Since repetitious shock effects tend to neutralize each other, the result is monotony rather than an increase of suspense. Nevertheless the film includes two brilliant episodes which testify to Lang's "uncanny genius for invoking terror out of the simplest things." [34] The first is the opening sequence. It shows a man cautiously moving about in an abandoned workshop that seems to be shaken by a perpetual, roaring drone. His apparent fear and this nerve-racking noise are bound to torment an audience which does not yet realize that the man is spying on Baum's counterfeiters and that the noise itself originates in their nearby printing press. Life under a terror regime could not be rendered more impressively, for throughout the sequence the imminence of doom is sensed and no one knows when and where the ax will fall. The other episode also features the spying man, who is one of Lohmann's detectives. After his capture by the gang this victim of Baum's sadistic cruelty, now insane, spends his days in a cell of the lunatic asylum. He imagines himself as living in a vacuum, and as Lohmann approaches him he shrinks back panic-stricken and sings with an animal voice, "Gloria—gloria!" Lang succeeds in making the vacuum seem real. Transparent walls of glass surround the mad detective, and the luminous immateriality breeds horrors more shattering than those of a shadow world.

Dr. Goebbels undoubtedly knew why he banned the film. However, it is hard to believe that average German audiences would have grasped the analogy between the gang of screen criminals and the Hitler gang. And had they even been aware of it, they would not have felt particularly encouraged to stand up against the Nazis, for Lang is so exclusively concerned with highlighting the magic spell of Mabuse and Baum that his film mirrors their demoniac irresisti-

[34] Weinberg, "Fritz Lang," program to the film, *ibid.*

bility rather than the inner superiority of their opponents. To be sure, Lohmann defeats Baum; but Lohmann himself is left without any halo. Like his predecessor, Dr. Wenk, who defeated the criminals in Lang's first Mabuse film, he is a colorless official and as such unfit to represent a cause involving political issues. His victory lacks broad moral significance. As so often with Lang, the law triumphs and the lawless glitters. This anti-Nazi film betrays the power of Nazi spirit over minds insufficiently equipped to counter its peculiar fascination.

21. NATIONAL EPIC

THE second major group of pre-Hitler films served as an outlet for the existing authoritarian tendencies. These films ignored the suffering masses and of course shunned any solution that recalled humanization, progress and democracy. Their sole concern was the individual. They usually glorified some potential or full-fledged rebel, without, however, neglecting the figures of the war hero and the omnipotent leader. Sometimes their main character amounted to a blend of all three.

A subterranean affinity for the rebel theme shows even in films which, judging by their milieus or surface designs, seem remote from it. One of them was DER MÖRDER DIMITRI KARAMASOFF (KARAMAZOV, 1931), staged by the former Soviet film director Fedor Ozep.[1]

Indifferent to the pseudo-religious moods which had engendered the KARAMAZOV of 1920, this pre-Hitler film exploited the Dostoievsky novel for the sole purpose of dramatizing the story of Dimitri Karamazov. Fritz Kortner's impetuous young Dimitri abruptly leaves his well-to-do bride to make love to Grushenka, a kept girl who plays with the idea of marrying his father. This senile old fool is so infatuated with Grushenka that he promises her a fortune if she complies. Dimitri in a fury sets out to kill him, but eventually shrinks from the murder. While he rushes in a troika back to Grushenka, the old Karamazov is murdered by his servant Smerdjakov (Fritz Rasp), a weird epileptic possessed with greed for the treasure his master hides behind an icon. No one yet knows about the crime when Grushenka decides to accept Dimitri as her permanent lover. After a turbulent night the happy hotspur spends with her and a licentious crowd in a sort of brothel, he is arrested on suspicion of having committed parricide. Even though Smerdjakov hangs himself, the court doubts Dimitri's innocence. They sentence him to Siberia. Grushenka, admirably portrayed by Anna Sten, accompanies him.

[1] *Film Society Programme,* April 17, 1930.—Cf. p. 109.

It was a story which had little in common with Dostoievsky or with Soviet mentality. Ozep seemed to sense it; for he refrained from using Russian "montage" methods, except, perhaps, for the magnificent troika episode in which he juxtaposed treetops and horse's hoofs in fast cutting so as to increase the impression of speed. But this had been done on the European screen before. On the whole, KARAMAZOV is patterned after the German silent films. Inanimate objects assert themselves imperiously whenever human passions boil over. A shining clock with four revolving pendulums is the chief witness of that scene in which Dimitri reviles Grushenka for luring his father and somewhat later leaves her as her lover. The clock appears while he is still alone in the room, watches the two raging against each other and re-emerges at the moment of their first embrace.

Made in the early days of sound, the film suffers from the stage habits of its actors who continually fall into declamation. But the visual part is not yet reduced to a mere accompaniment of the dialogue, and at least in one instance Ozep combines sounds and pictures in a truly cinematic way. As Grushenka assures Dimitri of her love, both laugh and laugh in a fit of happiness and their laughter is so contagious that soon the whole brothel joins in. Before this uproar has completely died away, the close-up of a big chandelier fills the screen—a sea of whirling candle flames, anticipating the subsequent revelry with its shooting, dancing and singing.

Stripped of its Russian apparel, KARAMAZOV has all the traits of those street films which during the stabilized period reflected, after the manner of dreams, the longing for authoritarian rule. Dimitri is the rebellious son who, driven by his instincts, exchanges bourgeois security for life on the street. And Grushenka represents the prostitute who is a well of love in a world grown cold. The film would be nothing but a late street film if it were not for its finale which marks an important change of pattern. Although ASPHALT and other old street films concluded with the promise of continued rebellion, their middle-class runaways eventually returned to the plush parlors from which they had sprung.[2] At the end of KARAMAZOV, rebellion not only remains a hope, but is symbolized as a fact. Unlike his wavering predecessors, Dimitri, this bourgeois lover, goes on living with Grushenka, the prostitute, and his submission to an unjust sentence is so far from being an act of resigned retreat that, conversely, it

[2] Cf. p. 159 f.

indicates his determination once for all to turn his back upon the paternal world. He is a rebel for good. Since he is not the sole die-hard rebel to appear on the contemporary German screen, this variation of the street films tends the more to show that the atmosphere of the pre-Hitler era was pregnant with the idea of rebellion. Characteristically, the spirit of violence which sweeps through the film materializes in Dimitri himself.

DANTON (1931), a historical film by Hans Behrendt, also revived a theme of the early postwar years. This picture resembled ALL FOR A WOMAN, Buchowetski's Danton film of 1921, in its indifference to the French Revolution and its emphasis on the private life of the revolutionary leaders.[3] The pre-Hitler Robespierre is an arid, jesuitical schemer who envies Danton's immense popularity and the broad scope of his uninhibited nature. Danton on his part has a sanguine temperament and is open-minded rather than doctrinaire. He liberates an imprisoned aristocrat and marries her; he overtly expresses his disgust of Robespierre's terror regime. His careless conduct offers his archenemy a welcome opportunity to arraign him for high treason. In the convention episode Kortner as Danton is at his best. With the skill of a born demagogue he turns the tables on Robespierre, accusing him and Saint-Just of procedures bound to choke the Revolution in blood. Since the masses, first hostile to Danton, fiercely acclaim him at the end of his speech, Robespierre resorts to the expedient of having them removed by force of arms. "Long live liberty!" Danton shouts before his execution.

In the course of the film this character undergoes an interesting metamorphosis. He begins as a genuine Jacobin who calls for, and obtains, the death of Louis XVI. Later, when France is invaded by the enemy, Danton turns patriot; in his successful negotiations with the Duke of Koburg he promises to spare the life of Marie Antoinette if the invasion armies under the Duke's command effect a retreat. It is not his fault that Robespierre thwarts this agreement by sending the Queen to the guillotine. In addition, Danton, the patriot, reveals himself as a champion of humanity concerned not so much with the further pursuit of the Revolution as with freedom from any kind of oppression. His ardent opposition to Robespierre's dictatorship makes him appear the counterpart of Schiller's liberty-loving heroes. The revolutionary Jacobin grows into a noble rebel.

[3] Cf. p. 50 f.

As such Danton, it is true, sides with democracy against tyranny. But at the same time he is so patriotic and emotional that he strongly recalls those rebellious German idealists who, loathing Versailles and the Weimar Republic, were predestined to become Nazi sympathizers. This screen rebel is a paradoxical blend of a potential Hitlerite and a democratic fighter. Such a blend seemed to prove attractive; DANTON is said to have been enthusiastically received on the occasion of its Berlin première.[4]

The rebel theme also loomed in Kurt Bernhardt's DER MANN DER DEN MORD BEGING (THE MAN WHO MURDERED, 1931). Made after a novel by Claude Farrère, this Terra-United Artists production dealt with a scandal in the diplomatic circles of Constantinople. The exotic scenery was beautiful, the treatment subtle, the action slow. A French attaché—Conrad Veidt in one of his seducer roles—falls in love with Mary, the wife of an English lord, and after a while discovers that she is mistreated by her husband and his cousin, a domineering woman. In a tête-à-tête he suggests a divorce. Mary shrinks from the mere thought of it, for then she would have to give up her little boy. After this exposition of her plight the drama takes its course: no sooner does the lord find out about Mary's love affair with a charming and decadent Russian prince (Gregory Chmara) than he forces her to agree to the divorce she dreads so much. She screams in her despair and is overheard by the Frenchman who, as Mary's protector, has secretly followed her. Later the lord is found murdered. At the end, the French attaché, conversing with the Turkish police minister, casually mentions that he himself is the man who did it. The Turk, too, is a man of the world. Intent on hushing up the unpleasant affair, he intimates that his visitor should return to Paris at his earliest convenience, and dismisses him with an understanding handshake.

Despite its aloofness, this upper-crust story had a bearing on current attitudes. The "man who murdered" commits his crime in the conviction of righting a wrong brought about by the existing laws. They destroy the woman he loves and he cannot stand such an injustice. To be sure, as a diplomat this desperate lover is surrounded with a halo of extraterritoriality; but in taking the law into his own hands he nevertheless assumes the character of a rebel. The so-called "*Feme*-murderers" also deemed it their holy duty to rid

[4] According to Magnus, "Danton," *Variety*, Feb. 1931(?).

themselves of their opponents by killing them. This analogy is not as far-fetched as it seems, for, like the German judges who never punished any of those murderous rebels, the Turkish police minister absolves the Frenchman and moreover expresses his sympathy for him.

Here, as in other cases, the objection suggests itself that undoubtedly neither the film-makers nor the German audiences were aware of such parallels. Yet these parallels exist, and that they passed unnoticed increases rather than invalidates their significance. The less an individual knows why he prefers one subject to another, the more one is safe in assuming that his choice has been determined by powerful tendencies below the dimension of consciousness. Any tendency of that kind asserts itself in the most remote ideas and perceptions, so that these necessarily reflect it, no matter what is dealt with or what on the surface appears to be said. Although Bernhardt's film is exclusively concerned with love and crime among high-ranking dignitaries, it betrays a state of mind which favors rebels and conniving authorities.

In the film credits for THE MAN WHO MURDERED, Carl Mayer is listed as the dramaturgic supervisor. Since his script for SUNRISE (1927), Murnau's first Hollywood film, Mayer had on the whole confined himself to advisory work, as if unable, or unwilling, to cope with a period which ran against his inmost experiences and sensibilities. Mechanization had leveled all deep emotions, collective interests had weakened the sense of individual values, and with the rising Nazi tide petty-bourgeois mentality more and more pervaded the atmosphere. Something like resignation may have driven him to collaborate in films which fell short of his own standards.

Mayer joined Czinner and, first in Berlin, then in Paris, helped to prepare two films starring Bergner. In ARIANE (1931), she portrays a young Russian student who, posing as an experienced woman, captivates a man about town with a penchant for casual liaisons.[5] In DER TRÄUMENDE MUND (THE DREAMING MOUTH, 1932), a picture reminiscent of her first film, HUSBANDS OR LOVERS?, she wavers between passion for a famous violinist and devotion to her husband, and after having wavered long enough evades the dilemma by the old stratagem of drowning herself.[6] It was all love

[5] Bryher, "Berlin, April 1931," *Close Up*, June 1931, p. 131; synopsis in *Illustrierter Film-Kurier*.

[6] *Film Society Programme*, Jan. 22, 1933; Weiss, "Elizabeth Bergner Again," *Close Up*, Dec. 1932, pp. 254–55.

and psychology, and to make it seem still more so, music was called upon. Ariane listens to the *Don Giovanni* overture, and the famous violinist contributes part of Beethoven's violin concerto.

That Mayer realized the questionable social implications of these films is highly improbable. In 1932, he went to London where he continued to serve as an adviser in documentary and theatrical films. A much-cherished project of his own was another city film, this time about London; but no one would produce his script. He died of cancer, in 1944.

Paul Rotha, Mayer's intimate friend, who more than anyone else understood and appreciated his unique merits, wrote to me about him: "To look at, he was like Beethoven, but with a more sensitive, a more fragile face. In comparison with his small body (he was about 5 ft. 2 ins.) his head seemed unnaturally big. He would stroll along—almost meandering—as if blown here and there by the wind. You never knew where you would meet him next. In little cafés in Soho, . . on a park bench, in a book shop. . . . He endeared all people to him; his nurses during his illness, barmen in pubs, caretakers. He had a habit—rare in cities—of saying 'Good morning' to everyone, whether he knew them or not." [7] This devotee of the big cities, who "first made the camera move for inherent script purposes," [8] was animated by Dickens' love of aimless vagabondage, his sympathetic concern with cobblestones and stray souls alike—the very impulses which prompt the camera itself into action.

In Erich Waschneck's ACHT MÄDELS IM BOOT (EIGHT GIRLS IN A BOAT, 1932), a film in the wake of MÄDCHEN IN UNIFORM, the rebel motif asserted itself openly. Christa, a college girl, lives through a veritable nightmare because she is expecting a child. Her student lover's medical friend agrees to give her an abortion, but she is so appalled by the surgical atmosphere in his room that she runs away before he can even start. Since she dreads her unsuspecting father no less than the doctor, she escapes to the rowing club of which she is a member. There Hanna, a vigorous blonde, is coaching the girls under her command for a boat race. When after a heroic attempt to conceal her condition Christa finally confesses, the whole team glows with desire to shield the girl from her father.

[7] Mr. Rotha's letter to me, of Sept. 3, 1944. See also Rotha, "Carl Mayer, 1894–1944," *Documentary News Letter*, no. 3, 1944, p. 39; Rotha, "It's in the Script," *World Film News*, Sept. 1938, p. 205.

[8] Mr. Rotha's letter to me, Sept. 3, 1944.

Hanna calls on him, and there is a violent clash between the two generations. For the sake of a happy ending, the father straightens matters out. Informed by Hanna of his daughter's predicament, he appears at the club along with the student lover to fetch Christa home, and all the girls enjoy the prospect of a wedding.[9]

The film, an average product ornamented by nice landscape shots, features not so much Christa as the militant Hanna. She is an outright rebel figure. When the father refuses to adopt her view of the case, she bluntly tells him that his stubbornness will force the club to take care of Christa and her future child. It is as if the club were a stronghold of the young in the hostile territory of the adults. Furious at Hanna's provocations, the father threatens her with the police; whereupon she calls all fathers brutal tyrants. An offspring of the earlier Youth Movement, Hanna illustrates its affinity with Nazi spirit [Illus. 58]. Her idea of the club as Christa's guardian anticipates the repudiation of family bonds under Hitler; moreover, her arrogance and sadism mark her as the prototype of an S.S. leader. To punish Christa for continually lagging behind, she orders her to jump off the diving board ten times; observing the girl's difficulties, she still insists that the order be carried out to the full. It is only after she has collapsed that the tortured Christa reveals her secret to this redoubtable female. The implied marital solution obviously serves as a compromise with traditional ethics.

The surge of pro-Nazi tendencies during the pre-Hitler period could not better be confirmed than by the increase and specific evolution of the mountain films. Dr. Arnold Fanck, the uncontested father of this species, continued along the lines he himself had developed. Besides a pleasing comedy, DER WEISSE RAUSCH (THE WHITE FRENZY, 1931), in which Leni Riefenstahl is initiated into the secrets of skiing, he made STÜRME ÜBER DEM MONTBLANC (AVALANCHE, 1930), one of those half-monumental, half-sentimental concoctions of which he was master.[10] The film again pictures the horrors and beauties of the high mountains, this time with particular emphasis on majestic cloud displays. (That in the opening sequence

[9] Jahier, "42 Ans de Cinéma," *Le Rôle intellectuel du Cinéma*, p. 70; Kalbus, *Deutsche Filmkunst*, II, 57–58; etc.

[10] For WHITE FRENZY, see "Der Weisse Rausch," *Filmwelt*, Dec. 20, 1931, and Weiss, "Sonne über dem Arlberg," *Close Up*, March 1932, pp. 59–60. For AVALANCHE, see Fanck, *Stürm über dem Montblanc*, and *Der Kampf mit dem Berge*; Kalbus, *Deutsche Filmkunst*, II, 36–38; synopsis in *Illustrierter Film-Kurier*. Significantly, the film's original title was ÜBER DEN WOLKEN ("Above the Clouds").

of the Nazi documentary TRIUMPH OF THE WILL, of 1936, similar cloud masses surround Hitler's airplane on its flight to Nuremberg, reveals the ultimate fusion of the mountain cult and the Hitler cult [11] [Illus. 59 and 60].) Impressive sound effects supplement the magnificent photography: fragments of Bach and Beethoven from an abandoned radio on Mont Blanc intermittently penetrate the roaring storm, making the dark altitudes seem more aloof and inhuman. For the rest, AVALANCHE duplicates THE WHITE HELL OF PITZ PALÜ in reiterating Ernst Udet's stunt flights, diverse elemental catastrophes and the inevitable rescue party. The man to be rescued in this case is a young Mont Blanc meteorologist threatened with freezing to death in his storm-wrecked observatory on the peak. But why, then, does he stay up there over Easter instead of joining the girl he secretly loves in the valleys? Because his best friend, a Berlin musician, has sent him a letter which clearly indicates that he, too, adores this girl. The letter suffices to make the meteorologist give up his love. He does not think of asking the girl how she herself feels about him; full of self-pity and noble sentiments, he leaves her to his friend. May they be happy! His own lot is to remain above the clouds and all mortals. And there he would have died were it not for the girl, alias Leni Riefenstahl, who, mountain-possessed as ever, loves this hero on Mont Blanc and braves all dangers to save him. An American reviewer called the plot "woefully inadequate." [12] As a matter of fact, it follows a typically German pattern, its main character being the perpetual adolescent well-known from many previous films. The psychological consequences of such retrogressive behavior need no further elaboration.

In the course of the pre-Hitler years, Leni Riefenstahl embarked upon a career of her own. She directed DAS BLAUE LICHT (THE BLUE LIGHT, 1932), cooperatively produced by her, Béla Balázs, and the photographer Hans Schneeberger. The film is based on an old legend of the Italian Dolomites. On nights when the moon is full, the peak of Mount Cristallo radiates a marvelous blue light that lures all the young villagers to it. Even though their parents try to keep them home behind closed window shutters, they are drawn away like somnambulists and fall to death among the rocks. Only Junta (Leni Riefenstahl), a sort of gypsy girl, is said to reach the light safely and is therefore considered a witch [Illus. 62]. The super-

[11] Cf. p. 290.

[12] Boehnel, "Avalanche," *New York World Telegram*, March 29, 1932.

stitious village people insult the girl and throw stones at her whenever she comes down from her cabin high in the mountains. A young Viennese painter staying for a day or so in the village witnesses such a scene and feels so attracted by Junta that he goes to live with her in her mountain refuge. One night, she leaves him and climbs the moon-lit cliffs of Mount Cristallo. Secretly following her to the peak, the painter discovers that the mysterious blue light emanates from a stretch of precious crystals. He enlightens the villagers, who under his guidance remove the treasure, now turned from a source of fright into a promise of wealth. Next full moon, Junta, unsuspecting, resumes her ascent; but since the blue light is gone, she misses her way and falls down a precipice. The painter, too late to rescue her, bends over the shining face of the dead girl.[13]

Beautiful outdoor shots stress the insoluble ties between primitive people and their natural surroundings. The statues of saints are carved in a rock by the road; the mute Dolomites partake of the life in the village. Close-ups of genuine peasant faces thread through the whole of the film; these faces resemble landscapes molded by nature itself, and in rendering them, the camera achieves a fascinating study in facial folklore. While the peasants are merely related to the soil, Junta is a true incarnation of elemental powers, strikingly confirmed as such by the circumstances of her death. She dies when sober reasoning has explained, and thus destroyed, the legend of the blue light. With the glow of the crystals her very soul is taken away. Like the meteorologist in AVALANCHE, this mountain girl conforms to a political regime which relies on intuition, worships nature and cultivates myths. To be sure, at the end the village rejoices in its fortune and the myth seems defeated, but this rational solution is treated in such a summary way that it enhances rather than reduces Junta's significance. What remains is nostalgia for her realm and sadness over a disenchanted world in which the miraculous becomes merchandise.

Luis Trenker, the model mountaineer of THE HOLY MOUNTAIN, also emancipated himself from Fanck. He enacted the main characters of two films made from his own scripts and staged by him in collaboration with experienced directors. These pictures are particularly important: they mark the junction of the mountain films and

[13] Kalbus, *Deutsche Filmkunst*, II, 65–66; Weiss, "The Blue Light," *Close Up*, June 1932, pp. 119–22.

the national films. In them, the political implications of AVALANCHE and THE BLUE LIGHT appear as overt themes.

The first of the two was BERGE IN FLAMMEN (THE DOOMED BATTALION, 1931), much praised for Sepp Allgeier's brilliant camerawork. It dealt with an isolated combat episode of World War I set against the snow peaks of the Austrian Tyrol. A mountain top is held by an Austrian battalion, and since it proves inaccessible to direct attacks, the Italians below start drilling a tunnel into the rocks so as to dynamite this position. While the Austrians, unable to forestall the enemy action, listen helplessly to the ominous tapping in the mountain, one of their officers (Trenker) goes on a daredevil ski patrol down to his native village, which serves the Italians as headquarters. There he learns the date set for the explosion and returns in time to warn his comrades. His exploit enables the "doomed battalion" to evacuate the position just before it is blown into the air.[14]

Whereas Pabst's WESTFRONT 1918 accumulates war horrors to advance pacifism, the Trenker war film devotes itself to the praise of martial virtues. War in THE DOOMED BATTALION is nothing but a background for a mountain climber who seems to fulfill his natural destiny by turning war hero. Both the pacifist and the heroic film disregard the causes of World War I; but, unlike Pabst, Trenker is justified in ignoring them, for he glorifies the ideal soldier, and soldiers are not supposed to encroach upon politics. The image of the war hero is completed by two sequences framing the combat episode proper. In the opening sequence, the Austrian officer and the Italian commander, his future antagonist, are seen together on a mountain excursion immediately before the outbreak of hostilities—two friends elevated above nationalistic prejudices; in the finale, the ex-enemies resume their old friendship a few years after the war.

In emphasizing this survival of personal bonds, the Trenker film defies chauvinism even more energetically than did such films as THE EMDEN and U-9 WEDDIGEN.[15] Yet while they were affected by the paralysis of minds during the stabilized period, THE DOOMED BATTALION reflects the surge of national passions bound to result in war. How is its antichauvinistic attitude compatible with its inherent nationalism? This attitude makes wars appear as superindividual

[14] Cf. reviews in *New York Herald Tribune* and *New York Post*, both of June 11, 1932, Museum of Modern Art Library, clipping files. See also Kalbus, *Deutsche Filmkunst,* II, 83, and Arnheim, *Film also Kunst,* p. 278.

[15] Cf. p. 155 f.

events which have to be accepted, whether we sanction or condemn them. Considered thus as products of inscrutable fate, there is no danger that emotional fervor in their interest may yield to doubt. Friendship between soldiers of different countries in the lulls of peace does not weaken the friends' determination to fight each other in wartime; rather, it ennobles this fight, transforming it into a tragic duty, a superior sacrifice. Trenker's mountain climber is the type of man on whom regimes in need of war can rely.

The second Trenker film was DER REBELL (THE REBEL), a German-made Universal production released as late as January 17, 1933. It again was concerned with a war episode, this time drawn from the Tyrol's revolt against the Napoleonic occupation army. A Tyrolese student (Trenker) returning home finds his native village plundered and his mother and sister killed. After killing a French officer in retaliation, he goes underground and helps to organize the resistance. Simultaneously, he continues his romance with a Bavarian girl (Vilma Banky) who shields him from the occupation authorities and even does a bit of spying for him. The student profits by her information. Disguised as a Bavarian officer, he attends a ball given by the French at Innsbruck and there gathers sufficient intelligence to prepare a gigantic trap for Napoleon's legions. While this indoor episode and the amorous interlude are not particularly stirring, the sequence which shows how the trap is sprung can hardly be surpassed in violent realism. The Tyrolese peasants, hidden high in the mountains, let loose masses of rocks and tree trunks on the French troops passing along the road below. It is an elaborate, roaring wholesale slaughter, with the mountains as the allies of the rebels. Of course, at the end the French win out and the student is shot.[16]

With Trenker, the rebel enters upon the final stage of a screen career inseparable from the evolution of the German cinema [Illus. 61]. A definite historic role is assigned to him: he leads, or takes part in, the people's rebellion against an enemy that subjugates the nation. This reveals him to be a nationalist rather than a revolutionary. The analogy between the Tyrol's revolt and the Nazi movement is obvious; Trenker in his film only reflects what the Nazis themselves called a national uprising. Napoleon stands for the hated "system" and the student has the traits of a Hitlerite. Here it becomes clear why during the pre-Hitler years the German film rebel

[16] Kalbus, *Deutsche Filmkunst,* II, 66–67; review in *New York Post,* July 28, 1933.

no longer conformed to the old pattern which had invariably led him from rebellion to submission. Now that the Nazis prepared for the ultimate assault upon the crumbling Republic, he, too, was bound to embody the idea of rebellion. This idea excludes surrender, even though it does not preclude defeat. Such pre-Hitler figures as Dimitri Karamazov and Danton therefore fight it out to the last. It was the hour of decision, and the plush parlors of the past lay far behind.[17]

There is pictorial evidence that the Trenker film was nothing but a thinly masked pro-Nazi film. Photographed by Sepp Allgeier,[18] it introduced symbols which were to play a prominent part on the early Hitler screen. To enhance national passion, elaborate use is made of close-ups of flags, a device common with the Nazis. In the visionary concluding sequence, the resurrected student, who along with two other rebel leaders has been executed by the French, moves onwards, a flag in his hands. "The squad fired, and the rebels . . . were seen, fallen sprawling in the dust. But now the sound of a patriotic song was faintly heard, ghostly figures of the three men rose from their prostrate bodies and, valiantly singing their song, marched at the head of the peasant forces, ascending along the rim of a distant cloud, until finally, as the song swelled to its conclusion, they disappeared into the skies." [19]

This apotheosis of rebellious ardor is all but duplicated in HITLERJUNGE QUEX (September 1933; camera: Konstantin Tschet), a Nazi propaganda film which features the Nazis' eleventh-hour struggle for power, resounding with their "Youth Song": "Our flag billows before us! . . ." In the film's finale, the militant Hitler boy Heini, surnamed Quex, distributes leaflets in one of Berlin's proletarian quarters and there is stabbed by a communist. Abandoned, he lies on a dark street. "The Nazis come and find Heini dying. His last words are, 'Our flag billows before . . .' The sound track takes up the Youth Song and the flag appears on the screen, giving place to marching columns of Hitler Youth." [20] Through similar images

[17] Cf. Erikson, "Hitler's Imagery," *Psychiatry*, Nov. 1942, p. 480.

[18] A few years later, Allgeier collaborated as chief cameraman in TRIUMPH OF THE WILL, which, as has been pointed out above, reverted to the cloud effects of his AVALANCHE. According to Leni Riefenstahl, this collaboration meant "more than only an artistic task" to him. Cf. Riefenstahl, *Hinter den Kulissen des Reichsparteitag-Films*, p. 16.

[19] Quoted from Spottiswoode, *A Grammar of the Film*, pp. 228–29. See also Iros, *Wesen und Dramaturgie des Films*, p. 348.

[20] Quoted from Bateson, "Cultural and Thematic Analysis of Fictional Films," *Transactions of the New York Academy of Sciences*, Feb. 1943, p. 76.

both the Trenker film and the Nazi film point at the imminent triumph of national rebellions—a coincidence which strikingly confirms the identical nature of the rebellions themselves.

The national films of the pre-Hitler period surpassed those of the stabilized period in number and significance. Like THE REBEL, the bulk of them drew upon the Napoleonic era to substantiate the idea of a national uprising. Prussia vs. Napoleon was their central theme, and Prussia invariably appeared as the protagonist of the united German nation. On the whole, these films constituted a sort of national epic, fabricated for domestic mass consumption.

The epic dwelt upon Prussia's humiliation, with a view to her future redemption. Kurt Bernhardt, Trenker's collaborator in THE REBEL, made DIE LETZTE KOMPAGNIE (THE LAST COMPANY, 1930), an Ufa film detailing a combat episode of Napoleon's Prussian campaign. A captain and twelve men engage in a hopeless rear-guard action against the advancing French so as to cover the retreat of the defeated Prussian army across the river Saale. They all are killed. After conquering the position, the French salute their dead enemies, whose bravery has succeeded in relieving the rest of the Prussians. The film breathed the same spirit as THE DOOMED BATTALION. Rudolf Meinert's DIE ELF SCHILL'SCHEN OFFIZIERE (1932), a sound version of his silent film of 1926, depicted the doom of Prussian officers shot by order of the French for having participated in Schill's premature revolt. Gerhard Lamprecht in his DER SCHWARZE HUSAR (BLACK HUSSAR, 1932; Ufa) chose to render the rebellious mood of French-occupied Prussia in the form of a comedy. For reasons of state Napoleon orders a princess of Baden to marry a Polish prince. But Veidt as an officer of the Black Hussars, an outlawed Prussian regiment, plays a trick on the Emperor: he kidnaps the princess as she travels eastward, saving her from the unwanted husband.[21]

Representative of the whole series was Carl Froelich's LUISE, KÖNIGIN VON PREUSSEN (LUISE, QUEEN OF PRUSSIA, 1931), produced by Henny Porten, who also enacted the unhappy Queen. This decorative historical panorama, which culminated in the famous meeting of Luise and Napoleon, abounded with allusions to Ver-

[21] For THE LAST COMPANY, see synopsis in *Illustrierter Film-Kurier* and Kalbus, *Deutsche Filmkunst,* II, 15; for BLACK HUSSAR, Kalbus, *ibid.,* p. 44; for DIE ELF SCHILL'SCHEN OFFIZIERE, Kalbus, ibid., p. 77. See also diverse New York reviews of the first two films.

sailles and the actual German situation. Two reviews in the *New York Herald Tribune* not only mentioned the film's "grim frown in the direction of the Third French Republic" and its "insistence on the brotherhood of all Germans," but went so far as to advance an outright suspicion: "The Emperor, the film reminds you with particular pointedness, once robbed Germany of the Baltic port of Danzig and set it up as a free city, and when you recall how the Polish corridor rankles at the moment, it is difficult to believe that the photoplay . . . only recalls the historical precedent by accident." [22] Whether accidentally or not, the film popularized the political claims of the Hitler-Hugenberg front and, by implication, foretold a victorious rebellion.

Concentrating upon the theme of rebellion itself, Gustav Ucicky's Ufa production YORK (1931) featured a personal union of war hero and rebel. While Napoleon is engaged in his Russian campaign, King Frederick Wilhelm III of Prussia, in strict observance of his treaty with the Emperor, puts a Prussian army corps at the disposal of the French high command. He orders General von York (Werner Krauss), the preceptor of Prussia's new citizens' army, to take charge of this corps. York is the prototype of a Prussian soldier, imbued with a sense of duty and utterly devoted to his King. He obeys and joins the French in Kurland, even though his restive young officers implore him to turn the tables on their allies. The crisis in the Prussian camp reaches its climax as soon as the news of Napoleon's Russian defeat leaks out. But York still refuses to break his allegiance to the King. Only when this weakling proves deaf to his patriotic arguments does he cross the Rubicon. York, the rebel, signs the Convention of Tauroggen with the Russians. The War of Liberation against Napoleon commences.

This film about the Prussian military caste discriminates between two types of soldier rebels. The emotional young officers are of much the same kind as those "*demi-soldes*" who after World War I filled the cadres of the notorious Freikorps and somewhat later formed the nucleus of the Nazi movement. But during the pre-Hitler period topical interest lay not so much in their well-known affiliations as in possible reactions of the army High Command. York is symptomatic of this clique. He turns rebel when it becomes apparent that Napoleon is on the decline and that therefore any further loy-

[22] Quoted from Watts, "Luise, Queen of Prussia," *New York Herald Tribune*, Oct. 5, 1932.—In Grune's silent Luise film, of 1927, Mady Christians had played the Queen.

alty to him might prove disastrous to Prussia. His decision, unhampered by sentimental impulses, springs from his exclusive concern with Prussia's grandeur. "York was a soldier," as the program to the film puts it, "who rebelled against his King for the sake of his King." [23] Nothing could be more to the point; for in the eyes of the military tribe national power politics served the true interests of the King. There is no doubt that the case of this illustrious soldier was intended to demonstrate the historic legitimacy of an alliance between the Reichswehr and the rebellious forces represented by Hitler and Hugenberg. In idealizing York of all generals, Hugenberg's Ufa clearly suggested that such an alliance would be for the sake of the "King," the King now being Hindenburg as the symbol of Germany.[24]

In York and other pre-Hitler films, unyielding rebels defy the submissive conduct of their numerous screen predecessors so resolutely that they might almost be mistaken for champions of individual freedom. Trenck, a Phoebus production of 1932, nips this misconception in the bud. Made after a novel by the late German refugee-writer Bruno Frank, the film belonged to the Fridericus series. For even though Frederick the Great remained too much in the background to be played by his usual impersonator, Otto Gebühr, he was the true center of the action, which concerns the abortive love affair between his sister Amalie and Trenck, his aide-de-camp. Both dare oppose him. When Frederick tells Amalie that he wishes her to marry the Swedish Crown Prince, she retorts with the question: "And my happiness?" Frederick answers that as the daughter of a King of Prussia she has to suppress such thoughts. Angry at Amalie's insubordination, he once and for all forestalls her aspirations to happiness by making her the abbess of a provincial convent.

Trenck on his part is portrayed as an unruly character who, violating the King's express orders, goes on a dangerous patrol during the war. Later, he escapes from the fortress in which he has been put for his disobedience, and after sundry adventures in Austria settles down at the Russian court as the declared favorite of the Empress. The film emphasizes that he never commits any treacherous

[23] Quoted from Watts, "York," *New York Herald Tribune*, Nov. 4, 1932.

[24] The War of Liberation itself, which seemed rather remote at a time still preoccupied with Hitler's ascent, was treated in Theodor Körner (1932), a mediocre screen biography of this patriotic soldier-poet, who joined Luetzow's corps of volunteers and died in action at the age of 22.

action against his King. Yet the King considers him a deserter, and as Trenck is careless enough to pay a visit to Danzig, he is arrested there by Frederick's henchmen. They bring their captive back to Prussia, imprisoning him in the dungeon of Magdeburg. In vain Amalie entreats the King to show mercy. Only after endless years is Trenck released; but he has to leave Prussia forever. Time passes and the King dies. His successor permits the old, broken exile to return home.[25]

A few changes in the distribution of lights and shadows, and the steadfast Amalie as well as Trenck, so hungry for freedom, might have transformed themselves into heroic rebels engaged in breaking Frederick's ruthless tyranny. In fact, they are potential rebels. But far from acknowledging these unhappy lovers as such, the film strips them of their moral significance, bestowing all glamour on the King. Amalie is stigmatized for preferring her private happiness to her sacred duty, and Trenck is made to appear an erratic soldier of fortune. Authoritarian mentality, eager to glorify the rebel when he fights for national liberation, thus distorts and soils his image when he offends the sovereignty of the "King" in the interest of individual liberty.

The ideal rebel has to submit to authoritarian rule. Trenck himself is shown surrendering, although he is never recognized as a true rebel. Back in Prussia, he goes to see Amalie—a late and sad tête-à-tête after a separation of thirty years. Since the King has destroyed their love and happiness, one might expect Trenck to answer in the affirmative Amalie's question as to whether he hates Frederick. His answer consists in handing to her the manuscript of his memoirs. A close-up, marking the end of the film, impresses upon the audience Trenck's dedication. The words read: "To the Spirit of Frederick the Unique, King of Prussia, my Life." This unfathomable surrender corroborates the meaning of York's rebellion and moreover intimates that the other rebels of the pre-Hitler screen are also intrinsically authoritarian-minded. In the last analysis, the philistine of THE STREET is the archetype of all German film rebels. Reincarnated in Trenck, he finally meets the Frederick of his dreams, who redeems him from the horrors of the plush parlor.

An elaborate image of the inspired leader supplemented that of the rebel. Besides TRENCK, three full-fledged Fridericus films, all of

[25] Kalbus, *Deutsche Filmkunst*, II, 74; synopsis in *Illustrierter Film-Kurier*; etc.

them starring Otto Gebühr, featured Frederick as such a leader: Gustav Ucicky's DAS FLÖTENKONZERT VON SANSSOUCI (THE FLUTE CONCERT AT SANS SOUCI, 1930); Friedrich Zelnik's BARBERINA, DIE TÄNZERIN VON SANSSOUCI (THE KING'S DANCER, 1932); and DER CHORAL VON LEUTHEN (THE ANTHEM OF LEUTHEN, March 7, 1933), produced and staged by Carl Froelich in collaboration with A. von Cserèpy, the creator of the first Fridericus film. The series continued under Hitler. FRIDERICUS, drawn from a novel by Walter von Molo and released in the early days of the Nazi regime, focused upon the King of the Seven Years' War—a King who, if possible, surpassed all previous Fredericks in his resemblance to Hitler. Artistically on an average level, these pictures with their propagandistic implications found little understanding abroad. An American reviewer called THE KING'S DANCER a "fine German costume piece" in an obvious attempt at indulgence.[26]

On the whole, the new Fridericus films harped on the motifs of the old ones and, like them, overflowed with rationalizations of retrogressive behavior. But what once were unsubstantiated desires developed into topical allusions. Frederick's aggressive power politics, itself a compensation for retrogression, appears as a sustained defense action against an overwhelming enemy conspiracy. Interesting in this respect is the introductory caption of FRIDERICUS, which anticipates the official language of such Nazi war films as BAPTISM OF FIRE and VICTORY IN THE WEST all down the line: "Encircled by the hereditary Great Powers of Europe, rising Prussia has aspired for decades to her right to live. The whole world is amazed at the King of Prussia who, first ridiculed, then feared, has maintained himself against forces many times superior to his own. Now they seem to crush him. Prussia's fateful hour has come." After such apologetic remarks, found in every Fridericus film, the expected victories and parades pour down with a rapidity certain to delight the immature.

The endeavor to rationalize feelings of inferiority was particularly strong. All Fridericus films confront Prussia's poverty and rudeness with the wealth and polished manners of her enemies, and in doing so persistently deprecate the latter. The Austrians continue

[26] Quoted from "Barberina," *Variety*, Nov. 1, 1932. For THE FLUTE CONCERT AT SANS SOUCI, *see* Kalbus, *Deutsche Filmkunst*, II, 72–73, and program to the film; for THE KING'S DANCER, Kalbus, *ibid.*, p. 74, and program to the film; for THE ANTHEM OF LEUTHEN, Kalbus, *ibid.*, p. 75, and *Illustrierter Film-Kurier;* for FRIDERICUS, *Illustrierter Film-Kurier*. See also the New York reviews of these films.

in their role of effeminate operetta figures; one of them, a colonel, excels in pleasing love songs (ANTHEM OF LEUTHEN). The French, in turn, are represented as born courtiers, fond of intrigues and puns. Who could envy these people? It is the case of Prussia-Germany against the Western Powers; of the "have-nots" against the plutocracies; of what in Germany is called culture against a rotten civilization. Compared with their enemies, these films imply, the Germans have all the traits of a master race entitled to take over Europe and tomorrow the world.

The whole series was a thorough attempt to familiarize the masses with the idea of a *Führer*. None other than Voltaire is called upon to recommend him. When, in TRENCK, Frederick advocates sovereignty of the law, Voltaire replies that good sovereigns are preferable to good laws—enlightened reason paying homage to the absolute ruler. The King justifies this flattering opinion by playing, as before, the part of the people's father. His patriarchal regime is a mixture of old-Prussian feudalism and Nazi sham socialism. He promises oppressed farmers to punish the Governor of their province for partially favoring the big-estate owners (TRENCK); he cancels all victory celebrations, urging that the money provided for them be given to the war victims (KING'S DANCER); he thinks of allotting funds for cultural purposes on the eve of a decisive battle (ANTHEM OF LEUTHEN). Everybody will have to admit that the security Frederick's subjects enjoy is inaccessible to the citizens of a democracy, for in his protective zeal the King generously helps lovers (KING'S DANCER) and even goes so far as to prevent the wife of an absent major from committing adultery (FLUTE CONCERT).

This model King is a veritable genius. As such he succeeds in thwarting conspiracies, outwitting slick diplomats, and winning battles where all the chances are against him. In THE FLUTE CONCERT AT SANS SOUCI, he secretly issues mobilization orders to his generals during a flute concert attended by the unsuspecting ambassadors of Austria, France and Russia, thus stealing a march on these three powers which, he knows, are all set to attack Prussia. In THE KING'S DANCER, he invites Barberina to Berlin, so as to make his enemies believe that he whiles his time away with a flirtation. THE ANTHEM OF LEUTHEN reveals the relations between this genius and plain mortals. When the King decides to venture upon a battle near Leuthen, his devoted old generals fiercely advise against it in view of their desperate situation. Of course the battle is won, and the moral is that the "intuitions" of a genuine *Führer* prove superior to normal reasoning—a moral well established in German hearts until Stalingrad. Always right in the end, the inspired King is surrounded with a dense aura. Both THE KING'S DANCER and THE ANTHEM OF LEUTHEN capitalize on the authenticated episode of his sudden appearance at Austrian headquarters on the occasion of one of his dashing reconnoitering rides: the Austrians are so spellbound by their legendary enemy that they forget to capture him, and when they come to their senses, relief arrives in the form of a Prussian detachment.

The reverse of the leader's grandeur is his tragic solitude, played up in all Fridericus films [Illus. 63]. No one is able to understand Frederick, and amidst cheering crowds he misses the sense of warmth and nearness which any lover enjoys. At the end of THE KING'S DANCER, "you see the great king, who has graciously turned Barberina over to her lover, walk to the window of his palace to greet his people, and you leave him, standing there, a lonely, unhappy old man." [27] It has been pointed out in earlier contexts that this insistence upon the *Führer's* loneliness meets the needs of a juvenile mind.

On February 2, 1933, one day after Hitler had been appointed Chancellor of the Reich, Ufa released MORGENROT (DAWN), a film about a submarine during World War I. Gustav Ucicky, a specialist in nationalistic productions, directed this film from a script by Gerhard Menzel, winner of a high literary award (*Kleistpreis*). The composer was Herbert Windt, who in the years to come did the scores of many important Nazi films. "At the Berlin first night," *Variety's* Berlin correspondent reported on the première of MORGENROT, "the new Cabinet with Hitler, Dr. Hugenberg and Papen, were present. . . . The picture was received with tremendous applause. . . ." [28]

The film is a mingling of war exploits and sentimental conflicts. Liers, the sub commander (Rudolf Forster), and his first lieutenant, Fredericks, are on home leave in their small native town, and as they depart it becomes apparent that both have fallen in love with the same girl. Then the submarine is seen in action, torpedoing and sinking a British cruiser. After this victory, Liers for the first time opens

[27] Quoted from Watts, "The King's Dancer," *New York Herald Tribune*, Oct. 27, 1932.

[28] "Morgenrot," *Variety*, Feb. 28, 1933.

his heart to Fredericks who, without showing how much he suffers, tacitly realizes that the girl he loves feels more attached to Liers than to himself. In pursuit of its mission, the submarine challenges a seemingly neutral vessel which, however, reveals itself as a British decoy boat. Signaled by the decoy, a British destroyer rams the sub. A crucial problem arises, for in the sinking hull ten men are left alive with only eight divers' suits available. Two shots solve the problem: Fredericks and another crew member, grieved for reasons of his own, commit suicide to save their comrades. The final sequence resumes the theme of home leave. Liers again departs from his native town, and the war goes on.

The American reviews not only praised this film for its brilliant acting and its abundance of realistic battle details, but showed themselves very impressed by its absence of any hatred.[29] In fact, Liers' mother, who has already lost two sons in the war, is singularly lacking in patriotic ardor, and the submarine crew reacts to the British ruse of a decoy without the slightest animosity. DAWN is no Nazi film. Rather, it belongs to the series of such war films as THE LAST COMPANY and THE DOOMED BATTALION which precisely through their impartiality elevate war to the rank of an unquestionable institution.[30]

That Hitler saw DAWN at the dawn of his own regime is a strange coincidence. He might have enjoyed this film with its smell of real war as a lucky omen, a providential sanction of what he himself planned to bring about [Illus. 64]. Moreover, it told him unmistakably that Liers and his kind, even should they fail to become his partisans, were predestined to become his tools. Liers, a conservative-minded professional soldier, says to his mother: "Perhaps we Germans do not know how to live, but how to die, this we know incredibly well." [31] His words frankly acknowledge the process of retrogression reflected by the German screen throughout its whole development. The desire to mature, they admit in a scarcely veiled manner, has faded away, and the nostalgia for the womb is so definite that it stiffens to pride in dying a good death. People such as Liers were indeed bound to submit to the *Führer*.

[29] Cf. Barrett, "Morgenrot," *National Board of Review Magazine*, June 1933, pp. 10–12, 15; Tazelaar, "Morgenrot," *New York Herald Tribune*, May 19, 1933; Boehnel, "Morgenrot," *New York World Telegram*, May 17, 1933.

[30] In a similar vein was Emelka's KREUZER EMDEN (CRUISER EMDEN, 1932), a sound version of THE EMDEN of 1926.

[31] Quoted by Kalbus, *Deutsche Filmkunst*, II, 82.

Comparison of the two major groups of pre-Hitler films reveals that in the conflict of antiauthoritarian and authoritarian dispositions, the odds are against the former. To be sure, the films of the first group are, in part, on a high artistic level, and no matter whether they indulge in pacifism or socialism, they all turn against the tyranny of authoritarian rule. But these films are only loosely connected with each other and, much more important, they fail to carry power of conviction. In MÄDCHEN IN UNIFORM, Fräulein von Bernburg does not succeed in radically defeating the disciplinarian headmistress; HELL ON EARTH with its emphasis on international fraternization is thoroughly evasive; COMRADESHIP spreads Social Democratic ideals in a way that testifies to their actual exhaustion.

Unlike this first major group, the second consists of films which, except for a few scattered products, are closely interrelated. They belong together; they concur in establishing a national epic which centers round the rebel and is dominated by the figure of an inspired *Führer*. In addition, the story these films tell resists criticism from within. While the pacifist message of Pabst's WESTFRONT 1918 sounds unconvincing because of its complete disregard of the diverse causes of war, the war heroism in Trenker's DOOMED BATTALION is not a credo that has to be substantiated but an attitude that simply exists. One may condemn it for well-founded external reasons, but one cannot hope to analyze away its reality or possible appeal. The fact that all films of the second group are internally invulnerable and allied in a common effort indicates the superior weight of their underlying authoritarian tendencies. The power of these tendencies is confirmed by the fusion of the mountain films and the national films which could take place only under the pressure of irresistible impulses.

Considering the widespread ideological opposition to Hitler, there is no doubt that the preponderance of authoritarian leanings was a decisive factor in his favor. Broad strata of the population, including part of the intelligentsia, were psychologically predisposed to the kind of system Hitler offered; so much so that their craving for it made them overlook their welfare, their chance of survival. During those years, many an unbiased observer warned white-collar workers and employers alike against the Nazis, holding that in its own economic interest the middle class would do better to associate itself with the Social Democrats. History has corroborated this warning. In the spring of 1943, *Das Schwarze Korps*, the official S.S. organ, bluntly proclaimed that "the middle class is dead and should not rise again after the war." [32] And yet this very middle class formed the backbone of the Hitler movement. The impact of pro-Nazi dispositions seemed to upset all sober considerations.

A further symptom of the essential role of these dispositions is the magic spell that the Nazi spirit cast over youth and the unemployed—two groups which because of their remoteness from fixed class interests were particularly sensitive to a propaganda appealing to their longings for totalitarian leadership. Hitler, if anyone, knew how to play upon such longings. Finally, it can be assumed that the discrepancy between these ever-smoldering desires and the political convictions of the Weimar parties contributed much to the collapse of the "system." The catholic Center as well as the Social Democrats was increasingly drained of its vital energies. It was as if they were both paralyzed. The tenets they advocated lacked the support of strong emotions, and in the end their will for power degenerated into impotent formal scruples.

Irretrievably sunk into retrogression, the bulk of the German people could not help submitting to Hitler. Since Germany thus carried out what had been anticipated by her cinema from its very beginning, conspicuous screen characters now came true in life itself. Personified daydreams of minds to whom freedom meant a fatal shock, and adolescence a permanent temptation, these figures filled the arena of Nazi Germany. Homunculus walked about in the flesh. Self-appointed Caligaris hypnotized innumerable Cesares into murder. Raving Mabuses committed fantastic crimes with impunity, and mad Ivans devised unheard-of tortures. Along with this unholy procession, many motifs known from the screen turned into actual events. In Nuremberg, the ornamental pattern of NIBELUNGEN appeared on a gigantic scale: an ocean of flags and people artistically arranged. Souls were thoroughly manipulated so as to create the impression that the heart mediated between brain and hand. By day and night, millions of feet were marching over city streets and along highways. The blare of military bugles sounded unremittingly, and the philistines from the plush parlors felt very elated. Battles roared and victory followed victory. It all was as it had been on the screen. The dark premonitions of a final doom were also fulfilled.

[32] Quoted from "The Middle Class Is Dead . . ," *New York Times,* April 12, 1943.

SUPPLEMENT

PROPAGANDA AND THE NAZI WAR FILM

AUTHOR'S NOTE

THIS Supplement is, except for some changes in style, arrangement and the transposition of tense from the present to the past, a reprint of my pamphlet "Propaganda and the Nazi War Film," issued, in 1942, by the Museum of Modern Art Film Library, which kindly permitted its incorporation into the present book. Originally serving the purposes of psychological warfare, the pamphlet was made possible by a Rockefeller grant and written under the auspices of Miss Iris Barry. My debt of gratitude also extends to Professor Hans Speier of the Department of State, Dr. Ernst Kris of the Graduate Faculty of the New School for Social Research, Dr. Hans Herma of the City College of New York, and Mr. Richard Griffith, Executive Director of the National Board of Review of Motion Pictures. As an analysis of official screen activities under Hitler, this supplement may afford some insight into developments beyond the scope of the book proper.

S. K.

1. NAZI VIEWS AND MEASURES

THE following pages are devoted to the analysis and interpretation of totalitarian film propaganda, in particular of Nazi film propaganda after 1939. To be sure, all Nazi films were more or less propaganda films —even the mere entertainment pictures which seem to be remote from politics. However, in this study only those propaganda films will be examined which were produced for the express purpose of bolstering Nazi Germany's total war effort.

The Nazis carried out their direct war film propaganda through two types of films:

I. The weekly newsreels—including a compilation of newsreels entitled BLITZKRIEG IM WESTEN (BLITZKRIEG IN THE WEST);

II. The feature-length campaign films, two of which were shown in this country:

 (a) FEUERTAUFE (BAPTISM OF FIRE), dealing with the Polish campaign, and

 (b) SIEG IM WESTEN (VICTORY IN THE WEST), dealing with the French campaign.[1]

Before embarking upon my investigation proper, which refers almost exclusively to the aforementioned material, I should like to present an account of how the Germans handled their war film production. Most official announcements and administrative measures were concerned with the shaping and distribution of newsreels, but what holds true of them also applies to the feature-length documentaries.

Immediately after the outbreak of war, the German Propaganda Ministry employed every possible means to make of newsreels an effective instrument of war propaganda. It is true that, long before the war began, the Nazis used newsreels for the dissemination of propaganda messages; but the emphasis they put on newsreels after September 1939 goes far beyond their former achievements and cannot easily be overestimated.

Three principles asserted themselves in the German war newsreels.

First, they had to be true to reality; i.e., instead of resorting to staged war scenes, they had to confine themselves to shots actually taken at the front. Because of their documentary intention, the campaign films

[1] The date of the original release of BLITZKRIEG IN THE WEST is unknown to me. It was shown for the first time in New York on November 30, 1940. BAPTISM OF FIRE (with a first run in Berlin at the beginning of April 1940) is a version of a film unknown in this country, FELDZUG IN POLEN (CAMPAIGN IN POLAND), released in Berlin on February 8, 1940. VICTORY IN THE WEST was shown to the German and foreign press for the first time in Berlin on January 29, 1941.

Baptism of Fire and Victory in the West, both of which consist almost entirely of newsreel material, were also subject to this restriction. Official accounts as well as press reviews never forgot to stress their realism. On February 6, 1940, the *Licht Bild Bühne* stated that the Polish campaign film matched the newsreels of the first weeks of the war in that it gave the spectator the impression of being an eyewitness to the battle scenes. Official sources became eloquent whenever they pondered the dangerous mission of the film reporters. Mr. Kurt Hubert, export director of Tobis, said in the fall of 1940, on a German short-wave broadcast in English, that the regular army cameramen ". . . are regular soldiers, doing a soldier's full duty, always in the first lines. . . . This explains the realistic pictures which we show. . . ."[2] For the enhancement of this realism, the losses among front-line reporter formations were readily announced—by people ordinarily reluctant to admit the presence of death in their "realistic" pictures. On April 26, 1940, the Berlin correspondent of the *New York Times* was authorized to report that twenty-three war correspondents had met death since the outbreak of the war, and the opening caption of the main part of Victory in the West takes care to increase the thrill of subsequent scenes by stressing similar facts. On the strength of them, Mr. Hubert labeled the Nazi war film a "perfect document of historical truth and nothing but the truth, therefore answering the German demand for a good substantial report in every way."[3] But it will be seen that the death of brave cameramen did not prevent a clever editor from composing their shots into films that, if necessary, blurred reality and set aside historical truth.

The second principle concerned the length of newsreels. After the ominous September days they were considerably enlarged. On May 23, 1940, the *Licht Bild Bühne* announced the forthcoming newsreel as a top event of 40 minutes' length. This inflation of the newsreel made it possible to produce on the screen much the same effects as those obtained through steady repetition in speeches. It was one of many devices which served to transform German audiences into a chain-gang of souls.

The third principle was speed. Nazi newsreels had not only to be true to reality but to illustrate it as quickly as possible, so that the war communiqués were not forgotten by the time their content appeared on the screen. Airplanes flew the negatives from the front—a dynamic procedure apparently designed to parallel and support the radio front reports.

Distribution of newsreels, the production of which was unified at the

[2] *Sight and Sound,* 1941, Vol. 10, No. 38.
[3] *Ibid.*

beginning of the war, was most thoroughly organized. In 1940, Goebbels said that films must address people of all strata.[4] Following his instructions, the Nazis managed to impose their propaganda films upon the entire German population, with the result that within Germany proper no one could possibly escape them. Film trucks were sent all over the country; special performances were arranged at reduced prices. Since exact timing of the pictorial suggestions was desirable, the Propaganda Ministry moreover decreed that each official front newsreel be released on the same day everywhere in the Reich. Thus the domestic market was completely held under control.

As to export, the effort of the Nazi authorities to flood foreign countries with their official pictures is sufficiently characterized by the fact that the Propaganda Ministry prepared versions in sixteen different languages. The Summer 1941 issue of *Sight and Sound,* cited previously, completes this information. It states: "The U.F.A. office in New York reports that, despite blockade difficulties, a German film reaches this country on an average of once every two weeks." Of particular interest is the well-known use Hitler diplomats made of propaganda films to undermine the resistance of foreign peoples and governments. In Bucharest, Oslo, Belgrade, Ankara, Sofia—to mention but a few—official showings of these pictures served as psychological holdups. Thus on October 11, 1941, the *New York Times* reported that Herr von Papen had left Istanbul with a film of the German invasion of Russia, and that he "will have a large party at the German Embassy during which he will show the film to Turkish leaders." Propaganda films as a means of blackmail—the gangster methods of the Nazis could not be better illustrated.

2. FILM DEVICES

The film devices of Nazi propaganda are numerous and frequently subtle. This does not imply that the Nazi propaganda films necessarily surpassed similar films produced in other countries; the British film Target for Tonight realized artistic effects one would seek vainly in any of the Nazi films. Moreover, these films suffered somewhat from excessive use of newsreel shots, and they included sequences which proved to be more tiresome than convincing. Through such sequences certain weak points of Nazi propaganda betrayed themselves.

But despite these deficiencies, which resulted from the problematic

[4] Cf. *Licht Bild Bühne,* Feb. 3, 1940.

structure of Nazi propaganda rather than from awkwardness of technique, the Nazis managed to develop effective methods of presenting their propaganda ideas on the screen. There is hardly an editing device they did not explore, and there exist several means of presentation whose scope they enlarged to an extent hitherto unknown. They were bound to do so, for their propaganda could not proceed like the propaganda of the democracies and appeal to the understanding of its audiences; it had to attempt, on the contrary, to suppress the faculty of understanding which might have undermined the basis of the whole system. Rather than suggesting through information, Nazi propaganda withheld information or degraded it to a further means of propagandistic suggestion. This propaganda aimed at psychological retrogression to manipulate people at will. Hence the comparative abundance of tricks and devices. They were needed for obtaining the additional effects upon which the success of Nazi film propaganda depended.

The art of editing had been cultivated in Germany long before 1933, and Leni Riefenstahl's Triumph of the Will, for example, drew heavily upon former achievements. Owing to these traditions, the Nazis knew how to utilize the three film media—commentary, visuals and sound. With a pronounced feeling for editing, they exploited each medium to the full, so that the total effect frequently resulted from the blending of different meanings in different media. Such polyphonic handling is not often found in democratic war films; nor did the Nazis themselves go to great pains when they merely wished to pass on information. But as soon as totalitarian propaganda sprang into action, a sumptuous orchestration was employed to influence the masses.

To begin with the commentary of the two campaign films, it expresses in words the ideas that cannot be communicated by means of the visuals, such as historical flashbacks, accounts of military activities and explanations of strategy. These explanations, which recur at regular intervals, deal with the German and enemy army positions and report, in somewhat general terms, encirclements just achieved or encirclements in the offing. Their whole make-up shows that they are intended to impress people rather than to instruct them; they seem to be advertising the efficiency of some enormous enterprise. Besides this pseudo-enlightenment typical of the two campaign films, the linkages between statements are repeatedly entrusted with propagandistic functions. In Victory in the West they are used to build ellipses: the announcement of an action is immediately followed by its result, and long developments are supposed to have been consummated in the tiny period between two verbal units. Thus a great deal of reality and enemy resistance disappears in the "pockets" of the commentary, giving the audience a sense of ease of accomplishment and increasing the impression of an indomitable German blitz.[1] Actually the blitz has flashed through an artificial vacuum.

Within the visuals, much use is made of the fact that pictures make a direct appeal to the subconscious and the nervous system. Many devices are employed for the sole purpose of eliciting from audiences certain specific emotions. Such effects may be obtained by means of maps. I wish to supplement the remarks in Professor Speier's excellent article "Magic Geography,"[2] which also refers to the propagandistic value of maps in the Nazi war films. These maps accompany not only the strategic explanations, but appear whenever symbolic presentation is called for and can be considered the backbone of the two campaign films. They stress the propaganda function of the statements about strategic developments inasmuch as they seem to illustrate, through an array of moving arrows and lines, tests on some new substance. Resembling graphs of physical processes, they show how all known materials are broken up, penetrated, pushed back and eaten away by the new one, thus demonstrating its absolute superiority in a most striking manner. Since they affect all the senses, they are bound to terrorize the opposite camp—at least so long as the tests have not been invalidated. In addition, these tests are performed on expanses that resemble areas seen from an airplane—an impression produced by the camera always panning, rising and diving. Its continual motion works upon the motor nerves, deepening in the spectator the conviction of the Nazis' dynamic power; movement around and above a field implies complete control of that field.

Other important devices in this medium are: the exploitation of physiognomical qualities by contrasting, for instance, close-ups of brute Negroes with German soldier faces; the incorporation of captured enemy film material and its manipulation in such a way that it testifies against the country of origin; the insertion of leitmotivs for the purpose of organizing the composition and stressing certain propagandistic intentions within the visuals. While BAPTISM OF FIRE presents these leitmotivs only in the bud, VICTORY IN THE WEST shows them flourishing. In this film, marching infantry columns betoken an advance; in it, the ideal type of the German soldier emerges time and again in close-up, a soft face that involuntarily betrays the close relationship of soul and blood, sentimentality and sadism.

The use of visuals in connection with verbal statements is determined by the fact that many propaganda ideas are expressed through pictures alone. The pictures do not confine themselves to illustrating the commentary, but, on the contrary, tend to assume an independent life which, instead of paralleling that of the commentary, sometimes pursues

[1] Cf. p. 294 f.

[2] *Social Research,* Sept. 1941.

a course of its own—a most important and extensively utilized device. In employing it, totalitarian propaganda could manage to shape, on the one hand, a rather formal commentary which avoided heretical or overexplicit statements, and yet, on the other hand, could give audiences to understand that Britons were ridiculous and that Nazi Germany was pious and adored peace above all. The Nazis knew that allusions may reach deeper than assertions and that the contrapuntal relation of image to verbal statement is likely to increase the weight of the image, making it a more potent emotional stimulus.

Where the visuals follow the line of the commentary, much care is taken that the depiction of battle scenes does not go so far as to reveal the military operations clearly. Except for a few sequences, the pictures of German warfare have no informative character. Instead of adequate illustration of the verbally indicated activities, they mostly confine themselves to exemplifications which frequently remain indistinct or prove to be universally applicable stereotypes. Whenever artillery goes into action, a series of firing guns appear in quick succession. Since such patterns are not specific, the impression of a vacuum is reinforced. Whole battles develop in a never-never land where the Germans rule over time and space. This practice works in the same way as do a number of other devices: it helps confuse the spectator by a blurred succession of pictures so as to make him submit more readily to certain suggestions. Many a pictorial description is actually nothing more than an empty pause between two propagandistic insinuations.

A conspicuous role is played by the music, particularly in Victory in the West. Accompanying the procession of pictures and statements, it not only deepens the effects produced through these media, but intervenes of its own accord, introducing new effects or changing the meaning of synchronized units. Music, and music alone, transforms an English tank into a toy. In other instances, musical themes remove the weariness from soldier faces, or make several moving tanks symbolize the advancing German army. A gay melody imbues the parade and decoration scene in Paris with a *soupçon* of "*la vie parisienne.*" Through this active contribution of the music the visuals affect the senses with intensified strength.

3. THE SWASTIKA WORLD

In their war propaganda films the Nazis, of course, pictured themselves exactly as they wanted to be seen, and when, with the passing of time, some trait or other lost its attraction, the propaganda experts did not hesitate to suppress it. The meeting of Hitler and Il Duce shown in

BLITZKRIEG IN THE WEST was eliminated in the fall of 1941[1]; and it goes without saying that the Russian-German conference on the division of Poland in BAPTISM OF FIRE had to disappear from a second version of this film released in Yorkville in August 1941. But for interpretation it makes little difference whether or not such self-portraits are true to life; obvious distortions prove to be particularly enlightening, and, on the whole, reality cannot be prevented from breaking through its delusive images, so that these vanish like the enemy armies on the maps in Nazi war films.

All propaganda films were unanimous in emphasizing the dominance of the army over the Party. In his *Pattern of Conquest*, Joseph C. Harsch dwells upon the fact that, instead of letting the Party penetrate the army, Hitler preferred to satisfy the army by setting aside Party claims. For the period in question the propaganda films coincided with Hitler's actual policy in that they devoted to Party activities during the war only a few references and shots. After having mentioned the role played by Danzig's SA and SS formations, BAPTISM OF FIRE confines itself to showing Hitler's bodyguard being reviewed by its chief, and that is all. In VICTORY IN THE WEST, the two statements acknowledging the presence of armed SS are synchronized with pictures which pass much too hastily to make their presence evident. What a contrast with the Russian MANNERHEIM LINE, in which Party officials address the encamped soldiers and shake hands with a newly enlisted recruit! Such a scene would have been impossible in any of the Nazi films. On the other hand, these films overlook nothing that might glorify the army. In VICTORY IN THE WEST, which bears the subtitle "A Film of the High Command of the Army," special effects are called upon to make it the Song of Songs of the German soldier: impressive mass-ornaments of soldiers prelude the two parts of the film, and it ends with the banner-oath scene with which it begins. Here as well as in BAPTISM OF FIRE the army occupies all the strategically important points of the composition.[2]

[1] This scene is mentioned in the article "The Strategy of Terror: Audience Response to *Blitzkrieg im Westen*" by Jerome S. Bruner and George Fowler (*The Journal of Abnormal and Social Psychology*, Vol. 36, October 1941, No. 4). The description refers to a performance of the film on April 9, 1941.

[2] Regarding the various arms of the service, the frequency of their appearance in the different propaganda films undergoes interesting changes. The ratio of air force scenes to the total footage in BAPTISM OF FIRE is almost double the ratio in VICTORY IN THE WEST. This is all the more surprising as BLITZKRIEG IN THE WEST—which supplied VICTORY IN THE WEST with a certain quantity of newsreel shots—presents, relative to the total amount of shots, air force activities to an even larger extent than does BAPTISM OF FIRE; the ratio of the latter comes to merely a half of the same ratio in BLITZKRIEG IN THE WEST. It is quite inevitable to draw from these figures the conclusion that in VICTORY IN THE WEST the share of the air force has been deliberately reduced. The question remains as to whether or not this shift resulted from the High Command's desire to boast about tank warfare, for tanks do prevail in VICTORY IN THE WEST, while, compared with the air force, they play but a minor role in BAPTISM OF FIRE and BLITZKRIEG IN THE WEST.

This could not be done without presenting Hitler as the war lord. There is, however, an interesting difference between his appearance in Baptism of Fire and Victory in the West—a difference pointing to a development which, as a matter of fact, had been confirmed by reports from Germany. While the commentary of the Polish campaign film mentions Hitler but a few times and then in a laconic manner, the visuals zealously indulge in showing him as the ubiquitous supreme executive: he presides over a war council, gives soldiers his autograph, increases his popularity by having lunch at a military kitchen and shows pleasure in parades. In Victory in the West the ratio of pictures to statements is somewhat reversed: here the army praises as a strategic genius the man who has launched the attack against the Western powers. The war lord exceeds the executive to become a war god—and of a god images must not be made. Thus Hitler disappears almost completely behind clouds that disperse only on the most solemn occasions; but the commentary is enthusiastic about the Führer's ingenious plans and idolizes him as the one who alone knows when the hour of decision has come.

The introductory part of Victory in the West contains a shot of Hindenburg and Ludendorff during the first World War, presenting them as leaders upon whom the outcome of the war depended. They have weight; they seem to be conscious of a destiny beyond mere technical considerations. According to the Nazi films, none of the generals of the present war equals in rank or responsibility those two old army leaders whose functions apparently are assumed by Hitler himself. From time to time the real position of his generals is revealed through shots showing them all together as his subordinates—the staff assembled around its "Führer." And when they appear isolated, bending over maps, pacing through columns of soldiers and issuing orders on the field, they always give the impression of being high functionaries rather than commanders-in-chief. But it is quite natural that increased mechanization fosters the organizer type and tends to elevate technical experts to the top. Moreover, the fact that in all these films warfare itself is described as but a part of a larger historical and political process somewhat circumscribes the role of the generals.

For the rest, soldiers fill up the propaganda pictures to such an extent that there remains little room for civilians; even cheering crowds are closely rationed. In Victory in the West, this space is almost entirely given over to the workers. "The best comrade of the German soldier is the ammunition worker," to quote the commentary, and the synchronized shots amount to several close-ups of worker types in the manner of former German leftist films which, for their part, were influenced by the classic Russian productions. The propagandistic reasons for the insertion of these flattering photographs are plain enough.

Commentary and visuals of the two campaign films collaborate in advertising the martial virtues of the Germans: their bravery, their technical skill, their indefatigable perseverance.[3] But since such virtues appear in the war films of all belligerent countries, they can be neglected here in favor of certain other traits more characteristic of the behavior of German soldiers. Pictures alone imply this behavior; there is a complete lack of dialogue, discussion or speeches to tighten and bolster the impressions which the silent life on the screen may evoke. While the English aviators in TARGET FOR TONIGHT speak frankly about what they feel and think, the German soldiers even refrain from echoing any official propaganda ideas. In earlier propaganda films, such as HITLERJUNGE QUEX and TRIUMPH OF THE WILL, people were not so discreet in this respect. The later attitude may be due to the influence of the High Command: talking politics would have offended venerable army tradition.

Numerous pictorial hints build up the propagandistic image of the German soldier, among them the "camping idylls" of both BAPTISM OF FIRE and VICTORY IN THE WEST—rather drawn-out sections or passages that show the troops during their rest period, exhibiting what is left to the privates of their private life. Besides the routine work, which consists mainly of cleaning weapons, the soldiers wash their shirts and their bodies, they shave and enjoy eating, they write letters home or doze. For two reasons Nazi film propaganda thus emphasizes general human needs. First, in doing so it utilizes an old lesson taught by the primitive film comedies—that the gallery likes nothing more than the presentation of vulgar everyday procedures. Each of the six times I attended VICTORY IN THE WEST in a Yorkville theater, people around me were noticeably amused and refreshed when, after a terrific accumulation of tanks, guns, explosions and scenes of destruction, a soldier poured cold water over his naked comrade. Secondly, such scenes have the advantage of appealing specifically to instincts common to all people. Like spearheads, they

[3] It should be noted that in the two campaign films members of the elite alone are mentioned by name; words of praise are very cautiously distributed and, with a few exceptions, apply mostly to the German soldier in general or to army units as a whole. German army tradition seems to have been decisive in this respect. Single soldiers or small groups of soldiers are nowhere explicitly praised except in four possible instances in VICTORY IN THE WEST, while both films (and the newsreels as well) speak highly of the different branches of the service. The exploits of the air force and the infantry receive special recognition. With regard to vilification and ridicule of the enemy, there exists no reluctance whatever. The enemy is rarely mentioned without being criticized; and whenever his bravery is acknowledged, praise is designed to stress a subsequent blame. These deprecations are carried out less by verbal statements than through pictures and synchronization of pictures with musical themes. Exploring the polyphonic potentialities of the medium to the full, Nazi propaganda excels in blending official suggestions with confidential intimations, of knitting the brow and winking the eye at one and the same time.

drive wedges into the defense lines of the self, and owing to the retrogression they provoke, totalitarian propaganda conquers important unconscious positions.

To fashion the screen character of the German soldier the Nazi films sometimes have recourse to indirect methods; they single out and criticize, through pictures, the alleged qualities of the various enemy types, and, since they always draw upon contrasts, the naïve spectator automatically attributes the complementary qualities to the Germans. Thus the elaborate scene in BAPTISM OF FIRE in which several Poles are charged with having tortured and murdered German prisoners attempts to impose upon audiences the conviction that Germans themselves are indulgent towards their own victims. Could Nazis possibly be as flippant and degenerate as the French soldiers who are shown mingling with Negroes and dancing in the Maginot Line? The presentation of their conduct invites unfavorable comparison with the Germans'. And when English soldiers appear as funny, ignorant and arrogant creatures, there is no doubt about the conclusions to be drawn from their vices regarding the catalogue of virtues in the opposite camp. The more Polish, Belgian, French and English prisoners pass over the screen, the more this imaginary catalogue expands.

Its contents are supplemented by some indications to the effect, for instance, that German soldiers ardently love peace. It is not by accident that the beginning of VICTORY IN THE WEST presents a series of peaceful German landscapes between soldier crowds and inflammatory maps; that each verse of the song of the "Lieselotte," which is sung by moving infantry columns or accompanies their advance, concludes with the refrain "Tomorrow the war will be over." That the Nazis also wanted soldiers to be attached to home and family is implied by the camping idyll of the same film, in which a soldier, playing the organ in an old French church, seems to dream intensely of his dear ones at home; the organ music dissolves into a folk-song, and on the screen appear the soldier's mother, father and grandmother, whose carefree existence is protected against aggressive enemies by the German army. It is well known that in reality the Nazis followed quite another line with respect to such ideas as home, peace, family; no one familiar with their methods can overlook the cynicism with which they concocted all these sentimental episodes for the purpose of answering popular trends of feeling and, perhaps, the demands of the High Command. To round out the counterfeit, the Nazis used every opportunity to insert churches and cathedrals, with soldiers entering or leaving them during their rest period. Thus the films tacitly intimated that Germany fostered Christianity. They also suggested the cultural aspirations of German soldiers by showing, for instance, the Organization Todt taking care of historical buildings threatened by the progress of war. But these aspirations were never directed towards personal achievements. During the first years of World War I, the boast was spread through Germany that her soldiers carried Nietzsche's *Zarathustra* and Goethe's *Faust* in their knapsacks. When, in BAPTISM OF FIRE, soldiers read newspapers while marching, the possibility that they might be reading for sheer relaxation is denied by the commentary which states: "The German soldiers are so news-starved that they jump at every paper they can get hold of . . . enjoying the reports from the front, from the work at home."

On the whole, the "Reichswehr" soldier prevails over the Nazi creation of the "political soldier." There is, in this respect, a striking difference between film propaganda and printed or broadcast propaganda. While the Nazis always spoke and wrote of the revolutionary war that the Axis powers—the have-nots—had undertaken against the rich plutocracies, their films anxiously avoided corroborating such a contention. Except for a somewhat eased discipline and the suppression of the Prussian lieutenant type, the soldiers on the screen behave in so traditional a manner that nobody could suspect them of being the military vanguard of a revolution. The newsreel shots depicting these soldiers are certainly true to reality. Why did the Nazis hesitate to change the image further? Perhaps for the reason that the rendering of a revolutionary army on the screen would have prevented them from conveying through the word "revolution" its opposite meaning. Pictures alone can be misused as much as words alone; but as soon as they begin to cooperate, they explain each other, and ambiguity is excluded. Since the Nazis obviously could not afford to give up the advantage of covering their real aims with such attractive slogans as "Revolution" or "New Order," they were, indeed, forced to show in their films soldiers of rather neutral behavior. The extensive use made of silent newsreel soldiers was to paralyze audience attention and, moreover, to appeal to certain strata abroad that Nazi propaganda wished to influence.

The achievements of the German army resulted from the organizational abilities of a people which, as a consequence of its history, so deeply desires to be shaped that it mistakes organization for shape and submits to organization as readily as the wax to the seal. Nazi war films, of course, parade the perfection with which, thanks to such abilities, the blitz campaigns were prepared and accomplished. The episode of Hitler's war council in BAPTISM OF FIRE includes the following statement: "Continued information on the course of operations is passed on. . . . The decisive orders and instructions are returned at once"—sentences that refer to some shots of soldier typists and telephonists inserted in this episode. Like the series of firing guns, telephonists belong among the stereotypes within the visuals; their appearance infallibly indicates that orders are being issued and an attack is in the making. VICTORY IN THE WEST adds to this cliché a few innovations: a shot of a "firing-schedule" (*Feuerplan*) which characterizes the subsequent artillery bombardment as being "according to plan," and a little scene illustrating the last staff conference before the offensive against the *Chemin des Dames.* In the field of strategic measures, the swiftness of army regroupments as well as the admirable functioning of the supply lines are strongly emphasized. But, strangely enough, all these scenes treat organization in a somewhat perfunctory manner. Compared with the British film TARGET FOR TONIGHT, which really illustrates the preparation and the accomplishment of a bomber raid over Germany, even the purposefully informative sequence of the air attack in BAPTISM OF FIRE is poor in organizational details. This negligence parallels the deliberate superficiality with which military actions are exemplified in the medium of the visuals. In both cases, the withholding of full information must be traced to the inhibitions of a propaganda which lives in constant fear of arousing the individual's intellectual faculties. However, this explanation is too general to be sufficient. Fortunately, VICTORY IN THE WEST offers a clue to the problem.

Captured French film material is used in this film to depict the organization of the Maginot Line with surprising care. The main sequence devoted to the French defense system offers an account of its construction and also includes a series of pictures that dwell extensively upon the technical installations of this subterranean fortress. Towards the end of the film, the Maginot Line appears again: French soldiers serve a gun in one of the mechanical forts, and the synchronized statement announces: "For the last time the clockwork of this complicated defense machinery is in action." By exhibiting that machinery to the full, the Nazis wanted not only to heighten the significance of the German victory, but also to specify its unique character. The term "defense," used in the statement, is particularly revealing. Nazi propaganda in the film of the French campaign sets defensive against offensive warfare and, moreover, manages to present these two kinds of warfare as belonging to two different worlds. That of the French defenders appears as an obsolete static world with no moral right to survive. Since the shots of the French soldiers in the Maginot Line were made before the outbreak of the war, it was easy to evoke this impression by contrasting them with shots of German soldiers taken during the actual campaign. Here it becomes clear why the Nazis focused upon the French defense organization, instead of stressing their own organizational techniques. They wanted to show that the *deus ex machina* can never be the machine itself; that even the most perfect organization proves useless if it be regarded as more than a mere tool, if it be idolized by a generation-on-the-decline as an autonomous force. The whole presentation aims at implying that the Maginot Line was precisely that to the French, and that, in consequence, the German victory was also a victory of life over death, of the future over the past.[4]

In accordance with their emphasis on Germany's offensive spirit, the Nazi war films characterize organization as a dynamic process within pictures of continual movement spreading over enormous spaces. The big control-room from which, in TARGET FOR TONIGHT, British air force activities are directed and supervised would be impossible in any of the Nazi war films; it is too solid a room, it has too much the savor of defense. In these films, on the contrary, no room is more than an improvised shelter—if there exist shelters at all. Railway cars serve as Hitler's headquarters or for conferences with the delegates of capitulating nations; fields and highways are the very home of generals and troops alike. The soldiers eat on the march and sleep in airplanes, on traveling tanks, guns and trucks, and when they occasionally stop moving, their surroundings consist of ruined houses no longer fit to harbor guests. This eternal restlessness is identical with impetuous advance, as the Nazi films never fail to point out through moving maps and marching infantry columns—devices already commented upon. Significantly, the frequent appearance of infantry columns in the two campaign films seems to exceed the use actually made of infantry in the campaigns. Such columns were undoubtedly less effective than the columns of tanks and air squadrons, but their appearance on the screen is particularly appropriate to impress the idea of advance upon the audience. This impression is deepened by repeated close-ups of waving swastika banners, which serve the additional purpose of hypnotizing audiences.

To sum up: all Nazi war films insistently glorify Germany as a dynamic power, as dynamite. But, as if the Nazis themselves suspected that their sustained presentation of blitz warfare would hardly be sufficient to suggest a war of life against death, of the future against the past, they supplemented it by politico-historical records adding to the parades of goose-stepping soldiers a panoroma of thoroughly manipulated topical events. While BAPTISM OF FIRE modestly contents itself with reviewing current world events, VICTORY IN THE WEST widens the perspective by an ambitious retrospect which goes back to the Westphalian Peace of 1648. Hitler's speeches encouraged people to think in terms of centuries. The accounts of current events as a rule illustrate "history" through newsreel shots of notables and weighty incidents:

[4] This is fully confirmed by the statement that accompanies the last appearance of the Maginot Line: "Here, too, the heroism of the single soldier and the enthusiasm of the young national-socialist German troops entirely devoted to the Führer and his ideas triumph over technique, machinery and material."

Herr von Ribbentrop boards an airplane bound for Moscow to sign there the nonaggression pact; displays of French, English and Polish troops serve to demonstrate the war preparations of their countries; Professor Burckhard, delegate to the League of Nations for Danzig, leaves his office after Danzig's annexation by the Reich; King Leopold of Belgium negotiates armistice conditions with a German general. By shaping the world situation with the aid of such anecdotal scenes, the Nazis may also have intended to flatter audiences, to give them the proud feeling of being introduced to sovereigns, statesmen, diplomats and other celebrities. It was a sort of cajolery which made the implications of these screen editorials the more acceptable.

What implications did they convey? On the one hand, they make the Western democracies appear as evil powers animated, for centuries, by the design to destroy Germany; on the other, they suggest a sadly wronged and innocently suffering Germany who, on the point of being overwhelmed by these world powers, is only defending herself in attacking them. The whole myth was to give the impression that Germany's war and triumph were not accidental events, but the fulfillment of an historic mission, metaphysically justified. Thanks to the introduction of this myth, both BAPTISM OF FIRE and VICTORY IN THE WEST expand beyond the limits of mere documentary films to totalitarian panoramas connecting the march of time with the march of ideas. Such panoramas certainly answered the deep-rooted German longing to be sheltered by a *Weltanschauung*. In transferring them to the screen, the Nazis tried to conquer and occupy all important positions in the minds of their audiences, so as to make their souls work to the interest of Nazi Germany. They treated souls like prisoners of war; they endeavored to duplicate in the field of psychology Germany's achievements in Europe.

4. SCREEN DRAMATURGY

THE structure of the two Nazi campaign films is particularly important. Unlike the newsreels, they are the outcome of compositional efforts designed to make them documents of permanent value that would survive the more ephemeral weekly reports. Lieutenant Hesse, Chief of the Press Group attached to the German High Command, asserted in a radio talk on January 20, 1941: "VICTORY IN THE WEST has been deliberately planned and produced for the general public." The significance of this statement, which might have been applied to the Polish campaign film as well, is illustrated by the fact that both films were the product of intense condensation: the 6,560 feet of BAPTISM OF FIRE were drawn from about 230,000 feet of newsreel shots, and VICTORY IN THE WEST—according to Lieutenant Hesse—profited by film material of about one million feet. The Nazi experts would not have made a selection on such a vast scale without a definite idea as to the choice and the arrangement of the comparatively few subjects admitted.[1]

Except, perhaps, for the *March of Time* shorts and certain travelogs which, in the manner of Flaherty's NANOOK and MOANA, rely on some sort of story to animate the presentation of facts, most films of fact affect audiences not so much through the organization of their material as through the material itself. They are rather loosely composed; they prove to be more concerned with the depiction of reality than with the arrangement of this depiction. The two Nazi campaign films differ from them in that they not only excel in a solid composition of their elements but also exploit all propagandistic effects which may be produced by the very structure. VICTORY IN THE WEST goes so far as to entrust special leitmotivs and staged sequences with the function of reinforcing the weight of the interior architecture. This evidently cannot be done unless certain forceful ideas determine the composition, imbuing it with their vigor. The strong will underlying the two Nazi campaign films is of course more likely to work upon audience imagination than the mentality behind documentaries which simply meander from one point of information to the next. TARGET FOR TONIGHT was one of the first British war films to draw practical conclusions from this rule.

In approaching their main subject, both Nazi campaign films follow the classic Russian films rather than those of the Western democracies; at any rate, they are exclusively concerned with the destiny of a collectivity—Nazi Germany. While American films usually reflect society or national life through the biography of some hero representative of his epoch, these German films, conversely, reduce individuals to derivatives of a whole more real than all the individuals of which it consists. Whenever isolated German soldier faces are picked out in the campaign films, their function is to denote the face of the Third Reich. Hitler himself is not portrayed as an individual with a development of his own but as the embodiment of terrific impersonal powers—or better, as their meeting-place; in spite of many a reverential close-up, these films designed to idolize him cannot adapt his features to human existence.

It was Goebbels who praised POTEMKIN as a pattern and intimated that the Nazi "Revolution" should be glorified by films of a similar structure. As a matter of fact, the few representative films of Hitler Germany are as far from POTEMKIN as the Nazi "Revolution" was from a revolution. How could they be otherwise? Like the great silent Russian

[1] The following considerations are founded upon versions available in this country. Other versions may differ from them. It can be assumed, however, that these differences do not affect the basic principles of structural organization discussed here.

films, they naturally stress the absolute dominance of the collective over the individual; in POTEMKIN, however, this collective is composed of real people, whereas in TRIUMPH OF THE WILL spectacular ornaments of excited masses and fluttering swastika banners serve to substantiate the sham collective that the Nazi rulers created and ran under the name of Germany. Despite such basic differences, Goebbels' reference to the Russian pattern was not precisely a blunder. Not so much because of their allegedly revolutionary conduct as in consequence of their retrogressive contempt for individual values, the Nazis were, indeed, obliged to rely in their films more on Russian than on Western methods, and had even this perverted affinity not existed, the unquestionable propagandistic success of the early Soviet pictures would have been sufficient to bring them to the attention of the German Propaganda Ministry. As if finding their inspiration in such models as THE END OF ST. PETERSBURG and TEN DAYS THAT SHOOK THE WORLD, the two Nazi campaign films assumed the form of epics.

The traditional German penchant for thinking in antirational, mythical terms was never entirely overcome. And it was, of course, important for the Nazis not only to reinforce this tendency, but to revive old German myths; in doing so, they contributed to the establishment of an impregnable intellectual "West Wall" against the dangerous invasion of democratic ideas. The opening sequence of TRIUMPH OF THE WILL shows Hitler's airplane flying towards Nuremberg through banks of marvelous clouds—a reincarnation of All-Father Odin, whom the ancient Aryans heard raging with his hosts over the virgin forests. In keeping with their documentary functions, both BAPTISM OF FIRE and VICTORY IN THE WEST avoid evoking such reminiscences; but they are deliberately organized in an epic way, and the surface resemblance between them and the Eisenstein and Pudovkin films is striking.

It is for propagandistic reasons that both campaign films not merely render the course of battles and the succession of victories. Intent on producing a totality of effects, Nazi propaganda had to enlarge its program and offer a multifaceted composition rather than a simple account of military events. To attain their aim, the Nazis endowed their hero, i.e. Nazi Germany, with the traits of the old mythical heroes. Since these inevitably had to suffer before they could rise like the sun, Germany is shown suffering at the beginning of BAPTISM OF FIRE and VICTORY IN THE WEST as well. Weakened and alone, she stands against a conspiracy of powers that have fettered her by the Treaty of Versailles, and who would not sympathize with her attempt to shake off her chains and get rid of her oppressors? As propaganda pictures these films, of course, do not charge their hero with a mythical guilt; they represent him as an entirely innocent, harmless creature—on the maps in the Polish campaign film the white of the German territory is in symbolic contrast to the black of Poland, England and France—and they supplant for the motif of guilt that of justification. The Nazis are so intent on justifying Germany's aggression that vindications appear everywhere in the film; towards the end of BAPTISM OF FIRE, the commentary points to posters in occupied Warsaw through which the Polish Government had summoned "the population to fight the German army as irregulars." [2]

Now it becomes clear why these films include the totalitarian panoramas mentioned above: any such panorama is nothing more than the mirage of epic structure transmitted in terms of propaganda. The campaign films follow the laws of epics also in that they portray war as the hero's struggle for liberation, for *Lebensraum.* Having introduced him into the family of epic heroes, they throw a dazzling light on all his feats. Germany's infallibility and invincibility are duly streamlined, and a number of smaller apotheoses precede the final one which gives the full taste of triumph. This world of light is opposed by one of darkness with no softening shades. The enemies do not appear as normal foes with whom Germany once maintained and afterwards will resume relations; rather, they are presented as the eternal adversaries of the hero, concocting sinister plans to ruin him. Incarnations of opposing moral or natural principles, in these films both Germany and her enemies belong to the everlasting realm of the epics in which time does not enter. Between the powers boiling in the democratic inferno differences are made: France is an evil spirit in a state of decomposition; England has all the traits of the devil incarnate, and Poland serves as her wicked helper. A clever device is used to characterize these malignant specters as epic figures—Nazi film propaganda attributes to them a mythical lust for destruction. Numerous verbal statements in the campaign films stigmatize the enemy's demoniac sadism by imputing to him the burnings, havocs and wrecks abundant in the synchronized pictures; whereas the demolitions obviously caused by the Nazis assume the function of revealing the supremacy of German weapons.[3] Germans also are shown re-

[2] Cf. p. 306.

[3] The ratio of destruction to the total footage in the newsreel compilation BLITZKRIEG IN THE WEST is about 1:5; in BAPTISM OF FIRE about 1:8; in VICTORY IN THE WEST about 1:15. Since newsreels—even German newsreels—are released before final victory is assured, Nazi propaganda, always on the look-out for stimulants, here (more than in the feature films) depended upon the accumulation of catastrophes, provided they endangered the enemy. Such a catastrophe as the burning of a big oil tank had the additional advantage of being photogenic. That VICTORY IN THE WEST exhibits far less destruction than BAPTISM OF FIRE must be traced to the different intentions behind these films. While the Polish campaign film, issued during the period of the "phony" war, attempted to spread panic among future enemies, the film of the French campaign, with its elliptic construction, aimed, not without hilarity, at demonstrating an incomparable military performance—as if the happy ending were

building destroyed bridges, protecting endangered architecture and saving the Cathedral of Rouen. The positive nature of the hero is systematically played off against the destructive ego of his antagonists.

To sum up: the Nazi campaign films can be considered propagandistic epics. They are not concerned with portraying reality, but subordinate its insertion, and the method of its insertion, to their inherent propaganda purposes. These purposes constitute the very reality of the Nazi films. It is interesting to compare BAPTISM OF FIRE and VICTORY IN THE WEST with the early Eisenstein and Pudovkin films, which also picture the suffering and ultimate triumph of a heroic collectivity. That the Russian films have no less propagandistic significance than their German counterparts is obvious; but unlike the Nazi films they preserve the character of true epics because of their allegiance to reality. In these Russian films, the existing distress of the people is rendered with such attention to detail that its reality impresses itself upon the audience. How carefully the Nazis for their part avoid mobilizing reality can be inferred from the superficial way they deal with the same distress. Contrary to the Russians, they assign to a few commonplace shots the task of bearing out the verbal statements that in the opening parts of both campaign films publicize Germany's sufferings prior to Hitler's rise to power. These shots, which never succeed in quickening the commentary's complaints with a semblance of life, recall the conventional illustrations in advertisements for some standard article.[4] It is as if the Nazis were afraid of impinging on reality, as if they felt that the mere acknowledgment of independent reality would force them into a submission to it that might imperil the whole totalitarian system. On the other hand, maps profusely illustrate the disastrous consequences of the Westphalian Peace and the Treaty of Versailles. In these films the suffering of the hero Germany is purely cartographic. Through their

just around the corner. It is noteworthy that with regard to the presentation of destruction radio propaganda and film propaganda differ essentially. According to Professor Speier, Nazi broadcasters generally refrained fom announcing the destruction of military objectives which, in their belief, would not appeal to popular imagination; to thrill the average listener they preferred a demolished city hall to heavily damaged fortifications. Propaganda films, of course, did not omit any spectacular disaster; they moreover profited by their specific possibilities in depicting perforated steel plates and other strictly technical effects of German arms—destruction that, if presented through words, would hardly have interested people.

[4] True, in such films as SA-MANN BRAND, HANS WESTMAR, HITLERJUNGE QUEX and UM DAS MENSCHENRECHT (FOR THE SAKE OF THE RIGHTS OF MAN), Nazi propaganda details to some extent the sufferings of the middle class and the "misled" workers to popularize the Freikorps, the SA and the "national revolution." But these sequences appear in films that are political screen plays rather than epic documentaries after the Russian manner. At any rate, the classic Russian films never confined themselves to illustrating the misery of the people through a few stereotyped shots, as the German campaign films do.

maps the Nazi propagandists revealed that they recognized no reality other than that of their pattern of conquest.

This difference between the Russian and German screen epics affects their whole structure. Since the two campaign films shun the very reality through which the Russian films work upon audiences, they have to use other means to develop their story.

In actual political practice Nazi propaganda never was content with simply spreading suggestions, but prepared the way for their acceptance by a skillful combination of terrorist and organizational measures which created an atmosphere of panic and hysteria. On the screen, these preparatory measures are the task of the arrangement. Both films include a number of compositional tricks designed to manipulate the mind of the spectator. While the spectator's instincts and emotions are kept alive, his faculty of reasoning is systematically starved. Only one single sequence challenges the intellect: that of the air attack in BAPTISM OF FIRE, which indulges in information. This exceptional sequence can be explained by the fact that BAPTISM OF FIRE was made during the period of the "phony" war when the R.A.F. had not yet raided Germany, and Germany herself was still convinced of her absolute air superiority. By detailing the air attack in an unusually instructive way, the Nazis presumably wanted to adjust the film to the English mentality in the hope of impressing upon England the incomparable might of the German air force.[5] In this one case, information is identical with threat, and panic is to be produced by a sober appraisal of facts.

The two campaign films had not only to prepare the audience for the acceptance of their suggestions, but, above all, had to dramatize the story they told, so as to compensate for its lack of reality. Outright dramatization was, if possible, to produce artificially the thrills that in the Russian films resulted from the rendering of real-life events. Dramatic techniques resort to intermissions, vacant spaces between the power centers of the plot. Profiting by its liberty to time the narrative at will, Nazi film propaganda endeavored to obtain through mere organization the striking effects of drama.

The introductory parts of both campaign films are particularly revealing in this respect. They use all compositional means available to characterize the prewar period as a dramatic struggle between the powers of light and darkness. At the beginning of VICTORY IN THE WEST, this struggle is presented in the form of continual ups and downs designed to produce a quick succession of tensions. After Versailles, Germany seems annihilated, but Hitler appears and the prospect is

[5] According to Professor Speier, the German war communiqués broadcast to England in English generally omitted all words and phrases of a merely emotional appeal.

changed. Is it really changed? The democracies persist in conspiring against the young Third Reich, and each new German advance is followed by a new assertion of its enemies' diabolic intentions. This steadily accelerating series of tensions, increasing in dramatic weight as it approaches the present time, leads straight to the ultimate catastrophe —war. But even the Polish campaign proves to be only an episode, for Hitler's peace offer is immediately used as a means of suspense, preparing for the next turn of the action, and thus making the drama continue. Nazi propaganda always tended to work with such oscillations. They would be more effective in this case if they were not presented by means of pictorial stereotypes.

The narration of the two successful campaigns themselves is split up into a number of sequences, most of which follow the same pattern. The typical sequence opens with a map of pending strategic projects which as a rule are realized in the sequence itself. Maps in this context assume the function of dramatic exposition: they herald what is to come and canalize the audience's anticipations. Once all is laid out, the action takes shape as a process that piles up dramatic effects to compensate for the omission of substantial documentation.

Either of two methods is employed to this end. First, in the interest of increased suspense many sequences emphasize difficulties that delay the happy ending in the offing or even pretend to frustrate it. Ilya Ehrenburg reported the Russian General Gregory Zukhoff to have said about Germany's military achievements in Poland and France: "For them war was merely manoeuvres." [6] This contention is borne out by the spurious nature of those difficulties. The shots of French soldiers in the Maginot Line, inserted towards the end of VICTORY IN THE WEST, distinctly serve the propagandistic purpose of postponing again and again a conclusion reached long before. In the same film, a far-fetched "montage" sequence appears directly after the sequence of the Maginot Line; resuming motifs of the introductory part, this interlude blends maps of the world, toy soldiers and real soldiers, French statesmen and their speeches, the "Marseillaise" and a parade on the Champs-Elysées to strengthen, through fabricated testimony of Germany's hopeless situation, the importance of her subsequent victories. All these insertions owe their existence merely to the necessities of dramatic composition.

A second method of increasing suspense is the already-mentioned "ellipse." [7] Many sequences in VICTORY IN THE WEST skip the whole development that leads from the announcement of an action to its completion. Sometimes, the two methods are used jointly: an expository map is followed by some obstacle that seems to block the way—then a sudden

[6] Cf. *New York Times,* Jan. 26, 1942.

[7] Cf. p. 278 f.

jump and the trumpets of victory sound. To compensate for the suppression of reality, no better compositional device could be used than that of elliptic narration: it symbolizes the German blitz and makes credulous spectators overlook all that has been removed by juggler's tricks. The ellipse is often practiced with the aid of polyphonic technique, which will be discussed later. This is exemplified in the following instance: a verbal statement announcing a forthcoming action is combined with a series of shots not commented upon. They illustrate, more or less distinctly, several military operations, the precise meaning of which no one would be able to decipher. Since these shots pursue a vague course of their own with no connection with the statement to which they belong, audience imagination is led astray by them. The verbal announcement of attained success therefore comes as a shock to the distracted spectator—a most desirable effect for Nazi propaganda.

The triumph typical of the end of a sequence is not simply recorded, but adorned and savored to the full—except for those rare cases in which its mention is passed over to deepen the significance of a subsequent triumph. Frequently this concluding part is much longer than the preceding main part devoted to the military actions themselves. In BAPTISM OF FIRE, the battle of Radom is shown only by a moving map and several flimsy pictures, while the report on the consequences of the German victory covers a good deal more footage. In VICTORY IN THE WEST the scene of Holland's capitulation prevails over the few shots of her invasion, and in the same way the victory parade in Paris overshadows the troops' approach to the French capital. These apotheoses duplicate the old triumphal processions: first the victorious heroes move in, and then—while the commentary gloats over the tremendous booty and summarizes the strategic outcome—an immense multitude of prisoners and captured munitions pass in review. Never did the Nazis tire of assembling, to their own glorification, these masses of human and iron material. The technique used in their presentation is the pan-shot. After having focused upon a small group of marching or standing prisoners, the camera begins to pan, with the result that the visual field expands to include infinite columns or a huge camp: a well-known method cleverly exploited, for enormous masses most impress the spectator if he can compare them with groups of normal size.

As a whole, the typical dramatic sequence of the two campaign films mirrors—consciously or not—the typical procedures of a regime in which propaganda has been invested with such power that no one is sure whether it serves to change reality or reality is to be changed for the purposes of propaganda. What alone counts here is the Nazi rulers' desire for conquest and domination. The Nazis utilized totalitarian propaganda as a tool to destroy the disturbing independence of reality, and wherever they succeeded in doing so, their maps and plans were actually projected in a kind of vacuum. Thus their formula "according to plan" acquired a specific meaning, and many a dramatic and surprising effect was obtained. Practice itself furnished the pattern for the stereotyped sequences that helped to shape the campaigns on the screen.

Drama needs moments of rest to underline the vehemence of subsequent storms. Even more do the campaign films depend upon breaks in the tension; for they are not so much dramas as dramatized epics, and their epic tendency counteracts excessive dramatization. The Nazi dramaturgists had not only to supply such apparent "pauses" as the "camping idylls," but to insert everywhere brief breathing-spaces for the audiences in their upward flight. Here a grave problem arises. As soon as the spectator is permitted to relax, his intellectual faculties may awake, and the danger is that he become aware of the void around him. And in this frightening situation he might feel tempted to approach reality and, approaching it, experience the emotions of that German pilot who, after having bombed Leningrad from a great height, too high to see it, was forced down by a Soviet plane. The *New York Times* (Feb. 26, 1942) retailed the story of this pilot as told by the Russian writer Tikhonoff: "He landed on the roof of a high apartment house and was found gazing wonderingly down onto the moonlit city. As he was brought downstairs in the tall building past apartments in which the dwellers were leading busy lives it was apparent from his expression . . . that he had never thought of Leningrad as a real live place but only as a target on the map. The pilot then said he believed Leningrad could never be taken or bombed into submission."

It is evident that, despite the compositional necessity of inserting pauses in the campaign films, Nazi propaganda could not afford to let up on its constant pressure. If, on the screen or in life, the dynamic power of that propaganda had slackened only for one single moment, the whole system might have vanished in a trice.

This accounts for the extensive use made in the Nazi films of polyphonic techniques. Well aware that propaganda must work continuously upon the mind of audiences, the Nazis handled it as farmers do the soil. The wise farmer does not always sow the same crop, but contrives to alternate them; thus his soil is saved from exhaustion and yet with each season he reaps his harvest. The campaign films parallel this procedure. Instead of ever halting the succession of propaganda ideas, they merely change the medium through which these ideas are transmitted. When the commentary is reticent for a moment, one can be sure that the visuals or the music take over, and often two or three independent meanings, assigned to diverse media, run contrapuntally like themes in a score. Since each of these media affects the spectator's psychological constitution in a different way, their skillful variation is continually relieving other regions of his mind. He is relieved without, however, being released from the steady impact of propaganda.

The "camping idyll" in VICTORY IN THE WEST, not synchronized with any verbal statements, either predisposes the audience to suggestions or spreads its own insinuations. After the commentary in this film has denounced the alleged invasion of Belgium by French and English troops, the visuals not merely depict it, but point derisively at the Negroes in the French army and then with the aid of music ridicule the British. Propaganda currents arising alternately or jointly from the three media impose upon the spectator a kind of psychic massage that both eases and strains him at the same time. By this method, polyphony achieves its structural task of preventing his escape. Throughout the whole of the dramatized pseudo-epics this technique attempts to maintain in the spectator vacillations that, if they really could be maintained, would make him indifferent to truth or untruth and alienate him from reality forever.

5. CONFLICT WITH REALITY

THE outright use Nazi propaganda films make of newsreel shots seems to be influenced by certain techniques favored in the leftist camp. In 1928, the Popular Association for Film Art (*Volksverband für Filmkunst*) transformed, through mere editing procedures, a set of colorless Ufa newsreels into a red-tinged film that stirred Berlin audiences to clamorous demonstrations. The censor soon prohibited further performances, even though the *Volksverband* based its protest upon the demonstrable assertion that the film contained nothing but newsreel shots already shown in all Ufa theaters without scandalizing anyone.

The Nazi film propagandists practiced leftist montage technique in reverse order: they did not try to elicit reality from a meaningless arrangement of shots, but nipped in the bud any real meaning their candid-camera work might convey. Nothing was neglected in camouflaging this procedure and in bolstering the impression that, through unfaked newsreel material, reality itself was moving across the screen. All Nazi war films include shots and scenes that, from a merely photographic standpoint, are quite undesirable; Nazi propaganda, however, retained them, because they testified to the authenticity of the film as a whole and thereby supported confusion of veracity and truth. For the same reason, the Nazis speeded the release of their newsreels, at least in Germany,[1] reducing to a minimum the time interval between war events

[1] Cf. p. 276.

and their appearance on the screen. Owing to such speed, audiences involuntarily transferred the impressions they received from reality itself to the newsreels, which, like parasites, fed on the real-life character of the events they reflected.

It is not easy to understand why the Nazi film experts obstinately insisted upon composing their campaign films from newsreel shots. The average spectator, of course, believed their loudly proclaimed desire to be true to reality. But actually the wholly staged bombardment in the British film TARGET FOR TONIGHT seems more real—and is aesthetically more impressive—than any newsreel of a similar bombardment in the Nazi films. And the Nazis themselves knew quite well that life photographed is not necessarily synonymous with the image of life. In the *Licht Bild Bühne* of May 16, 1940, an article on films from the front is followed by another one, "Truth to Life—the Basic Law of the Artistic Shaping of Films," the author of which contends: "Truth to life—this does not mean the mere photography of life. It rather means the artistically shaped representation of condensed life." Precisely by piling up their newsreel shots, the Nazis betrayed how little they were concerned with reality.

Since they wanted to remove reality, one would expect them to stage films freely, instead of following so closely the pictorial records of their front-line reporters. It is true that they resorted to moving maps and did not hesitate to include in VICTORY IN THE WEST a number of special effects. But maps and editing devices disappear amid the overwhelming mass of candid-camera work. Why then this predominance of newsreel material? The answer does not lie in the aesthetics of film, but is found in the structure of the totalitarian system as such.

Totalitarian propaganda endeavored to supplant a reality based upon the acknowledgment of individual values. Since the Nazis aimed at totality, they could not be content with simply superseding this reality —the only reality deserving the name—by institutions of their own. If they had done so, the image of reality would not have been destroyed but merely banished; it might have continued to work in the subconscious mind, imperiling the principle of absolute leadership. To attain their aim, the Nazi rulers had to outdo those obsolete despots who suppressed freedom without annihilating its memory. These modern rulers knew that it is not sufficient to impose upon the people a "new order" and let the old ideas escape. Instead of tolerating such remnants, they persistently traced each independent opinion and dragged it out from the remotest hiding-place—with the obvious intention of blocking all individual impulses. They tried to sterilize the mind. And at the same time they pressed the mind into their service, mobilizing its abilities and emotions to such an extent that there remained no place and no will for intellectual heresy. Proceeding ruthlessly, they not only managed to prevent reality from growing again, but seized upon components of this reality to stage the pseudo-reality of the totalitarian system. Old folk-songs survived, but with Nazi verses; republican institutions were given a contrary significance, and the masses were compelled to expend their psychic reserve in activities devised for the express purpose of adjusting people's mentality, so that nothing would be left behind.

This is precisely the meaning of the following statement by Goebbels: "May the shining flame of our enthusiasm never be extinguished. This flame alone gives light and warmth to the creative art of modern political propaganda. Rising from the depths of the people, this art must always descend back to it and find its power there. Power based on guns may be a good thing; it is, however, better and more gratifying to win the heart of a people and to keep it."

Goebbels, an expert at combining journalistic rhetoric and smart cynicism, defined modern political propaganda as a creative art, thereby implying that he considered it an autonomous power rather than a subordinate instrument. Could his propaganda possibly meet the real wants of the people? As a "creative art," it excelled in instigating or silencing popular wants, and instead of promoting valuable ideas, it opportunistically exploited all ideas in its own interest. Goebbels, of course, was too great an artist to mention that this interest coincided with the lust for domination. Nevertheless, his definition is sufficiently sincere to intimate that a world shaped by the art of propaganda becomes as modeling clay—amorphous material lacking any initiative of its own. What Goebbels said about the necessity of an intimate relation between propaganda and people reveals how artistically he manipulated this emptied world. He rejected "power based on guns," because power that fails to invade and conquer the soul is faced with ever-impending revolution. Here Goebbels' genius asserted itself: propaganda, he declared, has "to win the heart of a people and to keep it." In plain language, Goebbels' propaganda, not content with forcing the Nazi system upon the people, endeavored to force the heart of the people into this system—and to keep it there. Goebbels thus confirmed that Nazi propaganda drew upon all the capacities of the people to cover the void it had created. Reality was put to work faking itself, and exhausted minds were not even permitted to dream any longer. And why were they exhausted? Because they had incessantly to produce the "shining flame of . . . enthusiasm," to which Goebbels attributed the faculty of keeping Nazi propaganda alive. Bismarck once said: "Enthusiasm cannot be pickled like herrings"; but he did not foresee the art of continuously creating it anew. Goebbels was, indeed, obliged to feed the "shining flame" that gave "light and warmth" to his propaganda with ever more propaganda. Cynic that he was, he himself admitted that his propaganda must always return to the "depths of the people" and "find its power there." Obviously it found its power there by stirring up enthusiasm. This is an important point, for the fact that Goebbels' artistic efforts were founded on abnormal conditions of life once again testifies to the hollowness of the Nazi system: air whizzes when it streams into a vacuum, and the more untenable a social structure is in itself, the more "enthusiasm" must be aroused lest it collapse. Enthusiasm? Whenever the Nazi propaganda films detailed their cheering crowds, they picked out close-ups of faces possessed by a fanaticism bordering on hysteria. In calling this fanaticism enthusiasm Goebbels was for once being too modest; in reality, it was the "shining flame" of mass hysteria that he fanned so assiduously.

Goebbels spoke these words at the Nuremberg Party Convention in 1934; and TRIUMPH OF THE WILL, the film about this Convention, illustrates them overwhelmingly. Through a very impressive composition of mere newsreel shots, this film represents the complete transformation of reality, its complete absorption into the artificial structure of the Party Convention. The Nazis had painstakingly prepared the ground for such a metamorphosis: grandiose architectural arrangements were made to encompass the mass movements, and, under the personal supervision of Hitler, precise plans of the marches and parades had been drawn up long before the event. Thus the Convention could evolve literally in a space and a time of its own; thanks to perfect manipulation, it became not so much a spontaneous demonstration as a gigantic extravaganza with nothing left to improvisation. This staged show, which channeled the psychic energies of hundreds of thousands of people, differed from the average monster spectacle only in that it pretended to be an expression of the people's real existence. When, in 1787, Catherine II traveled southward to inspect her new provinces, General Potemkin, the Governor of the Ukraine, filled the lonely Russian steppes with pasteboard models of villages to give the impression of flourishing life to the fast-driving sovereign—an anecdote that ends with the highly satisfied Catherine bestowing on her former favorite the title of Prince of Tauris. The Nazis also counterfeited life after the manner of Potemkin; instead of pasteboard, however, they used life itself to construct their imaginary villages.

To this end people as the incarnation of life must be transported in both the literal and metaphoric sense of the word. As to the means of transportation, TRIUMPH OF THE WILL reveals that the Convention speeches played a minor role. Speeches tend to appeal to the emotions as well as the intellect of their listeners; but the Nazis preferred to reduce the intellect by working primarily upon the emotions. At Nuremberg, therefore, steps were taken to influence the physical and psychological condition of all participants. Throughout the whole Convention masses already open to suggestion were swept along by a continuous, well-organized movement that could not but dominate them. Significantly, Hitler reviewed the entire five-hour parade from his standing car instead of from a fixed dais. Symbols chosen for their stimulative power helped in the total mobilization: the city was a sea of waving swastika banners; the flames of bonfires and torches illuminated the nights; the streets and squares uninterruptedly echoed with the exciting rhythm of march music. Not satisfied with having created a state of ecstasy, the Convention leaders tried to stabilize it by means of proved techniques that utilize the magic of aesthetic forms to impart consistency to volatile crowds. The front ranks of the Labor Service men were trained to speak in chorus—an outright imitation of communist propaganda methods; the innumerable rows of the various Party formations composed *tableaux vivants* across the huge festival grounds. These living ornaments not only perpetuated the metamorphosis of the moment, but symbolically presented masses as instrumental superunits.

It was Hitler himself who commissioned Leni Riefenstahl to produce an artistically shaped film of the Party Convention. In her book on this film,[2] she incidentally remarks: "The preparations for the Party Convention were made in concert with the preparations for the camera work." This illuminating statement reveals that the Convention was planned not only as a spectacular mass meeting, but also as spectacular film propaganda. Leni Riefenstahl praises the readiness with which the Nazi leaders facilitated her task. Aspects open here as confusing as the series of reflected images in a mirror maze: from the real life of the people was built up a faked reality that was passed off as the genuine one; but this bastard reality, instead of being an end in itself, merely served as the set dressing for a film that was then to assume the character of an authentic documentary. TRIUMPH OF THE WILL is undoubtedly the film of the Reich's Party Convention; however, the Convention itself had also been staged to produce TRIUMPH OF THE WILL, for the purpose of resurrecting the ecstasy of the people through it.

With the thirty cameras at her disposal and a staff of about 120 members, Leni Riefenstahl made a film that not only illustrates the Convention to the full, but succeeds in disclosing its whole significance. The cameras incessantly scan faces, uniforms, arms and again faces, and each of these close-ups offers evidence of the thoroughness with which the metamorphosis of reality was achieved. It is a metamorphosis so radical as to include even Nuremberg's ancient stone buildings.

[2] *Hinter den Kulissen des Reichsparteitag Films,* Franz Eher, München, 1935.

Steeples, sculptures, gables and venerable façades are glimpsed between fluttering banners and presented in such a way that they too seem to be caught up in the excitement. Far from forming an unchangeable background, they themselves take wing. Like many faces and objects, isolated architectural details are frequently shot against the sky. These particular close shots, typical not only of TRIUMPH OF THE WILL, seem to assume the function of removing things and events from their own environment into strange and unknown space. The dimensions of that space, however, remain entirely undefined. It is not without symbolic meaning that the features of Hitler often appear before clouds.

To substantiate this transfiguration of reality, TRIUMPH OF THE WILL indulges in emphasizing endless movement. The nervous life of the flames is played upon; the overwhelming effects of a multitude of advancing banners or standards are systematically explored. Movement produced by cinematic techniques sustains that of the objects. There is a constant panning, traveling, tilting up and down—so that spectators not only see passing a feverish world, but feel themselves uprooted in it. The ubiquitous camera forces them to go by way of the most fantastic routes, and editing helps drive them on. In the films of the Ukrainian director Dovzhenko, motion is sometimes arrested for a picture that, like a still, presents some fragment of motionless reality: it is as if, by bringing all life to a standstill, the core of reality, its very being, were disclosed. This would be impossible in TRIUMPH OF THE WILL. On the contrary, here total movement seems to have devoured the substance, and life exists only in a state of transition.

The film also includes pictures of the mass ornaments into which this transported life was pressed at the Convention. Mass ornaments they appeared to Hitler and his staff, who must have appreciated them as configurations symbolizing the readiness of the masses to be shaped and used at will by their leaders. The emphasis on these living ornaments can be traced to the intention of captivating the spectator with their aesthetic qualities and leading him to believe in the solidity of the swastika world. Where content is lacking or cannot be revealed, the attempt is often made to substitute formal artistic structures for it: not for nothing did Goebbels call propaganda a creative art. TRIUMPH OF THE WILL not only explores the officially fabricated mass-ornaments, but draws on all those discovered by the wandering cameras: among them such impressive *tableaux vivants* as the two rows of raised arms that converge upon Hitler's car while it slowly passes between them; the bird's-eye view of the innumerable tents of the Hitler Youth; the ornamental pattern composed by torchlights sparkling through a huge cloth banner in the foreground. Vaguely reminiscent of abstract paintings, these shots reveal the propagandistic functions pure forms may assume.

The deep feeling of uneasiness TRIUMPH OF THE WILL arouses in unbiased minds originates in the fact that before our eyes palpable life becomes an apparition—a fact the more disquieting as this transformation affected the vital existence of a people. Passionate efforts are made to authenticate the people's continued existence through multifold pictures illustrating Germany's youth and manhood and the architectural achievements of their ancestors as well. Nazi Germany herself, prodigally embodied, passes across the screen—but to what end? To be immediately carried away; to serve as raw material for the construction of delusive villages *à la* Potemkin. This film represents an inextricable mixture of a show simulating German reality and of German reality maneuvered into a show. Only a nihilistic-minded power that disregarded all traditional human values could so unhesitatingly manipulate the bodies and the souls of a whole people to conceal its own nihilism. The Nazi leaders pretended to act in the name of Germany. But the Reich's eagle, frequently detailed in the film, always appears against the sky like Hitler himself—a symbol of a superior power used as a means of manipulation. TRIUMPH OF THE WILL is the triumph of a nihilistic will. And it is a frightening spectacle to see many an honest, unsuspecting youngster enthusiastically submit to his corruption, and long columns of exalted men march towards the barren realm of this will as though they themselves wanted to pass away.

This digression may explain why the Nazis in their campaign films clung so desperately to newsreel shots. To keep the totalitarian system in power, they had to annex to it all real life. And since, in the medium of the film, the authentic representation of unstaged reality is reserved to newsreel shots, the Nazis not only could not afford to set them aside, but were forced to compose from them their fictitious war pictures.

Unlike those of TRIUMPH OF THE WILL, the events in BAPTISM OF FIRE and VICTORY IN THE WEST form part of an independent reality. Whereas the cameramen at Nuremberg worked on a well-prepared ground, the army film reporters could shoot only what they happened to find on their expeditions. Or overlook it. Of this latter possibility the Nazis made persistent use, even though they must have been aware that the average spectator knows enough of present warfare to sense an incompleteness. The two campaign films as well as the newsreels avoid touching on certain subjects inseparable from the war they pretend to cover. Such omissions are the more surprising as they seem to conflict with the basic design of Nazi propaganda.

One German newsreel issued after the French campaign vividly illustrates the hearty reception given to the troops returning home. Little boys climb upon a standing tank, girls in white strew flowers, and the town's whole population is afoot to welcome back the regiment to its old garrison. This sequence, however, seems to be an exception within the newsreels. At any rate, neither campaign film exhibits people in their natural state, but only—and then rarely—in the form of cheering crowds. They differ in this respect from the Russian MANNERHEIM LINE which concludes with the Leningrad people happily applauding the return of their victorious army. Theoretically, the end of VICTORY IN THE WEST could have been composed in the same way, for, according to William L. Shirer,[3] all Berlin turned out on July 18, 1940, to attend the victory parade through the Brandenburg Gate. "I mingled among the crowds in the Pariserplatz," he notes. "A holiday spirit ruled completely. Nothing martial about the mass of the people here. They were just out for a good time." The rejection of such scenes and of people in general may be connected with the particular character of the campaign films. As descriptions of blitz wars and conquests they could pretend to be uninterested in the civil life within their national boundaries. In addition, both of them are films of the German High Command and are thus obliged to glorify the soldier rather than the citizen. Hence, they end in parades—military apotheoses which also indicate that the war is to be continued. Nevertheless, the almost complete exclusion of people from these representative films remains a puzzling fact; it betrays the Nazi leaders' genuine indifference to the people they officially praised as the source of their power.

The American versions of BAPTISM OF FIRE and VICTORY IN THE WEST suppress even the slightest allusion to the anti-Jewish activities of the Nazis in wartime. Other versions may be less reticent: the German edition of the Polish campaign film is said to contain a scene with caricature-like Polish Jews sniping at German soldiers from behind doors and trees. Here, as in other cases, the newsreels are more communicative than the feature-length films. One newsreel bestows on George VI the title "King of Judaea" and calls Mr. Mandel "the Jew Mandel," further characterizing him as "the hangman of France." Another, likewise released after the French debacle, represents deserted cars on the highway as the property of "Jewish warmongers and Parisian plutocrats" who wanted to flee in them, their luggage filled with "ingots of gold and jewelry." Except for the aforementioned Polish war episode, however, these vituperations are confined to a few hints that, unseconded by visuals, disappear in the mass of verbal statements. While the Nazis continued practicing, printing and broadcasting their racial anti-Semitism, they reduced its role in the war films, apparently hesitant to

[3] Cf. *Berlin Diary,* pp. 451–52.

spread it through pictures. On the screen, anti-Jewish activities were almost as taboo as, for instance, concentration camps or sterilizations. All this can be done and propagated in print and speech, but it stubbornly resists pictorial representation. The image seems to be the last refuge of violated human dignity. Only one scene, the identification of alleged Polish murderers in BAPTISM OF FIRE, points to the unseen background of the system—an isolated instance designed to terrorize audiences.

The omission of death in the German war films has struck many observers. In this field, the two campaign pictures offer nothing but two dead horses of enemy nationality, two graves of soldiers and several wounded soldiers who pass by too quickly to make an impression. The newsreels practice similar abstinence. In one of them, badly injured soldiers appear in a hospital, but since their Führer honors them with a visit, they are the elect rather than victims. This cautious line never seems to have been abandoned. The *New York Times* of June 14, 1941, mentions a Nazi newsreel dealing with the blitzkrieg in the Balkans and the German North African campaign "which did not show any German dead or wounded." And in the *New York Times Magazine* of March 1, 1942, Mr. George Axelsson notes among other impressions: "The newsreels show the German Army sweeping forward against the usually invisible enemy without the loss of a single man or vehicle." [4]

A side-glance at Russian war pictures proves the pictorial abolition of death to be a peculiarity of Nazi propaganda. The campaign film MANNERHEIM LINE not only includes pan-shots over dead Russian soldiers, but goes so far as to emphasize the horrors of war through relentless close-ups of fragmentary corpses. In their ardent realism, these Russian cameramen and film editors did not repudiate the most terrifying details. Their later documentary, THE ROUT OF THE GERMAN ARMIES BEFORE MOSCOW, reportedly contains a scene with a Red Army general "addressing his men against a background of eight dangling figures of civilians of Volokalamsk who had been hanged by the Nazis." [5]

Shirer's *Berlin Diary* makes it evident that the Nazis proceeded "according to plan" in withholding from general audiences the calamities of war. On May 16, 1940, Shirer wrote: "I just saw two uncensored newsreels at our press conference in the Propaganda Ministry. Pictures of the German army smashing through Belgium and Holland. Some of the more destructive work of German bombs and shells was shown. Towns laid waste, dead soldiers and horses lying around, and the earth

[4] George Axelsson: "Picture of Berlin, Not by Goebbels."

[5] See the report cabled from Moscow: "Film of the Defense of Moscow Depicts Army's and People's Fight," in the *New York Times* of Feb. 17, 1942.

and mortar flying when a shell or bomb hit." This record is followed on June 10, 1940, by some remarks on another newsreel likewise presented at a press conference: "Again the ruined towns, the dead humans, the putrefying horses' carcasses. One shot showed the charred remains of a British pilot amid the wreckage of his burnt plane." Shirer's notes testify to the pictorial presence of death in the original German newsreels and to the occasional interest of the Propaganda Ministry in impressing war horrors upon the minds of a selected group of foreign correspondents. Presumably the Nazi authorities wanted them to write or broadcast reports that would spread panic abroad; but, of course, the Nazi authorities did not want to upset people at home. It is noteworthy that the Nazis, while suppressing death in their films, once allowed a radio broadcast from the front to include the cries of a dying soldier[6]; this proves conclusively that they were well aware of the immediate and striking reactions pictorial documents might provoke in audiences. Although the whole totalitarian system depended upon its ability to transfigure all reality, the Nazis did not dare to deal with the image of death. FÜR UNS (FOR US, 1937), a short Nazi film presenting the grandiose Munich commemoration for fallen partisans of the movement, culminates in the following scene: a speaker calls the roll of the dead, and at each name he shouts, the masses of living partisans respond in unison, "Here." But this was a staged ceremony with everything under control. How would uncontrollable audiences react to pictures of dead German soldiers on the screen? The lack of corpses in the Nazi war films reveals the leaders' secret fear that possibly no "Here" would be audible then. Their fear was undoubtedly well-founded. The sight of death, this most definitive of all real facts, might have shocked the spectator deeply enough to restore his independence of mind, and thus have destroyed the spell of Nazi propaganda.

What actually appears on the screen should be expected to achieve its propagandistic mission unequivocally. But the Nazis do not always succeed in mastering their material. For instance, the carefully polished commentary of the two campaign films overflows with self-justifications which cannot but arouse the suspicions of unprejudiced spectators. Besides the already-mentioned vindication,[7] BAPTISM OF FIRE offers such a mass of arguments in favor of Germany that the alleged legitimacy of her war against Poland is not only made clear, but too clear. After Danzig's return to the Reich the commentator introduces the subsequent war episodes with the words: "Poland . . . is threateningly taking up arms against the just cause of the German nation," and the bombardment of Warsaw is made to appear the work of its defenders. Simi-

[6] I owe this information to the Research Project on Totalitarian Communication.
[7] Cf. p. 291.

larly, the verbal statements of VICTORY IN THE WEST overdo their attempt to transform Germany's blitz attacks into measures of self-defense and in this way get entangled in patently dubious assumptions. It was precisely by detailing the proofs of their innocence that the Nazi leaders exposed themselves as the aggressors. Experienced criminals are rich in alibis.

The visuals are even more refractory than the commentary. The reason is that unstaged reality carries a meaning of its own which sometimes undermines the propagandistic meaning imposed upon the newsreel shots. Infinite columns of prisoners yield a monotony that counteracts their task of substantiating glowing German triumphs. Instead of feeling overwhelmed, audiences soon tire; the more so as all columns, including those of the German soldiers, resemble each other. The confused depiction of military operations not only produces the intended effect, but also leads spectators to realize that the Nazis, far from giving information, are merely seeking to impress them. In such scenes, the Nazi rulers' contempt for the individual becomes apparent. No less revealing are the incoherent shots that frequently fill the interlude between the verbal announcement of a victory and its actual achievement. In all these cases—they could easily be increased—images of genuine reality indict totalitarian propaganda for their manipulation.

The void behind this propaganda also manifests itself. It rises to the surface in a German newsreel sequence in which Hitler, accompanied by his architect, Professor Speer, and several other members of his staff, pays a visit to Paris early in the morning. The columns of the Madeleine sternly watch as he paces up the steps. Then the Nazi cars pass before the Opéra. They cross La Concorde, drive along the Champs-Elysées and slow down in front of the Arc de Triomphe, a close shot of which shows Rude's "Marseillaise" emerging from its cover of sand bags. On they drive. At the end, Hitler and his retinue stand on the terrace of the Trocadéro, steadfastly gazing at the Eiffel Tower in the rear. The Führer is visiting the conquered European capital—but is he really its guest? Paris is as quiet as a grave. Except for a few policemen, a worker and a solitary priest hastening out of sight, not a soul is to be seen at the Trocadéro, the Etoile, the huge Concorde, the Opéra and the Madeleine, not a soul to hail the dictator so accustomed to cheering crowds. While he inspects Paris, Paris itself shuts its eyes and withdraws. The touching sight of this deserted ghost city that once pulsed with feverish life mirrors the vacuum at the core of the Nazi system. Nazi propaganda built up a pseudo-reality iridescent with many colors, but at the same time it emptied Paris, the sanctuary of civilization. These colors scarcely veiled its own emptiness.

STRUCTURAL ANALYSIS

A. DEFINITION OF CONCEPTS

A FILM is as a rule divided into sequences, scenes and shots. This division, however, cannot be used here, for it would unnecessarily complicate the task of eliciting from the Nazi films all their propagandistic functions.

Since the analysis of a whole presupposes the analysis of its elements, we have to trace the smallest units that—either isolated or in relation to other units—imply intended propagandistic functions. They may be called basic units.

Complexes of these basic units compose what we call sections, passages and parts.

To begin with the basic units, they appear in the three media of which each propaganda film consists. These media are:

the commentary—including both verbal statements and occasional captions;
the visuals—including camera reality and the numerous maps;
the sound—composed of sound effects and music, including songs (words spoken by characters on the screen are so rare that they can be ignored).

In the medium of the commentary, the basic unit may be called a verbal unit or, more specifically, a

statement. Each statement consists of one or more sentences. The whole commentary of a propaganda film is a succession of such explicit verbal statements, each separated from the other by an interval during which visuals appear or continue to appear.

Example 1: BAPTISM OF FIRE opens with the

STATEMENT: "As far back as the time of the Templars, the city of Danzig used to be a German stronghold against the East. The Hanseatic League, a merchant guild of Free German towns formed to protect their trade in the Baltic region, developed the city into an important and beautiful trade center. Beautiful old houses and gates still bear witness to a proud past, and today as ever demonstrate the Germanic character of the place."

FUNCTION: The intended propagandistic function of this statement is to emphasize Germany's historical right to Danzig.

In the medium of the visuals, we call the basic unit a *picture unit*. The picture unit consists of one or more shots. Shots form a picture unit if they represent a unity of subject, of place, of time, of action, a symbolic unity or any combination of several of these factors.

Example 2: Maps are sometimes represented through one and the same traveling shot, which then constitutes a picture unit.

PICTURE UNIT: constituting a symbolic unity.

Example 2a: The statement of Example 1 is synchronized with a picture unit.

PICTURE UNIT: A number of shots showing old Danzig houses from different angles. These shots represent a unity of subject and place. Its intended propagandistic
FUNCTION: A romantic-aesthetic appeal.

In the medium of the sound the basic unit may be called a *sound unit*. The sound unit consists of a uniform noise or a musical motif—a sad tune, a gay song, a terrific bombardment.

These three kinds of basic units cover whatever is communicated within the three media. Since their propagandistic function originates in the content of the commentary, the visuals and the sound, they may be called *content units*.

In addition to the content units, there are basic units whose functions do not originate in any content, but in the relations between content units. These units may be called *relation units*. But before defining them, we have once more to examine the content units.

Each explicit statement (verbal unit) is usually synchronized with one or more picture units and/or sound units. We call such a complex a *section*. Each section normally extends over all three media.

Example 3: The statement about the German character of Danzig—Example 1—and the picture unit representing old Danzig houses—Example 2a—are accompanied by a sound unit. These three synchronized content units form a section.

For practical purposes we assign to the commentary the leading role within any section. Since the commentary differs from the other media in that it is composed of explicit verbal statements, its propagandistic functions are less ambiguous. This methodological preference, however, does not imply that the commentary's propagandistic appeal is more important than that of the visuals or the sound. The contrary will frequently prove true.

To sum up: each statement determines a section. A section is composed of one statement, one or more picture units and possibly one or more sound units.

We now revert to the relation units, which can be divided into three types: the linkage, the synchronization and the cross-linkage.

A *linkage* is the relation between successive content units within one and the same medium. Such linkages may also occur between already-linked content units.

Example 4: taken from the visual part of BAPTISM OF FIRE. We shall consider two successive sections of this film.

SECTION I

STATEMENT: "Hundreds of thousands of Polish prisoners are assembling for transportation into the camps." Synchronized with

PICTURE UNIT: About eight shots representing moving Polish prisoner columns. The last shot shows a prisoner column retreating towards the rear.

SECTION II

STATEMENT: "The German troops are still following the retreating enemy on all fronts, advancing steadily eastward."

PICTURE UNIT: Several shots representing a moving German infantry column. The first two shots show the column moving towards the foreground.

FUNCTION: The intended propagandistic function of this linkage between two picture units is to emphasize symbolically the contrast of German advance with Polish retreat.

A *synchronization* is the relation between simultaneous content units or linkages of different media within one section.

Example 5: taken from the historical part of VICTORY IN THE WEST.

STATEMENT: (dealing with the events in Germany after the first World War) "The tributes extorted by the enemy, inflation and unemployment dragged the German people into the deepest kind of want. Exhausted, disrupted and in need of a leader, they drifted towards extinction." This statement is synchronized with one

PICTURE UNIT: consisting of about three shots:

1. Demonstrating worker processions with banners and signs: "Revolution Forever."
2. Same, with signs claiming "General Strike."
3. Crowd with signs: "Dictatorship of the Proletariat." A (Jewish-looking) speaker instigating the crowd.

FUNCTION: The intended propagandistic function of this synchronization of a picture unit with a simultaneous statement is obviously to identify the moral collapse, emphasized in the commentary, with the "Marxist Revolution" for the purpose of slandering this revolution.

A *cross-linkage* is the relation between a content unit in one of the three media of a section and a content unit in another medium of a neighboring section.

Example 6: taken from the media of the commentary and the visuals of VICTORY IN THE WEST. Towards the end of this film the following two successive sections appear:

SECTION I

STATEMENT: "Up to the last moment the heavy forts of the Maginot Line are fighting."
(This statement is followed by another one that can be neglected here.)

PICTURE UNIT a: A shot of a French gun-crew in a fort of the Maginot Line.

PICTURE UNIT b: Several shots exemplifying the German attack against the fort and its surrender.

SECTION II

STATEMENT: It sums up the balance of the campaign: almost two million prisoners have been taken, and there is no end of captured material.

PICTURE UNIT: It consists of four shots:

1. Two captured French officers
2. Pan-shot over a multitude of prisoners
3. Close shot of encamping Negroes
4. A group of Negroes, picked out in medium close-up.

DESCRIPTION: There is a distinct relation between the statement of Section I praising French bravery, and the picture unit of Section II pointing to the number of Negroes in the French army.

FUNCTION: The intended propagandistic function of this cross-linkage between the statement of Section I and the picture unit of the subsequent Section II is presumably to invalidate the praise of French bravery by the pictorial suggestion that the same French army is so decadent as to rely on Negroes. Thus Germany's triumph appears to be the outcome of moral as well as military superiority.

We have yet to define the concepts of passage and part.

The *passage* is composed of two or several successive sections, the number of which depends upon the length of the linkages and cross-linkages connecting these sections. If a cross-linkage covers two sections and a simultaneous visual linkage three sections, the passage is determined by the linkage comprising three sections. (It must be noted, however, that only linkages within the media of the commentary and the visuals determine the length of a passage; linkages in the medium of sound serve also as linkages of passages.)

Example 7: Both Example 4 and Example 6 contain two successive sections which form passages. In the first case, the passage is determined by a linkage; in the second, by a cross-linkage.

A *part* is a succession of passages.

Example 8: The introduction of VICTORY IN THE WEST, which surveys German history from the Nazi viewpoint, must be considered a part of this film.

Concepts of Structural Analysis

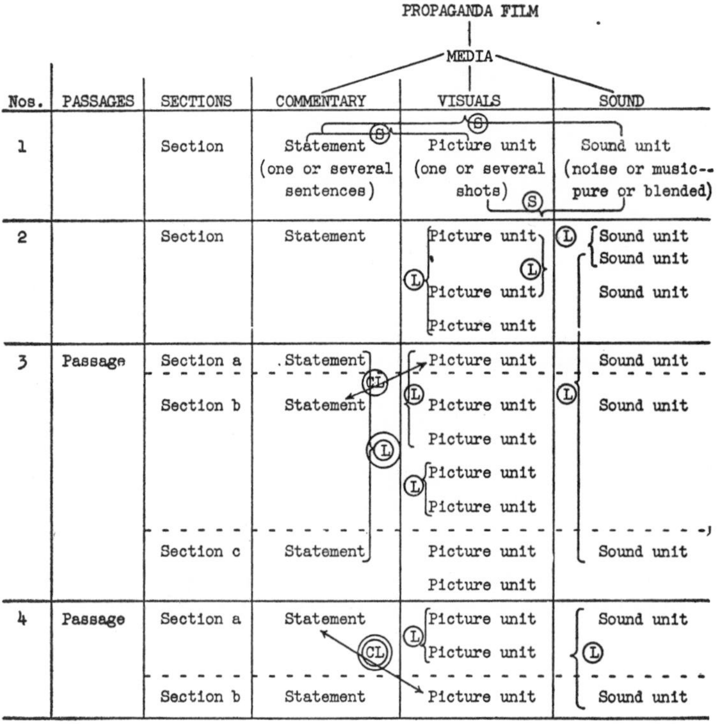
PROPAGANDA FILM
MEDIA
Nos.
PASSAGES
SECTIONS
COMMENTARY
VISUALS
SOUND
1
Section
Statement (one or several sentences)
Picture unit (one or several shots)
Sound unit (noise or music--pure or blended)
S
2
Section
Statement
Picture unit
Picture unit
Picture unit
Sound unit
Sound unit
Sound unit
L
3
Passage
Section a
Section b
Section c
Statement
Statement
Statement
Picture unit
Picture unit
Picture unit
Picture unit
Picture unit
Picture unit
Picture unit
Sound unit
Sound unit
Sound unit
CL
4
Passage
Section a
Section b
Statement
Statement
Picture unit
Picture unit
Picture unit
Sound unit
Sound unit

S = Synchronization (indicated only in No. 1)
L = Linkage
CL = Cross-Linkage

The length of passage 3 is determined by linkage (L)

The length of passage 4 is determined by cross-linkage (CL)

B. SCHEME OF ANALYSIS

A scheme has to be established through which all basic units of Nazi propaganda films can be analyzed. Since any large unit is not merely the sum of its components, such an analysis does not anticipate that of the "parts" of a film or of the film as a whole. On the other hand, this scheme will enable us to discover all film devices within the dimension of basic units.

The scheme is designed to be followed through any propaganda film from beginning to end.

In applying the scheme, for instance, to the analysis of a passage, one has first to consider the units within each medium of this passage—i.e., the content units (statements, picture units and sound units) and the linkages (relations between content units within each of the three media). Only then can the basic units which connect media, i.e., synchronizations and cross-linkages, be taken into account.

Units Within Each Medium

The commentary being the starting-point for the analysis of a section, the media will have to be considered in the following order: commentary—visuals—sound.

COMMENTARY

The commentary includes statements and linkages of statements.

Statements:

Each statement has to be listed. Sometimes a statement is followed by one or several others that simply exemplify it. These exemplifying statements will be put in parentheses to indicate their subordinate character.

Example 9: taken from BAPTISM OF FIRE

STATEMENT: "Reconnaissance flights are producing valuable information, and snapshots are taken of the movements and positions of the enemy." This statement is followed by

STATEMENT: ("The snapshots are developed immediately, and form the basis for decisive operations initiated on account of information received.")

It is advisable to summarize, by means of generalization, the propagandistic content of most statements. This will be done under the heading

CONTENT.

The intended propagandistic function of the statement is pointed out in the subsequent column

FUNCTIONS.

This column appears, of course, in each division of the scheme. It should never contain anything but the presumed function of the basic unit under consideration.

Like Nazi propaganda in general, Nazi film propaganda attempts to reduce the intellectual faculties of audiences, so as to facilitate the acceptance of its appeals and suggestions. Many basic units—particularly linkages—assume such preparatory functions. Others are intended to enlist sympathies for Nazi Germany or to terrify audiences through a demonstration of the German army's striking power. Whenever necessary, we characterize the type of the function.

REMARKS.

This column is reserved for all such remarks as may prove valuable later.

Example 10: taken from the historical part of VICTORY IN THE WEST.

STATEMENT: "Willingly the Belgian customs guards open the frontier barriers to the troops of the Western Powers."
CONTENT: Belgium actually violating neutrality.
FUNCTIONS: Statement serves as moral justification of Germany's attack against Belgium. (Vindication motif.)
REMARKS: Falsification of facts.

Linkages:

They have to be considered under the headings
DESCRIPTION and
FUNCTIONS.

VISUALS

The visuals include picture units and linkages of picture units.

Picture units:

The shots of which each picture unit consists have to be listed and described. (See Examples 4, 5 and 6.)

As in the case of most statements, it is useful to summarize the propagandistically effective content of most picture units. This will be done in the column

CONTENT.

Note on "additional" picture units: Frequently, a statement is synchronized with a series of picture units, several of which are not covered by the statement. These "additional" picture units, which may elaborate on it or take a course of their own, seem to refer to a statement omitted in the commentary. The summary of their content, as listed in the column "Content," can be considered a substitute of this missing statement. Such implicit statements will be put within quotation marks.

Example 11: taken from VICTORY IN THE WEST

STATEMENT: "In the gray light of dawn the German armies advance along a wide front." The following picture units are synchronized with this statement:

PICTURE UNIT a: About eight shots, showing several running soldiers and moving tanks that, like the soldiers, clear away obstacles.

CONTENT: Actions necessitated by the advance of the armies.

PICTURE UNIT b: Several shots of soldiers running across a field swept by enemy fire, seeking cover and machine-gunning.

CONTENT: "Soldiers crossing a field under enemy fire." (Implicit statement.)

PICTURE UNIT c: Several shots of an empty village street, with soldiers running and machine-gunning.

CONTENT: "Soldiers taking possession of a village." (Implicit statement.)

Linkages:

Like the linkages of statements, the linkages in the medium of the visuals have to be taken into account under the headings

DESCRIPTION and

FUNCTIONS.

SOUND

The sound includes sound units and linkages of sound units.

Sound units:

They have to be examined in the column

CHARACTERIZATION.

Many sound units are definitely associated with certain images or ideas. Marching music, for instance, conveys the idea of military life, dance music that of festive occasions. In addition, if a musical unit is synchronized once or twice with picture units representing scenes of advance, it will later serve as a "leitmotiv," and this "leitmotiv" will automatically evoke the notion of advance. We mention all such fixed associations in the column "Characterization."

Example 12: taken from VICTORY IN THE WEST and supplementing Example 10.—The

STATEMENT: (of Example 10) "Willingly the Belgian customs guards open the frontier barriers to the troops of the Western Powers," determines a section composed of two picture units not to be listed here. The second picture unit is synchronized with two sound units:

SOUND UNIT a: Music imitating the chatter in a chicken-yard.

CHARACTERIZATION: Funny.

SOUND UNIT b: English song, "The Siegfried Line," thinly instrumented and sung by a chorus.

CHARACTERIZATION: Satirical variation of a popular British soldiers' song.—Here we have an exception: the music alone assumes the function of ridiculing English soldiers.

Since, as a rule, sound alone does not impart propaganda messages, the column "Functions" is omitted here.

Linkages:

Linkages of sound are not considered in this scheme.

Units Connecting Media

SYNCHRONIZATIONS

There are three kinds of synchronizations (i.e., relations between simultaneous content units or linkages of different media within one section):

Relation of the visuals to the commentary
Relation of the sound to the commentary
Relation of the sound to the visuals.

We consider first the

Relation of visuals to commentary:

Picture units or linkages in the medium of the visuals refer to statements in different ways, each of which may assume a specific propagandistic function. We characterize these different relations under the heading

CHARACTERIZATION.

With regard to the statement to which they refer, picture units (or linkages) may be symbolic, exemplificative, illustrative or explicative. The exemplification is either clear or indistinct. All kinds of representation can be elaborative.

As to the "additional" picture units, we refer to the note, page 316. The relations of these "additional" picture units to their "implicit" statements can be characterized, of course, in exactly the same manner as the relations to explicit statements.

Relation of sound to commentary and visuals:

These relations need only be examined with respect to their intended

FUNCTIONS.

CROSS-LINKAGES

They have to be checked in the columns

DESCRIPTION and

FUNCTIONS.

The scheme will be completed by the division

COMPOSITION OF THE SECTIONS AND PASSAGES

Within this division we define the role each medium plays in producing the total effect of the section or passage under discussion.

C. *FIVE ELABORATE EXAMPLES*

Preliminary remark: In case several basic units and their functions are intermingled, it is only the most important function that counts.

EXAMPLE I

taken from VICTORY IN THE WEST

STATEMENTS	*PICTURE UNITS*	*SOUND UNITS*
1) "The German Command has received information that a strong enemy force in the vicinity of Lille, consisting of a large number of French and English divisions, has been ordered to advance against the lower Rhine and on into the Ruhr District, in violation of Belgian and Dutch neutrality."	1) One shot of a map representing this intention. Arrows symbolizing enemy groups cross Belgium's boundaries and begin to advance towards a point marked "Ruhr."	
2) ("Willingly the Belgian customs guards open the frontier barriers to the troops of the Western Powers.") The beginning of this statement coincides with the shot of Belgian customs guards in Picture Unit 2a.	2a) About 19 shots representing the advance of various French army units: motorcyclists, cyclists, artillery, moving tanks, soldiers in a freight train.—One of the first shots shows Belgian customs guards opening the barriers. The final shots represent marching French infantry, mostly Negroes, from different angles.	
	2b) British troops: Shot 1: Medium shot of two English officers standing together. Shot 2: Close-up of an English tank moving towards the left.	2b) Sound unit synchronized with Shots 1 and 2: music imitating the chatter in a chicken-yard.
	Shot 3: English infantry column advancing towards the left. Shot 4: Same from another angle. Shot 5: English infantry slowly moving in Indian file towards the rear. Shot 6: Close shot of moving tank.	2b) Sound unit synchronized with Shots 3–6: variation of the English soldiers' song, "The Siegfried Line," thinly instrumented and sung by chorus.

ANALYSIS OF EXAMPLE I

COMMENTARY

Statements

1) CONTENT: Enemy's intention to violate Belgium's neutrality and to invade the Ruhr on the point of being realized.

   FUNCTIONS: Enemy stigmatized as aggressor.

   REMARKS: Statement a falsification.

2) CONTENT: Belgium actually violating neutrality.

   FUNCTIONS: Hint at Belgium's guilt implies moral justification of German attack against Belgium.

   REMARKS: Statement a falsification.

Linkages

None

VISUALS

Picture units

1) CONTENT: See description of picture unit.

   FUNCTIONS: Threat to Ruhr symbolically stressed.

   REMARKS: Moving map.

2a)
and
2b) CONTENT: Through linkage with map (see *Linkages*) and relation of map to Statement 1 (see *Synchronizations*), content is defined as "Enemy enters Belgium" (Implicit statement).

   FUNCTIONS: a) Aggression is a fact.
   b) Shots of Negro troops intended to arouse race bias and deprecate French racial behavior.

   REMARKS: Arrangement of captured French and English film material.

Linkages

DESCRIPTION: Immediately following the map in Picture Unit 1, Picture Unit 2 seems to substantiate the symbolic advance of the arrows. Both picture units linked.

FUNCTIONS: See Function a) of Picture Units 2a and 2b.

SOUND

2b) CHARACTERIZATION: Funny.

2b) CHARACTERIZATION: Satirical variation. In ridiculing English soldiers, music assumes a propagandistic function—an exceptional case.

REMARKS: Use of the popular English song, "The Siegfried Line."

SYNCHRONIZATIONS

Relation of visuals to commentary

1) CHARACTERIZATION: Map symbolizes Statement 1.

FUNCTIONS: Symbolic representation gives the impression that enemies were already about to carry out intentions denounced by statement.

2) CHARACTERIZATION: Illustrative with reference to implicit statement "Enemy enters Belgium."

FUNCTIONS: See Function a) of Picture Units 2a and 2b.

Relation of sound to visuals

2b) FUNCTIONS: Ridiculing big English tank.

2b) FUNCTIONS: Ridiculing English soldiers.

COMPOSITION OF PASSAGE

COMMENTARY: Enemy intending aggression. Moral justification of German attack.

VISUALS: They mark enemy aggression as a fact and, moreover, arouse race bias (through relation of map to commentary, linkage and picture units).

SOUND: Ridiculing English arms and troops (through sound alone and relation of sound to visuals).

EXAMPLE II

taken from VICTORY IN THE WEST

STATEMENTS	*PICTURE UNITS*	*SOUND UNITS*
1) "Up to the last moment, the heavy forts of the Maginot Line are fighting." (This statement is followed by another one that can be neglected here.)	1) Shot 1: Long shot of a fort. Shot 2: In the fort of the Maginot Line: French soldiers tending a gun. Shot 3: Battlefield: German soldiers cutting barbed wire. Shot 4: Flashes of fire shooting over the fort. Shot 5: Clouds of smoke rising from the fort. Shot 6: Barbed wire before clouds of smoke. Shot 7: Medium shot of fort. Shot. 8: German soldiers entering the fort. Shot 9: French commander surrendering the fort to the German officer. Shot 10: The destroyed fort with swastika banner hoisted.	
2) "Almost two million prisoners . . . and the total materiel of more than 130 divisions . . . fall into German hands."	2) Shot 1: Two French officers (prisoners) with an orderly. Shot 2: Camera pans over a multitude of prisoners. Shot 3: Close shot of encamping Negroes. Shot 4: A group of Negroes picked out in medium close-up.	2) Negro music reminiscent of jazz tunes.

ANALYSIS OF EXAMPLE II

COMMENTARY

Statements

1) CONTENT: Praise of French bravery.

FUNCTIONS: Appreciation of French bravery does credit to Germany and emphasizes German strength.

REMARKS: Praise of enemy.

2) CONTENT: Overwhelming proof of German victory.

FUNCTIONS: Appeal of triumph.

REMARKS: Use of statistics.

VISUALS

Picture units

1) CONTENT: French soldiers fighting and Germans conquering fort.
FUNCTIONS: Pictures show German bravery.
REMARKS: Shot 2 taken from captured film material—a faked insert. Shot 10 shows a swastika banner.

2) CONTENT: Prisoners, with emphasis on Negroes.
FUNCTIONS: See functions of cross-linkage.

SOUND

2) CHARACTERIZATION: Music reminds audiences of jazz bands.

SYNCHRONIZATIONS

Relation of visuals to commentary

1) CHARACTERIZATION: Shot 2 vaguely exemplificative. Other shots illustrative.

Relation of sound to visuals

2) FUNCTIONS: Coloring pictures of French prisoners, the music hints at French flippancy.

CROSS-LINKAGE

DESCRIPTION: Cross-linkage between Statement 1 and Picture Unit 2 synchronized with Sound Unit 2.

FUNCTIONS: Cross-linkage suggests the following thought: French soldiers may be brave, but French people are decadent. They deserve to be defeated. German victory proves moral superiority.

COMPOSITION OF PASSAGE

COMMENTARY: Emphasis on German efficiency. Appeal of triumph.

VISUALS: German bravery (through picture unit).

SOUND: Hint at French flippancy (through relation of sound to visuals).

COMBINATION OF COMMENTARY AND VISUALS: Germany's moral superiority (through cross-linkage).

EXAMPLE III

Opening of Baptism of Fire

STATEMENTS	*PICTURE UNITS*
1) "As far back as the time of the Templars, the city of Danzig used to be a German stronghold against the East. The Hanseatic League, a merchant guild of Free German towns formed to protect their trade in the Baltic Region, developed the city into an important and beautiful trade center. Beautiful old houses and gates still bear witness to a proud past, and today as ever demonstrate the Germanic character of the place."	1) A series of shots of Danzig architecture: Façades behind the river—among them a granary Close-up of the upper part of this granary Parts of an old fountain in close-up Traveling around the fountain and its fence towards a steeple Another steeple Upper parts of several patrician houses Tilting up to the upper part of an old house Tilting down façade to the portal.
2) "This memorable German town was cut off from the mother country by the Treaty of Versailles and was formed into a so-called 'Free State' under the control of the League of Nations. Various restrictions and obligations were imposed upon this new political structure such as exportation customs, postal and railway sovereignty allotted to Poland within the Green Line. A district especially needed for the Territory of the Free State, the Westernplatte, guarding the entrance to Danzig's harbor, was equipped with extensive munition dumps, and the little fishing village of Gdynia, in a direct contradiction to the agreement underlying the constitution of the Danzig Free State, was enlarged into a harbor admitting seagoing ships, thus aiming at gradually averting and battling the trade connections of Danzig property."	2a) Map representing the Danzig territory. Camera travels up from the map. At the left appears the territory of Poland colored entirely black and thus contrasted with the little white Danzig region. The word *"Polen"* appears white on the black ground. Then we see the boundaries of the Free State region and the words: *Freistaat Danzig. Westernplatte. Gdingen.* 2b) Map representing Eastern Europe. At the right of the Free State region the black Polish territory with the word *"Polen"* in white letters. Camera travels up from the map, so as to encompass almost all Europe with England and France. The words *"England"* and *"Frankreich"* appear against black background.
3) "The German fraction among the conglomerate of nationalities was ruthlessly persecuted. German schools were closed, industrials and landowners expropriated and large parts of the German populace were driven from the country. In steadily growing numbers, they tried to escape from Polish terror and seek protection	3) Picture unit representing German refugee procession: German refugees with bag and baggage moving through wood They advance (about 20 to 30) towards the foreground A big column of refugees moving on road towards the rear, where, at one point,

STATEMENTS	*PICTURE UNITS*
on Reich territory. Hundreds of thousands of worn-out, distressed and panic-stricken people poured daily into German refugee camps."	there is a sign with inscription, *"Lager Rummelsburg"* Medium shot of a refugee group moving towards the foreground Medium close-up: Refugees getting out of buses Two or three shots of a go-cart handed down from the deck of a bus Medium shot: group of refugees standing, a crying woman with child in their midst. Then a similar group Another group with a man with a child in his arms; at his left a crying girl.

ANALYSIS OF EXAMPLE III

COMMENTARY

Statements

1) CONTENT: Statement puts emphasis on Germanic character of Danzig and on beauty of its architecture.
   FUNCTIONS: Germany a civilized nation (Appeal of culture). Her historical right to Danzig.
2) CONTENT: Germany wronged by Versailles and the Poles.
   FUNCTIONS: To arouse sympathy for Germany's sufferings.
3) CONTENT: Germans victimized by Polish terror.
   FUNCTIONS: Same as above, with emphasis on Poland's guilt.
   REMARKS: Use of statistics.

Linkages

A) DESCRIPTION: Statements 1 and 2.
   FUNCTIONS: Contrast between Germany's economic and cultural achievements in Danzig (Statement 1) and Germany's sufferings (Statement 2) assumes the preparatory function of stirring emotions. Thus the spectator's intellectual faculties will be somewhat weakened. This kind of manipulation, found also in the opening part of VICTORY IN THE WEST, is the more needed here as the subsequent Statement 3 invites unprejudiced audiences to think of the millions Nazi Germany herself drove away from their homes.

B) DESCRIPTION: Statements 2 and 3.
   FUNCTIONS: Intensification of the propagandistic effect of each statement.

VISUALS

Picture units

1) CONTENT: See description of picture unit.
   FUNCTIONS: Romantic-aesthetic appeal.
   REMARKS: Two steeples.
2) CONTENT: Representation of Danzig's predicament and Poland's dependence on England and France.
   FUNCTIONS: Black and enormous, Poland is made to appear an uncanny threat to the tiny Free State region which, through its white color, is marked as the innocent victim. The later appearance of black England and France symbolizes these powers as pulling the strings from behind.
   REMARKS: Moving maps.
3) CONTENT: See description of picture unit.
   FUNCTIONS: To arouse pity for German refugees.

Linkages

Same as verbal linkages, with same functions.

SYNCHRONIZATIONS

Relation of visuals to commentary

1) CHARACTERIZATION: Illustrative, with reference to mention of Danzig's beauty.
   FUNCTIONS: Collaboration with statement.
2) CHARACTERIZATION: Symbolic and elaborative.
   FUNCTIONS: Collaboration with statement.
3) CHARACTERIZATION: Clearly exemplificative, with reference to mention of German refugees.
   FUNCTIONS: Collaboration with statement.

COMPOSITION OF PASSAGE

COMMENTARY: Appeal of culture. Historical right to Danzig. Demanding understanding of Germany's sufferings (through statements).—Stirring emotions and thereby reducing intellectual faculties. Intensification of propagandistic effects (through linkages).

VISUALS: Picture units and linkages supporting statements and linkages of statements.

Moreover: Romantic-aesthetic appeal. Poland an uncanny threat. England and France pulling the strings (through picture units).

EXAMPLE IV

taken from BAPTISM OF FIRE. The section deals with the attack against the *Westernplatte.*

Remark: The sound consists of noise without particular significance.

STATEMENTS	*PICTURE UNITS*
"After the fortifications have been covered by steady fire, a debarcation corps is sent ahead to attack. The men spread out in a hand-to-hand fight."	Shot 1: Soldiers looking through peepholes in a wall at the right. Shot 2: Close shot of several soldiers passing from left to right. The harbor of Gdynia in the background, with a battleship. Shot 3: Soldiers running around a ruined building. Shot 4: Soldiers moving through wood towards the rear. Shot 5: Infantry with hand grenades moving towards the rear, through smoking wood. Shot 6: Same from another angle. Shot 7: Long shot of same, with much smoke. Shot 8: Woods. White smoke rising. Explosion in a remote glade. Shot 9: Same, with river in the foreground.

ANALYSIS OF EXAMPLE IV

Statement

CONTENT: Description of a military operation.
FUNCTIONS: ——

Picture unit

CONTENT: Soldiers—action indistinct.
FUNCTIONS: ——

SYNCHRONIZATIONS

Relation of picture unit to statement

CHARACTERIZATION: Indistinctly exemplifying.

FUNCTIONS: It is of course difficult for film-makers to cope with what has been called the intangibility of modern war. A battle covers enormous space, and there is no longer a general's hill from which to survey and direct operations. In addition, the mechanization of warfare has contributed much towards transforming the battlefield into a vacuum. However, all these difficulties do not prevent the British film TARGET FOR TONIGHT from offering exhaustive information about a bomber raid. Similarly, the air-attack episode in BAPTISM OF FIRE proves that the Nazis themselves are quite able to enlighten the audience if they want to do so. But, as a matter of fact, they do want just the opposite, as can be inferred from the preponderance, in both campaign films, of battle scenes edited after the manner of Example IV. Blurred depictions of military actions, these scenes seem designed to confuse the mind, so as to prepare it for the acceptance of propaganda suggestions.

COMPOSITION OF SECTION

SYNCHRONIZATION OF PICTURE UNIT WITH STATEMENT: Preparatory function of weakening intellectual faculties.

EXAMPLE V

taken from Victory in the West

STATEMENTS	*PICTURE UNITS*	*SOUND UNITS*
1) "Just as on the Somme, the battle of June 9 on the Aisne begins with attacks against the fortified villages of the Weygand Line. As soon as they are overcome, the road to the Marne is clear."	1a) A series of shots devoted to moving German tank units: Soldiers passing a village Tank moving towards rear Same Tank moving towards foreground, with a soldier on it. Shot taken from below (in Russian manner) to heighten the soldier's significance; he looks noble—an incarnation of the ideal German soldier. Guns and trucks moving from left to right Close-up of a moving tank with soldiers on it House at the road, with signboard *"Reims 41 km"* Moving tanks Same from another angle Close-up of tank wheels.	1) The frequently repeated "leitmotif" of a marching theme.
	1b) Infantry column moving (right to left) Same (left to right) Same (towards foreground) Close shot of same, picking out soldier faces, with horses in the rear Close shot of same, showing marching legs, wheels and wounded soldiers in the background Infantry column moving in Indian file	March music ceases.
2) "German troops reach the Marne—the river of destiny of the World War."	2) A number of cars parking; between the cars a soldier. Stone bridge; on its balustrade the word *"Marne."*	

ANALYSIS OF EXAMPLE V

COMMENTARY

Statements

1) CONTENT: Intimation of German advance to the Marne.
FUNCTIONS: ——

2) CONTENT: The Marne reached.
FUNCTIONS: ——

Linkages

DESCRIPTION: Statements 1 and 2 form an elliptic linkage; i.e., the intimation of German advance is abruptly followed by the announcement of its success.

FUNCTIONS: To produce the impression of irresistible lightning advance and thus to overwhelm audiences.

VISUALS

Picture units

1a) CONTENT: Troops moving, particularly tanks.

FUNCTIONS: The shot of the advancing tank with the noble soldier on it is obviously intended to substantiate the idea of German advance. (Proof: the same shot is resumed in the film's important final passage.) Through this shot the whole picture unit, insignificant in itself, assumes a symbolic meaning.

1b) CONTENT: Moving infantry column.

FUNCTIONS: Since such columns appear whenever the commentary emphasizes advance, they play the role of a pictorial leitmotif designed to evoke the impression of advancing German armies.

REMARKS: Moving infantry column.

2) CONTENT: Germans at the Marne.

FUNCTIONS: ——

SOUND

CHARACTERIZATION: Usually synchronized with advancing infantry columns, march music assumes the character of a stimulating leitmotif impregnated with the meaning "advance."

FUNCTIONS: ——

SYNCHRONIZATIONS

Relation of visuals to commentary

1) CHARACTERIZATION: Elaboration of statement in an exemplificative way.

FUNCTIONS: The pictures are to imbue the audience with the conviction that the verbal intimation of further advance will come true.

2) CHARACTERIZATION: Sufficiently exemplificative.

FUNCTIONS: Collaboration with statement.

Relation of sound to visuals

1) FUNCTIONS: The musical leitmotif not only deepens the impression of advance evoked by the pictures, but makes audiences overlook the wounded soldiers and tired faces that might invalidate this impression.

COMPOSITION OF PASSAGE

COMMENTARY: Irresistible lightning advance (through elliptic linkage).

VISUALS: Representation of advance (through picture units that include a shot of the ideal German soldier and the leitmotif of moving infantry columns).

SOUND: Deepening impression of advance (through musical leitmotif alone and its relation to visuals).

BIBLIOGRAPHY

Most of the books and articles listed here are available in the Museum of Modern Art Library, New York.

"Abwege (Crisis)," *Close Up*, III (Territet, Switzerland, Sept. 1928), no. 3: 72–75.

"Achtung, Liebe—Lebensgefahr! (Where's Love There's Danger)," *Close Up*, V (Territet, Switzerland, Nov. 1929), no. 5: 441–42.

Ackerknecht, Erwin, *Lichtspielfragen*, Berlin, 1928.

"All for a Woman," *Exceptional Photoplays*, I (New York, Nov. 1921), bulletin no. 10: 4–5.

Alten, W. V., "Die Kunst in Deutschland," J. Meier-Graefe, ed., *Ganymed: Blätter der Marées Gesellschaft*, II (München, 1920), 145–51.

Altenloh, Emilie, *Zur Soziologie des Kinos*, Schriften zur Soziologie der Kultur, Jena, 1914.

Altman, Georges, "La Censure contre le Cinéma," *La Revue du Cinéma*, III (Paris, 1er Février 1931), no. 19:33–42.

Amiguet, Fréd.-Ph., *Cinéma! Cinéma!*, Lausanne and Genève, 1923.

Arnheim, Rudolf, *Film als Kunst*, Berlin, 1932.

"Auch Murnau . . ," *Filmwelt* (Berlin, 22. März 1931), no. 12.

B., W., "Geschlecht in Fesseln," *Close Up*, III (Territet, Switzerland, Dec. 1928), no. 6: 69–71.

Balázs, Béla, *Der sichtbare Mensch: Eine Film-Dramaturgie*, Halle, Germany, 1924. 2nd ed.

———, *Der Geist des Films*, Halle, Germany, 1930.

———, "Der Film sucht seinen Stoff," *Die Abenteuer eines Zehnmarkscheins*, Berlin. [A publicity program to this film issued by Deutsche Vereins Film A.-G.]

Balthasar, "Die Dekoration," Hugo Zehder, ed., *Der Film von Morgen* (Berlin-Dresden, 1923), pp. 73–90.

"Barberina," *Variety*, New York, Nov. 1, 1932.

Bardèche, Maurice, and Brasillach, Robert, *The History of Motion Pictures*, New York, 1938.

Barr, Alfred H., Jr., "Otto Dix," *The Arts*, XVII (New York, Jan. 1931), no. 4: 235–51.

Barrett, Wilton A., "Grey Magic," *National Board of Review Magazine*, I (New York, Dec. 1926), no. 7: 4–6.

———, "Morgenrot," *ibid.*, VIII (June 1933), no. 6: 10–12, 15.
Barry, Iris, *Program Notes*, Museum of Modern Art Film Library. [Reviews of and commentary on films.]
———, "The Beggar's Opera," *National Board of Review Magazine*, VI (New York, June 1931), no. 6: 11–13.
Bateson, Gregory, "Cultural and Thematic Analysis of Fictional Films," *Transactions of the New York Academy of Sciences*, Series II, V (New York, Feb. 1943), no. 4: 72–78.
Berr, Jacques, "Etat du Cinéma 1931: Etats-Unis et Allemagne," *La Revue du Cinéma*, III (Paris, 1er Juillet 1931), no. 24: 40–51.
Berstl, Julius, ed., *25 Jahre Berliner Theater und Victor Barnowsky*, Berlin, 1930.
Birnbaum, Leonhard, "Massenscenen im Film," *Ufa-Blätter*, Programm-Zeitschrift der Theater des Ufa-Konzerns (Berlin, 1921?).
Blakeston, Oswell, "An Epic—Please," *Close Up*, I (Territet, Switzerland, Sept. 1927), no. 3: 61–66.
———, "Lusts of Mankind," *ibid.*, III (Nov. 1928), no. 5: 38–41.
———, "The Adventures of a Ten-Mark Note," *ibid.*, pp. 58–61.
———, "Interview with Carl Freund," *ibid.*, IV (Jan. 1929), no. 1: 58–61.
———, "Dracula," *ibid.*, pp. 71–72.
———, "Snap," *ibid.* (May 1929), no. 5: 38–42.
Boehmer, Henning von, and Reitz, Helmut, *Der Film in Wirtschaft und Recht. Seine Herstellung und Verwendung*, Berlin, 1933.
Boehnel, William, "Avalanche," *New York World Telegram*, March 29, 1932.
———, "Morgenrot," *ibid.*, May 17, 1933.
Brody, Samuel, "Paris Hears Eisenstein," *Close Up*, VI (Territet, Switzerland, April 1930), no. 4: 283–89.
Bryher, *Film Problems of Soviet Russia*, Territet, Switzerland, 1929.
———, "The War from Three Angles," *Close Up*, I (Territet, Switzerland, July 1927), no. 1: 16–22.
———, "G. W. Pabst. A Survey," *ibid.* (Dec. 1927), no. 6: 56–61.
———, "A German School Film," *ibid.*, VI (Feb. 1930), no. 2: 128–33.
———, "Berlin, April 1931," *Close Up*, VIII (London, June 1931), no. 2: 126–33.
———, "Notes on Some Films," *ibid.*, IX (Sept. 1932), no. 3: 196–99.
Buchner, Hans, *Im Banne des Films. Die Weltherrschaft des Kinos*, München, 1927.

"Cabinet of Dr. Caligari, The," *Exceptional Photoplays*, I (New York, March 1921), bulletin no. 4: 3–4.

Caligari-Heft. Was deutsche Zeitungen über den Film berichten, Berlin. [A publicity pamphlet issued by Decla-Bioscop-Konzern.]

Canudo, *L'Usine aux Images,* Paris, 1927.

Carter, Huntly, *The New Spirit in the Cinema,* London, 1930.

Chavance, Louis, "Trois Pages d'un Journal," *La Revue du Cinéma,* II (Paris, 1er Juin 1930), no. 11: 52–54.

Chevalley, Freddy, "Mickey Virtuose—La Mélodie du Monde," *Close Up,* VI (Territet, Switzerland, Jan. 1930), no. 1: 70–73.

Chowl, H., "The French Revolution," *Close Up,* IV (Territet, Switzerland, May 1929), no. 5: 46–51.

Coböken, Jos., "Als ich noch rund um die Friedrichstrasse ging . . ," *25 Jahre Kinematograph* (Berlin, 1931?), pp. 13–14.

"Comment and Review," *Close Up,* II (Territet, Switzerland, Feb. 1928), no. 2: 64–71.

———, *ibid.* (May 1928), no. 5: 80–82.

"Crime and Punishment," *National Board of Review Magazine,* II (New York, June 1927), no. 6: 10–11.

Crisler, B. R., "The Friendly Mr. Freund," *New York Times,* Nov. 21, 1937.

D., H., "Conrad Veidt: The Student of Prague," *Close Up,* I (Territet, Switzerland, Sept. 1927), no. 3: 34–44.

"Die Dame mit der Maske," *Ufa-Leih,* Berlin. [An undated brochure.]

Davidson, Paul, "Wie das deutsche Lichtspieltheater entstand," *Licht Bild Bühne. 30 Jahre Film* (Berlin, 1924), pp. 7–10.

"Deception," *Exceptional Photoplays,* I (New York, April 1921), bulletin no. 5: 3–4, 7.

Decla-Bioscop Verleih-Programme, Berlin, 1923. [These illustrated programs include short synopses of various films.]

Deming, Barbara, "The Library of Congress Project: Exposition of a Method," *The Library of Congress Quarterly Journal,* II (Washington, Nov. 1944), no. 1: 3–36.

Diaz, P., *Asta Nielsen. Eine Biographie unserer populären Künstlerin,* Berlin, 1920?.

"30 Kulturfilme," *Ufa-Leih,* Berlin. [An undated brochure.]

Dreyfus, Jean-Paul, "Films d'épouvante," *La Revue du Cinéma,* II (Paris, 1er Mai 1930), no. 10: 23–33.

———, "La Femme sur la Lune," *ibid.,* pp. 62–63.

Eger, Lydia, *Kinoreform und Gemeinden,* Veröffentlichungen der sächs. Landesstelle für Gemeinwirtschaft, Heft IV, Dresden, 1921.

Ehrenburg, Ilya, "Protest gegen die Ufa," *Frankfurter Zeitung*, 29. Feb. 1928. [Reprint in Museum of Modern Art Library, clipping files.]

"Emelka-Konzern," *Das grosse Bilderbuch des Films* (Filmkurier, Berlin, 1926), pp. 49–64.

"Die entfesselte Kamera," *Ufa-Magazin*, IV (Berlin, 25.–31. März 1927), Heft 13.

Epardaud, Edmond, "Faust," *Cinéa-Ciné* (Paris, 15 Mars 1927), pp. 19–20.

Erikson, Erik Homburger, "Hitler's Imagery and German Youth," *Psychiatry: Journal of the Biology and Pathology of Interpersonal Relations*, V (Baltimore, Nov. 1942), no. 4: 475–93.

"Erläuterungen," [Szenen aus dem 'Faust'-Film], *Film-Photos wie noch nie* (Frankfurt a.M., 1929), pp. 51–62.

Evans, Wick, "Karl Freund, Candid Cinematographer," *Popular Photography*, IV (Chicago, Feb. 1939), no. 2: 51, 88–89.

Ewers, Hanns Heinz, Dr. Langheinrich-Anthos, and Noeren, Heinrich, *Der Student von Prag: Eine Idee von Hanns Heinz Ewers*, Berlin, 1930.

Fanck, Arnold, *Der Kampf mit dem Berge*, Berlin.

———, *Stürme über dem Montblanc. Ein Filmbildbuch*, Basel, 1931.

Farrell, James T., "Dostoievsky and 'The Brothers Karamazov' Revalued," *New York Times Book Review*, Jan. 9, 1944.

———, "Will the Commercialization of Publishing Destroy Good Writing?" *New Directions* (Norfolk, Conn., 1946), no. 9: 6–37. [Reprinted as a pamphlet under the title: "The Fate of Writing in America."]

"Faust," *National Board of Review Magazine*, I (New York, Nov. 1926), no. 6: 9–10.

Fawcett, L'Estrange, *Die Welt des Films*, Unter Mitwirkung des Wiener Filmbunds für die deutsche Ausgabe frei bearbeitet und ergänzt von C. Zell und S. Walter Fischer, Zürich, Leipzig, Wien, 1929?.

Film Forum, New York, March 19, 1933, program 3.

Film Index. A Bibliography, New York, 1941.

Film Society Programmes, issued by The Film Society, London. [1925–34].

Fønss, Olaf, *Krig, Sult Og Film*, Filmserindringer Gennem 20 Aar, II, Copenhagen, 1932

"Frau im Mond," *Close Up*, V (Territet, Switzerland, Nov. 1929), no. 5: 442–44.

Freedley, George, and Reeves, John A., *A History of the Theatre*, New York, 1941.

Freeman, Joseph, *Never Call Retreat*, New York, Toronto, 1943. [A novel.]
"Freie Fahrt," *Close Up*, IV (Territet, Switzerland, Feb. 1929), no. 2: 97–99.
"Fritz Lang Puts on Film the Nazi Mind He Fled From," *New York World Telegram*, June 11, 1941.
Fromm, Erich, *Escape from Freedom*, New York and Toronto, 1941.
"25 Jahre Filmatelier," *25 Jahre Kinematograph* (Berlin, 1931?), pp. 65–66.

"Gassenhauer," *Filmwelt* (Berlin, 5. April 1931), no. 14.
"Geheimdienst," *Filmwelt* (Berlin, 21. Juni 1931), no. 25.
"The Golem," *Exceptional Photoplays*, I (New York, June 1921), bulletin no. 7: 3–4.
Gregor, Joseph, *Das Zeitalter des Films*, Wien, 1932. 3rd ed.
Grune, Karl, "Wie ein Film entsteht: Von der Idee bis zum Drehbuch," *Ufa-Magazin*, II (Berlin, 29. April—5. Mai 1927), Heft 18.
———, "Was Karl Grune, der Regisseur, über den Russenfilm zu sagen weiss," *Film-Photos wie noch nie* (Frankfurt a.M., 1929), p. 15.

H., D. L., "Films in the Provinces," *Close Up*, IV (Territet, Switzerland, June 1929), no. 6: 52–57.
Haas, Willy, "Das letzte Filmjahr," *Das grosse Bilderbuch des Films* (Filmkurier: Berlin, 1925?), pp. 6–12.
Häfker, Hermann, *Der Kino und die Gebildeten. Wege zur Hebung des Kinowesens*, Gladbach, 1915.
Hain, Mathilde, *Studien über das Wesen des frühexpressionistischen Dramas*, Erhard Lommatzsch, ed., Frankfurter Quellen und Forschungen zur germanischen und romanischen Philologie, Heft V, Frankfurt a.M., 1933.
Hamilton, James Shelley, "Das Lied vom Leben," *National Board of Review Magazine*, VI (New York, Nov. 1931), no. 9: 7–9.
———, "M," *ibid.*, VIII (March 1933), no. 3: 8–11.
———, "Hell on Earth," *ibid.* (April 1933), no. 4: 8–9.
Hamson, Nina, "Une Nouvelle Œuvre de Ruttmann," *La Revue du Cinéma*, II (Paris, 1er Juillet 1930), no. 12: 70–71.
Harbou, Thea von, "Vom Nibelungen-Film und seinem Entstehen," *Die Nibelungen* (Berlin, 1924?), pp. 6–11. [A program brochure to this film.]
Hartlaub, G. F., "Zur Einführung," *Die neue Sachlichkeit: Wanderausstellung der Städtischen Kunsthalle zu Mannheim* (Sächsischer Kunstverein, Dresden, 18. Okt.–22. Nov. 1925), pp. 3–4.

Hauptmann, Carl, "Film und Theater," Hugo Zehder, ed., *Der Film von Morgen* (Berlin-Dresden, 1923), pp. 11–20.

Hegemann, Werner, *Frederick the Great*, London, 1929.

"Heimweh," *Close Up*, I (Territet, Switzerland, Dec. 1927), no. 6: 74–76.

Hellmund-Waldow, Erich, "Alraune and Schinderhannes," *Close Up*, II (Territet, Switzerland, March 1928), no. 3: 45–51.

———, "Combinaison: Le Film et la Scène," *ibid.* (April 1928), no. 4: 23–30.

Herring, Robert, "La Tragédie de la Rue," *Close Up*, III (Territet, Switzerland, July 1928) no. 1: 31–40.

———, "Reasons of Rhyme," *ibid.*, V (Oct. 1929), no. 4: 278–85.

Hildebrandt, Paul, "Literatur und Film," Dr. E. Beyfuss, ed., *Das Kulturfilmbuch* (Berlin, 1924), pp. 83–86

"Hochverrat," *Film-Magazin* (Berlin, 29. Sept. 1929), no. 39; and (17. Nov. 1929), no. 46.

Hoffman, Carl, "Camera Problems," *Close Up*, V (Territet, Switzerland, July 1929), no. 1: 29–31.

Holländer, Felix, "The Road to Beauty and Strength," *Wege zu Kraft und Schönheit* (Berlin, 1926?), pp. 47–50. [Publicity pamphlet issued by Kulturabteilung der Ufa.]

"Homecoming," *National Board of Review Magazine*, III (New York, Dec. 1928), no. 12: 7, 10.

Horkheimer, Max, "Theoretische Entwürfe über Autorität und Familie," Horkheimer, ed., *Studien über Autorität und Familie*, Forschungsberichte aus dem Institut für Sozialforschung (Paris, 1936), pp. 3–76.

Illustrierter Film-Kurier, Berlin. [Issues devoted to synopses and stills of specific productions. Usually undated.]

"Inhaltsangabe für die Nibelungen . . ," *Die Nibelungen* (Berlin, 1924?), pp. 17–24. [A program brochure to this film.]

Iros, Ernst, *Wesen und Dramaturgie des Films*, Zürich, 1938.

"Isn't Life Wonderful?" *Exceptional Photoplays*, V (New York, Dec.-Jan. 1925), nos. 3 and 4: 5.

Jacobs, Lewis, *The Rise of the American Film. A Critical History*, New York, 1939.

Jahier, Valerio, "42 Ans de Cinéma," *Le Rôle intellectuel du Cinéma*, Société des Nations, Cahier 3 (Paris, 1937), pp. 13–151.

Jahrbuch der Filmindustrie (Berlin, 1923), 1. Jahrgang: 1922/3.

———, (Berlin, 1926), 2. Jahrgang: 1923/25.

Jannings, Emil, "Mein Werdegang," *Ufa-Magazin*, I (Berlin, 1.–7. Okt. 1926), Heft 7.
Jason, Alexander, "Zahlen sehen uns an . . ," *25 Jahre Kinematograph* (Berlin, 1931?), pp. 67–70.
Jeanne, René, "Le Cinéma Allemand," *L'Art Cinématographique*, VIII (Paris, 1931), 1–48.

Kalbus, Oskar, *Vom Werden deutscher Filmkunst* (Altona-Behrenfeld, Germany, 1935), I: Der stumme Film; II: Der Tonfilm.
Kallen, Horace M., *Art and Freedom*, New York, 1942. 2 vols.
Kaufmann, Nicholas, *Filmtechnik und Kultur*, Stuttgart, 1931.
Kracauer, Siegfried, *Die Angestellten. Aus dem neuesten Deutschland*, Frankfurt a.M., 1930.
———, "Der heutige Film und sein Publikum," *Frankfurter Zeitung*, 30. Nov. and 1. Dez. 1928.
———, " 'Kuhle Wampe' verboten!" *ibid.*, 5. April 1932.
———, "Courrier de Berlin," *La Revue du Cinéma*, III (Paris, 1er Août 1931), no. 25: 62–66.
———, "Trop luxueux Passe-Temps," *ibid.* (1er Octobre 1931), no. 27: 54–55.
Kraszna-Krausz, A., "The Querschnittfilm," *Close Up*, III (Territet, Switzerland, Nov. 1928), no. 5: 25–34.
———, "A Letter on Censorship," *ibid.*, IV (Feb. 1929), no. 2: 56–62.
———, "G. W. Pabst's 'Lulu,' " *ibid.* (April 1929), no. 4: 24–30.
———, "Exhibition in Stuttgart, June, 1929, and Its Effects," *ibid.*, V (Dec. 1929), no. 6: 455–64.
———, "Production, Construction, Hobby," *ibid.*, VI (April 1930), no. 4: 311–18.
———, "A Season's Retrospect," *Close Up*, VIII (London, Sept. 1931, no. 3: 225–31.
———, "Four Films from Germany," *ibid.*, IX (March 1932), no. 1: 39–45.
Krieger, Ernst, "Wozu ein Weltkriegsfilm?" *Ufa-Magazin*, Sondernummer: Der Weltkrieg, ein historischer Film (Berlin).
Kurtz, Rudolf, *Expressionismus und Film*, Berlin, 1926.

Lang, Fritz, "Kitsch—Sensation—Kultur und Film," Dr. E. Beyfuss, ed., *Das Kulturfilmbuch* (Berlin, 1924), pp. 28–31.
———, "Worauf es beim Nibelungen-Film ankam," *Die Nibelungen* (Berlin, 1924?), pp. 12–16. [A program brochure to this film.]
———, "Screen Foreword to 'The Last Will of Dr. Mabuse,' " *Program* to THE LAST WILL OF DR. MABUSE, issued by World Theatre, New York, March 19, 1943.

Lejeune, C. A., *Cinema*, London, 1931.

Leprohon, Pierre, "Le Cinéma Allemand," *Le Rouge et le Noir*, cahier spécial (Paris, Juillet 1928), pp. 134–43.

Lewis, Lloyd, "Erich von Stroheim of the Movies . . ," *New York Times*, June 22, 1941.

Leyda, Jay, *Program Notes*, Museum of Modern Art Film Library. [Reviews of and commentary on Russian films.]

"The Loves of Pharaoh," *Exceptional Photoplays*, II (New York, Jan.–Feb. 1922), bulletin no. 1: 2–3.

Lubitsch, Ernst, "Wie mein erster Grossfilm entstand," *Licht Bild Bühne. 30 Jahre Film* (Berlin, 1924), pp. 13–14.

Mack, Max, *Wie komme ich zum Film?*, Berlin, 1919.

McKechnie, Samuel, *Popular Entertainments Through the Ages*, London, 1931.

MacPherson, Kenneth, "Die Liebe der Jeanne Ney," *Close Up*, I (Territet, Switzerland, Dec. 1927), no. 6: 17–26.

———, "As Is," *ibid.*, III (Aug. 1928), no. 2: 5–11.

———, "A Document of Shanghai," *ibid.* (Dec. 1928), no. 6: 66–69.

———, "*Times* Is Not What They Was!" *ibid.*, IV (Feb. 1929), no. 2: 33–36.

———, "Überfall (Accident)," *ibid.* (April 1929), no. 4: 70–72.

"Mädchen in Uniform," *National Board of Review Magazine*, VII (New York, Sept.–Oct. 1932), no. 7: 9–10.

Magnus, Max, "Danton," *Variety*, New York. [Clipping in Museum of Modern Art Library files, dated Feb. 1931?.]

"The Man Who Cheated Life," *National Board of Review Magazine*, IV (New York, Feb. 1929), no. 2: 10–11, 23.

"Martin Luther," *National Board of Review Magazine*, III (New York, Oct. 1928), no. 10: 4.

Martini, Wolfgang, "Nature and Human Fate," *Close Up*, I (Territet, Switzerland, Nov. 1927), no. 5: 10–14.

Mayer, Carl, "Technische Vorbemerkungen des Autors," Ernst Angel, ed., *Sylvester: Ein Lichtspiel von Carl Mayer*, Das Drehbuch, Band I (Potsdam, 1924), pp. 15–16.

———, "Sylvester," *ibid.*, pp. 17–96. [Scenario of this film.]

Meisel, Edmund, "Wie schreibt man Filmmusik?" *Ufa-Magazin*, II (Berlin, 1.–7. April 1927), Heft 14.

Messter, Oskar, *Mein Weg mit dem Film*, Berlin, 1936.

Metzner, Erno, "German Censor's Incomprehensible Ban," *Close Up*, IV (Territet, Switzerland, May 1929), no. 5: 14–16.

———, "A Mining Film," *Close Up*, IX (London, March 1932), no. 1: 3–9.

"Middle Class Is Dead, Says Official Nazi Paper," *New York Times*, April 12, 1943.

"Das Modell von Montparnasse," *Film-Magazin* (Berlin, 21. April 1929), no. 16.

Möllhausen, Balduin, "Der Aufstieg des Films," *Ufa-Blätter*, Programm-Zeitschrift der Theater des Ufa-Konzerns, Berlin, 1921?.

Molo, Walter von, *Das Fridericus Rex-Buch*, Berlin, 1922.

"Montmartre," *Exceptional Photoplays*, IV (New York, Feb.–March 1924), nos. 5 and 6: 5.

Moore, John C., "Pabst—Dovjenko—A Comparison," *Close Up*, IX (London, Sept. 1932), no. 3: 176–82.

Moreck, Curt, *Sittengeschichte des Kinos*, Dresden, 1926.

"Morgenrot," *Variety*, New York, Feb. 28, 1933.

Moussinac, Léon, *Panoramique du Cinéma*, Paris, 1929.

———, "Introduction" [to "Dziga Vertov on Film Technique"], *Filmfront*, I (New York, Jan. 28, 1935), no. 3: 7.

Mühsam, Kurt, "Tiere im Film," *Ufa-Blätter*, Programm-Zeitschrift der Theater des Ufa-Konzerns, Berlin, 1921?.

Mungenast, Ernst Moritz, *Asta Nielsen*, Stuttgart, 1928.

Museum of Modern Art Library, New York, clipping files. [These include film reviews, programs, program brochures, prospectuses, publicity booklets or sheets, etc., relating to a multitude of films, and many pertinent notes.]

" 'Mütterchen' Russland," *Ufa-Magazin*, I (Berlin, 27. August–2 Sept. 1926), Heft 2.

Neumann, Carl, Belling, Kurt, and Betz, Hans-Walther, *Film- 'Kunst,' Film-Kohn, Film-Korruption*, Berlin, 1937.

Neumann, Franz, *Behemoth: The Structure and Practice of National Socialism*, Toronto, New York, London, 1942.

"Das Netz der Indizien," *Filmwelt* (Berlin, 22. März 1931), no. 12.

"New Educational Films from UFA," *Close Up*, V (Territet, Switzerland, Sept. 1929), no. 3: 252–54.

Noldan, Svend, "Die Darstellung der Schlachten," *Ufa-Magazin*, Sondernummer: Der Weltkrieg, ein historischer Film (Berlin).

Olimsky, Fritz, *Tendenzen der Filmwirtschaft und deren Auswirkung auf die Filmpresse*, Inaugural Dissertation, Berlin, 1931.

"Out of the Mist," *Close Up*, I (Territet, Switzerland, Oct. 1927), no. 4: 84–86.

Pabst, G. W., "Servitude et Grandeur d'Hollywood," *Le Rôle intellectuel du Cinéma,* Société des Nations, Cahier 3 (Paris, 1937), pp. 251–55.

Pabst, Rudolf, "Die Bedeutung des Films als Wirtschafts-Propaganda-Mittel," Dr. Friedrich Rudolf Pabst, ed., *Moderne Kinematographie,* Amtliches Organ der Internationalen Kinematographischen Gesellschaft (München, 1920), 1. Januarheft: 25–32.

Panofsky, Erwin, "Style and Medium in the Moving Pictures," *transition* (Paris, 1937), no. 26: 121–33.

"Passion," *Exceptional Photoplays,* I (New York, Nov. 1920), bulletin no. 1: 3.

"Peter the Great," *Exceptional Photoplays,* IV (New York, Feb.–March 1924), nos. 5 and 6: 1–2.

Petzet, Wolfgang, *Verbotene Filme. Eine Streitschrift,* Frankfurt a.M., 1931.

Pick, Lupu, "Vorwort des Regisseurs," Ernst Angel, ed., *Sylvester: Ein Lichtspiel von Carl Mayer,* Das Drehbuch, Band I (Potsdam, 1924), pp. 9–11.

Pordes, Victor E., *Das Lichtspiel: Wesen—Dramaturgie—Regie,* Wien, 1919.

Porten, Henny, "Mein Leben," *Ufa-Magazin,* II (Berlin, 22–28. April 1927), Heft 17.

Potamkin, Harry Alan, "Kino and Lichtspiel," *Close Up,* V (Territet, Switzerland, Nov. 1929), no. 5: 387–98.

———, "The Rise and Fall of the German Film," *Cinema,* I (New York, April 1930), no. 3: 24–25, 57, 59.

———, "Pabst and the Social Film," *Hound & Horn,* VI (New York, Jan.–March 1933), no. 2: 293–305.

"Les Présentations de l'Alliance Cinématographique Européenne," *Cinéa-Ciné* (Paris, 1er Avril 1927), pp. 14–16.

"Die Produktion des Jahres, Emelka-Konzern," *Das grosse Bilderbuch des Films* (Filmkurier: Berlin, 1925?), pp. 161–78.

Programs, program brochures, prospectuses, publicity booklets or sheets, etc., relating to various films: *see* Museum of Modern Art Library, New York, clipping files. In addition, I have used similar material in the possession of Dr. Kurt Pinthus, Washington, D. C.

Pudovkin, V. I., *Film Technique,* London, 1933.

Ray, Man, "Answer to a Questionnaire," *Film Art,* III (London, 1936), no. 7: 9–10.

"Der Regisseur F. W. Murnau," *Ufa-Magazin,* I (Berlin, 15.–21. Okt. 1926), Heft 9.

Reiniger, Lotte, "Lebende Schatten: Kunst u. Technik des Silhouettenfilms," *Film-Photos wie noch nie* (Frankfurt a.M., 1929), pp. 45–46.

Reviews of films: *see* Museum of Modern Art Library, clipping files.

Richter, Hans, "Ur-Kino," *Neue Zürcher Zeitung* (25. Feb. and 2. April 1940).

Riefenstahl, Leni, *Hinter den Kulissen des Reichsparteitag Films*, München, 1935.

Robson, E. W. and M. M., *The Film Answers Back*, London, 1939.

Rohde, Alfred W., "German Propaganda Movies in Two Wars," *American Cinematographer*, XXIV (Hollywood, Jan. 1943), no. 1:10–11, 28.

"Rose Bernd," *National Board of Review Magazine*, II (New York, Feb. 1927), no. 2:16.

Rosenberg, Arthur, *Geschichte der Deutschen Republik*, Karlsbad, 1935.

Rotha, Paul, *The Film Till Now*, London, 1930.

———, *Celluloid: The Film To-day*, London, New York, Toronto, 1933.

———, *Documentary Film*, London, 1936.

———, "Plastic Design," *Close Up*, V (Territet, Switzerland, Sept. 1929), no. 3:228–31.

———, "It's in the Script," *World Film News*, III (London, Sept. 1938), no. 5:204–5.

———, "Carl Mayer, 1894–1944," *Documentary News Letter*, V (London, 1944), no. 3:39.

"Rund um die Liebe," *Film-Magazin* (Berlin, 27. Jan. 1929), no. 4.

Ruttmann, Walter, "La Symphonie du Monde," *La Revue du Cinéma*, II (Paris, 1er Mars 1930), no. 8:43–45.

Samuel, Richard, and Thomas, R. Hinton, *Expressionism in German Life, Literature and the Theatre (1910–1924)*, Cambridge, Eng., 1939.

"Saucy Suzanne," *Close Up*, I (Territet, Switzerland, Nov. 1927), no. 5:65–66.

Schapiro, Meyer, "Nature of Abstract Art," *Marxist Quarterly*, I (New York, Jan.–March 1937), no. 1:77–98.

———, "A Note on Max Weber's Politics," *Politics* (New York, Feb. 1945), pp. 44–48.

Schlesinger, E. R., "Das moderne deutsche Lichtspieltheater," *Das grosse Bilderbuch des Films* (Filmkurier: Berlin, 1925?), p. 28.

Schmalenbach, Fritz, "The Term *Neue Sachlichkeit*," *The Art Bulletin*, XXII (New York, Sept. 1940), no. 3:161–65.

Schwartzkopf, Rudolf, "Volksverband für Filmkunst," *Close Up*, II (Territet, Switzerland, May 1928), no. 5: 71–75.

Schwarzschild, Leopold, *World in Trance*, New York, 1942.

Seeber, Guido, "Szenen aus dem Film meines Lebens," *Licht Bild Bühne. 30 Jahre Film* (Berlin, 1924), pp. 15–19.

"Shattered," *Exceptional Photoplays*, II (New York, Jan.–Feb. 1922), bulletin no. 1: 4–5.

"Silberkondor über Feuerland," *Close Up*, V (Territet, Switzerland, Dec. 1929), no. 6: 542–43.

"Skandal um Eva," *Close Up*, VII (Territet, Switzerland, Sept. 1930), no. 3: 221–22.

Spottiswoode, Raymond, *A Grammar of the Film: An Analysis of Film Technique*, London, 1935.

Stenhouse, Charles E., "Die Wunder des Films," *Close Up*, IV (Territet, Switzerland, May 1929), no. 5: 89–91.

———, "The World on Film," *ibid.*, VI (May 1930), no. 5: 417–18.

———, "A Contemporary," *ibid.*, pp. 418–20.

"The Street," *National Board of Review Magazine*, II (New York, June 1927), no. 6: 9–10.

"Stürme der Leidenschaft," *Filmwelt* (Berlin, 27. Dez. 1931), no. 52.

Tannenbaum, Eugen, "Der Grossfilm," Hugo Zehder, ed., *Der Film von Morgen*, Berlin-Dresden, 1923), pp. 61–72.

"Tartuffe, the Hypocrite," *National Board of Review Magazine*, III (New York, May 1928), no. 5: 5–6.

Tazelaar, Marguerite, "Morgenrot," *New York Herald Tribune*, May 16, 1933.

Thomalla, Curt, "Der Kulturfilm," *Das grosse Bilderbuch des Films* (Filmkurier: Berlin, 1925?), pp. 23–27.

Bilderbuch "Ufa," *Das grosse des Films* (Filmkurier: Berlin, 1925?), pp. 323–80.

"Ufa, *Das grosse Bilderbuch des Films* (Filmkurier: Berlin, 1926), pp. 157–206.

Ufa, *Kultur-Filme*, Berlin. [Catalogs, issued Jan. 1929, June 1929, Jan. 1930, March 1930, Oct. 1930, March 1931, Feb. 1932, July 1932, Jan. 1933.]

Ufa Verleih-Programme, Berlin, 1923; 1923/24; 1924/25. [These illustrated volumes include short synopses of various films.]

Ullman, James Ramsay, *The White Tower*, Philadelphia and New York, 1945. [A novel.]

Veidt, Conrad, "Mein Leben," *Ufa-Magazin*, II (Berlin, 14.–20. Jan. 1927), Heft 3.
Vertov, Dziga, "Dziga Vertov on Film Technique," *Filmfront*, I (New York, Jan. 28, 1935), no. 3: 7–9.
Vincent, Carl, *Histoire de l'Art Cinématographique*, Bruxelles, 1939.

Wagner, Fritz Arno, "I Believe in the Sound Film," *Film Art*, III (London, 2nd quarter, 1936), no. 8: 8–12.
"Was ist los?" *Ufa-Magazin*, II (Berlin, 4.–10. Feb. 1927), Heft 6.
———, *ibid.* (8.–14. April 1927), Heft 15.
———, *ibid.* (15.–21. April 1927), Heft 16.
Watts, Richard, Jr., "Mädchen in Uniform," *New York Herald Tribune*, Sept. 21, 1932.
———, "Luise, Queen of Prussia," *ibid.*, Oct. 5, 1932.
———, "The King's Dancer," *ibid.*, Oct. 27, 1932.
———, "York," *ibid.*, Nov. 24, 1932.
———, "Kuhle Wampe," *ibid.*, April 25, 1933.
Weinberg, Herman G., Scrapbooks of film reviews and illustrations. 3 vols. [I: 1925–27; II: 1927; III: 1928.] [In the Museum of Modern Art Library, New York. Clippings are mostly undated.]
———, "Fritz Lang," *Program* to THE LAST WILL OF DR. MABUSE, issued by World Theatre, New York, March 19, 1943.
———, *An Index to the Creative Work of Fritz Lang*, Special Supplement to "Sight and Sound," Index Series No. 5, London, Feb. 1946.
———, *An Index to the Creative Work of Two Pioneers: I. Robert J. Flaherty; II. Hans Richter*, Special Supplement to "Sight and Sound," Index Series No. 6, London, May 1946.
Weiss, Trude, "Mutter Krausen's Fahrt ins Glück," *Close Up*, VI (Territet, Switzerland, April 1930), no. 4: 318–21.
———, "The Secret of the Egg-Shell," *ibid.* (May 1930), no. 5: 421–22.
———, "A Starring Vehicle," *ibid.*, VII (Nov. 1930), no. 5: 333–35.
———, "Achtung Australien! Achtung Asien!" *ibid.*, VIII (London, June 1931), no. 2: 149–50.
———, "Sonne über dem Arlberg," *ibid.*, IX (March 1932), no. 1: 59–60.
———, "The Blue Light," *ibid.* (June 1932), no. 2: 119–22.
———, "Das keimende Leben," *ibid.* (Sept. 1932), no. 3: 207–8.
———, "The First Opera-Film," *ibid.* (Dec. 1932), no. 4: 242–45.
———, "Elizabeth Bergner Again," *ibid.*, pp. 254–56.
"Der weisse Rausch," *Filmwelt* (Berlin, 20. Dez. 1931), no. 51.
Weniger, Erich, "Die Jugendbewegung und ihre kulturelle Auswirkung,"

Dr. Erasmus, ed., *Geist der Gegenwart* (Stuttgart, 1928), pp. 1–54.

Wesse, Curt, *Grossmacht Film. Das Geschöpf von Kunst und Technik*, Berlin, 1928.

Weyher, Ruth, "Wir drehen in Paris," *Ufa-Magazin*, II (Berlin, 25.–31. März 1927), Heft 13.

White, Kenneth, "Film Chronicle: F. W. Murnau," *Hound & Horn*, IV (New York, July–Sept. 1931), no. 4: 581–84.

"The White Hell of Piz Palu," *Close Up*, V (Territet, Switzerland, Dec. 1929), no. 6: 543–45.

"Wissen Sie schon?" *Das grosse Bilderbuch des Films* (Filmkurier: Berlin, 1926), p. 145.

Zaddach, Gerhard, *Der literarische Film. Ein Beitrag zur Geschichte der Lichtspielkunst*, Inaugural Dissertation, Breslau, Berlin, 1929.

Zimmereimer, Kurt, *Die Filmzensur*, Abhandlungen der Rechts- und Staatswissenschaftlichen Fakultät der Universtät Königsberg (Breslau-Neukirch, 1934), Heft 5.

"Zuflucht," *Ufa-Leih*, Berlin. [An undated brochure.]

INDEX

A

E

F

G

N

Y

Z

1. PASSION: The threat of mass domination.

2. CALIGARI: Insane authority.

3. CALIGARI: A draftsman's imagination.

4. CALIGARI: The three flights of stairs in the lunatic asylum symbolize Dr. Caligari's position at the top of the hierarchy.

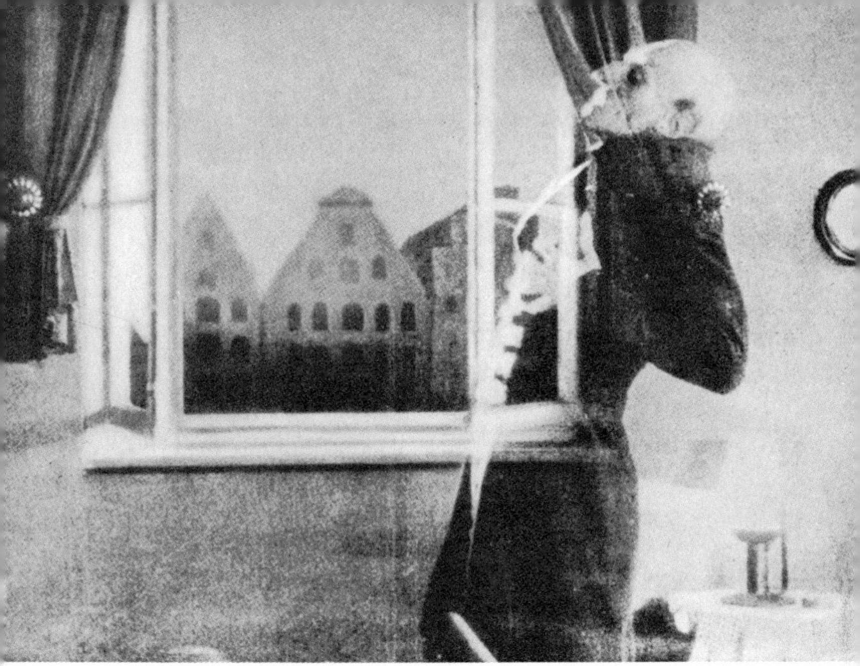

5. Nosferatu: The vampire, defeated by love, dissolves into thin air.

6. Dr. Mabuse, the Gambler: Interpenetration of realistic and expressionist style, betraying the close relationship between Mabuse and Caligari.

7. WAXWORKS: A phantasmagoria—Jack-the-Ripper pursuing the lovers.

8. WAXWORKS: Ivan the Terrible, an incarnation of insatiable lusts and unheard-of cruelties

9. DESTINY: The huge wall symbolizing Fate's inaccessibility.

10. NIBELUNGEN: Triumph of the ornamental over the human.

11. Nibelungen: }
12. Triumph of the Will: } The patterns of *Nibelungen* are resumed in Nazi pageantry.

13. New Year's Eve: The suicide of the café-owner.

14. The Last Laugh: Humiliation incarnate.

15. The Last Laugh: The revolving door—something between a merry-go-round and a roulette wheel.

16. A Glass of Water: With its stress on symmetry the décor breathes romantic nostalgia.

17. Peak of Destiny: Mountain climbers are devotees performing the rites of a cult.

18. The Golem: The Golem, a figure of clay, animated by his master, Rabbi Loew.

19 WARNING SHADOWS: Magical therapy—the Count and his guests

20

21. The Street: Mute objects take on life.

22. The Street: This gesture—recurrent in many German films—is symptomatic of the desire to return to the maternal womb.

23. VARIETY: Jannings' bulky back plays a conspicuous role in the prison scene

24. VARIETY: The inquisitive camera breaks into the magic circle of action.

25. WAYS TO STRENGTH AND BEAUTY: *Tableau vivant* of a Greek gymnasium.

26. TARTUFFE: The grand-style manner.

27. METROPOLIS: Sham alliance between labor and capital.

28. METROPOLIS: Ornamental despair.

29. The Joyless Street: Asta Nielsen in one of the roles in which she discards social conventions in her abundance of love.

30. Kampf der Tertia: One of the many youth films expressing a longing for adolescence.

31. The Joyless Street: The ghastliness of real life.

32. The Joyless Street: Realism, not symbolism.

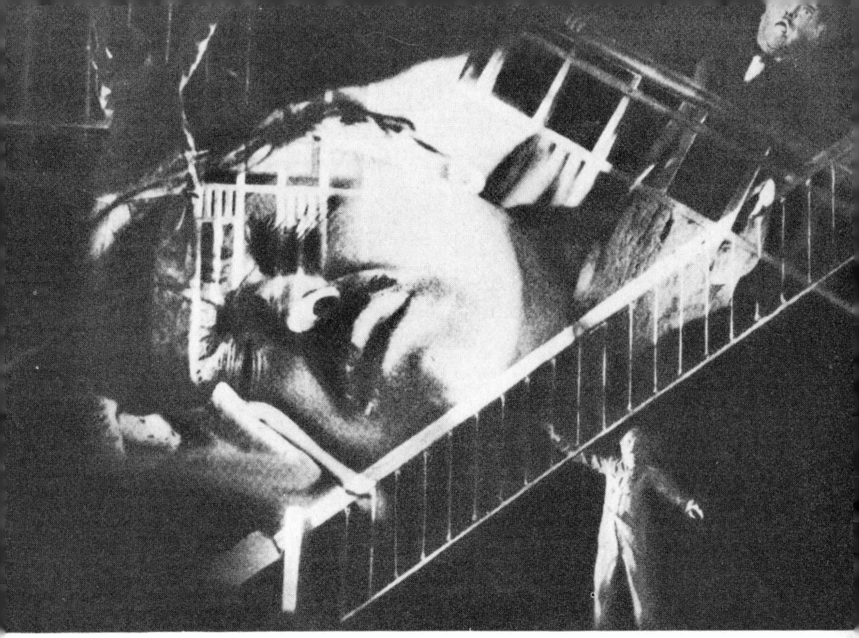

33. SECRETS OF A SOUL: Dreams cinematically externalized.

34. THE LOVE OF JEANNE NEY: The orgy of anti-Bolshevist soldiery—a scene elicited from life itself.

35. THE LOVE OF JEANNE NEY: The broken mirror, a silent witness, tells of glamour and destruction.

36. THE LOVE OF JEANNE NEY: Casual configurations of life.

37. **Berlin**: Patterns of movement.

38. **Berlin**: What once denoted chaos is now simply part of the record—a fact among facts.

39. BERLIN: A close-up of the gutter illustrates the harshness of mechanized life

40. ACCIDENT: The use of distorting mirrors helps to defy deep-rooted conventions.

41. Drei von der Tankstelle: A playful daydream woven of the materials of everyday life.

42. Song of Life: A symbolic scene which glorifies vitality.

43. The Man without a Name: The nightmarish workings of bureaucracy.

44. The Victor: Hans Albers, the embodiment of popular daydreams.

45. The Blue Angel: Jannings as the professor taunted by his pupils.

46. The Blue Angel: Marlene Dietrich as Lola Lola—provocative legs and an over-all impassivity.

47. M: The empty stairwell echoing with the cries of Elsie's mother.

48. M: The knives reflected around Lorre's face define him as a prisoner of his evil urges.

49. M: The group of criminals, beggars and street women sitting in judgment on the child-murderer.

50. Emil und die Detektive: The thief, a Pied Piper in reverse, pursued by the children under a radiant morning sun.

51. Mädchen in Uniform: The headmistress—a feminine Frederick the Great

52. Mädchen in Uniform: To prepare the audience for this scene, the staircase is featured throughout the film.

53. WESTFRONT 1918: Field hospital filled with moans and agonized cries.

54. THE BEGGAR'S OPERA: Glass screens transform the crowded and smoky café into a confusing maze.

55. Comradeship: Three German miners about to remove the iron fence set up since Versailles.

56. Comradeship: German miners in the shower room—the audience is let into one of the arcana of everyday life.

57. Kuhle Wampe: Young athletes at the Red sports festival which glorifies collective life.

58. Eight Girls in a Boat: This film betrays the affinity of the earlier Youth Movement with the Nazi spirit.

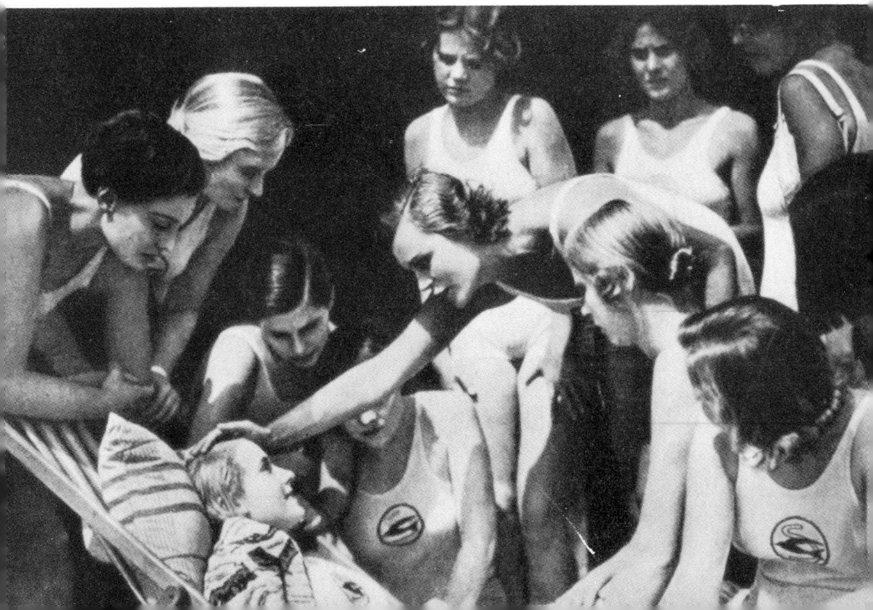

59. Avalanche:
60. Triumph of the Will:
Emphasis on cloud conglomerations indicates the ultimate fusion of the mountain- and the Hitler-cult.

61. THE REBEL: A thinly masked Hitlerite.

62. THE BLUE LIGHT: Junta, an incarnation of elemental powers.

63. THE ANTHEM OF LEUTHEN: The old king.

64. DAWN: The smell of real war.